King Lear

The Garland
Shakespeare Bibliographies
(General Editor: William Godshalk)
Number 1

Garland Reference Library
of the Humanities
Volume 230

The Garland
Shakespeare Bibliographies

William Godshalk
General Editor

Number 1:
King Lear
compiled by Larry S. Champion

King Lear
An Annotated Bibliography

compiled by
Larry S. Champion

in two volumes
Volume II

GARLAND PUBLISHING, INC.
NEW YORK & LONDON
1980

Library of Congress Cataloging in Publication Data

Champion, Larry S
  King Lear, an annotated bibliography.

  (The Garland Shakespeare bibliographies ; no. 1)
(Garland reference library of the humanities ; v. 230)
  Includes index.
  1. Shakespeare, William, 1564–1616. King Lear—
Bibliography. I. Title. II. Series: Garland
Shakespeare bibliographies ; no. 1.
Z8812.L4C47 [PR2819]   016.8223'3   80-8489
ISBN 0-8240-9498-0

Printed on acid-free, 250-year-life paper
Manufactured in the United States of America

CONTENTS

Volume I

Volume II

II. SOURCES

II. SOURCES

1237 Hazlitt, William Carew, ed. *Shakespeare's Library.* 6 vols. London: Reeves and Turner, 1875. Reprint. New York: AMS Press, 1965.

These volumes reprint the plays, romances, novels, poems, and histories "employed by Shakespeare in the composition of his works." Volume 6 includes *King Leir* and Volume 2 includes "An Account of Lear, Tenth Ruler of Britain" (from Holinshed's *Chronicles*), "The Story of Lear, King of Britain" (from *Gesta Romanorum*), "How Queene Cordila, in dispaire, slewe her selfe, the yeere before Christ, 800" (from the *Mirror for Magistrates*), "the story of the Paphlagonian King" (from Sidney's *Arcadia*), and "A Lamentable Song of the Death of King Leir and His Three Daughters" (to the tune of "When Flying Fame").

1238 Sykes, Henry Dugdale. *"King Leir." Sidelights on Shakespeare.* Stratford-Upon-Avon: The Shakespeare Head Press, 1919. Reprint. Folcroft, Pa.: Folcroft Library Editions, 1972, pp. 126-142.

The popularity of *King Leir* is attested by Henslowe's record of receipts from a production (1605) leading to its presumed second publication. Internal evidence clearly reveals the play to be by George Peele. Numerous words are common to Peele's vocabulary, various passages recall the diction of his accredited dramas, plot elements are similar, and diffuseness and tautology characterize the syntax in every case. The argument that Robert Greene collaborated in the composition cannot be convincingly demonstrated.

1239 Freud, Sigmund. "The Theme of the Three Caskets." *Collected Papers.* 4 vols. London: Hogarth Press, IV, 1925, 244-256. Reprint. *The Design Within: Psychoanalytic Approaches to Shakespeare.* Ed. Melvin D. Faber. New York: Science House, 1970.

3

The opening scene of *Lear* is based on the old myth of a man's having to choose among three women. In most of the variants of this myth the third woman is silent, a representation of death. As the goddess of death she also is related to the Fates, Moerae, Parcae, or Norns. Lear, more precisely, is an old, dying man, but he is unwilling to renounce life and the love of women. Thus, he responds to the adulation of Goneril and Regan, rejecting death in Cordelia. When Lear carries the dead Cordelia on stage in the final act, by a reverse situation Death is claiming him. "Eternal wisdom, clothed in the primeval myth, bids the old man renounce love, choose death, and make friends with the necessity of dying" (p. 256). See items 294, 689, 839, 1720, 2509.

1240   Noble, Richmond S. H. *"King Lear." Shakespeare's Biblical Knowledge and Use of the Book of Common Prayer.* New York: Society for Promoting Christian Knowledge, 1935, pp. 229-232.

Passages throughout *King Lear* apparently are directly inspired by Shakespeare's close knowledge of the Bible. Passages cited are spoken by Lear (six), Cordelia (two), Edgar (three), Kent (two), the Fool (one), and France (one). Following the catalogue of allusions and their scriptural counterparts, a list is provided of Biblical proper names alluded to by Shakespeare (pp. 261-280). See item 1313.

1241   Henderson, W. B. Drayton. "Montaigne's *Apology of Raymond Sebond* and *King Lear." Shakespeare Association Bulletin,* 14 (1939), 209-225 and 15 (1940), 40-54.

Montaigne's *Apology* is the spiritual source of *King Lear.* Shakespeare transformed the old man of *Leir* into a Renaissance God-King; Montaigne describes such a man as characterized by egregious folly; man's only salvation is in revealed religion, not in some king as a symbol of God's providential order. Montaigne is probably directly responsible also for the leitmotiv, "Nothing will come of nothing." The Renaissance God-King must be completely denied in some important business; he as an overweening creature must be shown his own true nature, his close relationship to beastliness itself; madness must on occasion be a part of the curative process.   Gloucester's leap from the imaginary cliffs was probably

suggested to Shakespeare by Montaigne's experience of vertigo
in the Alps. In numerous instances, in brief, Montaigne's essay
provides both the narrative frame and the philosophic spirit for
Lear. "It helped Shakespeare to reform the naive pietism of the
donnée, and helps us to see why he did it" (p. 51). See item 1462.

1242   Taylor, George Coffin. "Two Notes on Shakespeare." *Philologi-*
       cal Quarterly, 20 (1941), 371-376.

       "Shakespeare and the Prognostications"—Shakespeare was
thoroughly conversant with both sides of the argument concerning
astral influence on mundane events. In I, ii, 111-145, Gloucester's
claim that the evils besetting England result from the maleficent
position of the stars parallels the conventional assertions of Elizabethan prognosticators. On the other hand, Edmund's counter-
claims against astral influence closely parallel the contentions of
William Fulke, an English Renaissance skeptic who in 1563 attacked
the "supernatural in a fashion which can hardly be distinguished by
a hair's breadth from a modern skeptic" (p. 371).

1243   Perkinson, Richard H. "Shakespeare's Revision of the Lear
       Story and the Structure of *King Lear." Philological Quar-*
       terly, 22 (1943), 315-329.

       Shakespeare through modification of his sources for *King Lear*
carefully prepares the reader for the tragic ending. He compresses,
for example, four scenes from *Leir* into a long opening scene emphasizing the improbability and foolishness of Lear's actions. Cordelia
appears more innocent than does her counterpart in the anonymous
play. Moreover, Shakespeare focuses on an internal process of
change in Lear with a gradually mounting tragic tension. He gives
far less attention to Cordelia's invasion, ominously announcing its
defeat almost at the point it begins. The subplot is attached to
lend complexity. In a word, Shakespeare took a slight episode in
British history and by careful reshaping, largely in characterization,
achieved a powerful tragic effect. It is certainly not, as some critics
have suggested, a case of a sudden wrenching of the story to the
tragic catastrophe.

1244   Hammer, J. "Remarks on the Sources and Textual History
       of Geoffrey of Monmouth's *Historia." Quarterly Bulletin*

of the Polish Institute of Arts and Sciences, January, 1944, pp. 501-564.

This article examines the development of the Lear story in the twelfth century. See item 1247.

1245   Martin, L. C. "Shakespeare, Lucretius and the Commonplaces." *Review of English Studies,* 21 (1945), 174-182.

Various passages in *King Lear* (as well as in *Hamlet* and *Measure for Measure*) suggest that Shakespeare was familiar with Lucretius' *De Rerum Natura.* Although the work was not translated into English by the time of the Shakespearean plays, the playwright might have had access to a translation from the Latin in manuscript form.

1246   Parr, Johnstone. "A Note on the 'Late Eclipses' in *King Lear.*" *Shakespeare Association Bulletin,* 20 (1945), 46-48.

Attempts to determine topicality in the passage on the "late eclipses" in I, ii, 98 ff., should focus on prognostications rather than actual events. One such pamphlet was issued in 1604 by Himbert de Billy, *Certaine Wonderful Predictions for seven yeeres ensuing, shewing the Strange and Wonderful Comets and Meteors, beginning this present yeere 1604.* This ephemeral literature might well have provided Shakespeare the source for his astrological passage and would weaken any assumption that the composition of the play would have to postdate the actual occurrence of eclipses in 1605. See item 1270.

1247   Hammer, J. "Note sur l'histoire du roi Lear dans Geoffrey de Monmouth." *Latomus: R. d'Etudes Latines* (1946), pp. 299-301.

See item 1244.

1248   Hankins, John E. "Lear and the Psalmist." *Modern Language Notes,* 61 (1946), 88-90. Reprint. *Backgrounds of Shakespeare's Thought.* Hamden, Conn.: Archon Books, 1978.

The source of Lear's adjuration to the elements to destroy the earth in III, ii ("Blow, winds, and crack your cheeks"), is Psalms

144: 4-8. Destruction and elemental imagery are basic to both passages; the biblical passage, moreover, calls for the heavens to remove the writer from the "hande of straunge chyldren."

1249   Sitwell, Edith. "Nero is an Angler." *Times Literary Supplement,* 2 February 1946, p. 55.

The source for Edgar's babbling comment as Tom o' Bedlam ("Frateretto calls me, and tells me Nero is an angler in the lake of darkness" [III, i, 6-7]) is apparently a passage in Pausanius II, 37, describing Nero's inability to plumb the depths of the Alcyonian Lake.

1250   Smith, Grover. "The Tennis-Ball of Fortune." *Notes and Queries,* 190 (1946), 202-203.

The metaphor of man as a tennis ball buffeted by Fortune's waves is apparently from a misreading of a passage in Plautus' *Captivi.* Specifically, the passage in *Lear* referring to the relentless hounding of the gods ("As flies to wanton boys are we to the gods. / They kill us for their sport") is reminiscent of the fickle and cruel destiny of Euripidean tragedy.

1251   Smith, Roland M. *"King Lear* and the Merlin Tradition." *Modern Language Quarterly,* 7 (1946), 153-174.

The source for the mad scenes in *King Lear* in all likelihood is Arthurian material such as Richard Johnson's *Tom a Lincolne,* published several years earlier, and *The second parte of the famous history of Tom a Lincolne the Redd Rose Knight,* entered in the Stationers' Register in 1607 only twenty entries above Shakespeare's tragedy. Both parts of the tale include accounts of the "wild man of the woods," and numerous passages (cited in the article) bear resemblance to *Lear.* Other available sources for the Wild Man legend are the romance *Valentine and Orson,* the Latin *Vita Merlini,* and the Irish *Bevile Subihne* ("The Frenzy of Subihne" or "The Adventures of Subihne"). Again, there are numerous significant resemblances between *Lear* and these materials, especially the Latin and Irish materials. These sources apparently furnished material not only for Lear's mad scenes but for the Fool and Edgar as Tom o' Bedlam as well. The names in the subplot may well derive from the lost play *Uter Pendragon,* presumably a source for the later *The Birth of Merlin,* which features "The Earl of Gloster" and "Edwyn" his son. Indeed, the subtitle of *The Birth of Merlin* is "The Childe Hath Found His Father." The seeds of all of this material can be traced back to Geoffrey of Monmouth's *Historia.* Clearly Shakespeare for his madness scenes draws from some version of the Wild Man of the Woods story. "Only the Arthurian materials could give him what he needed. And in those materials the hysterical despair of the Celtic madman was bound to catch his attention" (p. 174).

1252   Lange, Günther. "Der Autor des vorsh-n Chronikspieles vom *König Leir.*" Ph.D. dissertation, University of Erlangen, 1947. (not seen)

1253   Harrison, Thomas P. "The Folger *Secret of Secrets.*" *Joseph Quincy Adams Memorial Studies.* Washington, D. C.: Folger Shakespeare Library, 1948, pp. 601-620.

Lear's dialogue with the Fool, specifically the series of questions and answers in I, v, and III, v (incorrectly stated as III, iv), may be a parody of the Sydrac question-and-answer book that appears with the *Secret of Secrets,* a pseudo-Aristotelian work of which a unique copy of the 1572 edition is in the Folger Shakespeare Library. Shakespeare probably also used the book as a source for Henry's advice to Prince Hal concerning the proper manner of conducting himself among his subjects.

1254   Pyle, Fitzroy. "*Twelfth Night, King Lear,* and *Arcadia.*" *Modern Language Review,* 43 (1948), 449-455.

Both *Twelfth Night* and *King Lear* draw significant inspiration from Sidney's *Arcadia.* For *Twelfth Night* Sidney furnished material for the function and action of the entire subplot, previously considered wholly original with Shakespeare; and for *King Lear* he provided not only the prototype for the characters, incidents, and situation of the Gloucester plot but also the tragic tone for transforming the *Leir* story. It is likely that the seeds of *Lear* were sown in Shakespeare's mind when he wrote *Twelfth Night,* though they could not come to maturity until he had come into contact with *King Leir.* At that time he was probably sent back to Sidney and, in turn,

reminded of *Twelfth Night,* which was revised at about that time.
"So the evidence linking the revision of the comedy with the composition of *King Lear* would seem to be confirmed" (p. 455).

1255   Rubow, Paul Victor. *Shakespeare og Hans Samtidige.* Copen-
       hagen: Gyldendale, 1948.

This volume includes an essay on the anonymous *King Leir.*
Particular attention is on Shakespeare's adaptation of themes and
characters for *King Lear.*

1256   Armstrong, William A. *"King Lear* and Sidney's *Arcadia." Times
       Literary Supplement,* 14 October 1949, p. 665.

Not only did Shakespeare use Sidney's *Arcadia* as a source for
the subplot of *King Lear*; he found in it also the germ of the concept
of epicurean atheism that he develops into Edmund's pronounce-
ment of self-sufficiency.   Specific parallels are cited for his line
"Thou, Nature, art my goddess" (I, ii, 1) from Cecropia's argument
to induce her niece Pamela to accept her son as husband in defiance
of a father's wishes. Pamela's response is possibly a source for Edgar's "clearest gods, who make them honours / Of men's impossibili-
ties" (IV, vi, 73-74).

1257   Atkinson, A. D. "Additional Florio-Shakespeare Resemblances."
       Notes and Queries, 194 (1949), 356-358.

Shakespeare's general familiarity with John Florio's translation
of Montaigne is obvious in numerous spots in the plays. A single
paragraph in Florio (II, 12), for example, deals with precipices, the
fear of heights, and a philosopher's pulling out his eyes. Surely this
paragraph served as a general source for the "Dover Cliff" scene in
King Lear.

1258   D[avenport], A[rnold]. "Possible Echoes from Sidney's *Arcadia*
       in Shakespeare, Milton, and Others." *Notes and Queries,* 194
       (1949), 554-555.

Sidney's *Arcadia* is generally accepted as the source of Shakespeare's subplot in *King Lear.* Not noticed before, however, is the
fact that the Paphlagonian king, like Gloucester, died from an excess
of joy after too much tribulation.

1259   Fischer, Walther P. "King Lear at Tuebingen: Johannes Nau-
       clerus and Geoffrey of Monmouth," *Philologica: The Malone
       Anniversary Studies.* Edited by T. A. Kirby and H. B. Woolf.
       Baltimore: Johns Hopkins University Press, 1949, pp. 208-
       227.

       This study of pre-Shakespearean versions of the Lear story re-
prints and analyzes the pertinent portions of Geoffrey of Monmouth's *Historia Regum Britanniae* and Johannes Nauclerus' *Universal History.*

1260   Hewitt, Douglas. "The Very Pompes of the Divell—Popular and
       Folk Elements in Elizabethan and Jacobean Drama." *Review
       of English Studies,* 25 (1949), 10-23.

       The Lear story is found as a folk-tale in many parts of the
British Isles, most strikingly, perhaps, in the story of "Cap of
Rushes." More importantly, Shakespeare's treatment of the story
makes the principal issue the prolonged suffering of Lear, not the
external conflict with his daughters. This treatment links Lear with
the annual village ritual of the expulsion of the scapegoat. Certainly
Shakespeare's contemporary spectators would not approve of Lear's
expulsion and suffering because of this folk memory, but the feeling
of the inevitability of his expulsion and the human revulsion against
it may have created a greater tension.

1261   Muir, Kenneth. "*King Lear,* IV, i, 10." *Times Literary Supple -
       ment,* 3 June 1949, p. 365.

       One of the worst cruxes in *King Lear* is IV, i, 10—"Who's here,
my father poorlie, leed" (Q uncorrected), "Who's here, my father
parti-eyd" (Q corrected), "But who comes heere? My father poorely
led?" (F). A clue to Shakespeare's original intention may come
from the similar moment in Sidney's *Arcadia,* Shakespeare's source—
"an aged man, and a young, scarcely come to the age of a man, both
poorely arayed." Shakespeare may, then, have written "But who
comes heere? My father poorely 'rayed?"

1262   Elton, William. "Timothy Bright and Shakespeare's Seeds of
       Nature." *Modern Language Notes,* 65 (1950), 196-197.

The source of Lear's roar upon the heath (III, ii, 9-10) as well as of Macbeth's command to the witches to let "nature's germens tumble all together" need not be the Stoics and Neo-Platonists, as W. C. Curry argues in *Shakespeare's Philosophic Patterns.* Instead it may be Timothy Bright's *A Treatise of Melancholie* (1586).

1263   Law, Robert Adger. "Holinshed's Leir Story and Shakespeare's." *Studies in Philology,* 47 (1950), 42-50.

Holinshed's *Chronicles* is generally overrated as Shakespeare's source for *King Lear.* A careful analysis reveals that Holinshed used Fabyan, Matthew Paris, Geoffrey of Monmouth, and John Higgins' material in the *Mirror for Magistrates* to construct his prose narrative. At the same time he effected changes to place the focus on "Cordeilla, her genuine affection for her father, and the help she with her husband gave him" (p. 48) rather than on the cruelties inflicted on Leir. Shakespeare's emphasis, to the contrary, is on the agony and development of the old king. While he was surely familiar with Holinshed's account, he apparently set it totally aside in favor of the play on *Leir,* Geoffrey, and other versions of the story.

1264   Muir, Kenneth and John F. Danby. *"Arcadia* and *King Lear." Notes and Queries,* 195 (1950), 49-51.

The full extent of Shakespeare's borrowings from Sidney's *Arcadia* for *King Lear* has not been appreciated. Not only does the playwright develop his subplot from the narrative of the Paphlagonian king; he also derives more general thematic hints concerning the rights and wrongs of suicide, the justice of the gods, and the slaughter of the innocent from the debate between Plangus and Basilius in Chapter XII of Book 2.

1264a Craig, Hardin. "Motivation in Shakespeare's Choice of Materials." *Shakespeare Survey,* 4 (1951), 26-34.

Two steps are normally involved in the creative process, "the abstractive ability which sees and grasps a central form and a later mental operation in which imagination adds to this concept the subsidiary details which complete the picture or the play" (p. 26). Once the Elizabethan dramatist established his concept, his imagination was free to amplify and expand. Critical to Shakespeare's mental progress with *King Lear* is his bringing the tragic concept of the blind king of Paphlagonia from Sidney's *Arcadia* to bear upon the essentially bright and cheerful *Chronicle History of King Leir.* The cruelty, the filial ingratitude, the deceit and dark intrigue, the theme of fugitives exposed to a storm, the death of the prototype of Gloucester—this material which establishes the tragic tone and temper of *Lear* is part of the concept later to be amplified with appropriate details.

1265   Muir, Kenneth.   "Samuel Harsnett and *King Lear.*" *Review of English Studies,* n.s. 2 (1951), 11-21.

Shakespeare's debt in *King Lear* to Samuel Harsnett's *A Declaration of Egregious Popish Impostures* is more extensive than previous editors have realized.   This article presents "a complete collection of passages which Shakespeare may have echoed" (p. 21). Especially notable is Harsnett's detailed knowledge of the theater; references are constant to actors, comedians, tragedians, performing, and the like.   The tract describes the supposed exorcism of devils from three chambermaids in the family of Edmund Peckham in 1585. Many of Edgar's allusions as Tom o' Bedlam are drawn from Harsnett, as is much of the material in the storm scene.

1266   Sisson, Charles Jasper.   "Elizabethan Life in Public Records." *The Listener,* 21 June 1951, pp. 998-999.

The chancery records comprise an invaluable source of information for understanding Shakespeare and his contemporaries. They reveal, for instance, a situation parallel to that of *King Lear* in Brian Annesley and his three daughters. See items 95, 383, 530, 705, 876, 1276, 1310, 1319, 1343.

1267   Muir, Kenneth.   "Shakespeare and Harsnett." *Notes and Queries,* 197 (1952), 555-556.

Additional small parallels are noted between *King Lear* and Samuel Harsnett's *Declaration of Egregious Popish Impostures.* For instance, several words used by Shakespeare for the first time are in Harsnett (propinquity, auricular).   Also, a passage in Harsnett is reminiscent of Lear and his companions in the storm and of Lear's comment on Edgar's (Tom's) garments.

1268   Ribner, Irving. "Sidney's *Arcadia* and the Structure of *King Lear.*" *Studia Neophilologica,* 24 (1952), 63-68.

Shakespeare in *King Lear* borrowed not only the subplot from Sidney's *Arcadia* but the structural function as well. Sidney's main plot relates the evils that befall a kingdom when its ruler refuses to accept his responsibilities, a theme probably topically motivated by Queen Elizabeth's projected marriage to the Duc D'Alencon. The story of the blind Paphlagonian king functions to reinforce and amplify this basic theme. Such is the case also in *King Lear.* The subplot reinforces and provides cosmic application for the theme of the main plot, the sin of resigning royal authority.

1269   Stevenson, Robert. "Shakespeare's Interest in Harsnett's *Declaration.*" *PMLA,* 67 (1952), 898-902. Reprint. *Shakespeare's Religious Frontier.* The Hague: Martinus Nijoff, 1958, pp. 62-66.

Harsnett's *A Declaration of Egregious Popish Impostures* is the one piece of polemical divinity we know Shakespeare to have digested with some care. The main purpose of the book is to ridicule the exorcising activities of a band of Jesuits, among them a certain Robert Debdale, a neighbor of the Hathaways at Shottery. Possibly Debdale was even one of Shakespeare's former schoolmates. The *Declaration* attracted him, then, not as religious polemic or a source of devil's names but as "the record of the last days of an early Shottery connection" (p. 902).

1270   Parr, Johnstone. "The 'Late Eclipses' in *King Lear*" and "Edmund's Birth under Ursa Major." *Tamburlaine's Malady and Other Essays on Astrology in Elizabethan Drama.* Tuscaloosa: University of Alabama Press, 1953, pp. 70-84.

The Renaissance assumptions concerning both the eclipse in the first essay and the astrological table in the second are drawn from Claudius Ptolemy. In particular, the *Quadripartitum* describes the manner in which various kinds of people are affected by cosmological events such as eclipses. Edmund, despite his protestations of independence and self-determination, accurately reflects Ptolemy's assertion that one born under Ursa Major, under the respective influences of Mars and Venus, was liable to develop a personality characterized by villainy and adulterous lechery.

1271   Isham, Gyles. "The Prototypes of King Lear and His Daughters." *Notes and Queries,* n.s. 1 (1954), 150-151.

It is likely that the plot of *King Lear* was inspired by the story of Brian Annesley of Lee and his three daughters, the youngest of whom (Cordell) is called Cordelia both in her marriage and death records. Cordell's husband, Sir William Harvey, may have been the model for Kent. At the time of the composition and the first re-corded performance of *Lear* the story of Cordell's saving her father from being declared insane and from having his estate confiscated would have been fresh in the mind.

1272   Salter, K. W.   *"Lear* and the Morality Tradition." *Notes and Queries,* n.s. 1 (1954), 109-110.

The deeply religious content of *King Lear* is a matter of con-siderable critical record. Further evidence of that fact is the similari-ty between IV, ii, 46 ff., and *Everyman* (11. 47-50). The essence of both passages is that man, without the check of divine sanctions, is bestial.

1273   Muir, Kenneth.   *"King Lear* IV. 6." *Notes and Queries,* n.s. 2 (1955), 15.

The episode of Gloucester's leap from the "cliffs of Dover" was probably suggested by the description in Holinshed of the wrest-ling match between Corines and Gogmagog, in which the latter was thrown over a cliff afterwards called "The Fall of Dover."

1274   Loske, Olav. "The Story and the Play." *Orbis Litterarum,* 11 (1956), 237-244.

This article describes the nature of the alterations Elizabethan dramatists made in their source materials, in part the demands of dramatic form and in part the expectations of contemporary audi-ences. Particular attention is focused on *Lear* and *Macbeth* and the metaphysical ambiguities that reflect the philosophic tensions of the age.

1275   Musgrove, S.   "The Nomenclature of *King Lear.*"   *Review of English Studies*, n.s. 7 (1956), 294-298.

Shakespeare, in addition to traditional sources cited for *King Lear*, probably also consulted Camden's *Remains*   either in print or manuscript.   From Camden's glossary of Saxon names he could have gotten Oswald, Edgar, and Edmund, whereas the names of the other principal characters have British names derived ultimately from Geoffrey of Monmouth; the names Gloucester, Kent, and even Caius occur in close proximity.   Moreover, several passages markedly resemble lines in *Lear*, such as Lear's bitter quip to Cordelia that nothing will come of nothing or Lear's description of the rights of his kingdom at the beginning of the play or his speech beginning "O reason not the need" (II, iv, 266).

1275a Ekeblad, Inga-Stina.   *"King Lear* and *Selimus."*   *Notes and Queries*, n.s. 4 (1957), 193-194.

The blinding of Gloucester in *King Lear* seems to echo a parallel situation in *Selimus*, a play written in the early 1590's probably by Robert Greene.   Whereas in *Arcadia* the Paphlagonian king is blinded by his son and the action is reported in the narrative, in *Selimus* the blinding occurs on stage, and it is carried out, as in *Lear*, by a child of the king in retaliation for his loyalty to that king. *Selimus*, moreover, involves a king with three sons, two of them evil and one faithful; a follower of one of the evil sons is named Regan.

1276   Muir, Kenneth. "Great Tragedies II: *King Lear." Shakespeare's Sources: Comedies and Tragedies.* London: Methuen, 1957, pp. 141-166.   Reprint. *William Shakespeare: The Great Tragedies.* London: Longmans, Green (for the British Council and National Book League), 1961.

Shakespeare created *King Lear* from the most heterogeneous materials—a chronicle play, a prose chronicle, two poems, and a pastoral romance.   The result is perhaps the most impressive evidence of his dramatic craftsmanship.   Above all the play is closely knit; he does not employ the loose episodic structure of the chronicle play.   The sources include Holinshed's *Chronicles, The Mirror for Magistrates*, Spenser's *The Faerie Queene*, the anonymous *King Leir*,

Sidney's *Arcadia,* and Harsnett's *Declaration of Egregious Popish Impostures.* A few details are also drawn from *Titus Andronicus* and *The London Prodigal.* Additional possible sources are Geoffrey of Monmouth's history, Gerard Legh's *Accedens of Armoury,* and William Camden's *Remains.* Muir directs detailed attention to Shakespeare's use of Harsnett and *Leir.* See items 1267, 1343.

1277   Cauthen, I. B., Jr. " 'The Foule Flibbertigibbet': *King Lear,* III. iv. 113; IV. i. 60." *Notes and Queries,* n.s. 5 (1958), 98-99.

Edgar's references to Flibbertigibbit are uniformly traced to Harsnett's *A Declaration of Egregious Popish Impostures* (1603), where the term is used as the name of a devil. Also, in Latimer's *Second Sermon Before Edward IV* (1549) and in John Heywood's *Proverbs and Epigrams* (1562), the word means gossipy person and wretch respectively. In the earlier *The Castell of Perseverance* (c. 1425) the word is used three times in a context which seems to involve both meanings, that of the devil and of the gossipy person. Although Shakespeare probably did not know the earlier morality play, his meaning of Flibbertigibbit does seem to retain the multiplicity of meaning found in it.

1278   Goldsmith, Robert Hillis. "Did Shakespeare Use the Old Timon Comedy?" *Shakespeare Quarterly,* 9 (1958), 31-38.

As a number of parallel passages reveal, Shakespeare may have used an English academic play, *Timon,* as a source for *King Lear* as well as for *Timon of Athens.* The old play was not published until 1842 and the date of composition is uncertain, but the similarities suggest that Shakespeare was familiar with it.

1279   Law, Robert Adgar. "*King Leir* and *King Lear*: An Examination of the Two Plays." *Studies in Honor of T. W. Baldwin.* Edited by Don Cameron Allen. Urbana: University of Illinois Press, 1958, pp. 112-124.

As both Furness and Greg agree, *Leir* is Shakespeare's major source for *Lear.* The anonymous playwright follows the general outline of the narrative from Geoffrey of Monmouth; key added scenes involve Cordell's wooing by Gallia, the messenger's threatening to kill Leir, and Leir's meeting Cordell with mutual forgiveness.

Shakespeare in adapting the romance to tragedy adds the ending with the defeat and death of Cordelia and the Gloucester plot from Sidney. Act III, with the events of the storm on the heath, and Act V, with the battle, Cordelia's defeat and hanging, and Lear's death, owe little or nothing to the old play. Shakespeare generally eliminates the easy poetic justice and the tedious expositional soliloquies.

1280   McNeal, Thomas H. "Shakespeare's Cruel Queens." *Huntington Library Quarterly*, 22 (1958-1959), 41-50.

The murderous woman who figures in Shakespeare from Queen Margaret in the *Henry VI* plays to Lady Macbeth finds its origin in Gonorill and Ragan of *King Leir.* "To watch this progress of Shakespeare's wicked queens out of *Leir*—from Margaret, through Beatrice and Goneril and Regan, and finally to the completely realized Lady Macbeth—is to follow the artist from his youth into his full maturity, out of his late twenties into his early forties" (p. 50).

1281   Potts, Abbie Findlay. "The Book of Holiness as a Design for Tragedy." *Shakespeare and The Faerie Queene*. Ithaca: Cornell University Press, 1958, pp. 174-207.

The experience of spiritual wholeness or fragmentation furnishes the central archetype in poetry, especially drama. Spenser's Book of Holiness is the most elaborate statement of the dilemma in English literature, and Shakespeare's major tragedies are its supreme illustration. The successive stages in Spenser's Book of Holiness are reflected in the succession of five major tragedies: *Othello, King Lear, Macbeth, Coriolanus,* and *Antony and Cleopatra*. Edmund reflects Sansjoi, and Goneril's hypocrisy reflects Duessa. The struggle between Albany-Edgar and Goneril-Edmund echoes the battle between the Redcrosse Knight and Sansjoi in the lists of Lucifera at the House of Pride. The most arresting similarities involve Spenser's House of Pride, Cave of Despair, and House of Holiness; the Redcrosse Knight's departure from the first, escape from the second, and ascent to the third provide the allegorical design behind the experiences of Lear and Gloucester. In the House of Pride Lucifera and Duessa reflect Goneril and Regan. The Knight and his Dwarf escaping from the Cave of Despair prefigure Lear and the Fool emerging from the control of the evil sisters; Gloucester's experience in despair also finds its source here with Sir Trevisan furnishing the allegorical type. Una is Lear's Cordelia in ministering to the Knight in the House of Holiness; both Spenser's and Shakespeare's principals have achieved a kind of New Jerusalem.

1282   Seng, Peter J. "An Early Tune for the Fool's Song in *King Lear.*" *Shakespeare Quarterly,* 9 (1958), 583-585.

The musical setting for the Fool's song "Then they for sudden joy did weep" (I, iv, 191-194) is preserved in *Pammelia, Musicks Miscellanie* (1609) in the British Library. The original of the song and of its manuscript fragment is the "Ballad of John Careless." That Shakespeare should have adopted it for one of the Fool's songs is not surprising since contemporary references indicate that it was extremely popular. The *Pammelia* preserves the only near-contemporary melody for the song thus far discovered.

1283   Hubbell, Lindley Williams. *"King Lear."* Lectures on Shakespeare. Tokyo: Nan'Un-Do, 1959, pp. 103-118.

Wilfrid Perrett, in *The Story of King Lear From Geoffrey of Monmouth to Shakespeare* (1904), traces over fifty versions of the Lear story from Geoffrey of Monmouth around 1130 to Shakespeare in the early seventeenth century. Certainly Shakespeare's most important source was the anonymous *Leir* play, first mentioned in 1594 and possibly by the author of *Locrine.* The fundamental differences are Shakespeare's tragic ending and his addition of the Gloucester double plot. Shakespeare improves on the opening scene by having Goneril's and Regan's comments unpremeditated and hence psychologically more revealing. The storm scene is another illustration of a powerful moment based on a trivial incident in the old play. The adaptations imposed on *Lear* by Nahum Tate are shocking and manifold.

1284   De Mendonça, Barbara Heliodora Carneiro. "The Influence of *Gorboduc* on *King Lear.*" *Shakespeare Survey,* 13 (1960), 41-48.

The tragic tone of Shakespeare's *King Lear* is alien to all of the sources. Moreover, Shakespeare establishes a philosophic backdrop

involving the question of the nature of man and the political implications of the disregard for hierarchical structure. In this respect
Gorboduc may very well have provided the controlling idea. Both
plays concern a rash decision by the king which leads to personal
and public disaster for both the guilty and the innocent. Both are
set in mythical classical environments, and they share numerous
verbal parallels not found in the other sources—death, rule, war,
governance, kingdom, treason, treachery, battery, foul, monster,
heinous, and numerous uses of animal imagery. Both possess a rapid
pace of action quite foreign to the leisurely progress of the source
stories; in both the nation is restored to hierarchic rule through an
agonizing process of destruction and catharsis. "There are altogether too many points of contact between *King Lear* and *Gorboduc*
in tone, general conception and language, for a close relationship
between them not to be admitted"(p. 47).

1285   Hyde, Isabel. "A Note on *King Lear* and *Timon of Athens.*"
       Notes and Queries, n.s. 7 (1960), 19-20.

       Shakespeare in *King Lear* utilizes a passage from Lucian's
Dialogue, *Timon or the Misanthrope,* which he does not use in
Timon of Athens. Lear's invocation to the gods to drench the earth
and punish the guilty through storm and lightning directly draws
upon Timon's plea to Zeus to blast the ingrates of Athens. This relationship does not settle the question of which is the prior play;
but, if Shakespeare wrote *Lear* first, he must already have read
Lucian or have heard his version of the Timon story in some detail.

1286   Law, Robert Adger. *"King John* and *King Leir."* Texas Studies
       in Literature, 1 (1960), 473-476.

       Shakespeare's use of *King Leir* as a source for *King Lear* is
generally accepted. Apparently, however, he had used the play
earlier as a source for *King John.* Particular similarities are noted in
Leir, 1. 1173, and *John,* IV, ii, 76, and in *Leir,* 1. 744, and *John,* IV,
iii, 23. The parallel extends beyond words to likeness of situation
and thought.

1287   Lloyd, Michael. "Plutarch's Daemons in Shakespeare." *Notes
       and Queries,* n.s. 7 (1960), 324-327.

Shakespeare was apparently familiar with Plutarch's theories of daemons as ministers of the gods. Albany, in *King Lear*, supposes the "visible spirits" as sent to tame men's offenses. A daemon also is the spirit of one dead; Lear imagines Cordelia to be a "spirit," a "soul in bliss."

1288   Entry Deleted.

1289   Garton, Charles. "Poor Tom in *King Lear*." *Times Literary Supplement*, 15 December 1961, p. 904.

Previous criticism has obscured the extent to which Shakespeare has Edgar as Poor Tom mimic the street cries of London. A first-hand version of such cries is provided in Orlando Gibbon's *The Cries of London*. Both "Tom's a cold" and Lear's line "Poor naked wretches" are apparently taken directly from one of the cries beginning "Poor naked Bedlam, Tom's a-cold."

1290   Pervaz, Draginja. "Legenda o kralju Liru." *Zbornik priloga istoriji jugoslovenskih pozorista*, special edition (1961), pp. 228-231.

This brief article surveys the development of the Lear legend with particular emphasis upon Shakespeare's treatment and the universal nature of his tragedy.

1291   Sampley, Arthur M. "Two Analogues to Shakespeare's Treatment of the Wooing of Cordelia." *Shakespeare Quarterly*, 12 (1961), 468-469.

None of the traditional sources of *King Lear* depicts rival wooers for Cordelia present at the English court. Burgundy is Shakespeare's addition, and the King of France is not at court when Cordelia is banished in any previous version. A close analogue appears in Dekker's *Old Fortunatus*, printed in 1600, in which Agripyne, daughter of King Athelstane of England, suddenly becomes deformed and in turn is rejected by the favored suitor, the Prince of Cypress, and subsequently accepted by the rival wooer, the Lord of Orleans. A more remote analogue appears in the anonymous *The Wisdom of Dr. Dodipoll*, also printed in 1600.

1292   Shapiro, I. A. "Shakespeare and Munday." *Shakespeare Survey,*
          14 (1961), 25-33.

          Possibly the basic plot and general outlook of *King Lear* was
       dictated to Shakespeare by the great success of *The Chronicle His-*
       tory of Leir, and possibly that work was supplied by Anthony
       Munday.

1293   Buckley, G. T.   " 'These Late Eclipses' Again." *Shakespeare*
          Quarterly, 13 (1962), 253-256.

          Although it is a physical, astronomical impossibility for eclip-
       ses to occur within fewer than fourteen days of each other, critical
       comments—those of E. K. Chambers, G. B. Harrison, W. A. Neilson
       and C. J. Hill among them—persist in dating the events possibly re-
       ferred to in *King Lear* as a partial eclipse of the moon on 27 Septem-
       ber 1605 and a nearly total eclipse of the sun on 2 October 1605.
       What started as a typographical error possibly was perpetuated by
       repetition. Some confusion is also evident in John Harvey's *A Dis-*
       coursive Probleme Concerning Prophecies printed in 1588 and avail-
       able in the Furness Variorum. Perhaps a simple confusion of Old
       Style and New Style dating is the answer. The dates of the eclipses
       by the Gregorian calendar were 27 September and 12 October. But
       the dates should be cited from the Julian calendar then in use in
       England as 17 September and 2 October.

1294   Sternfield, F. W.   "Poor Tom in *King Lear.*" *Times Literary*
          Supplement, 5 January 1962, p. 9.

          While the recent Arden and Cambridge editions of *King Lear*
       do not cite Orlando Gibbon's "London Cry" as a gloss on Edgar's
       line "Tom's a-cold," the point—Charles Garton's claim notwith-
       standing (see item 1289)—has been discussed previously by Sir
       Frederick Bridge, F. Allison and H. Just, E. H. Fellowes, and F. P.
       Wilson.

1295   Viola, Wilhelm. "Der Lear—Stoff bis zu Shakespeare." *Prisma*
          (Bochum) (1963/1964), pp. 6-7.

          This article sketches the development of the Lear story prior
       to Shakespeare.

1296   Alexander, Peter. *"King Lear." Alexander's Introductions to Shakespeare.* New York: Norton, 1964, pp. 164-166.

The tragic ending of the Lear story, contrary to popular assumption, is not original with Shakespeare. Indeed, Cordelia dies a tragic death in Holinshed, Spenser, and Higgins, among others. Only in the anonymous *King Leir* does Cordelia survive to restore the old king to his throne. Shakespeare gains a particular thematic focus, of course, by juxtaposing the deaths of Lear and Cordelia, a focus reemphasized through a second plot line drawn from Sidney. See item 1545.

1297   Alexander, Peter. "The Tragedies." *Shakespeare.* London: Oxford University Press, 1964, pp. 204-250.

It is unlikely, if *Leir* is the source of *Lear,* that Shakespeare could appropriate so much of someone else's play. More likely he was author of the older play a decade or so earlier while associated with Pembroke's men. Ingratitude is the force against which we measure Lear's progress as he passes through an ordeal that permits him to discover the hidden strength in his nature. The subplot is used to point out explicitly that Lear dies "not in despair but from an excess of joy" (p. 234).

1298   Bowen, Gwynneth. "Hackney, Harsnett, and the Devils in *King Lear." Shakespearean Authorship Review,* No. 14 (Autumn, 1965), pp. 2-7.

Since at every point that *King Lear* echoes Samuel Harsnett the latter is quoting *The Book of Miracles* (ca. 1585-1586), it is likely that that book is the playwright's source rather than *Egregious Popish Impostures.* Thus *King Lear* was probably written before the publication of Harsnett's pamphlet. Demonstrable connections between the Earl of Oxford and the Village of Hackney, where Roman Catholic priests resided, suggest Oxford's authorship.

1299   Jones, James Horace. "Shakespeare's Transformation of His Sources in *King Lear."* Ph.D. dissertation, Indiana University, 1965. *DA,* 26 (1966), 4630-4631.

Cordelia's answer and the father's lament, the two most important clues to the story's meaning, are handled differently in the various versions of the Lear story. In Geoffrey of Monmouth's *History of the Kings of Britain*, the king's love test expressed a quantitative demand for more than filial love. He banishes the daughter for suggesting in riddling fashion that love cannot be measured. The old play of *Leir*, on the other hand, substitutes Puritanism for Paganism and emphasizes the daughter's dutifulness rather than her perception of love. Shakespeare's Lear is misled by pagan pride (a craving for undue exaltation) in his quest for love; his egoism prevents him from understanding natural law, and only adversity can bring him to a discovery of love's transcendence of worth. Cordelia, unlike her earlier counterparts, is neither wise or loving initially; the potential for benevolent love develops in her character in the course of the play. In Shakespeare's version her rescue of her father is spiritual rather than temporal.

1300   Livermore, Ann. "Shakespeare and St. Augustine." *Quarterly Review*, No. 644 (April, 1965), pp. 181-193.

This article describes previously unnoticed parallels between St. Augustine's *City of God* and five Shakespearean plays, including *King Lear*. Parallels are also cited between the *Confessions* and *Hamlet* and *The Taming of the Shrew*.

1301   Rossiter-Smith, H. "Ripeness Is All." *Notes and Queries*, n.s. 12 (1965), 97.

While T. W. Baldwin admits that Shakespeare may well have read Cicero's *De Senectute* at school, he detects no use of this work in his plays. It would appear that a clear example of such usage is found in Edgar's advice to Gloucester that "Men must endure / Their going hence, even as their coming hither: / Ripeness is all" (V, ii, 9-11). The passage strikingly resembles one of Cicero's chapters, which at one point reads "but old men die by a certain ripeness and maturity."

1301a Schoff, F. G. "Ripeness Is All." *Notes and Queries*, n.s. 12 (1965), 353.

The suggestion by H. Rossiter-Smith (see item 1301) that Shakespeare drew Edgar's statement "Ripeness is all" from a clause in Cicero's *De Senectute* ("[O]ld men die by a certain ripeness and maturity") might be reinforced by comparison of yet another sentence from the same passage ("Old men die as it were fire . . .") with Sonnet 73. The entire process, however, of source hunting for such commonplace images of life can be a deceptive snare.

1302 Whitaker, Virgil K. "In Search of Shakespeare's Journal." *Studies in English Literature,* 5 (1965), 303-315.

Shakespeare's development as a playwright can be traced through a study of his use of sources. Especially revealing is his structural device of doubling, which reaches a peak in *Hamlet* and *King Lear.* Moreover, the concept of patience as the supreme virtue, fully developed in *Lear,* can also be traced back to *Hamlet.* Demonstrably Shakespeare grew in wisdom and skill through the years of his active work.

1303 Satin, Joseph. *"King Lear." Shakespeare and His Sources.* New York: Houghton Mifflin, 1966, pp. 445-532.

The direct sources of both the plot and the subplot of *King Lear* are clearly defined and richly detailed. Moreover, the main plot source can be traced back to its origin. The immediate source was the anonymous play *King Leir;* major points of divergence are Leir's and Perillus' (Kent's) going into France and the King of France's successful invasion of England and restoration of Leir to the throne. Behind the old chronicle play lies the earliest version (c. 1135) in Geoffrey of Monmouth and subsequent versions in Holinshed and Spenser (and possibly in Higgins' account in *Mirror for Magistrates* and a ballad, "King Leir and His Three Daughters"). The subplot is drawn from Sidney's *Arcadia. King Lear,* the most profound spiritual experience in Shakespeare, is of course greater than its sources; an addition of major significance is the protagonist's madness. Above all, Shakespeare universalizes the fable, raising it "from a little world whose main journey is across the Channel and back again aloft to a spacious and spiritual universe" (p. 447). Appropriate passages are included from Geoffrey of Monmouth, Holinshed, Spenser, and Sidney along with the full text of *The True Chronicle History of King Leir.*

1304 Snyder, Susan. *"King Lear* and the Prodigal Son." *Shakespeare Quarterly,* 17 (1966), 361-369.

The parable of the Prodigal Son was apparently a shaping force on *King Lear*. In broad outline *Lear* like the parable involves a protagonist who rejects the one who most loves him, "embarks on a reckless course which brings him eventually to suffering and want—and, paradoxically, to the self-knowledge he lacked before—and finally is received and forgiven by the rejected one" (pp. 362-363). Parallel, too, are the family relationships and the premature granting of portions. Lear like the prodigal is ashamed to face Cordelia; Cordelia like the father searches for him; he is welcomed with open arms and, as in the Biblical story, there is an explicit suggestion of rebirth. Goneril and Regan are agents for humbling and educating Lear. The parent figure is Cordelia, and the theme of the child as mentor is reinforced through Edgar's actions on behalf of Gloucester. The play is pagan in its setting, and the stern justice of the gods offers little comfort to man. Even so, Cordelia is a mortal embodiment of the Christ principle. Through her "Shakespeare shows that if there were no Christian ethic we should have to invent one. Regardless of the next world, man's salvation in this one depends only on love and forgiveness" (p. 368).

1305   Godshalk, William L. "Ripeness Is All." *Notes and Queries*, n.s. 14 (1967), 145.

E. K.'s remarks on the emblem to "November" in *The Shepheardes Calender* form a much more plausible source for Edgar's comment to Gloucester ("Ripeness is all") than Cicero (see items 1301 and 1301a). Shakespeare's audience would not have envisioned death as the supreme evil and hence not as the punishment for some ill-doing.

1306   Rosenberg, Marvin. "The Lear Myth." *Shakespeare Newsletter*, 17 (1967), 3.

Shakespeare's plot for *King Lear* is related to the mythic story of the parent who misjudges true love among his children, a story that can be traced back into Chinese, Indian, African, and Irish literature. Shakespeare moves beyond the mythic frame, however, imbuing his characters with a complexity and an ambiguity that provides them with the dimensions of compelling dramatic identity. This is an abstract of a paper delivered at the Shakespeare Section of the Modern Language Association meeting in New York in 1966.

1307   Stanley, E. G. "Ripeness Is All." *Notes and Queries,* n.s. 14 (1967), 228-229.

The Ciceronian concept of ripeness for death, maintained as a source for Edgar's comment to Gloucester by H. Rossiter-Smith (see item 1301) and F. G. Schoff (see item 1301a), is found elsewhere in seventeenth-century literature—for instance, in *Paradise Lost,* XI, 535-538. Thomas Newton, in his edition of Milton in 1749, specifically cites Cicero as the poet's source.

1308   Saner, Reginald A. " 'Gemless Rings' in *Purgatorio* XXIII and *Lear." Romance Notes,* 10 (1968), 163-167.

Edgar's comment in III, v, concerning his blinded father's "bleeding rings, / Their precious stones new lost" closely parallels Dante's description of Forese Donati in Purgatory. Both Edgar and Dante experience extreme misery and shock when first observing their woefully altered acquaintances. The similarity, both verbal and emotional, can hardly be coincidental.

1309   Vickers, Brian. *"King Lear* and Renaissance Paradoxes." *Modern Language Review,* 63 (1968), 305-314.

Since *King Lear* is characterized by paradoxical, riddling, contradictory elements, it is not surprising that apparently Shakespeare was reading the *Paradossi* of Ortensio Landi, first published in 1543, translated into French in 1553 by Charles Estienne, and in turn by Antony Munday in 1593 as *The Defence of Contraries.* The paradox for the Renaissance was essentially a serious mode of philosophical argument. The link between the philosophical and rhetorical applications is perhaps Cicero, for the "paradox became associated with the *Thesis* (a 'proposition' laid down to be proved by argument) and so with the *disputatio* or debate" (p. 306). As a rhetorical figure it was normally utilized to test a moral proposition through the shock tactic of inversion. The specific paradoxes which are reflected in *Lear* deal with *Omnia fieri ex nihilo,* the praise of bastards, the preference of prison to liberty, the necessity of blindness for sight, and the advantages of nakedness and poverty.

1310   Bullough, Geoffrey. *"King Lear* and the Annesley Case: A Reconsideration." *Festschrift Rudolf Stamm: zu Seinem*

Sechzigaten Geburstag am 12 April 1969. Edited by Eduard Kolb und Jörg Hasler. Bern: Francke Verlag, 1969, pp. 43-49.

Brian Annesley of Lee, Lewisham, Kent, had three children—Grace, Christian, and Cordell. On 1 April 1600 he made a will leaving most of his property to Cordell. In 1603 the father became senile, and Grace (Lady Wildgoose) sought to gain control of the estate by having him adjudged senile. This attempt was countered by Cordell, who in a letter to Lord Cecil writes that her father's many years of faithful service to the late Queen deserve better reconpense than his being declared a lunatic. Cordell's defense was upheld; but, after his death on 10 July 1604, Grace disputed the will. Again her effort was defeated, and Cordell erected a memorial slab for her father in the Chancel of Lee Parish Church. The revival of *King Leir* may well have been occasioned by the talk of the Annesley affair; Shakespeare, similarly, when he began his *Lear* shortly after the revival of the old play, may well have been familiar with the affair. As Groom of the Chamber in ordinary, he would have occasion to be at court at the time Annesley's will was being disputed. Possibly Shakespeare, in substituting the name of Kent for that of Perillus, has given evidence of his knowledge of "the county where the modern Lear was persecuted and protected" (p. 49). See item 1266.

1311   Cox, Roger L. "*King Lear* and the Corinthian Letters." *Thought,* 44, No. 172 (1969), 5-28. Reprint. *Between Earth and Heaven: Shakespeare, Dostoevsky, and the Meaning of Christian Tragedy.* New York: Holt, Rinehart, and Winston, 1969, pp. 71-95.

All of the important evidence for the Christian interpretation of *King Lear* is found in the Corinthian Letters. Paul sets forth both the problems that vex the critics of *Lear,* and their solutions as well. The overriding subject of the tragedy is love with most relationships paralleled in the two plots in order to reflect their worst and best aspects. Paul's definition of love precisely describes Cordelia; what love is not reflects Goneril and Regan. First Corinthians 13 is Shakespeare's source for the imagery, humor, and symbolic action in *Lear;* moreover, Corinthians 1-4 sets forth the paradoxical relationship between wisdom and foolishness, the second great theme of *Lear.*

Lear's experience involves his movement from a position of seeing Cordelia as foolish to a point at which he is able to discern her spiritual love and wisdom. The "suggestion of resurrection and the possibility of redemption through suffering are unmistakably present" (p. 88) in the final act. Yet another source, for the sight-blindness paradox, is found in Second Corinthians. Shakespeare, in a word, seems to have "molded the substance of the Corinthian Letters to the form of the old *Leir* play and by this transformation to have produced something entirely new" (p. 91). To speak of the ending as pessimistic or optimistic is rather beside the point; only the conception of grace keeps Christianity from being the most pessimistic philosophy imaginable.

1312   Jones, James H. *"Leir* and *Lear:* Matthew 5:33-37, The Turning Point, and the Rescue Theme." *Comparative Drama,* 4 (1970-1971), 125-131.

Both *Leir* and *Lear* echo Matthew 5:33-37—a passage counseling man not to swear presumptuously by heaven or earth but to accept the power and judgment of God—at a crucial point in the action of the play. The divergent perspectives, however, help to explain how the ethos of Shakespeare's tragedy differs from that of the source play and other accounts with which he may have been familiar. For the anonymous play the biblical reference supports the strongly Puritan sense of sin and Providence, the emphasis on God's absolute sovereignty and man's lack of merit; time and again throughout the action characters comment on the mercy of God in preventing disastrous consequences. Shakespeare uses the passage to focus on a spiritual rather than temporal crisis. Lear is not protected from physical pain and adversity, and this experience teaches him humility, the delusion of the pride of self-sufficiency. The characters of *Leir* "viewed themselves as 'elect' and expected, like the ancient Hebrews, to see in temporal events the special protective care of Divine Providence. Shakespeare's tragedy, on the other hand, implies man's fears to be answered not temporally but spiritually" (p. 130).

1313   Westhoven, Morris. "Biblical Material in Shakespeare's Great Tragedies." Ph.D. dissertation, Kent State University, 1970. *DAI,* 31 (1971), 6026A-6027A.

This study expands the examination of Shakespeare's biblical allusions in *King Lear, Hamlet, Macbeth,* and *Othello.* It also incorporates the earlier allusions cited by T. R. Eaton, J. B. Seekirk, Thomas Carter, and Richmond Noble. All citations (e.g., *Lear* IV, vi, 98-105, and Second Corinthians 1:17-20) are to the Geneva Bible, unless they specifically indicate the Bishops' Bible, the Great Bible (Rheims), or the like. See item 1240.

1314   Cutts, John P. "The Fool's Prophecy—Another Version." *English Language Notes,* 9 (1971-1972), 262-265.

Criticism regarding the Fool's prophecy as spurious and non-Shakespearean should be revised in light of the playwright's habit of adapting popular materials to his own use. A hitherto unnoticed version of the prophecy (Bodleian MSS. Ashmole 36/37, f. 60, item number 74) "represents a certain stage in the development of the 'Merlin's Prophecy' which is closer in structural organization to the medieval variety as represented by Puttenham and Trinity College Dublin MS. 576, but closer thematically to the breakdown of clear distinctions between fulfilled and unfulfilled as represented by the state of the text in *Lear.* And its overall value is to indicate the vitality of the riddling prophecy as a game for any parodist's ingenuity" (p. 265).

1315   Satin, Joseph. "The Symbolic Role of Cordelia in *King Lear.*" *Forum,* 9, No. 3 (1971), 14-17.

Cordelia symbolizes the religion of beauty in woman, a Renaissance motif nurtured in Italy that later branched out throughout the rest of Europe. Her very name would have suggested this role to Shakespeare's contemporaries. The name Delia in Samuel Daniel's sonnet sequence stood for "Ideal"; Drayton called his fair lady Idea; Maurice Scève, Daniel's source, wrote dizains in praise of Délie. *Cor,* the Latin and Italian for "heart," was inextricably bound up with concepts of "mind" and "soul." The ultimate source of the tradition is Dante's *Vita Nuova,* which narrates the story of the poet's love for the idealized Beatrice. Lear initially spurns a perfect love and thereby unleashes disorder in the world; later he accepts and is saved by this same love. "Like Beatrice Cordelia must die so that Lear's love for her may reach its proper heavenly plane"

(p. 17). The tradition was so commonplace by Shakespeare's time that a few touchstone characteristics would call to mind the host of associated meanings.

1316   West, Michael. "Skelton and the Renaissance Theme of Folly." *Philological Quarterly*, 50 (1971), 23-35.

In the development of the fool character who possesses a certain degree of wisdom and who satirically exposes the fatuity of others Skelton is Shakespeare's most important precursor in England. His figures are distant ancestors of Touchstone, Feste, and above all Lear's Fool. Skelton takes the small but vital step from the assumption that all sinfulness is folly to the conclusion that mankind is composed entirely of fools. Lear's Fool is the culmination of the wise fool tradition that follows.

1317   Nagarajan, S. *"King Leir* and *King Lear." Studies in Elizabethan Literature.* Edited by P. S. Sastri. Ram Nagar, New Delhi: Chand, 1972, pp. 29-42.

Several fundamental points reflect the major differences between Shakespeare's *Lear* and its source *Leir.* Leir is a pious man fully aware of his physical infirmities; Lear is an imperious individual still vigorous and active. Cordella is a young woman who refuses to play a father's game of arranged marriage; Cordelia is a maiden whose very nature is selfless love and whose inability to speak arises from her incapacity for engaging in hypocrisy. The thunder in *Leir* is an audible illustration of heaven's presence; in *Lear* it is a reflection of the chaos into which all nature has been cast. *Lear* in the final analysis is indeed a bleak play in which pain is real; at the same time it forces us to look beyond the play and beyond life itself in its confirmation of our "admiration of goodness irrespective of the rewards and griefs that it might bring" (p. 41).

1318   Bode, Emil. *Die Learsage vor Shakespeare mit Ausschluss des älteren Dramas und der Ballade.* Wiesbaden: Sandig, 1973. (not seen)

1319   Bullough, Geoffrey, ed. *"King Lear." Narrative and Dramatic Sources of Shakespeare.* 7 vols. London: Routledge and Kegan Paul, 1973, VII, 269-420.

The story of King Lear belongs to a class well known in European and Oriental folklore. Though the name Leir was that of a Celtic sea-god, the story does not appear in Welsh national literature. It was introduced into England in Geoffrey of Monmouth's *Historia regium Britanniae* (c. 1135), a work of widespread significance in England and on the continent (about 170 MSS. survive). Shakespeare might well have been familiar with the story as treated by various Tudor chroniclers and versifiers—a prose *Brut* printed by Caxton in the fourteenth century (the eleventh edition was issued in 1528), Polydore Vergil's *Anglicae Historiae* (1534), Robert Fabyan's *New Chronicles* (1516), John Stowe's *Summarie of Englyshe Chronicles* (1563) and *Annales* (1592), Raphael Holinshed's *Chronicles* (1577), William Camden's *Remains* (1605), John Higgins' additions to *The Mirror for Magistrates* (1574), Edmund Spenser's *The Faerie Queene*, and William Warner's *Albion's England* (1584-1606). The major source was apparently the anonymous play *The True Chronicle Historie of King Leir and his Three Daughters; Gonorell, Ragan, and Cordella* (first published in 1605 but probably not a new play when entered in the Stationers' Register in 1594). *Leir* is shaped by the Morality tradition (good and evil daughters, good and evil counsellors), and it is shot through with overt Christian reference. Thunder on the heath is a device by which God scares away the messenger who intends to murder the old king. The reconciliation of Leir and Cordella occurs in France shortly after the invading army is victorious, and Lear is restored to his throne. Shakespeare's Edmund-Edgar-Gloucester plot is drawn from Sidney's *Arcadia*. From such diverse sources Shakespeare constructs a drama dealing with "anger and despair, madness, the relations between parents and children, 'nature' and questionings of divine justice" (p. 297). Lear's madness is of special interest; indeed, the playwright surrounds the king with variations of mental aberration in the Fool, Gloucester's despair, and Tom o' Bedlam's demoniac possession, the latter influenced by Samuel Harsnett's *A Declaration of Egregious Popish Impostures ... Practised by Edmunds alias Weston, a Jesuit* (1603). Also of major importance, Shakespeare captures the polytheistic flavor of pre-Christian England by overlapping references to the Graeco-Roman gods, Nature in relation to the Divine, the concept of a divine power which should protect the innocent and punish the guilty, and Christian ideas. Source materials are reprinted from Cordell Annesley's defense of her father's sanity and property, Geoffrey of Monmouth, Holinshed, William Harrison, Camden, Higgins, Spenser, Warner, *Leir*, Sidney, and Harsnett. See items 1266, 1462.

1320   Glazier, Phyllis (Gorfain).   "Folkloristic Devices and Formal Structure in Shakespearean Drama."   Ph.D. dissertation, University of California—Berkeley, 1973.   *DAI*, 34 (1973), 3341A-3342A.

Shakespeare makes significant use of various forms of folklore such as the riddle, the proverb, and the game. In *King Lear*, for example, the love contest is intended to function as a rite of passage, but it fails to do so because Lear misuses irrationality. That is, he attempts to use the ritual for personal ends by forcing upon it meanings it will not accommodate. He subsequently must be educated through riddles, paradoxes, and proverbs. The folkloristic devices are also related to the play's use of disguises and deceptions. See item 1334.

1321   Jorgensen, Paul A.   "The Metamorphosis of Honesty in the Renaissance."   *English Literary Renaissance,* 3 (1973), 369-379.

The subplot of *A Knack to Know a Knave* employs abstractions drawn from the morality-play tradition, among them a character named Honesty, whose chief activity is to expose knaves through his satirical plain-speaking.   Not only does this play perhaps introduce a new meaning of honesty into Renaissance England ("a plain-speaking critic of society who is gifted in exposing knavery" [p. 370]); the character also apparently serves as a prototype for Kent in *King Lear*. As Honesty offers his service to King Edgar in *Knack*, so Kent (as Caius) offers his service to Lear as a "very honest-hearted fellow" (I, iv, 20); and, as Honesty quickly attacks a flattering courtier, Kent promptly victimizes the sycophant Oswald. It is his quality of satiric plainness that (as Kent) aggravates Lear and later (as Caius) enrages Cornwall.

1322   Hamilton, Donna B.   "Some Romance Sources for *King Lear:* Robert of Sicily and Robert the Devil." *Studies in Philology,* 71 (1974), 173-191.

Maynard Mack (see item 530) suggests convincingly that a major source of *King Lear* is the medieval legend of The Abasement of the Proud King, in particular that of Robert of Sicily, of which ten extant manuscripts exist from 1375 to 1500. An even more likely source is the tale of Robert the Devil, available in two editions by Wynkyn de Worde between 1500 and 1517 and retold by Thomas Lodge in 1591 in his prose romance, *The Famous true and historicall life of Robert second Duke of Normandy, surnamed for his monstrous birth and behaviour, Robin the Devill.* Robert's punishment for the folly of his pride involves his having to become the literal embodiment of stupidity and play the court fool, perhaps a source of Shakespeare's Fool as well. Both Lear and Robert "come to recognize their grievous errors, pass through periods of trial, suffering, and self-examination, and are ultimately rewarded" (p. 181). Also both the tale and Shakespeare's play connect evil with a deviant religious creed.

1323   Kaula, David. *"King Lear* and the *True Relation." Shakespeare and the Archpriest Controversy.* The Hague: Mouton, 1975, pp. 18-29.

The Jesuit conspiracy to seize control of the clergy in England began at Wisbech Castle in 1595 with William Weston's attempt, supported by Henry Garnet, to assume the leadership over his fellow prisoners. An account of Weston's conduct and of the ensuing quarrels at Wisbech was published in 1601, *A True relation of the faction begun at Wisbech . . . Against Us the Secular Priests their brethren and fellow Prisoners,* probably by Christopher Bagshan. Shakespeare in *King Lear* draws many specific words, phrases, and ideas as well as general similarities in character and incident from the pamphlet. Most significant perhaps are Goneril's repeated complaints about the conduct of Lear and his hundred knights, material not found in any of the play's other sources. Edmund, moreover, is quite similar to Weston in several prominent features. The issues involved in the Archpriest Controversy were still sufficiently compelling in 1605-1606 to influence Shakespeare, especially considering the tensions in the Catholic community provoked by the renewal of the recusancy laws in 1604 and the events of the Gunpowder Plot in 1605.

1324   Stewart, Alasdair M. "The Tale of King Lear in Scots." *Aberdeen University Review,* 46 (1975), 205-210.

A previously unpublished version of the Lear story is found in the MS. chronicle *The Roit or Quheill of Tyme,* written around 1537 by Adam Abell, a Franciscan Observant in Jedburgh. Obviously the tale warns of the general dangers of flattery, but it also seems to reflect upon the "pressing problems and contemporary themes current in the late 1530's in Scotland after Flodden and before the marriage and death of James V and the Rough Wooing of the 1540's" (p. 206).

1325   Cairncross, Andrew S. "Shakespeare and Ariosto: *Much Ado About Nothing, King Lear* and *Othello.*" *Renaissance Quarterly,* 29 (1976), 178-182.

Shakespeare's firsthand knowledge and use of Italian can be demonstrated by reference to cantos IV-VI of Ariosto's *Orlando Furioso,* material which—not available in all details in Sir John Harington's translation—the playwright utilized in *Much Ado About Nothing, King Lear,* and *Othello.* Specifically, the duel between Edmund and Edgar disguised as an anonymous knight seems to have its source in Ariosto. Ariodante in disguise as a plain knight challenges his brother Lurcanio in defense of Genevra, whose honor has been besmirched by a trick of the villain Polynesso and the maid Dalinda. At the sound of the third trumpet another plain knight, Rinaldo, who has discovered the truth of the deception, also appears to defend Genevra. He challenges and defeats the real culprit Polynesso, who confesses his machinations in his dying moments. Shakespeare compresses and simplifies this material for the Edmund-Edgar episode in *Lear.* The trial by combat does not occur in Holinshed or any other alleged source of the play; nor does it occur in the translated version of Ariosto. "This implies [Shakespeare's] knowledge of Ariosto in the Italian, which can be corroborated by his use of material that Harington omitted or paraphrased" (p. 180).

1326   Creeth, Edmund. "The King of Life in *King Lear*" and "The Uniqueness of *Othello, Macbeth,* and *King Lear.*" *Mankynde in Shakespeare.* Athens: University of Georgia Press, 1976, pp. 111-174.

In his great early Jacobean tragedies, Shakespeare returns to the structure of moral drama, thereby bringing literal and secular drama into intimate contact with the forms of Mankynde's temptations depicted in the moralities of the Macro MSS. This recrudescence of morality structure coincides with the Elizabethan twilight and in effect submits the standards of the age to an ethical test. *King Lear*, more specifically, appears to have its structural origins in the fragmentary moral *The Pride of Life*. Both plays utilize three basic movements—the protagonist's pride and wrath coupled with susceptibility to flattery and scorn for truth, especially as uttered by the woman nearest his heart; the chastening agony of the middle phase, during which time false friends desert him; and the restoration through kindness to a state of spiritual peace and grace. Both Rex Vivus and Lear are kings of Britain; other basic correspondences of character and theme are the boy Solas and the Fool, the queen and Cordelia as spokesmen of truth, the bishop and Kent, the false friends Strength and Health and Goneril and Regan, the debate between Body and Soul and Lear's intense introspection, the movement into the storm, and the virgin Mary and Cordelia in the role of spiritual renewal. The actual death of Lear and of Cordelia relate to the secular tragedy and is of no relevance to the comparison. "The Shakespearean avatar of the form of *The Pride of Life* yields the supreme tragedy of pride" (p. 151).

1327 Date, Toshihiro. *"King Lear* and Boethius." *Bulletin* (Otani Woman's University), 11 (1976), 1-18.

   King Lear is heavily influenced by Boethius, especially in the consolation of philosophy speeches of Edgar to his blinded father.

1328 Dundes, Alan. " 'To Love My Father All': A Psychoanalytic Study of the Folklore Source of *King Lear.*" *Southern Folklore Quarterly*, 40 (1976), 353-366.

   The "love like salt" folktale that lies behind the Lear story is a weakened version of the father who attempts to marry his daughter. In *Lear* the love test involves a daughter's declaring her total love of her father; it is a story of a daughter-father (not a father-daughter) incest. The play and its folktale source contain a girl unable to express this sexual love for the parent. Her later comment that she goes about her father's business is significant, as is her husband's absence in the final acts. The emotional reunion of daughter and father is the plot's logical and psychological denouement. In prison she "enjoys the culmination of her Electral Complex fantasy for but a brief instant" (p. 363).

1329   Jacobs, Edward Craney. "An Unnoted Debt to Kyd in *King Lear.*" *American Notes and Queries,* 14 (1976-1977), 19.

Edmund's comment to Kent in I, i, 31, "Sir, I shall study deserving," is best understood as highly ironic, implying not that he will aim at or seek to achieve deserving but that he will devise or meditate in a way to accomplish some revenge. The line is probably borrowed from Kyd's *The Spanish Tragedy,* in which the villain Balthazar also utters such an ironic comment, "And I shall study to deserve this grace," shortly before he murders Horatio.

1330   Nameri, Dorothy E. *Three Versions of the Story of King Lear Studied in Relation to One Another.* 2 Vols. Salzburg: Universität Salzburg, 1976.

While critics have explored the relationship, on the one hand, of Shakespeare's *King Lear* to the anonymous chronicle play *King Leir* and, on the other hand, of Shakespeare's play to Nahum Tate's adaptation, the significant relationship between *Leir* and Tate has not been examined. Demonstrably Tate borrowed thematic and structural elements from the old play—for example, the religious theme by which divine justice is vindicated through the restoration of order. "Tate follows the anonymous dramatist, and we find romance, religion and filial devotion linked, and functioning in the restoration of the king, thus conducing to the resolution of the plot which culminates in the happy ending" (p. 254). The love between Edgar and Cordelia is patterned after the relationship of Gallia and Cordella. Verbal parallels on numerous occasions reinforce the assumption that Tate drew from *Leir* as well as from Shakespeare. In all likelihood Tate was reluctant to announce his indebtedness to an anonymous author of a play not in vogue in the late seventeenth century; hence, he proclaimed only his zealous intention of rewriting Shakespeare's work.

1331   Uchiyama, Takado. "A Study of *King Lear* as a Christian Tragedy Considered as an Evolution from a Morality Play *Patience* in *King Leir.*" *Seishin Studies.* (University of Sacred Heart, Tokyo), 47 (1976), 1-29. (not seen)

1332   Cavalcanti, Leticiá Niederauer Tavares. "Raizes universals do teatro nordestino." *Correio das Artes,* supplement of *A União,* João Pessoa, Paraiba, Brazil, 23 December 1977, pp. 6-7.

An analysis of the theater of Northeastern Brazil reveals that in its roots it shares elements with Shakespeare and the best of the English tradition. *King Lear,* especially, with its symbolic characters and ritualistic themes, exemplifies several of these characteristics.

1333   Cary, Cecile Williamson. "The Problem of Evil in the *Arcadia* and *King Lear.*" *Shakespeare Newsletter,* 27 (1977), 30.

Sidney's *Arcadia* provided more than merely the narrative line of action for the subplot of *King Lear.* From it Shakespeare also drew the darkened philosophic atmosphere; it influenced his treatment of the problem of evil in the tragedy. This is an abstract of a paper delivered at the Ohio Shakespeare Conference in 1977.

1333a Donawerth, Jane. "Diogenes the Cynic and Lear's Definition of Man, *King Lear,* III. iv. 101-109." *English Language Notes,* 15 (1977-1978), 10-14.

The source of the definition of man given to Mad Tom in Act III is not Florio's translation of Montaigne but Plato, as known to the Renaissance through Diogenes Laertius' life of Diogenes the Cynic in *De vitis philosophorum.* Shakespeare might also have been familiar with the anecdote about Plato and Diogenes in Erasmus' *Apopthegmata.* Diogenes' mockery of Plato's definition is indeed related in Montaigne's "An Apology of Raymond Sebonde," but other details in the passage suggest that Shakespeare was drawing "also on the memory of his schoolboy's reading about Diogenes in either Erasmus or Diogenes Laertius" (p. 13). Lear's calling Tom a philosopher, more precisely a cynic, is appropriate, because the Renaissance believed such a philosopher could teach one properly to bear suffering.

1334   Gorfain, Phyllis (Glazier). "Contest, Riddle and Prophecy: Reflexivity through Folklore in *King Lear.*" *Southern Folklore Quarterly,* 41 (1977), 239-254.

Various folkloric forms in *King Lear* work reflexively to call attention to the nature and meaning of artifice; they work, that is, as metafolklore, contributing to the development of stage metaphors, disguise, and reflexive commentary. The initial love contest and the riddles exchanged between Lear and other characters establish certain expectations within the spectators; when the outcome is not that which is expected, the effect is to bring into question not only the conventional pattern of anticipation and result but also the very notions of justice and order upon which such conventional order is based. Through subtle "transformations of folkloric devices as well as with more literary means, such as poetry, characterization, and double plot, *King Lear* forces us to gain something through nothing" (p. 254). See item 1320.

1335   Greer, David. "A Spanish Song in *King Lear.*" *English Studies,* 58 (1977), 186-187.

The Fool's "Come o'er the broom, Bessie, to me" (Q_1 III, v, 27 ff.) refers to a popular song. While the words have not survived, its popularity is suggested by several moralizations, two broadside entries in the Stationers' Register, and a reference in Wager's *The Longer Thou Livest.* A song with a similar burden exists in a fifteenth-century Spanish collection. Possibly the song was transmitted to England at the time Katharine of Aragon and her entourage arrived in 1501.

1336   Jones, Emrys. "Shakespeare and the Mystery Cycles." *The Origins of Shakespeare.* Oxford: Oxford University Press, Clarendon Press, 1977, pp. 31-84.

In two scenes Lear is humiliated by the hostility of his evil daughters (I, iv; II, iv) who have now grown powerful. In each there is a progression from baiting by a single figure to mockery by two or more individuals. The scenes recall the "typical Caiphases and Annases of the Passion plays" (p. 57). Both the same ferocity and capacity for physical violence are present. The York "Second Trial before Pilate" is particularly analogous in structure. It would be wrong to push parallels too far, but in such scenes the "play seems to hold within itself memories of Passion sequences which Shakespeare had seen" (p. 59).

1337   Klinck, Dennis R. "Shakespeare's 'Tameness of a Wolf.' " *Notes and Queries,* n.s. 24 (1977), 113-114.

The Fool's comment, "He's mad that trusts in the tameness of a wolf" (III, vi, 18), draws upon two proverbial meanings as recorded by Simon Robson in *The Choice of Change* (1585)—the warning not to trust in dogs' (hounds') teeth and the warning not to trust in tamed wolves. See item 1234.

1338   Knight, W. Nicholas. "Patrimony and Shakespeare's Daughters." *Hartford Studies in Literature,* 9 (1977), 175-186.

Shakespeare's preoccupation with father-daughter relationships in his later plays reflects his own similar personal interests. *King Lear,* in particular, reflects his concern for justice and proper inheritance.   The main plot involves a father's dividing his estate upon his children's marriages, and the subplot involves an inheritance being stolen from the legitimate son. The latter may reflect the fact that a brother-in-law Edmund Lambert held from Shakespeare the inheritance he was to have gotten. The main plot may also reflect Shakespeare's personal concerns about inheritance when there is no living male issue. In another sense it celebrates an old man and his idealized daughter, perhaps a reflection of the joy of Susannah's marriage in 1607 to the prominent Dr. John Hall.

1338a Muir, Kenneth. *"King Lear." The Sources of Shakespeare's Plays.* New Haven: Yale University Press, 1977, pp. 196-208.

Whether Shakespeare was prompted to write *King Lear* by the contemporary incident of Brian Annesley and his daughters, he drew upon a wide range of sources—Geoffrey of Monmouth (possibly), Holinshed's *Chronicles* (both the 1577 and 1587 editions), Camden's *Remains* (probably published too late), Legh's *Accedens of Armory* (inconclusive), Spenser's *Faerie Queene,* Sidney's *Arcadia* (for the subplot), and above all the anonymous *King Leir.* The major alteration involved bridging the gap between Lear's restoration and Cordelia's death, making her murder causally connected with Lear's error, and bringing Lear to a full awareness of his folly. The subplot is more than a parallel to the Lear story. For one thing, Gloucester's conduct in the second scene helps the audience retrospectively accept Lear's foolish action in the first scene. For another, the meeting of the blind Gloucester and the mad Lear is the symbolic climax of the play. The storm is suggested by *Leir,* but the major inspiration for this scene comes from Harsnett's *Declaration of Egregious Popish Impostures.* Contrary to the charges of some critics, the structure is not loose; no lines can be deleted without distorting meaning and effect. The fusion of material from a chronicle play, one or more prose chronicles, two poems, and a pastoral romance is masterly, perhaps the single most impressive example of Shakespeare's skill as a dramatic craftsman.

1339   Seef, Adele. "Shakespeare's Medieval Heritage: Layamon's *Brut* as a Possible Source for *King Lear." Shakespeare Newsletter,* 27 (1977), 30.

Certain details in Shakespeare's *King Lear* which are found only in Layamon's treatment of the Lear story suggest that the *Brut* may have been a direct source for the playwright. Shakespeare, who had access to Layamon manuscripts, probably knew Middle English and possibly had some knowledge of Anglo-Saxon. This is an abstract of a paper delivered at the Ohio Shakespeare Conference in 1977.

1340   Duncan-Jones, Katherine. "Kent, Caius and Lear's Swordsmanship." *Notes and Queries,* n.s. 25 (1978), 151-153.

Kent's reference to Caius during his efforts to get Lear to recognize him ("The same; / Your servant Kent. Where is your servant Caius?" [V, iii, 282-83]) is an attempt to remind the king of games they played during swordpractice in former years. The name itself comes from a treatise on swordplay by Vincentio Saviolo, and Kent unsuccessfully uses the name—just following Lear's discussion of his own swordsmanship—in an attempt to gain full recognition from his master.

1341   Friedlander, Carolynn VanDyke. "The First English Story of King Lear: Layamon's *Brut,* Lines 1448-1887." *Allegorica,* 3 (1978), 42-49.

The original text and a translation into modern English are presented on facing pages. The material, if not precisely a source for Shakespeare's play, does present a provocative analogue.

1342   Kydryński, Juliusz.   "On Thomas Lodge's Rosalind."   *Zycie literackie* (Krakow), 32 (1978).

This article describes Lodge's influences on the anonymous chronicle play *King Leir*.

1343   Entry Deleted.

1344   Tobin, John J. M. "Apuleius and the Bradleian Tragedies." *Shakespeare Survey*, 31 (1978), 33-43.

Apparently Apuleius' *The Golden Asse* provided one of Shakespeare's early memorable reading experiences, and he drew on the story for a number of plays throughout his career, *King Lear* among them. The central episode of *The Golden Asse* involves three sisters, the youngest and best tormented by the other two. Moreover, one finds also an Edgar-like disguised madman possessed of fierce filial loyalty. Finally, the diction in the ending of the two works is too similar for it to be accidental—the repetition of the word *never,* the rhetorical question *why should,* words like *horse, lips, hanging.* Shakespeare no doubt had Apuleius' story in mind as he wrote of an impatient father and his laconic daughter.

1345   Weimann, Robert. "The English Folk Play and Shakespeare" and "Figurenposition: The Correlation of Position and Expression." *Shakespeare and the Popular Tradition in the Theater: Studies in the Social Dimension of Dramatic Form and Function.* Edited by Robert Schwartz. Baltimore: Johns Hopkins University Press, 1978, pp. 39-48, 224-236.

The reference to a barking dog in *Lear,* in the context of inverted values involving Lear's madness and the daughters' assumption of power, reflects "one of the most characteristic forms of topsy-turvydom in the Mummer's Play: 'I met a bark and he dogged at me' " (p. 40). Similarly the Fool's reference to the "little tiny wit" reflects the characteristic figure of the fool or saucy boy who introduces himself as one with a big head and a little wit. Language is consistently a means of distinguishing types of characters. The self-centered characters in *Lear,* for example, Edmund, Goneril, and Regan, speak without proverbial lore, while the speech of characters like Lear, Kent, and the Fool recalls the festival element and ritual origins of audience contact. Such characters are in a downstage position, reflecting the rapport they develop with members of the audience.

See also items: 7, 10, 21, 27, 28-29, 31, 53, 95, 102, 121, 135, 147, 194, 211, 222, 264, 269, 294, 298, 318, 332, 334, 346, 358-359, 368, 383, 393, 428, 432, 444, 446, 453-454, 460, 473, 503, 516, 524, 534, 549-550, 555, 557-559, 586, 608, 628, 648, 679, 693, 695, 705-706, 715, 766, 803, 814, 825, 861, 889, 916-917, 957, 986, 1011, 1052-1053, 1092, 1191, 1212-1213, 1346-1347, 1351, 1461-1463, 1465, 1473, 1475, 1480-1481, 1483, 1486, 1491-1492, 1498-1499, 1501-1502, 1507, 1513, 1518, 1524, 1528, 1533-1534, 1546, 1552-1553, 1571, 1574-1575, 1578, 1585, 1599, 1602, 1618, 1624, 1630-1631, 1640, 1651, 1656, 1669, 1683, 1686, 1689, 1693, 1695, 1701, 1703, 1705, 1708, 1711, 1713, 1718, 1723.

III. DATING

III. DATING

1346 Greg, W. W. "The Date of *King Lear* and Shakespeare's Use of Earlier Versions of the Story." *The Library*, 4th ser. 20 (1939-1940), 377-400.

King Lear was composed between 1603 (the publication of Harsnett's *Egregious Impostures*) and 1606 (the performance at Court on 26 December). The major source was *King Leir*, for which there is an entry in the Stationers' Register in 1594 and again in 1605. Publication followed the latter entry. It is a plausible conjecture that it was the popularity of Shakespeare's play (entered in the Stationers' Register in 1607 and published in 1608) that prompted the publication of *Leir*. If so, since the entry to *Leir* refers to it as a "tragicall history" and since no one treated it as a tragedy before Shakespeare, it would suggest that Shakespeare's *Lear* was on the stage by early 1605. Some forty passages in *Lear*, however, suggest that, when Shakespeare wrote *Lear*, "ideas, phrases, cadences from the old play still floated in his memory below the level of conscious thought" (p. 397). Shakespeare was not likely to have seen a production, but he well might have read the text.

1347 Greg, W. W. "Shakespeare and *King Leir*." *Times Literary Supplement*, 9 March 1940, p. 124.

It is generally assumed that *King Leir*, published in 1605, is a source for *King Lear* and, therefore, that Shakespeare's play could not have been written before that date. Two strong echoes of *Hamlet* in *King Leir*, however, suggest that Shakespeare must have read the play in manuscript before its publication. If so, the question of the date of *King Lear* is once again quite unsettled.

1348 Kojima, Nobuyuki. "Taimon no Nazo." *Essays in Literature and Thought* (Women's College, Fukuoka), 19 (1960), 20-35.

This Japanese article, entitled "Riddles in *Timon*," disputes the chronology of Shakespeare's plays that places *King Lear* after *Timon of Athens*. Specifically, there is no convincing evidence that Shakespeare found his *Timon* material too intractable to complete fully, that he cast it aside and returned to the theme of ingratitude in *King Lear.*

1349 Marder, Louis. "The Chronology of Shakespeare's Plays." *Shakespeare Newsletter,* 24 (1974), 23-25.

This article summarizes Andrew S. Cairncross' theories concerning the chronology of Shakespeare's plays. *King Leir,* he believes, followed rather than preceded *King Lear.*

1350 Slater, Eliot. "Word Links Between *Timon of Athens* and *King Lear.*" *Notes and Queries,* n.s. 25 (1978), 147-149.

An examination of the rare words linking *Timon of Athens* with other Shakespearean plays can act as an effective guide in dating the composition of the play. Such an examination reveals its closest verbal links to be with *King Lear,* and it leads to the conclusion that *Timon* was written either earlier than or at about the same time as *Lear.*

See also items: 264, 294, 444, 555, 814, 1009, 1092, 1246, 1351, 1462-1463, 1465, 1480-1481, 1483, 1486, 1491-1492, 1497, 1502, 1513, 1518, 1524, 1528, 1533-1534, 1545-1546, 1553, 1574-1575, 1585, 1599, 1602, 1624, 1630, 1640, 1651, 1656, 1659, 1683, 1689, 1692-1693, 1695, 1701, 1703, 1708, 1713.

IV. TEXTUAL STUDIES

IV. TEXTUAL STUDIES

1351 Chambers, E. K. *"King Lear."* William Shakespeare: A Study of
      Facts and Problems. 2 vols. Oxford: Oxford University Press,
      Clarendon Press, 1930, I, 463-470.

The Q and F texts of *Lear* are substantially derived from the
same original. Where there are variants, the F text must be preferred. The Q text (Q$_1$ 1608, the "Pide Bull" text of which Q$_2$
1619, falsely dated 1608, is a reprint) is a reported text, though it
is far superior to other bad quartos except that of *Richard III*. Possibly it was produced by shorthand and not memorization. Q omits
100 lines found in F, and F omits 300 lines found in Q. Probably
all of these passages with the exception of the reference to Merlin's
prophecy were a part of the original text. The various omissions
were apparently occasioned by errors of the printer, actor, or reporter, by the censor, and by the prompter. Of the earlier version
of the story, *Leir* was the most influential, and the play must tenta-
tively be dated 1605 even though it was not performed at Court
until late 1606. See items 814, 1389.

1352 Doran, Madeleine. *The Text of "King Lear."* Stanford: Stanford
      University Press, 1931. 148 pp.

The order of appearance for the quarto publications of *Lear*
prior to F$_1$ is generally settled—Q$_1$ in 1608, Q$_2$ (falsely dated 1608)
in 1619. The copy text for Q$_2$ was Q$_1$. The precise nature of the
texts, however, is still a matter of some debate. Q$_1$ is not a reported
version but rather is Shakespeare's original manuscript, extensively
revised. The F$_1$ text, omitting 300 lines from Q$_1$, is the more regular and satisfactory text; it is divided into acts and scenes, and the
stage directions are more complete and precise. The copy text for
F$_1$ was the promptbook, which had been transcribed from the
original (i.e., Q$_1$) and subsequently revised and shortened. Cuts in
the text were theatrical, namely to shorten the production. The
transcript itself was revised by Shakespeare, abridged for acting,
and finally prepared as the promptbook by the bookkeeper. Occasionally the bookkeeper referred to Q$_2$. See item 1389.

1353   Greg, W. W. "The Function of Bibliography in Literary Criticism
       Illustrated in a Study of the Text of *King Lear.*" *Neophilolo-
       gus,* 18 (1933), 241-262. Reprint. *The Practice of Modern
       Literary Scholarship.* Edited by Shelton Zitner. Glenview,
       Ill.: Scott, Foresman and Co., 1966, pp. 113-135.

       Of the three branches of literary criticism, textual criticism
   is the most fundamental since a knowledge of the true text is the
   basis of all proper interpretation. Textual criticism is concerned, not
   only with the reconstruction of the original text, but also with its
   history, how it was transmitted and how it reached its final form.
   Concerning *King Lear,* textual criticism has established the proper
   order of the quartos—that one was indeed published in 1608 and the
   other (falsely dated 1608) in 1619. Currently, one view holds that
   the quarto text is a reported text (see item 1351); another view
   holds that it is from the author's foul papers, much corrected, used
   as a promptbook and discarded (see item 1352). The one argues
   that the folio text was directly set up from this manuscript, the
   other that the printer worked from a copy of the quarto carefully
   collated and corrected from the promptbook. This study, though
   differences remain, will eventually lead to a text of *Lear* in which
   folio readings will generally replace quarto readings and in which
   more intelligent decisions can be made regarding emendations.

1354   Hubler, Edward. "The Verse Lining of the First Quarto of *King
       Lear.*" *Essays in Dramatic Literature: The Parrott Presenta-
       tion Volume.* Edited by Hardin Craig. Princeton: Princeton
       University Press, 1935, pp. 421-441.

       Bibliographical evidence does not support the view of J. Dover
   Wilson, W. W. Greg, and J. Q. Adams that Q_1 *Lear* is based on a
   stenographic report. The quarto text differs from the folio text in
   four significant ways—some prose is set as verse; much verse is set
   as prose; some verses are incorrectly divided; the verse lining of some
   passages is different from the lining of the folio. A comparison of
   these irregularities with the same characteristics in Thomas Heywood's *If You Know Not Me, You Know Nobody* (a play Heywood
   himself complains came to the printer from stenographic report)
   does not lead to the conclusion that Q_1 *Lear* is based on such a
   report. To the contrary, the irregularities found in Q_1 are found in

many other texts that are not stenographic reports. The irregularities of Q_1 are frequent simply because, demonstrably, the text is a singularly bad piece of printing.

1355   Greg, W. W. *The Variants in the First Quarto of "King Lear":*
       A Bibliographical and Critical Inquiry. Oxford: Oxford University Press (for the Bibliographical Society), 1940. 192 pp.
       Reprint. New York: Haskell House Pubs., 1966.

W. G. Clark and W. Aldis Wright in 1866 first established the fact that there were two prints of *Lear* dated 1608. P. A. Daniel established the "Pide Bull" quarto as the first and the "N. Butter" quarto as the second, and early in this century it was established that Q_2 actually was printed in 1619 with the false date on the title page. This study compares and analyzes the differences in the twelve extant copies of Q_1 (two in the British Library, two in the Bodleian, two in the Folger, one at Harvard, one at the Huntington, one at the New York Public Library, one in Trinity College, Cambridge, and two in private collections). The text consists of ten sheets (twenty formes) and a single half-sheet containing the title pages. Seven sheets involve variants (a total of 167), except for one instance confined to the outer formes. Of the seventy-two formes in all, thirty-two are in the original state, and forty-two are in corrected state. The variant readings are listed in one chart and compared to the superior folio reading in another. Also included are a list of errors in the Praetorius Facsimile (1885), misprints in the original text, doubtful readings, and manuscript corrections.

1356   Sledd, James. *"Hause* and *Slaves* in *King Lear."* Modern Language Notes, 55 (1940), 594-596.

In the Fool's mocking advice to Kent, concluding "I would hause none but knaves follow it, since a fool gives it" (II, iv, 77), the word *hause* has been universally rejected as a misprint for *have*. To the contrary, the word is correct, derived from old English *halsian* and meaning *abjure* or *beseech*. In Gloucester's line, "Let the superfluous and lust-dieted man, / That slaves your ordinance . . ." (F_1, slaves; Q_1, stands), editors accept the term as meaning *enslaves*, but they are bothered by it. The word probably derives from the Old English *slæfan* and means *cleave, split, rend,* or *tear apart.*

1357   Kirschbaum, Leo. "The True Text of *King Lear.*" *Shakespeare Association Bulletin,* 16 (1941), 140-153.

The single authoritative text of *King Lear* is that of F_1. It is based on a copy of Q carefully and purposively corrected against a theatrical manuscript which must have had Shakespeare's blessing. "The differences between Q and F are thus seen to be dynamically purposive. Where the two texts differ, the F reading *must* be adopted by editors" (p. 148). Far too many editors draw eclectically from these two texts on the basis of taste alone. Q itself is a bad quarto, a memorial reconstruction text.

1358   Tannenbaum, Samuel. "An Emendation in *King Lear.*" *Shakespeare Association Bulletin,* 16 (1941), 58-59.

Since Capell's emendation in the eighteenth century, most critics have accepted the reading of I, ii, 20-21, as "If . . . my invention thrive, Edmund the base / Shall top the legitimate." Clearly this is a wrong reading. Shakespeare no doubt intended to write "toe," meaning Edmund will kick Edgar out and supplant him.

1359   Greg, W. W. "Two Doubtful Quartos." *The Editorial Problem in Shakespeare.* Oxford: Oxford University Press, Clarendon Press, 1942, pp. 49-76.

Like that of *Richard III* the quarto text of *Lear* is textually corrupt, though not to the degree of the other bad quartos. One cannot credit Miss Doran's theory (see item 1352) that the Q text was printed from Shakespeare's foul papers, in spots illegible from much correction and alteration. The quarto, to the contrary, is derivative. Alexander Schmidt in 1879 was fundamentally correct in arguing that the text was a reported one, somehow based on an actual performance. All of the stigmas of a reported text are present —introduction of vocatives, expletives, or connective phrases, commonplace phraseology, paraphrase, anticipation, recollection, assimilation, vulgarization, and breakdown through memory failure. The folio text with few exceptions preserves the original reading. The differences in the length of the two texts (Q lacks 100 lines found in F; F lacks 300 lines found in Q) appear to be the result of two versions having been differently cut for acting. The quarto version is apparently based on a shorthand account; badly printed and arbitrarily corrected, it is of small textual value. The folio version, based on the quarto version carefully corrected against a prompt-book copy, is of prime textual significance.

1360   Kökeritz, Helge.   "Elizabethan che vore ye 'I warrant you.' "
       Modern Language Notes, 57 (1942), 98-102.

Edgar's comment to Oswald in *King Lear,* IV, vi, 245-246, should be translated "I warrant you," not "I warn you." The clause is from the Somersetshire dialect.

1361   Sisson, Charles J.   "Shakespeare Quarto as Prompt-Copies."
       Review of English Studies, 18 (1942), 129-143.

A number of Catholic recusants from Egton, Whitby, and Staithes were organized as an acting company in 1611 with authority under Sir Richard Cholmely. Two of the plays in their repertory were by Shakespeare—*King Lear* and *Pericles.* The Pide Bull quarto of *Lear* (1608) was beyond reasonable question the promptbook for this play. There would be no reason for the company to go to the expense of making a written transcript, and one of the members of the group, Richard Simpson, is on record as saying that the players acted from "a printed booke." Such a copy would also bear the approval of the Master of Revels, who had already sanctioned the play for performance in London. If the practice was widespread of using quarto copies for prompt copies, and evidence suggests it was, then the "staying" of the printing of a play could be a device by which a play was kept out of print (and thus out of circulation for the repertories of acting companies throughout the countryside) until the Master of the Revels had had time properly to examine it.

1362   Brown, B. Goulding.   *"King Lear,* IV, iii, 29-32." *Times Literary Supplement,* 23 December 1944, p. 619.

The reading "There she [Cordelia] shook / The holy water from her heavenly eyes / And dolour master'd" is far preferable to the "clamour moisten'd" reading admitted into the Cambridge Shakespeare.

1363   Kirschbaum, Leo.   "The Origin of the Bad Quartos." *PMLA,* 60 (1945), 697-715.

There was no system of shorthand sufficiently sophisticated to account persuasively for the texts of the Elizabethan bad quartos. The evidence points convincingly to a reported or memorial reconstruction text. It suggests, however, that the source was not the memory of an actor who had played a minor part since the memorial confusion seems to affect all parts more or less equally. Instead the source was a pirate who had memorized, from a written version, the theatrical manuscript. Only such a process will account for certain features of the bad quartos—the correctly lined blank verse, similarities between the bad and good text in matters of spelling and punctuation, similarities of stage directions, and the great length and relatively sound quality of certain texts such as the Pide Bull *Lear* (1608).

1364   Kirschbaum, Leo. *The True Text of "King Lear."* Baltimore: Johns Hopkins University Press, 1945. 81 pp.

The quarto text of *King Lear*, while not the shorthand report claimed by Greg (see item 1359), is a memorial reconstruction of the folio text. The F text was printed from a copy of Q emended by reference to a transcript that derived from Shakespeare's associates. Any substantive difference between Q and F indicates a change deliberately introduced by someone directly connected with the company; and hence, where the two texts differ, the F reading must be adopted. A careful analysis of the two texts reveals that the Q text is thoroughly undependable, plagued by omission, anticipation, recollection, assimilation, vulgarization, substitution, undependable designation of speakers' names, misunderstanding, and misinterpretation. The received text of *King Lear,* in a word, is the folio text except where it omits inadvertently or by design. Surprisingly, Alexander Schmidt based his edition in 1879 on just these principles. The edition promptly passed into scholarly oblivion—apparently only three copies exist in the United States—but his analysis of the Q-F textual relationships is a superb accomplishment for his time. See item 1381.

1365   Moses, S. W. "On IV, iii, 29-32." *Times Literary Supplement,* 24 February 1945, p. 91.

The reading of "clamour moisten'd" is preferable to "dolour master'd," as suggested by B. Goulding Brown (see item 1362), in

Cordelia's speech when she learns of her sisters' treatment of Lear and Kent.

1366   Greg, W. W.   "The Staging of *King Lear.*"   *Review of English Studies,* 22 (1946), 229.

The contention that the act and scene division in the F_1 *King Lear* is original can no longer stand. The folio division, it must now be admitted, was probably introduced by an editor working from an undivided Q text and an undivided manuscript.

1367   Small, S. A.   "The *King Lear* Quarto."   *Shakespeare Association Bulletin,* 21 (1946), 177-180.

The Pide Bull quarto of *King Lear* (Q_1, 1608) is the most puzzling of the publications of Shakespeare's plays, the result no doubt of the role of the scribe in either inserting emendations or making errors in his stenographic copying. Leo Kirschbaum's publication (see item 1364) has brought the problem closer to solution. His conviction is that Q_1 is a bad quarto based on memorial reconstruction, and his conclusion is based upon a detailed examination of seventy passages contaminated either by repetition or telescoping.

1368   Heilman, Robert B.   "Shakespeare's *King Lear,* IV, vi, 169." *Explicator,* 6 (1947-1948), Item 10.

The folio reading of IV, vi, 169 ("Place sins with Gold") is preferable to the usual emendation ("Plate sins with gold"), first introduced by Pope and Theobald. The line means "purchase an evil person an office with gold, and he becomes immune to justice." The folio reading accords convincingly with the play's general theme of corruption in office.

1369   Bowers, Fredson.   "Elizabethan Proofing."   *Joseph Quincy Adams Memorial Studies.*   Edited by James G. McManaway, Giles E. Dawson, and Edwin E. Willoughby.   Washington, D. C.:   Folger Shakespeare Library, 1948, pp. 571-586.

In this article Bowers extends his theories concerning the proofing and printing of *King Lear* (see item 1370) into the more general field of normal Elizabethan printing practice. Any such study demands consideration of the running-titles to determine how many skeletons were used to impose the formes. The two general methods for proofing involve one for one-skeleton books and another for two-skeleton books. With one skeleton correction was possible only after the printing of a number of incorrect states of the first forme, at this point occasioning a delay. Two-skeleton printing was able to fill this gap, and work could continue on a second forme while the first was being proofed. In two-skeleton work the "invariant" forme of a variant sheet would be proof-corrected.

1370   Bowers, Fredson.   "An Examination of the Method of Proof Correction in *Lear."* *Library,* 5th ser. 2 (1948), 20-44.

Bowers challenges W. W. Greg's theory (see item 1353) that the variant forms of Q_1 *King Lear* are explained by a method of proofreading involving two formes, an impression of the first forme being proofed while the second forme is being run, after which the press run of the second forme is interrupted and corrections made on it while the first forme is run. This hypothesis would involve excessive delays in printing and would have been too costly for the printer, Nicholas Okes. Bowers' theory is that the printing and proofing were carried out in a normal manner, with sheets being perfected only after the customary interval; the hypothesis "is based fundamentally on the bibliographical evidence provided by the headlines of this quarto which trace the progress and the manner of imposition" (p. 43).

1371   Williams, Philip.   "The Compositor of the Pied-Bull *Lear."* *Studies in Bibliography,* 1 (1948-1949), 59-68.

A study of the orthographic habits and peculiarities of individual compositors at work in Nicholas Okes' printshop reveals that a single compositor set the type for the Pide Bull quarto of *Lear* in 1608. Two compositors, designated A and B, worked on Robert Armin's *The History of the Two Maids of More-Clacke* in 1609; the same two set John Webster's *The White Devil* in 1612. The analysis clearly indicates that compositor B alone set Q_1 *King Lear.* On only two of eighty pages is the evidence inconclusive.

1372   Duthie, George Ian. *Elizabethan Shorthand and the First Quarto of "King Lear."* Oxford: Basil Blackwell, 1949. 82 pp.

We must accept the view that the folio text (1623) of *King Lear* was printed from a copy of Q (1608) which had been brought by a scribe into general agreement with an authentic playhouse text, probably the promptbook. The quarto text bears the marks of some form of memorial transmission. Alexander Schmidt, E. K. Chambers, and W. W. Greg, among others, postulate, to the contrary, that it is a stenographic report. Three systems of shorthand were available in 1608—Timothy Bright's *Characterie*, Peter Bale's *Brachygraphie*, and John Willis' *Stenographie*. A careful analysis of each of these systems reveals conclusively that none was sufficiently sophisticated to produce the text. One might capture the essence or summary through these systems, but nothing approaching the verbal detail.

1373   Owen, W. J. B. "A Dogge, so Bade in Office." *Notes and Queries,* 194 (1949), 141-142.

The Q reading of IV, vi, 164, "a dogge, so bade in office," is not logically a mishearing of the F reading, "a Dogg's obey'd in Office," as Greg, Kirschbaum and Duthie maintain. More likely, the Q reading results from a misreading of the copy, which probably read either "a dogges obaide in office" or "a dogges obeide in office."

1373a   Williams, George W. "A Note on *King Lear,* III, ii, 1-3." *Studies in Bibliography,* 2 (1949-1950), 175-182.

The opening lines of Lear's storm speech read in Q$_1$ "Blow wind & crack your cheekes, rage, blow / You caterickes, & Hircanios spout til you have drencht, / The steeples drown'd the cockes. . . ." The punctuation is essentially the same in F$_1$, but editors beginning with Pope in 1725 have tended to modify the punctuation of the first line to create an end-stopped line. Thus, "spout" becomes the imperative verb for cataracts and hurricanoes. The emendation creates a much superior Shakespearean reading. The corruption in the Q text, from which F was set, may well have been an actor's error, caused by his not pausing while reciting the line from memory. Or, perhaps the error was the compositor's; he may inadvertently have dropped the comma (end punctuation) to the line below or he may have omitted it in line one because of difficulties in justifying the line.

1374   Babler, O. F. "Shakespeare's *King Lear* in Czech Translations."
        Notes and Queries, 196 (1951), 55-56.

The first Czech translation of *King Lear*, at least by 1792, was by Prokop Frantisek Sedivy. The second was by Josef Kajetan and was first performed on 13 December 1835. The third was by the renowned botanist Ladislav Celakovsky in 1856. Josef V. Salder's translation appeared in 1900 and Bohumil Stapanek's in 1927. A new translation by O. F. Babler is soon to appear in print.

1375   Cauthen, Irby B., Jr. "Shakespeare's *King Lear:* An Investigation of Compositor Habits in the First Folio and Their Relation to the Text." Ph.D. dissertation, University of Virginia, 1951. *University of Virginia Abstracts of Dissertations,* 1951, pp. 13-18.

The text of F_1 *King Lear* is based on a copy of Q_1 1608 which had been extensively revised by a scribe using the theater prompt-copy. A study of the work of the compositor separates the authorized or scribal folio variants from the unauthorized or compositorial variants. Evidence reveals that only a single compositor worked on the F text of *Lear* and that only a single skeleton was used. A collation of the work of this compositor in other plays with Q texts of those respective plays yields substantive variants, a classification of which can be compared with a similar classification of the variants between Q_1 1608 *Lear* and F_1 *Lear*. Those variants conforming closely to the variants in the "control plays" can safely be rejected by an editor as compositorial; those that do not should be retained as scribal. The result is a text of *Lear* "free from the corruptions that were inadvertently included by an anonymous compositor" (p. 13). See item 1378.

1376   Muir, Kenneth. *"King Lear,* II, iv, 170." *Notes and Queries,* 196 (1951), 170.

The reading of II, iv, 170 should be "To fall and blister her" rather than "To fall and blast her pride" (Q) or "To fall, and blister"

(F). See item 1553; note that in Muir's edition the line number is 169.

1377   Stevenson, Allan H. "Shakespearian Dated Watermarks." *Studies in Bibliography,* 4 (1951-1952), 159-164.

Forty-two years after Pollard's convincing argument that the Pavier quartos (variously dated 1600, 1608, and 1619) were all printed in 1619, the discovery was made in the Huntington Library that Sheet F in the church copy of *Sir John Oldcastle* had a watermark dated 1608 and that sheet F of the church copy of *Henry V* had a watermark dated 1617 or 1619. Examination of the remaining Pavier quartos in various libraries turned up no additional evidence. Apparently, they are "intrusive" watermarks, the result of Jaggard's using up old paper from his stockroom. At any rate the 1608 watermarks on *Oldcastle* (dated 1600 on its title page) and the 1617/1619 date on *Henry V* (dated 1608 on its title page) add further empirical evidence that the dating in the Pavier quartos is on occasion falsified.

1378   Cauthen, Irby B. "Compositor Determination in the First Folio *King Lear.*" *Studies in Bibliography,* 5 (1952-1953), 73-80.

The folio text of *King Lear* was set by only one compositor, compositor B as identified by E. E. Willoughby in *The Printing of the First Folio* in 1932. Several kinds of evidence point to this conclusion. An examination of 600 variant spellings of 142 words does not indicate a two-compositor pattern. Since the plays surrounding *Lear* were set by compositor B, it is likely that he also worked on *Lear*. Only one skeleton-forme is utilized throughout, a likely indication of a single compositor. Finally, the examination of spelling preferences points directly to the work of compositor B. See item 1375.

1379   Hoepfner, Theodore C. "Sessa." *Notes and Queries,* 197 (1952), 502.

Both the word *Sesey* (III, iv, 104) and the word *sese* (III, vi, 77) mean *cease,* from the French cesser.

1380   J., R. "Sessa." *Notes and Queries,* 197 (1952), 437.

In *King Lear* III, iv, 104, *sesey* seems to mean *cease*, from a French context (*cesser*).

1381   Walker, Alice. "*King Lear*—The 1608 Quarto." *Modern Language Review*, 47 (1952), 376-378.

Copy for Q₁ 1608 *King Lear* is Shakespeare's foul papers as dictated by an actor familiar with the text and who, consequently, in certain spots relied on his memory rather than on his careful reading of the material.

1382   Davenport, A. "Notes on *King Lear*." *Notes and Queries*, 198 (1953), 20-22.

In II, i, 56, Gloucester intends to banish Edgar, not to kill him. In II, iv, 89, Lear's description of the reasons for Cornwall's and Regan's not seeing him as "mere fetches" means both subterfuges and, in the nautical sense, tactical evasions. Edgar's speech in III, iv, 85 ff. echoes Joseph Hall's *Virgidemiae*. Edgar's words when Gloucester enters in IV, i, 10, "My father, poorly led," probably should read "parti-eyed" (displaying various colors at the eyes); this reading was first suggested by Kenneth Muir in *TLS*, 3 June 1949. See p. 147 in item 1533.

1383   Jazayery, Mohammad Ali and Robert Adger Law. "Three Texts of *King Lear*: Their Differences." *Texas Studies in English*, 32 (1953), 14-24.

A line-by-line analysis of the text of *King Lear* in the Globe edition (1864), Kittredge's edition (1936), and Neilson's edition (1906) reveals interesting differences. All three texts are based primarily on the folio, but all allow quarto readings; Neilson in doubtful readings is more apt to follow the folio. Differences in punctuation reflect the standards of their particular times, while differences in stage directions (drawn from eighteenth-century editions) reveal editorial tastes and assumptions. Clearly, for example, Kittredge does not locate Edmund within hearing distance of Gloucester's discussion of his parentage. In punctuation Kittredge and Neilson tend to shorten sentences, utilizing periods where the Globe editors use semicolons or colons. All three attempt to adhere to what

Shakespeare wrote and to present a readable text for the contemporary reader. Neilson's text closely adheres to Greg's textual assumptions; Kittredge's is more eclectic; the Globe text possesses less authority in light of modern scholarship.

1384   Parrott, Thomas Marc. "Gods or 'gods' in *King Lear,* V, iii, 17." *Shakespeare Quarterly,* 4 (1953), 427-432.

The F_1 reading "Gods" should be emended to "gods" in order to render Shakespeare's pagan polytheism consistent throughout the play. See item 1392.

1385   Walker, Alice. *"King Lear." Textual Problems of the First Folio.* Cambridge: Cambridge University Press, 1953, pp. 37-67.

The evidence seems conclusive that the folio text of *Lear* is "mixed," that is, based on a copy of Q_1 collated with a playhouse manuscript. On the other hand, the theory that Q_1 itself is a memorially reconstructed text (whether the result of shorthand or the result of a corporate effort by the King's Men to replace a missing promptbook) is less convincing. Evidence suggests that the quarto is not based on an acting version of the play "but on the foul papers and that these were surreptitiously dictated to a scribe by an actor who, for some reason we can only guess at (haste, over-confidence, laziness, inattention), relied on his memory instead of his script for dialogue with which he was familiar" (p. 41). That the contaminating actor-reader was the boy playing Goneril (or perhaps the two boys playing Goneril and Regan) is suggested by the general accuracy of the text except for those scenes (I, i; II, iv; V, iii) in which Goneril and Regan are on stage (in which spots the boy[s] would dictate more from memory than from text), and that the scribe was not a professional is suggested by his atrociously poor spelling and his equally poor handwriting. Omissions from the quarto seem the result of carelessness rather than a systematic effort to shorten the play. These conclusions obviously affect the editing of the play. We must be prepared to conflate the two texts freely and to accept readings from the quarto (which is closer to Shakespeare's foul papers than is widely supposed) in those passages that do not reflect memorial contamination. See items 555, 1389, 1415.

1386   Williams, Philip. "Two Problems in the Folio Text of *King Lear.*"
       Shakespeare Quarterly, 4 (1953), 451-460.

It is generally accepted that Q_1 1608 *Lear* is a bad quarto (a
reported text), that Q_2 1619 (falsely dated 1608) is a reprint, that
F_1 was printed from a copy of Q collated with another manuscript
(probably the prompt copy), and that the F_1 text was set by a single
compositor (identified as Compositor B). Evidence now suggests,
however, that more than one compositor worked on the F_1 text and
that this F_1 text was not set directly from a corrected copy of Q.
Concerning the first point, there is a consistent inconsistency in the
spelling of Gloucester both in abbreviated and non-abbreviated
forms; one spelling uses "o," the other "ou." Also, all of the lines
are not centered in the same manner. Apparently, in other words,
two compositors were at work. Concerning the other point, differences in speech headings and the intrinsic difficulties of a heavily
annotated Q as printer's copy make it probable that the copy text
for F_1 was a promptbook that was "a conflation of 'good' pages
from Q_1 supplemented by inserted manuscript leaves to replace corrupt passages of Q_1. Reluctant to let the official promptbook leave
their possession, the company permitted a scribe to make a transcript of this conflated text to serve as copy for the First Folio"
(p. 460).

1387   Anderson, D. M. "A Conjecture on *King Lear* IV, ii, 57." *Notes
       and Queries,* n.s. 1 (1954), 331.

King Lear IV, ii, 57 ("With plumed helm thy state begins
thereat" [Q], "With plumed helm thy slayer begin threats" [un-
corrected Q]), should read "With plumed helm his state begins thy
rout(e)." The suggested reading is convincing, and it offers little
graphical difficulty.

1387a Hoepfner, Theodore. "We that are young." *Notes and Queries,*
       n.s. 1 (1954), 110.

Some editors, despite the folio reading, refuse to give the final
lines of *King Lear* to Edgar, preferring the quarto reading in which
Albany, as the person of highest rank, most appropriately speaks the
lines which indicate an assumption of kingship. Albany, however,

has refused the throne, offering it jointly to Kent and to Edgar. When Kent declines and Edgar, using the royal "we," accepts with "We who are young," he from that moment is the person of highest rank, as king outranking Albany the Duke. Moreover, the reference to young is most fitting to Edgar.

1388   Cairncross, Andrew S. "The Quartos and the Folio Text of *King Lear.*" *Review of English Studies*, n.s. 6 (1955), 252-258.

The fact that Q_1 and Q_2 (corrected from some authoritative manuscript) served as copy for F_1 "points rather to the printing-house than to the theatre, and to the bad rather than the doubtful status of the quarto text" (p. 255). The Company would certainly not resort to using two quartos alternately as promptbooks, but such alteration "is just the sort of device likely to suit the collaboration of editor and compositor—the editor correcting in advance on one quarto, and handling it to the compositor while he proceeded to correct the other" (p. 258). Evidence suggests that the *Lear* quarto is bad, only a degree better than, for example, Q_1 *Romeo and Juliet*.

1389   Greg, W. W. *"King Lear." The Shakespeare First Folio: Its Bibliographical and Textual History*. Oxford: Oxford University Press, Clarendon Press, 1955, pp. 375-388.

Approximately 300 lines of *King Lear* are unique to Q_1 1608, and approximately 100 are unique to F_1 1623. The Q text is clearly recognized as unsatisfactory. Doran argues that Shakespeare's confused foul papers served as the copy text (see item 1352); Van Dam maintains it is based on an early promptbook; E. K. Chambers sees it as a reported text from shorthand (see item 1351); Kirschbaum as a bad quarto (see item 1364); Duthie as an effort of communal memory (see item 1535); Walker as a surreptitious transcript of the foul papers by two boy actors (see item 1385). All things considered, no theory is totally convincing. The folio text was printed from a copy of the quarto collated with an authoritative text, probably the promptbook.

1390   Schaller, Rudolf. "Shakespeare in deutscher Sprache. Einige Probleme bei der Arbeit des Übersetzers." *Theater der Zeit*, 10, No. 11 (1955), 30-31, 34-37.

This article discusses the fundamental problems involved in translation, especially a creative work in which the subtleties of meaning and verse rhythm are virtually incapable of transmission.

1391   Sehrt, Ernst Theodore, Karen Kramp, and Wolfgang Stroedel. "Einzelbesprechungen." *Shakespeare Jahrbuch,* 91 (1955), 348-355.

Richard Flatter's translation of *King Lear* and seven other Shakespearean texts is discussed on pp. 353-355.

1392   Thaler, Alwin. "The Gods and God in *King Lear.*" *Renaissance Papers* (1955), 32-39.

T. M. Parrott's (see item 1384) suggestion that "God's spies" (V, iii, 17) should read "gods' spies" is untenable. For one thing, it ignores the fact that, in the more than 1000 references in Shakespeare to "God" and "the gods," there is not a single instance of the genitive plural without the article "the." More important, it refuses to recognize the spiritual drift of things in Lear toward Christianity and God, howevermuch it might be anachronistic. Lear and others gain in spiritual insight, and this regeneration brings the name of God inevitably to Lear's lips.

1393   Walton, James Kirkwood. *The Copy for the Folio Text of "Richard III." With a Note on the Copy for the Folio Text of "King Lear."* Monograph Series, No. 1. Auckland, New Zealand: Auckland University College, New Zealand, 1955. 164 pp.

The number of variants between the Q and F texts of *King Lear* is greatest at the beginning and the end of the play. The anomalies in the incidence of variants can be explained only by the assumption that the collator worked at varying levels of efficiency, specifically that he began carefully but grew progressively more careless, reached a decisively low ebb in Act IV, and then became closely attentive again in Act V. This conclusion is supported by a survey of the distribution of variants between Lear's speeches and those of the other characters, by evidence provided by the variant Q_1 sheets, by a list of the errors most common to Q and F, and by analogy with a similar situation in collation of the folio copy for

Richard III. Philip Williams' theory (see item 1386) that the F text was set from a transcript of a conflated promptbook (with ms. leaves inserted to replace corrupt passages) is untenable.

1394   Bolton, Joseph G. "Worn Pages in Shakespearian Manuscripts." *Shakespeare Quarterly,* 7 (1956), 177-182.

In six instances, *Hamlet, Othello, King Lear, Troilus and Cressida, Richard III,* and *2 Henry IV,* the quarto and folio texts supplement each other in important ways. It would appear by the somewhat regular spacing of textual problems in the quartos that quite possibly the printer was setting his type from manuscripts which from excessive use in the theater had suffered a gradual wearing or tearing away of the lower edge of the paper to the point that the last lines on both sides were illegible. The theatrical companies kept fair copies from which later the folio text was to be set. Careful analysis of the quarto and folio texts of *Lear* strongly support this theory. See item 1402.

1395   Schlösser, Anselm.   "Besser als Baudissin (Betrachtungen Zu Rudolf Schallers Ubersetzung des *King Lear*)." *Zeitschrift fur Anglistik und Amerikanistik* (Berlin), 4 (1956), 172-190.

This article examines Rudolf Schaller's translation of *Lear* and finds it superior to Baudissin's.

1396   Sisson, C. J. *"King Lear." New Readings in Shakespeare.* 2 vols. London: Dawsons, 1956, II, 230-244.

This volume provides annotations of difficult passages from the histories and tragedies. Specifically, thirty-seven passages from *Lear* are explicated. Sisson is primarily concerned with errors in transmission from manuscript to print. The material sprang from the work on his recent edition of Shakespeare's works. See item 1558.

1397   Hinman, Charlton.   "The Prentice Hand in the Tragedies of the Shakespeare First Folio: Compositor E." *Studies in Bibliography,* 9 (1957), pp. 3-20.

The publication of F_1 (1623) involved several compositors. Compositor E, who helped to set the text for *King Lear, Othello,* and *Hamlet,* was clumsy and inaccurate. Since *Lear* was set from an extensively correct quarto, it offered even greater difficulties than the other plays. Consequently, the copy for qq3^V, 5, 2 were manipulated to fall to Compositor B rather than Compositor E. All evidence points to the fact that Compositor E was an indentured apprentice of Jaggard's house.

1398   Musgrove, S. *"King Lear* I, i, 170." *Review of English Studies,* n.s. 8 (1957), 170-171.

A variant in the extant folios exists in I, i, 170 of *King Lear*— "To come betwixt our sentence/sentences and our power." The quarto reads "between our sentence and our powre." Evidence suggests that the corrected reading is "betwixt our sentences and our power" and that some copies of F were run off with "sentence" before the error was discovered.

1399   Rostenberg, Leona.   "Nathaniel Butter and Nicholas Bourne, First 'Masters of the Staple.' " *The Library,* 5th ser. 12 (1957), 23-33.

This account of the work of the printers Nathaniel Butter and Nicholas Bourne includes a reference to Butter's publication of Q_1 *King Lear* in 1608 at his shop at the Pide Bull near St. Austin's Gate. From 1602 to 1622 Butter published over 200 books. Bourne, three years Butter's junior, joined him in 1622.

1400   Brown, John Russell.   "A Proof-Sheet from Nicholas Okes' Printing-Shop." *Studies in Bibliography,* 11 (1958), 228-231.

The discovery of a proof-sheet for a book printed by Nicholas Okes (in the Folger Library copy of John Tichborne's *A Triple Antidote, against certaine very common Scandals of this time*) is significant in revealing the manner of proofreading in the shop in which, in 1608, Q_1 *King Lear* was printed. That Okes was concerned primarily with preferential changes and purely typographical improvements "lends some support to Professor Bowers' contention that Okes was the sort of printer who was likely to do his 'conscientious best to produce the best text he could' from the 'miserable' manuscript copy for *Lear* in 1608" (p. 230).

1401   Pasternak, Boris. "Translating Shakespeare." *Twentieth Century*, 164 (1958), 213-228.

The translation of Shakespeare involves matters of style and rhythm. The problems cannot be reduced to simple rules; instead, the translator must impressionistically attempt to achieve the inner meaning of a passage. Seven plays, including *King Lear*, are discussed in some detail.

1402   Bolton, Joseph S. G. "Wear and Tear as Factors in the Textual History of the Quarto Version of *King Lear.*" *Shakespeare Quarterly*, 11 (1960), 427-438.

Printer's copy for Q_1 *King Lear* was most likely the author's manuscript that had served as the players' promptbook. The scribe in editing Shakespeare's foul papers did a bit of editing now noticeable in the differences in the stage directions between Q and F and in numerous brief textual variants. This manuscript, serving as promptbook, was subject to extensive wearing by 1607. "As certain speeches grew illegible, the prompter or the scribe salvaged them in various ways [e.g., by copying out lines in the margins]. But when the lower portions of nine of its thirty-odd sheets had worn away, the manuscript was discarded as useless" (p. 438). Finding its way into the hands of Nathaniel Butter and John Busby, it was printed, and the consequence is the so-called bad quarto. Such a theory best accounts for the various textual differences between Q and F, the latter subsequently being set from the fair copy retained by the players. See item 1394.

1403   Ringler, William. "Exit Kent." *Shakespeare Quarterly*, 11 (1960), 311-317.

One of the puzzling moments in the text of *King Lear* occurs in III, i, in which Kent asks where Lear is and who is with him; he is told that the King has wandered onto the heath accompanied only by his Fool while the storm is at its height. The puzzle is that Kent would have to ask the question since only twenty-three lines earlier

Kent left the stage presumably in Lear's company. In all likelihood the text is faulty; the Q_1 stage direction at II, iv, 289 is wrong, and a necessary stage direction at II, iv, 135 has been omitted in both Q_1 and F_1. Kent should exit the stage following Lear's comment on seeing Caius (Kent) released from the stocks ("O are you free? / Some other time for that"); logic dictates that he should exit since he has no line in the remainder of the scene and would be out of character in keeping silent while Lear is berated by his daughter. Kent then might well ask of Lear's whereabouts when he re-enters in III, i. A careful examination of the text provides a reasonable explanation for each of these alterations.

1404   Craig, Hardin. "The Composition of *King Lear.*" *Renaissance Papers* (1961), 57-61.

Q_1 1608 *King Lear* is by no means the work of a pirate actor, a reporter, or a memorial reconstructer. Instead of a bad quarto, it represents Shakespeare's foul papers, and its textual vagaries in comparison with the folio text permit us a rare glimpse of Shakespeare's process of composition. The Lear material taken from Geoffrey, Holinshed, and others totals 1,234 lines, almost entirely in regular and uncontaminated verse. Material taken from Sidney, the moving force in the direction of tragic intensity, totals—along with the speeches of the Fool, of Edgar as Tom, and of the insane Lear, and the final 28 lines which provide the nexus of the two plots—just under 1300 lines. Only 1000 lines remain to be accounted for. These are the lines in which Shakespeare is developing his interrelationships and transitions, and in these lines occur seventy percent of the textual variants. The quarto, then, is an indispensable document revealing Shakespeare at work. The fair copy remained in the playhouse and, tempered by theatrical experience, became the basis for the folio text. The foul papers fell into the hands of Nathaniel Butter and John Busby and provided the basis for the quarto publication.

1405   Craig, Hardin. "Inadequate Methodology in Textual Criticism." *A New Look at Shakespeare's Quartos.* Stanford: Stanford University Press, 1961, pp. 90-120.

The theory that the folio text of *King Lear* is based on a corrected copy of the quarto text is not feasible. The necessary alterations (at least 2000) would be overwhelming. Given the mislineations of verse, the misprinting of prose as verse, the verbal variants, the differences in punctuation, the 300 lines unique to the quarto, the 100 lines unique to the folio, it is impossible to believe that the multitude of changes could have been physically entered on the soft paper of a printed quarto—or that so ordered a text as the folio version could have been prepared from such a text. Obviously, copy text for the folio was the promptbook. More generally, the entire theory of the reported or memorial reconstruction text is suspect; there is no testimony to support it, and furthermore the supposition is unnecessary. The various quarto versions most likely are the consequences of stage contamination, changes made by actors and managers in the texts of plays when they were acted on the stage.

1406   Gold, Charles H. "A Variant Reading in *King Lear.*" *Notes and Queries*, n.s. 8 (1961), 141-142.

Modern editions are divided in the reading of I, i, 151, in which the folio text is "When Majesty falls to folly" and the quarto text is "When Majesty stoops to folly." The quarto reading is inferior because it is inconsistent with the total meaning of the play and the character of Lear to have him stoop. In these critical expositional lines his character as a proud and impulsive ruler is being firmly established. The idea of his stooping, even in the physical sense, is unthinkable. Indeed, his tragedy is that he will break before he will bend.

1407   Hogan, J. J. "Cutting His Text According to His Measure: A Note on the Folio *Lear.*" *Philological Quarterly*, 41 (1962), 72-81.

Demonstrably on numerous occasions the printer for the folio *Lear* altered his material to fit it into a given line, not always without serious violation of the text. The contaminations cover a range of changes including spelling, punctuation, deletions, synonyms, and quasi-synonyms. Twelve verse and four prose passages from throughout the tragedy are compared with the comparable passages from Q_1. Given the evidence of this practice, we must seriously reconsider the assumed preference of the folio text, as on the whole superior to the quarto text, in all relatively small matters of variation.

1408   Tamaki, Ishitaro. "The Manuscripts of *King Lear.*" *Eigo Eibungaku Ronshu* (Kansai University), No. 6 (1962), pp. 1-21.

This article in Japanese examines the major differences between the quarto and folio texts.

1409   Elton, William. "Our Means Secure Us." *Neophilologus,* 47 (1963), 225-227.

"Means" in Gloucester's line, "Our means secure us" (IV, i, 19), refers not to "resources" and "power" or to "adverse condition" but to a sense of "occasion" or "opportunity" reflected in Elizabethan theological treatises. Specifically, Gloucester—recently blinded for his efforts on Lear's behalf—warns an old man who would befriend him of the peril of deeds.

1410   Jackson, MacD. P. " 'The Gods Deserve Your Kindness': *King Lear,* III, vi, 5." *Notes and Queries,* n.s. 10 (1963), 101.

The folio reading of III, vi, 5, "The Gods reward your kindness," is universally preferred over the quarto reading, "The Gods deserve your kindness." The folio reading may represent a change made by Shakespeare himself or by an actor, compositor, or editor, but in any case the quarto reading is logical. One meaning of "deserve" is "to give in return for service rendered, to requite." In this context the verb is the jussive subjunctive, and the meaning is precisely that rendered in the variant reading of the folio.

1411   Meszöly, Dezso. "Vörösmarty és Lear." *Kritika,* 2, No. 6 (1964), 33-41.

This discussion of Mihály Vörösmarty's Hungarian translation of *King Lear* observes that any word-for-word translation inevitably distorts the original meaning. Vörösmarty is wise to concentrate on a loose approximation of phrasing that captures the tone and spirit of the original.

1412   Smidt, Kristian. "The Quarto and the Folio *Lear*: Another Look
       at the Theories of Textual Deviation." *English Studies,* 45
       (1964), 149-162.

Despite the present witch-hunt concerning bad Shakespearean
quartos, neither Q_1 *Richard III* nor Q_1 *King Lear* belongs in that
category. Interestingly, those who claim Q_1 *Lear* to be bad cannot
agree on the cause—whether shorthand, group or individual memorial reconstruction, a boy actor surreptitiously dictating from foul
papers to a companion actor serving as scribe. Moreover, the evidence used to argue the case is too one-sided and is made to seem
too unequivocal. In truth, a close comparison of the Q and F texts—
in scene one, for example—reveals virtually equal touches of so-
called contamination—unmetrical lines, repetitions, variants, omissions, redundancy. The theory that F is a superior text is simply untenable. The two texts are remarkably similar considering the difficulty of many of the speeches, and the mistakes and anomalies
found in both would appear to argue for a common manuscript
source. Neither the Q nor the F text is likely to have been a stage
version; both are too long by a considerable amount. "It seems
distinctly possible that they furnish interesting examples of plays
which exist in equally authentic variant editions; authentic, that is to
say, in so far as they represent differences, accidental or otherwise,
in the author's own original papers and transcripts" (p. 162). A systematic study of the two texts will probably eliminate completely
the charge that Q *Lear* is contaminated by non-Shakespearean interference.

1413   Duthie, George Ian and Paul Gerhard Buchloh. *Shakespeares
       "King Lear": Historie oder Tragödie? Untersuchungen zur
       Textkritik.* Kiel: Verl. F. Hirt, 1965.

This volume contains two lectures giving contrasting views of
the play and its textual problems. Buchloh sees the quarto version
as a theater text of a history play with the primary political theme
of the proper duties of kingship; the folio text is a literary text and
is tragedy rather than history. Duthie argues that the quarto represents a surreptitious copy of Shakespeare's foul papers, while the
folio text is printed from the promptbook.

1414   Honigmann, Ernest Anselm Joachim. "Spelling Tests and the
        First Quarto of *King Lear.*" *Library,* 20 (1965), 310-315.

        Two compositors probably worked on Q$_1$ *King Lear* (1608),
        with compositor "B" setting Acts I-III and compositor "C" (just
        possibly the same as "B") setting Acts IV-V. An alteration in the
        spelling suggests that the division into acts was marked in the quarto.

1415   Honigmann, Ernest Anselm Joachim. *"King Lear."* *The Stability
        of Shakespeare's Texts.* London: Edward Arnold, 1965,
        pp. 121-128.

        The *Lear* quarto is probably not a reported or a memorial re-
        construction text; instead, it apparently is based on a copy taken by
        dictation from Shakespeare's foul papers. The folio version is gen-
        erally agreed to be based on a quarto collated with the prompt-copy
        cut for representation. The single most compelling argument for
        Shakespeare's interference in the quarto text is its occasional superi-
        ority in meter. Honigmann argues with Alice Walker (see item 1385)
        that the quarto text is much closer to Shakespeare's foul papers than
        has generally been assumed.

1416   Meagher, John C. *"King Lear,* I, iv: 'Exit an Attendant.'" *Notes
        and Queries,* n.s. 12 (1965), 97-98.

        Editors universally add stage directions something like "Exit
        an Attendant" in four places in *King Lear,* I, iv—following "Let me
        not stay a jot for dinner: go, get it ready" (8); "Go you and call my
        Fool hither" (42); "Go you and tell my daughter I would speak with
        her" (73); and "Go you, call hither my Fool" (74). To the contrary,
        the very point is that the attendants do not obey Lear; no doubt
        they have been instructed—like Oswald—to be deliberately inatten-
        tive to the old King's wishes. "The silence of the original texts on
        these four directions is the silence of insolence, and the dramatiza-
        tion of Lear's growing dishonour and impotence" (p. 98).

1417   Baldini, Gabriel. "Marginalia per L'Ultima Lettura di *Lear.*"
        *Friendship's Garland: Essays Presented to Mario Praz on His
        Seventieth Birthday.* Edited by Vittorio Gabrieli. Rome:
        Edizioni di Storia e Letteratura, 1966, pp. 161-174.

The first five notes deal with various editorial changes in *King Lear* which have tended to distort rather than clarify Shakespeare's meaning. The final note is a brief, somewhat scathing, comment on Victor Hugo's exegesis of the play, a reading which anticipates that of Freud. The first note, the longest, argues that Shakespeare knew little or no Anglo-Saxon or Middle English. Notes three, four, and five concern eighteenth-century revisions which in particular passages emasculate the imagery and transform poetry into banal utterance.

1418 McNeir, Waldo F. "The Last Lines of *King Lear*: V, iii, 320-327." *English Language Notes*, 4 (1966-1967), 183-188.

The quarto texts give the last four lines to Albany while the folio text assigns them to Edgar. Eighteenth-century editors disagreed on the assignment, and the problem continues to the present time. Since there is no textual basis for a decision, the choice must be made eclectically on analysis of the speeches within the context of the final dramatic movement. The lines are best distributed, following neither Q nor F_1 evenly between Albany (ll. 324-325) and Edgar (ll. 326-327). Such a distribution maintains the established couplet ceremonial tone; "Albany's reaction, in response to Kent's, is both personal and official, showing his growth in moral stature; and Edgar's reaction, in response to both [Albany and Kent], is official in its agreement with Albany and both personal and universal in its forecast for the future of the state" (p. 188).

1419 Ingham, Patricia. "A Note on the Aural Errors in the First Quarto of *King Lear.*" *Shakespeare Studies*, 3 (1967), 81-84.

Analysis of supposed aural errors in the quarto text of *King Lear* in the light of contemporary standard English pronunciation reveals the following categories: (1) errors of mishearing (i.e., errors not based on contemporary pronunciations), such as "I apprehend" for "Ile apprehend"; (2) true aural errors resulting from the listener's vulgar or advanced contemporary pronunciations, such as "ought" for "oft"; (3) instances of Q spellings that are different from F, such as "aurigular" (I, ii, 94). Evidence suggests that genuine aural errors are fewer than generally supposed and that they usually occur from someone's using an advanced or vulgar form of speech.

1420   McManaway, James G. "A Reading in *King Lear.*" *Notes and Queries,* n.s. 14 (1967), 139.

The line spoken by Goneril, in IV, ii, 28, after she dismisses Edmund with a kiss should read "My Foole usurpes my body" (as in the folio and uncorrected quarto texts) as opposed to "A foole usurps my bed" (as in the corrected quarto text).

1421   Mulholland, Joan. " 'Thou' and 'you' in Shakespeare: A Study in the Second Person Pronoun." *English Studies,* 48 (1967), 34-43.

Shakespeare's usage of thou/you distinguishes among four distinct social classes in *King Lear,* and further distinction is obvious within each class concerning men talking to men, men to women, women to men, and women to women. When a character chooses deliberately to flout conventional usage, as is the case in the disguised Kent's conversation with Lear, it is a grammatical clue to his character.

1422   Roston, Morray. "Shakespeare in Hebrew." *Israel Argosy* (Jerusalem), 9 (1967), 102-122.

With samples both from English and from Hebrew, this article surveys various Hebrew translations of Shakespeare. Textual illustrations are from six Shakespearean tragedies, including *King Lear.*

1423   Zitner, Sheldon P. "The Fool's Prophecy." *Shakespeare Quarterly,* 18 (1967), 76-80.

Since there is no compelling textual evidence that the Fool's prophecy concerning Merlin genuinely belongs in the folio text of *King Lear,* it must be supported or denied on the basis of its contextual relevance. The justification clearly seems to be thematic. The passage is essentially anti-Utopian, indicating that a Utopia with cutpurses, bawds, and whores is no Utopia at all; Albion tomorrow will be what it is today because the human condition is permanent. The first two lines ("This prophecy Merlin shall make; for I live before his time") is the humor of anti-climax. Thematically the passage is necessary, coming as it does when Lear is being led to shelter and Gloucester is determining to aid him, as a grim reminder that the ending will involve destruction and confusion. Moreover, the lines summarize the Stoical view that *Lear* both embodies and evokes.

1424   Fleissner, Robert F. "King Lear's Love Test: A Latin Derivation." *Notes and Queries*, n.s. 15 (1968), 143-144.

The quarto text of *King Lear*, at the point at which the king responds to Cordelia's solitary word with "Nothing can come of nothing," is in the folio text expanded so that the word *nothing* is repeated several times before Lear's "Nothing will come of nothing." Perhaps one reason for preferring the folio reading is that Shakespeare was borrowing from Corderius' Colloquy No. LXVIII, in which the word *nihil* is repeated twice in three consecutive sentences and once again after a three-word sentence gap. It is reasonable to assume that Shakespeare had studied Corderius' *Dialogues* in his schooling at Stratford.

1425   Meagher, John C. "The Fool's Brach." *English Language Notes*, 6 (1968-1969), 251-252.

One of the textual cruxes in *King Lear* occurs in I, iv, when the Fool observes that "Truth is a dog that must to kenell, hee must be whipt out, when Ladie oth'e brach [Q; Lady Brach, F] may stand by the fire and stincke." A more reasonable reading (and one manifestly susceptible to being misinterpreted by a reporter, scribe, or compositor is "Lady Oathe"; thus the lines become "Truth is a dog that must to kennel; he must be whipped out, when Lady Oath, the brach, may stand by the fire and stink" (p. 252).

1426   Spevack, Marvin. "A Concordance to *King Lear*." *A Complete and Systematic Concordance to the Works of Shakespeare*. Vol. III. Hildesheim: Georg Olms Verlagsbuchhandlung, 1968, pp. 892-1017.

A complete concordance to the text of *King Lear* is provided with tables indicating the word , its frequencies, its relative frequencies, whether in verse or prose, and the act-scene-line references. Line references are based upon the Riverside Shakespeare edited by G. B. Evans. See item 1708.

1427   Bentley, Gerald Eades. "Eleven Shakespeare Quartos." *Princeton University Library Chronicle*, 30 (1969), 69-76.

This description of eleven quartos presented to Princeton University includes a 1608 quarto of *King Lear*.

1428 McManaway, James G. "The Year's Contributions to Shakespearian Study: Textual Studies (1948-1965)." *Studies in Shakespeare, Bibliography, and Theater.* Edited by Richard Hosley, Arthur C. Kirsch, and John W. Velz. New York: Shakespeare Association of America, 1969, pp. 305-383.

G. I. Duthie's edition of *King Lear* (see item 1535) intends to establish a text as close to Shakespeare's version as possible. Assuming that the Q_1 text (1608) is a reported version based on a communal effort by the entire touring company, he accepts the folio as his copy text and eclectically allows quarto readings where desirable. He fails to address two basic problems— (1) that Nathaniel Butter's entry in the Stationers' Register in 1608 suggests nothing amiss even though certainly he would know the difference between a scribe's report and either a normal book of the play or the author's foul sheets and (2) that the one folio copy he uses as his basic text, without collation with the other extant copies, is subject to numerous variants as a consequence of the printer's method of proofreading and other printing-house practices.

1429 Kashahara, Masao. "A Note on Auxiliary Verbs Used in Shakespeare's Plays." *Bunka Report* (Kagoshima University, No. 6 (1970), pp. 1-49.

This discussion of Shakespeare's verb formations draws evidence from *King Lear* and five other Shakespearean plays. See item 1564.

1430 Miller, Paul W. "The 1619 Pavier Quartos of Shakespeare: A Recapitulation." *Michigan Academician,* 3, No. 1 (1970-1971), 95-99.

The so-called false folio of Shakespeare's plays in 1619, the oversized Pavier quartos, sharpens our perspective on the first folio in 1623. That the date on the title page of five of the ten plays, including that of *King Lear*, is false was not discovered until the early twentieth century. The abortive project probably spurred Heminge and Condell to publish a fitting monument to their friend.

Probably also Jaggard was encouraged to halt the 1619 project by being offered the right to print the 1623 collection. A. W. Pollard first recognized irregularities among the quartos, but it was W. W. Greg who discovered through watermarks on the paper that all were actually printed in 1619, a finding reinforced by William Neidig's meticulous study of the type-setting ("The Shakespeare Quartos of 1619," *Modern Philology*, 8 [1910], 145-163).

1431   Stetner, S. C. V. and Oscar B. Goodman. "Regan's Profession."
       English Studies, 51 (1970), 331-336.

Regan's line in her protestation of love for Lear in the opening scene—"Which the most precious square of sense possesses"—should actually read "Which the most precious sphere of sense professes." The "sphere" is a metaphor for the eye, and it refers backward to Goneril's claim that she loves Lear "dearer than eyesight" and forward to Kent's being ordered out of Lear's sight and later to Gloucester's blinding. The word "profess" suggests religious overtones; hypocritically, Regan claims to renounce all earthly things for her father's sake.

1432   Winterton, J. B. "*King Lear*, IV, vii: An Improved Stage Direc-
       tion." *Notes and Queries*, n.s. 17 (1970), 133-134.

A fusion of the quarto and folio texts in every modern version of *King Lear* creates an anomaly by placing a gentleman and Kent on stage together at the beginning of Scene vii; although Cordelia openly addresses Kent, the gentleman several lines later clearly does not know who he is. Since the quarto text leaves us a free hand for determining where the gentleman is brought in and since someone needs to attend Lear in his entrance at 1. 21, the gentleman's entry should be delayed to that point. Now, with Cordelia's conversation with Kent having passed, it is   credible that the gentleman not recognize him when they converse.

1433   Andrews, John Frank. "The Pavier Quartos of 1619—Evidence
       for Two Compositors." Ph.D. dissertation, Vanderbilt Uni-
       versity, 1971. *DAI*, 32 (1972), 6364A.

The Pavier quartos were typeset by two compositors (the first folio's compositor B and one we must now distinguish as

Compositor F). In fact, Compositor B set only approximately one-third of the material. *King Lear* represents a text in which the two compositors shared responsibility. The major thrust of the study is an examination of this Q_2 text of *Lear,* confirming Madeleine Doran's theory that the first eight quires and the last three quires were set by different compositors. Evidence is based on such matters as spelling patterns, punctuation patterns, patterns in the placement and punctuation of marginal stage directions, patterns in the alignment of verse and prose, and patterns in the introduction of certain kinds of substantive alterations in the language of the text.

1434   Dace, Letitia Skinner. "Prolegomena to a New Edition of *King Lear."*   Ph.D. dissertation, Kansas State University, 1971. *DAI,* 32 (1972), 5178A.

An old-spelling edition of *King Lear* is needed, based on a re-examination of the transmissions of the quarto and folio texts. The quarto text, despite previous conjectures, cannot adequately be explained as the result of either shorthand or memorial reconstruction. Instead it is more likely to derive from a pre-promptbook draft and thus possesses a high degree of authority. An analysis of the folio text reveals various forms of textual contamination. The ideal edition would accept the quarto text for accidentals and the folio text for substantives. Folio readings should be emended by reference to the quarto or, if necessary, conjecturally.

1435   Dace, Letitia Skinner. "Towards a New Edition of *King Lear:* The Place of the First Quarto." *Shakespeare Newsletter,* 21 (1971), 61.

Editors of *King Lear* should reexamine their prejudice against the Q_1 text. For those who conclude that the Q_1 text was printed from early holograph, "an informed and selective use for Q for some matters of word order, morphology (e.g., Q 'a' for F 'he'), spelling, etc., will be obligatory" (p. 61). This paper was read at the Midwest MLA Bibliography Section in Detroit on 5 November 1971.

1436   Halio, Jay L. "Editing an Old-Spelling Text of *King Lear."* *Shakespeare Newsletter,* 21 (1971), 54.

The editor of an old-spelling text of *King Lear* should adopt Q_1 as his copy text and correct it against F. The editor, in other words, must attempt to reproduce as nearly as possible the copy that B and E had before them in Jaggard's printshop, without deleting passages marked for stage abridgement or censorship. This paper was read at the World Shakespeare Congress in British Columbia.

1437 Howard-Hill, T. H., ed. *King Lear: A Concordance to the Text of the First Folio.* Oxford: Oxford University Press, Clarendon Press, 1971. 331 pp.

This volume, based on the copy-text for *King Lear* extablished by Alice Walker for the forthcoming Oxford Old Spelling Shakespeare, "takes account of every word in the text, and represents their occurrence by frequency counts, line numbers, and reference lines, or a selection of these according to the interest of the particular work" (p. v). This copy-text is the Chatsworth copy of the first folio; in this copy only qq6ᵛ and rr2 are in an uncorrected state.

1438 Ismail, Muhyi al-Din. "Al-Malik Lir al-ma'suf 'alayhi." *Al-Majella* (Cairo) (July, 1971), pp. 43-46.

This article ("The Lamented King Lear") discusses Jabra I. Jabra's Arabic translation of *King Lear.*

1439 "Shakespeare-Übersetzungen. (Text and Bochumer Diskussion). Teilnehmer: Bolz Engler, Karl Maurer, Barbara Puschmann-Nalenz, Bernd Santesson, Dieter Wessels, Ingeborg Heine. Text: Raimund Borgmeier und Ulrich Suerbaum." *Poetica,* 4 (1971), 82-119.

This general discussion of the possibilities and limitations of a prose translation of Shakespeare features, for comparative analysis, various drafts of *King Lear*, I, i.

1440 Walton, J. K. *"King Lear." The Quarto Copy for the First Folio of Shakespeare.* Dublin: Dublin University Press, 1971, pp. 269-281.

Q *Lear* has many features resembling Q *Richard III,* a fact leading G. I. Duthie to propose that the text is a memorial reconstruction made by the entire company while on provincial tour and without the promptbook (see item 1535). Alice Walker's theory that the two boys playing Goneril and Regan are guilty of a surreptitious transcript (see item 1385) is not convincing. It does seem clear that the F *Lear* is based on a version of Q that has been collated with the promptbook. An analysis of the distribution of verbal variants, however, reveals that the thoroughness of the collation of the copy for F varied. This collation was carried out (1) because it was recognized that Q was a memorial reconstruction and thus needed correction and (2) probably because no copy of *Lear* existed other than the promptbook and the company was unwilling to risk letting it out of their possession.

1441   Feather, J. P. "Some Notes on the Setting of Quarto Plays." *The Library*, 5th ser. 27 (1972), 237-244.

Various compositorial inconsistencies in *King Lear* can best be explained either by alternation of the measure or insertion of type in the furniture. There is also evidence of the use of quotation quadrats in the dramatic text.

1442   Ellis, John. "Scene Division in the Folio *King Lear*, Act II." *American Notes and Queries*, 12 (1973-1974), 142-143.

Whereas the folio text includes in a single scene (ii) all of the action in *King Lear*, Act II, from the meeting of Kent and Oswald through Edgar's soliloquy in which he declares his intention of masquerading as Tom o' Bedlam and through Lear's discovery of Kent in the stocks, modern editions normally divide the action into three scenes (ii, iii, iv) in order to avoid having Kent asleep in the stocks on stage while Edgar delivers his soliloquy. The folio arrangement, however, is preferable. Edgar has escaped by hiding in a tree near the castle; when he comes on stage again, he does not notice Kent behind him. After he moves off stage to go to the heath, Lear enters. Among other things, the juxtaposition of Edgar (with his suddenly changed fortune) and Lear (whose fortune is soon to change just as suddenly) is dramatically effective.

1443   McKenzie, D. F. " 'Indenting the Stick' in the First Quarto of *King Lear* (1608)." *Papers of the Bibliographical Society of America*, 67 (1973), 125-130.

Two distinct measures were not used by Okes in the printing of Q$_1$ *King Lear* to set verse lines of 80-81 mm. and prose lines of 93-94 mm. Instead, the printer, who was short of pica quads, used a single measure but left the composing stick set to a wider measure, indenting where possible by adding large quads at one end. The difference between the two line lengths "is regularly 3-ems and it results, not from a change of measure, but from the compositor's indenting his stick by using a quad which, running up the head of the stick, served to indent two, three, or four text lines at a time" (p. 127).

1444   Petrovic, Zivojin.   "Spor oko jednog prevoda *Kralja Lira.*" *Zbornik Matice srpake za Knijizevnost i jizik*, 21 (1973), 161-165.

The complex problems involved in translating *King Lear*, for which an eclectic text must first be established, is the subject of "Dispute over the Translation of *King Lear.*"

1445   Chakravorty, Jagannath.   " 'Blow, winds, and crack your cheeks! Rage! Blow!'–The Storm in *King Lear." Shakespeare Translation*, 2 (1975), 85-100.

Maintaining the proper tone and sustaining the tension of the storm scene in *King Lear* are especially difficult in translating the material into Bengali, Hini, and Marathi. The principal danger in translation is to overdo the rhetoric of the lines and consequently turn the scene into something only approximating tragedy.

1446   Kim, Yong-sung.   *A Study of the Uses of the Subjunctive in King Lear.*   Master's thesis, Korea University, 1975.

The text of *King Lear* is used as a corpus in a linguistic analysis of Elizabethan modal auxiliaries in the periphrastic subjunctive. The basis for classification is provided by G. O. Curme.

1447   Kopff, E. Christian. "An Emandation in Herodotus 7. 9. B. 2." *American Journal of Philology*, 96 (1975), 117-120.

Words in context occasionally are changed into their exactly opposite meaning. One example cited from *King Lear* is the quarto

reading "The gods are just, and of our pleasant *vertues* / Make in-
struments to plague us" (V, iii, 170-171). The reading in F is
"vices." See item 1450.

1448   Gjurin, Velemir. "Semantic Inaccuracies in Three Slovene Trans-
       lations of *King Lear.*" *Acta Neophilologica,* 9 (1976), 59-83.

       The three segments of this article list the Slovene translation
of *King Lear,* the principles for translation analysis, and the comparative strengths of the three translations. The first Slovene translation in book form was by Anton Funtek in 1904; Matej Bor's followed in 1964. A translation in script form by Zupancic is kept in
the Slovene Theatrical Museum in Ljubljana. In translation the unit
of source language (transferend) must be matched as nearly as possible with a unit of the native language (translate), with modification
occurring only where there are unavoidable discrepancies. Of the
three translations Bor's is the most semantically accurate.

1449   Johnston, Shirley White. "Samuel Johnson's Text of *King Lear:*
       'Dull Duty' Reassessed." *Year's Work in English Studies,* 6
       (1976), 80-91.

       A full collation of Samuel Johnson's text of *King Lear* with
the first folio text, the quarto text, the text of the eighteenth-century editions of Lewis Theobald, Thomas Hanmer, and William
Warburton, and the modern Duthie-Wilson Cambridge edition reveals that—contrary to popular critical opinion—Johnson was fully
conscientious as an editor. No one could argue that Johnson's text
is the equal of those that have profited from this century's study of
descriptive bibliography; but, like modern editors, he does establish
the folio as his basic copy text and fully and accurately annotate
all readings admitted from the quarto. He is alert to expunging the
capricious emendations of his predecessors; generally he is far less
permissive of emendations than his predecessors. "In the case of
King Lear, at least, Johnson's was in fact the most meticulous text,
as well as the most readable, that had so far been produced. And it
is doubtful that any single editor after Johnson can be shown to
have improved the text of *King Lear* as comprehensively as he did"
(p. 91).

1450   Maxwell, J. C. " 'Polar Errors' in Shakespeare." *American Journal of Philology* (Baltimore), 97 (1976), 170-171.

E. C. Kopff (see item 1447) is inaccurate in citing "pleasant virtues" (Q *King Lear*) for "pleasant vices" (F *King Lear*) as a polar error. The oxymoronic nature of "pleasant vice" is enough to give rise to the temptation for textual change. The Q error no doubt arises from memorial transmission.

1451   Oppel, Horst. "The Final Lines of *King Lear.* Problems of Textual Analysis, Interpretation, and Translating." *English and American Studies in German: Summaries of Theses and Monographs.* Edited by Werner Habicht. Tubingen: Niemeyer, 1977, pp. 52-53.

The final half-line is elliptical and can be read in three different ways. The lines are appropriately assigned to Edgar (as in F₁). See item 1452.

1452   Oppel, Horst. *Die Schlussverse von King Lear: Text-Interpretations-und Übersetzungprobleme.* Abhandlungen der Geistes— und Sozialwissenschaftlichten Klasse/Akad. der Wissenschaften und der Literatur. Jy. 1976, No. 6 Wiesbaden: Steiner, 1976.

On the reading of the final lines of *King Lear,* see item 1451. The section on problems of translation treats a number of examples from a broad spectrum of English literature.

1453   Ross, Gordon N. "Shakespeare's *King Lear*, I, i, 306." *Explicator*, 36, No. 4 (1978), 25-26.

Readers of Shakespeare have long been misled by Samuel Johnson's emendation *compliment* (formality, ceremony, formal courtesy) in *King Lear*, I, i, 306: "There is a further complement [Q₁ 1608, Q₂ 1619, F₁ 1623] of leave-taking between France and him [Lear]." Goneril, speaking to Regan, surely means, not to comment on some ceremonious parting that would be out of character in light of Lear's sharp words to France, but to observe that Lear's breaking with France complements (repeats in similar fashion, fills out in kind) his banishment of Kent.

1454   Warren, Michael J. "Quarto and Folio *King Lear* and the Inter-
        pretation of Albany and Edgar." *Shakespeare: Pattern of
        Excelling Nature.* Edited by David Bevington and Jay L.
        Halio. Newark, Del.: University of Delaware Press, 1978,
        pp. 95-107.

        Critics have assumed without sufficient evidence that Q_1 and
        F_1 *King Lear* are corruptions of some ideal text and a modern edi-
        tion must of necessity be a conflated text. Instead, they are proba-
        bly two equally sound versions of a single play. That significant
        modifications have occurred between the two is easily seen in the
        roles of Albany and Edgar. Albany is more fully developed in Q, in
        that version closing as a mature and victorious duke who assumes
        major responsibility in the kingdom; in F he is weaker and avoids
        responsibility. Edgar, to the contrary, is a young man overwhelmed
        by his experience in Q, whereas in F he seems to have assimilated his
        wisdom and emerges as a leader of the ravaged society. The evidence
        in general indicates that all further work on the play be based on
        either Q or F but not on the conflation of both.

1455   Stone, P. W. K. *The Textual History of "King Lear."* London:
        Scholar's Press, 1979. 256 pp.

        The text of *King Lear* exists in two different version—Q_1 1608
        and F_1 1623. The quarto text is based on a longhand report of the
        play made during visits to several performances. The folio text is
        based essentially on a revised version of the quarto text. Various
        new readings are proposed in a series of appendices.

See also items: 383, 407, 418, 444, 467, 482, 540, 555, 613, 636, 661,
        666, 671, 676, 684, 730, 735, 739, 783, 802, 814, 1261, 1457,
        1459, 1461-1463, 1465, 1468-1471, 1473-1475, 1477, 1480-1481,
        1484, 1486, 1490-1492, 1497-1498, 1501, 1503, 1507-1508, 1510,
        1513, 1521, 1524, 1528, 1533-1535, 1540, 1544-1546, 1550, 1552-
        1553, 1557-1558, 1561, 1569, 1571.

V. BIBLIOGRAPHIES

V. BIBLIOGRAPHIES

1456 Tannenbaum, Samuel A. *Shakespeare's "King Lear": A Concise Bibliography*. New York: Samuel A. Tannenbaum, 1940. 101 pp.

This volume cites 1,934 items, topically arranged, on *King Lear*. The divisions include editions and adaptations (235 entries), translations (186 entries), music, songs, operas (26 entries), commentary on music (17 entries), illustrations and costumes (13 entries), parodies, burlesques (4 entries), *King Leir* (11 entries), *King Lear* in the theater (154 entries), commentary on *Lear* (1,253 entries), and book titles from *Lear* (28 entries).

1457 Smith, Gordon Ross. *A Classified Shakespeare Bibliography 1936-1958*. University Park: Pennsylvania State University Press, 1963. 784 pp.

References to 305 works on *King Lear* are included, pp. 721-731, classified under Texts, Literary Genesis and Analogues, Use of Language, General Criticism of the Play, Characterization, Miscellaneous Items, and Subsequent History of the Play.

1458 Eastman, A. M. and G. B. Harrison, eds. *"King Lear." Shakespeare's Critics from Johnson to Auden: A Medley of Judgments*. Ann Arbor: University of Michigan Press, 1964, pp. 222-236.

In addition to sections on each of the plays, the general criticism includes sections on attitudes, approaches, unity and chaos, characters and characterization, style, gallimaufry, focus and vision, and poets on Shakespeare. The section on *King Lear* provides excerpts from ten critics—Coleridge (see item 4), Stauffer (see item 122), Heilman (see item 106), Murry (see item 25), Swinburne, Sewall (see item 288), Johnson (see item 168), Auden (see item 187), Bradley (see item 9), and Empson (see item 118). Swinburne calls *Lear* Shakespeare's most Aeschylean work, set in a world filled with death and life with no guidance. For Shakespeare's fatalism there is no glimmer of light; the key is found in Gloucester's words concerning the wanton cruelty of the gods.

1459   Marder, Louis, ed. *King Lear: A Supplementary Bibliography (1880-1964).* New York: American Scholar Publications, 1965. 30 pp.

Entries are included under the following categories: reproductions of the original folio editions, reproductions of quarto editions of *Lear*, a representative list of modern editions of *Lear*, and critical studies. The major section is the last, containing 589 entries. The entries are not annotated.

1460   Velz, John W. "The Tragedies." *Shakespeare and the Classical Tradition: A Critical Guide to Commentary, 1660-1960.* Minneapolis: University of Minnesota Press, 1968, pp. 285-335.

This volume gathers, classifies, and summarizes criticism on Shakespeare from 1660 to 1960 involving the playwright's knowledge and use of the classics in his drama. The general argument has persisted since Restoration critics interpreted Ben Jonson's comment on "small *Latine* and lesse *Greeke*" as a slur on Shakespeare's art. And the resultant criticism has touched virtually every aspect of his work—the characters, the philosophic backgrounds, the sources, his poetic and dramatic techniques, the mythological allusions and the folkloric context. Of the 2,487 entries (most of them annotated), 381 are on the tragedies, of which 32 are on *Lear*. The brief summary of each article or book is concerned, of course, with Shakespeare's specific use of the classics rather than with the general thesis.

1461   Berman, Ronald. *"King Lear." A Reader's Guide to Shakespeare's Plays.* Chicago: Scott, Foresman, 1965. Reprint. 1973, pp. 107-112.

Selective bibliographical information is listed under various headings—text, editions, sources, criticism, staging, and bibliography. Major emphasis is upon the critical material, with the most significant items annotated briefly.

1462   Muir, Kenneth. *"King Lear."* *Shakespeare: Select Bibliographical Guides.* Edited by Stanley Wells. London: Oxford University Press, 1973, pp. 171-188.

A general discussion of the text of *King Lear* and of criticism and commentary is followed by a bibliographical listing with 134 entries. The work of bibliographers and textual critics has established the folio text as superior to that of the quarto (1608); however, readings from Q must be allowed in various places. G. I. Duthie's old-spelling edition (see item 1535) is the most valuable; M. R. Ridley's (see item 1497) is unsatisfactory since it is based on the quarto text. Excellent editions for general use include the New Cambridge edition of Duthie and J. D. Wilson (see item 1599) and Alfred Harbage's Pelican edition (see item 1594). Selective criticism of the tragedy until Bradley's study is considered chronologically; but work in this century, for this play a particular proliferation, is described by categories. These major areas include characterization (Bradley, see item 9; E. E. Stoll; L. B. Campbell, see item 18), sources (W. Perrett; Muir, see item 1553); W. B. D. Henderson, see item 1241; G. Gordan, see item 53; Geoffrey Bullough, see item 1319), dramatic technique (G. W. Knight, see item 19; Murry, see item 25; H. A. Mason, see item 583; Harley Granville-Barker, see item 72), the philosophy as positive, even Christian (R. W. Chambers, see item 30; G. L. Bickersteth, see item 70; John M. Danby, see item 116; Terence Hawkes, see item 281; H. S. Wilson, see item 258; Virgil Whitaker, see item 547), the philosophy as nihilistic (Barbara Everett, see item 305; John Holloway, see item 345; Jan Kott, see item 348; J. Stampfer, see item 327), imagery (C. Spurgeon, see item 24; W. H. Clemen, see item 139; R. B. Heilman, see item 106; W. R. Keast, see item 119), and the Fool and foolishness (Enid Welsford, see item 27; William Empson, see item 118; R. H. Goldsmith, see item 207). Particularly valuable non-inclusive studies are those of W. R. Elton (see item 559), Russell Fraser (see item 368), G. W. Knight (see item 19), and Maynard Mack (see item 530). Each play in the canon is covered in similar fashion, and general introductory sections are provided on the study of Shakespeare (Stanley Wells), the text (Norman Sanders), and Shakespeare in the theater (Michael Jamieson).

1463   Quinn, Edward, James Ruoff, and Joseph Grennen, eds. *"King Lear." The Major Shakespearean Tragedies: A Critical Bibliography.* New York: Free Press, 1973, pp. 151-203.

This volume provides a selective annotated bibliography on criticism, sources, and date, textual criticism, editions, and staging for *Hamlet, Othello, Lear,* and *Macbeth.* Additionally there is a brief introductory essay on each of these plays and notes on bibliographies, reference works, biographies, the Elizabethan theater, Elizabethan life and times, general criticism, and imagery and language. For *Lear,* Edward Quinn provides seventy-five entries under the general criticism, ranging from Nahum Tate's adaptation in 1681 (see item 2494) to an article by Morris Weitz in 1971 (see item 832). Seven works on the sources, thirteen on staging, and three editions are cited. For most entries under criticism a brief evaluative comment is also provided. Quinn observes in his introduction that criticism on *Lear* tends to be more emotive than descriptive. Generally the eighteenth-century critics insisted on viewing the play as an affirmation of a moral order in the universe. The romantic critics shifted from the ethical to the philosophical, perceiving "the great Romantic agonist whose struggles issue in the birth of a terrible beauty" (p. 153). In the present century a critical dialectic has developed between those who claim an affirmation of Christian doctrine or at least spiritually redemptive potentiality on the one hand and those who claim a nihilistic, absurdist, existential, or apocalyptic interpretation. The most profound criticism has begun to produce a synthesis of these two polarized visions.

1464   Bergeron, David M. "A Guide to Resources: Tragedies." *Shakespeare: A Study and Research Guide.* New York: St. Martin's, 1975, pp. 64-81.

This chapter provides a discussion of twenty-six of the major book-length studies of Shakespeare's tragedy. Illustrations of the critical perspectives are drawn from *King Lear* in numerous instances.

1465   McManaway, James G. and Jeanne Addison Roberts. *"King Lear." A Selective Bibliography of Shakespeare: Editions, Textual Studies, Commentary.* Charlottesville: University

Press of Virginia (for the Folger Shakespeare Library), 1975,
pp. 108-115.

Included are five entries under editions, twenty-six entries
under commentary, in addition to a cross-reference to 152 additional entries. The entries are not annotated.

See also items: 238, 294, 365, 404-405, 445, 490, 516, 525, 527, 555,
598, 663, 679, 719, 767, 818, 857, 1480, 1528, 1533, 1553, 1571,
1600, 1602, 1605, 1614, 1618, 1620, 1630, 1638, 1659, 1670,
1672, 1686, 1689, 1692-1693, 1695, 1701, 1703-1705, 1708, 1711,
1727.

VI. EDITIONS

VI. EDITIONS

1466   Rowe, Nicolas, ed. *The Works of William Shakespeare.* 7 vols. London: Jacob Tonson, 1709. Reprint. New York: AMS Press, 1967.

Based upon the fourth folio, this edition establishes an inferior text that seriously vitiated later editions for the next sixty years. Rowe set up a systematic division of the plays into acts and scenes and is the first to indicate a localized setting for many of the scenes. Also, his "Life of Shakespeare" is the first serious attempt at a biography of the playwright.

1467   Pope, Alexander, ed. *The Works of William Shakespeare.* 6 vols. London: J. Tonson, 1723-1725. Reprint. New York: AMS Press, 1969.

In his Preface, Pope describes Shakespeare as not so much an imitator as an instrument of nature, both in his concept of characterization and in his control over our passion. The folio text is corrupt as a consequence of numerous emendations by the actors. The various readings are placed in the margins, with suspected passages relegated to the bottom of the page. See item 913.

1468   Theobald, Lewis, ed. *The Works of William Shakespeare.* 7 vols. London: A. Bettesworth and C. Hitch et al., 1733. Reprint. New York: AMS Press, 1968.

"Collated with the oldest copies, and corrected; with notes, explanatory, and critical," this edition includes *King Lear* in Volume 5. A "Table of the Several Editions of Shakespeare's plays collected by the Editor" in Volume 7 lists the 1608 quarto of *King Lear* and the folios of 1623 and 1632 as texts of authority, the 1655 quarto as a text of middle authority, and the editions of Rowe and Pope as texts of no authority.

1469   Hanmer, Thomas, ed. *William Shakespeare: Works of Shake-
       speare.* 6 vols. Oxford: Printed at the Theatre, 1743-44.
       Reprint. New York: AMS Press, 1969.

   This edition is "carefully revised and corrected by the former
edition [Pope's], and adorned with sculptures designed and executed by the best hands." Pope's Preface is also included, along with
Rowe's biographical sketch. *King Lear* is in Volume 3 (pp. 3-106).

1470   Warburton, William, ed. *The Works of William Shakespeare.*
       8 vols. London: F. and P. Knopton, 1747. Reprint. New
       York: AMS Press, 1968.

   Noting that his primary task is to restore the poet's genuine
text, Warburton disdains the "interpolations occasioned by the
fanciful extravagances of others." Both textual and explanatory
notes are provided, along with notes by Alexander Pope.

1471   Johnson, Samuel, ed. *The Plays of William Shakespeare.* 8 vols.
       London: J. and R. Tonson, 1765. Reprint. New York: AMS
       Press, 1968.

   This edition, based primarily on Warburton, features "the corrections and illustrations of Various Commentators," to which Johnson's notes are added. *King Lear* is included in Volume 6. On Johnson's "Preface," see item 168. The prefaces of Pope, Theobald, Warburton, Rowe, as well as notes from previous editions, are included
with the text of *Lear.* See item 913.

1472   Steevens, George, ed. *Twenty of the Plays of Shakespeare.* 4
       vols. London: J. and R. Tonson, 1766. Reprint. New York:
       AMS Press, 1968.

   "Being the whole number printed in quarto during his lifetime, or before the Restoration, collated where there were different
copies, and published from the originals." *King Lear* (Q, 1608) is
in Volume 2, and *King Leir* (Q 1605) is in Volume 4.

1473   Capell, Edward, ed. *Mr. William Shakespeare: His Comedies,
       Histories, and Tragedies: Set out by Himself in Quarto, or by
       his players in folio, and now faithfully republished from those*

editions. 10 vols. London: J. and R. Tonson, 1767-1768. Reprint. New York: AMS Press, 1968.

Capell argues that the basis of Rowe's edition, which provided a superstructure for those which came after, was faulty in that the text was based upon the fourth folio of 1685. In his introduction, he describes his attempt to establish a particular copy text, recognizing generally the superiority of the earliest printed texts. The source for the main plot of *King Lear,* which is included in Volume 10, is "a silly old play" entitled *King Leir,* while the subplot is based upon Sidney's *Arcadia.* See items 913, 1236.

1474 Malone, Edmund, ed. *The Plays and Poems of William Shakespeare.* 10 vols. London: H. Baldwin, 1790. Reprint. New York: AMS Press, 1968.

Malone's Preface illustrates in detail the nature of the textual corruption occurring in the second folio. The main task of the editor is not to choose among folio variants—F_1 must be the standard— but to choose judiciously between folio and quarto variants. Copious footnotes, as well as an appendix in Volume 10, describe the nature of the collation. See item 913.

1475 Boswell, James, the Younger, ed. *The Plays and Poems of William Shakespeare.* 21 vols. London: F. C. and J. Rivington et al., 1821. Reprint. New York: AMS Press, 1966.

This edition features the "corrections and illustrations of various commentators: comprehending the life of the poet and an enlarged history of the stage by the late Edmond Malone." The prolegomena in Volume 1 describes Boswell's dependence upon Malone's work and cites deficiencies in the earlier editions. Included also are the prefaces by Pope, Theobald, Hanmer, Warburton, and Johnson, and advertisements and proposals by Steevens, Reed, and Richardson. *King Lear* is in Volume 10. The "preliminary Remarks" note Shakespeare's sources as *King Leir,* Sidney's *Arcadia,* Spenser's *Faerie Queene,* Camden's *Remains,* Holinshed's *Chronicles,* the *Mirror for Magistrates,* and Geoffrey of Monmouth. The section "An Attempt to Ascertain the Order of Shakespeare's Plays," in Volume 2, sets the date of composition as 1605. Notes from earlier editors are printed with the text.

1476   Campbell, Thomas, ed. *The Dramatic Works of William Shake-*
       speare. New York: Routledge, Warne, and Routledge, 1863.
       Reprint. New York: AMS Press, 1972. 960 pp.

       A lengthy introduction includes a biographical sketch of
       Shakespeare and a critical introduction to each play. *King Lear*, spe-
       cifically, dramatizes with awesome power the weakness of senility
       in combination with the strength of despair. The meeting of Lear,
       Edgar, and the Fool—resulting in the mixing of real and pretended
       madness—is one of Shakespeare's master strokes. Included also are
       sections from the first folio ("To the Great Variety of Readers" and
       commendatory verses), a glossary, and several indices (historical
       characters, manners and passions, fictitious characters, thoughts or
       sentiments, speeches, descriptions or images, similes and allusions).

1477   Clark, William George and William Aldis Wright, eds. *The Works*
       of William Shakespeare. The Cambridge Shakespeare. 9 vols.
       London: Macmillan and Co., 1863-1865. Reprint. New York:
       Blue Ribbon Books, 1940. 1233 pp. Garden City, N. Y.:
       Garden City Publishing Co., 1940. 1527 pp. Philadelphia:
       The Bakiston Co., 1944. New York: Grosset and Dunlap,
       1951. 1420 pp. Chicago: Encyclopaedia Britannica, 1952.
       2 vols. New York: AMS Press, 1968. 9 vols. Doubleday and
       Co., 1974. 2 vols. Franklin Center, Pa.: Franklin Library,
       1978.

       This edition features the Cambridge text with the Temple
       notes by Israel Gollancz. Certain imprints include illustrations by
       Rockwell Kent and a preface by Christopher Morley. *King Lear* is
       described as the tragedy in which passions assume the largest pro-
       portions. Lear dies in an agony of grief, but he has been released
       from the bondage of pride and selfishness. Lear is the greatest suf-
       ferer in Shakespeare's plays, and the Fool is the most pathetic of the
       characters. The mad scene on the stormy heath is the boldest
       moment in poetry.

1478   Halliwell-Phillips, James Orchard, ed. *The Works of William*
       Shakespeare. 16 vols. London: J. E. Adlard, 1864-1865.
       Reprint. New York: AMS Press, 1970.

This edition features a historical introduction, explanatory and critical notes, a life of the poet, and an introductory essay on his phraseology and meter.

1479 Lacroix, Jules, trans. *Le roi Lear.* Paris: Michel Lévy frères, 1868. Reprint (on microcard). Louisville, Ky.: Falls City Press, 1959. 144 pp. (French—not seen)

1480 Furness, Henry Howard, ed. *A New Variorum Edition of Shakespeare: "King Lear."* New York: J. B. Lippincott Co., 1880. Reprint. New York: Dover Publications, 1963. 503 pp.

The text, based on the Globe Shakespeare, is accompanied by extensive notes that provide critical excerpts from commentators from the eighteenth and nineteenth centuries. Appendices include a description of the text (the 1605 text of *Leir* and the 1608 and 1623 texts of *Lear*) and various critical theories concerning them, of the date of composition, and of the source of the plot (with selections reprinted from Holinshed's *Chronicles,* Sidney's *Arcadia, The Mirror for Magistrates,* Spenser's *The Faerie Queene, King Leir,* and the ballad "King Leir and his three Daughters"). Additional sections cover the duration of the action and Lear's insanity, general selections from English critics on the play itself, on the actors, and on costumes, selections from German critics, from Victor Hugo, and selections from Nahum Tate's version of 1681. An extensive bibliography is also attached.

1481 Craig, W. J., ed. *The Tragedy of King Lear.* Indianapolis: Bowen-Merrill Co., 1889. Reprint. London: Methuen, 1942. 250 pp.

The text is eclectic, a result of a collation of the two quarto and the four folio versions. While the F_1 text is generally preferred, it can be in no way absolute. Both the date (between Harsnett's *Egregious Popish Impostures* and an entry in the Stationers' Register) and the multiple sources (ultimately from Celtic lore) are discussed at length. Shakespeare's primary modifications of his material include the tragic ending, Kent's interference with Cordelia's banishment, the role of the Fool, Burgundy as a rival to France for Cordelia's hand, and Lear's madness. *Lear* is "one of the greatest miracles in art" (p. xxxv), a deeply pathetic tragedy unlocking the gates of pity and terror. Out of the depths of darkness and despair, "Love, ardent and unconquerable, asserts itself like a diamond" (p. lix). Textual and explanatory notes accompany the text. See items 1490, 1574.

1482   Vietor, W., ed. *King Lear.* Marburg, Germany: N. C. Elevert, 1892. 178 pp. Reprint. *Shakespeare Reprints, 1* (microfilm copy). Ithaca, N. Y.: Photo Science, Cornell University, 1973.

This volume provides parallel texts of the quarto and folio versions of *King Lear.*

1483   Verity, A. W., ed. *King Lear.* Pitt Press Shakespeare for Schools. Cambridge: Cambridge University Press, 1897. 260 pp.

Introductory material includes a discussion of the date (1605-1606), the early editions (two identical quarto texts in 1608, a folio text which provides "substantially the abridged acting edition" [p. xii]), the sources, and various critical aspects of the play. Notes and a glossary follow the text. The double plot creates an essential unity of effect. Although either story alone might seem unnatural, together they effectively delineate a general upheaval. Lear's death is artistically correct; any continued life would be in a state of general enfeeblement little better than dotage. Cordelia, the Antigone of English drama, dies; but mysteriously the effect is one of a beginning. If the good are defeated, the loss is but temporary and there are worse things than defeat.

1484   Craig, W. J., ed. *The Complete Works of William Shakespeare.* The Arden Shakespeare. London: Oxford University Press, 1903.

The text, established by the editor, is based on a collation of quartos and the folios. Most helpful in this task were the editions of Capell, Theobald, Delius, Dyce, and Clark and Wright. In the early impressions the general introduction is by A. C. Swinburne, and introductions to the individual plays are by Edward Dowden.

1485   Rhys, Ernest, ed. *Shakespeare: The Tragedies.* Everyman's Library. 3 vols. New York: E. P. Dutton, 1906. 981 pp.

King Lear is included in Volume 3. The prefatory note is by
D. C. Browning.

1486   *The Aldus Shakespeare.*   40 vols.   New York: Bigolow Smith,
       1909. Reprint.   New York: Funk and Wagnalls Co., 1967.

   King Lear, comprising Volume 16, features a preface by Israel
Gollancz, an introduction by Henry Norman Hudson, a selection of
previous critical commentary, copious notes by Hudson, Gollancz,
and C. H. Herford, a synopsis by J. Ellis Burdick, and a glossary.
The preface covers such matters as the early editions, the date,
Tate's version, the sources, and the duration of the action. Extracts
from the major sources are included in the introduction. Previous
critical commentary is drawn from Ferris-Gettemy, Coleridge,
Hallam, Jameson, Knight, Gervinus, Clarke, Ransome, Heuse,
Schick, Snider, Hazlitt, Rapp, Bradley, Luce, and Boas.

1487   Chiarini, Cino. trans. *Re Lear.* Florence: G. C. Sansoni, 1910.
       Reprint. 1948, 270 pp.

   This bilingual edition of *King Lear* features Italian and English
on opposite pages. Both a critical introduction and illustrations by
the translator are included.

1488   *Elizabethan Drama.* The Harvard Classics, Vol. 46. New York:
       P. F. Collier, 1910. Reprint. 1961. 442 pp.

   King Lear (pp. 201-302), Shakespeare's most overpowering
work, reveals the terrible costs of defects of character. The key to
the power of the tragedy is the intensity of the characters: "The
imperiousness and intellectual grasp of Lear, the force and subtlety
of Edmund, the venom of the wicked daughters, the tenderness of
Cordelia, the impassioned loyalty of Kent, the unselfishness of Edgar, and the poignant candor of the faithful Fool" (p. 202).

1489   Benavant, Jacinio, trans. *El rey Lear.* Madrid: Ediciones de La
       lectura, 1911. Reprint. Buenos Aires: Emecé Editores, 1949.
       187 pp.

   The introduction for this Spanish translation is by Ignacio B.
Anzoetequi. The philosophic complexity of the tragedy is a point
of special concern, as is the universality of the story.

1490   Craig, W. J., ed. *The Tragedies of Shakespeare.* London: Oxford
       University Press, 1912. Reprint. 1945.

       The introductions by Edward Dowden and the text for this
volume are drawn from Craig's Oxford edition (see item 1481).
King Lear occupies pp. 735-837.

1491   Brooke, C. F. Tucker, John William Cunliffe, and Henry Noble
       MacCracken, eds. *Shakespeare's Principal Plays.* New York:
       Century Co., 1914. Reprint. New York: D. Appleton-Cen-
       tury Co., 1941. 933 pp.

       The text of *King Lear* (pp. 601-656), included with nineteen
other plays, is eclectic, with spelling modernized. The first folio
text is the primary copy, but passages unique to the quarto are inserted, marked with a dagger. The sources of the play are described
with particular attention to *The True Chronicle History of King Leir*
and to Shakespeare's modifications. Other sections cover matters of
date, text, critical comment, and stage history. The actability of the
tragedy is not a point at issue; however, it is observed that only a
great actor can bring the role effectively to life.

1492   Phelps, William Lyon, ed. *The Chronicle History of the Life and
       Death of King Lear and His Three Daughters.* The Yale Shake-
       speare. New Haven: Yale University, 1917. Reprint. 1941.
       154 pp.

       Aside from extensive notes and a glossary, this edition includes
appendices on the sources of *King Lear*, the history of the play, the
text, and suggested collateral readings. The present text is a reprint
of Craig's Oxford Shakespeare, with the addition of several pages
from the first folio text. The composition may be dated no more
certainly than some time between 1603, the appearance of Harsnett's *Popish Impostures,* and 1606, the year of the first recorded
performance (26 December) in the Stationers' Register. Following
Nahum Tate's adaptation in 1681, Shakespeare's *Lear* was not seen
in London until 1823, when Edmund Kean in large part returned to
the original. The most notable American performances were those
of Edwin Booth and Robert Mantell. Even so, there is still much
truth in Charles Lamb's comment that the "Lear of Shakespeare
cannot be acted. . . . [T]he play is beyond all art" (p. 145).

1493   Bogdanović, Milan, trans. *Kralj Lear.* Zagreb: Izvanredno
        izdanje Matice hrvatske, 1919. Reprint. 1950. 198 pp.
        (Serbian—not seen)

1494   Losey, Frederick D., intro. *The Complete Dramatic and Poetic
        Works of William Shakespeare.* Philadelphia: John C. Win-
        ston Co., 1926. Reprint. The Kingsway Shakespeare. Lon-
        don: G. G. Harrap, 1949. 1331 pp. Philadelphia: John
        C. Winston Co., 1952. 1344 pp.

        Frederick D. Losey provides a general introduction, a bio-
graphical sketch, and a critical introduction to each play. Color
plates are by Sir Frank Dicksee. The text is based on that of Delius.
King Lear he describes as the salvation of a great soul. His tragic
flaw is a pride in his own authority to which even truth must yield.
In his suffering and madness he realizes his own helplessness, and
wisdom comes with his ability to feel compassion for others. The
tragedy is that he gained such wisdom so woefully late.

1495   Mee, Arthur, arr. *The Children's Shakespeare.* London: Hodder
        and Stoughton, 1926. Reprint. London: Amalgamated Press,
        1941. 976 pp.

        Twelve plays, including *King Lear*, are arranged for a juvenile
audience. Famous paintings are used as illustrations.

1496   Craig, Hardin, ed. *Shakespeare: A Historical and Critical Study
        with Annotated Texts of Twenty-one Plays.* Chicago: Scott,
        Foresman, and Co., 1931.

        The Globe text of *King Lear* (pp. 845-897) is included, along
with a full range of critical apparatus. In addition to a general introduction ("The Middle Ages and the Renaissance," "Life in England in Shakespeare's Time," "Pre-Shakespeare Drama," "London
Theaters and Dramatic Companies," "The Order of Shakespeare's
Plays," "Shakespeare Criticism," "Editions, Editors, and Actors,"
and "Shakespeare's English"), a specific introduction is provided for
each of the four chronological periods of Shakespeare's work. The
critical analysis of *King Lear* (pp. 717-720), in "The Period of the
Tragedies," covers matters of publication, date, sources, political
background, ethical interpretation, and stage history. Craig assumes

that the copy for Q_1 1608 is Shakespeare's manuscript, rendered somewhat illegible through revision. The folio text was presumably published from a clean copy that stayed in the playhouse and subsequently underwent additional alteration. Lear, in abdicating his throne, commits a crime against Nature and sets in motion the chaos which destroys the royal family and the kingdom. *Lear* is described as rather unfortunate in its stage history; only the greatest of actors have been able to perform it successfully.

1497   Ridley, M. R., ed. *King Lear.* The New Temple Shakespeare. London: J. M. Dent, 1935. Reprint. 1957. 171 pp.

This modernized spelling text is based on the earliest reliable version, Q_1. Though Q_1 contains disparate passages, it is essentially a good quarto and clearly is in close relation to an original manuscript. The folio text was probably set from a better manuscript than was available for Q_1, but it is not based on an independent and superior text. The date of composition can be narrowed no further than between 1603 (the publication of Samuel Harsnett's *A Declaration of Egregious Popish Impostures*) and December, 1606 (the entry in the Stationers' Register). The duration of the action is seven days. *Lear* is Shakespeare's cry *De profundis, fractus illabitur orbis.* Two characteristics set this tragedy apart from the other tragedies—the Fool is bitter and scornful, not conventional comic relief; this play reaches its climax not with the death of the protagonist but with Lear's irretrievable insanity with Cordelia dead in his arms. Critical excerpts are featured from Johnson, Lamb, Hazlitt, and Bradley. Also included are explanatory notes and a glossary. See items 1462, 1602.

1498   Holzknecht, Karl Julius and Norman E. McClure, eds. *Selected Plays of Shakespeare.* 3 vols. New York: American Book Company, 1936-1941.

King Lear is in Volume 2, published in 1937, pp. 397-522. The play is based on a story thoroughly familiar to the audience, a legend treated by every chronicler from Layamon to Holinshed. Compared to the older play of *King Leir,* the opening scene of Shakespeare's tragedy is weak in motivation. In *Leir,* for example, the love test is designed expressly to trick the youngest daughter into marriage. In *Lear,* the test is of no value except as the pageant-ry of an old man's vanity. Shakespeare adds both the subplot thematically to reinforce the main action and the Fool to provide bitter, clear-eyed commentary. Lear's madness, too, as well as the tragic ending, is a Shakespearean modification. *Lear* operates with a remorseless logic, with a satanic force crushing everything before it. The date of 1604-1605 cannot be fixed with greater precision. The text is based upon Q_1 1608, but the lines unique to F_1 are ad-mitted as well as obviously preferable folio readings. Textual and explanatory notes are also included.

1499   Kittredge, George Lyman, ed.   *The Complete Works of Shake-speare.* Boston: Ginn, 1936. 1528 pp.

Copy text for this edition of *King Lear* is the first folio, sup-plemented by the lines unique to the quarto. The introduction to the play discusses the Lear legend but stresses the additions (the Gloucester plot from Sidney, Lear's madness, the Fool, the tragic ending) which characterize Shakespeare's treatment. An unusually full glossary is also included. See items 1507, 1517, 1521, 1667, 1689.

1500   Harrison, George Bagshaw, ed.   *The Tragedy of King Lear.* The Penguin Shakespeare. London: Penguin Books, 1937. Re-print. Harmondsworth, Middlesex, 1949. 160 pp. (not seen)

1501   Parrott, Thomas Marc, ed.   *Shakespeare: Twenty-three Plays and the Sonnets.* New York: Scribner's, 1938. Reprint. Madison, Wis.: Charles Scribner's Sons (for the United States Armed Forces Institute), 1944. 1116 pp.

Copy text for this edition is a collation of the folio and quarto texts.   Subheadings in the introductory essay are the text, date, *Leir,* sources, Shakespeare's alterations, the theme, the characters, character and destiny, the redemption of Lear, atmosphere, final appreciation, and stage history. Essentially, Parrott views the play as more the redemption than the tragedy of Lear. The protagonist completely casts aside his kingly robes, pride, and self-will in his reconciliation with Cordelia. The lesson learned is too late to save his life, however, and the evil loosed by Lear's folly destroys him and his faithful daughter even as it also recoils upon its perpetrators. A general introduction and numerous illustrations are included.

1502   *The Works of William Shakespeare*. The Shakespeare Head Press Edition. New York: Oxford University Press, 1938. Reprint. 1940, 1263 pp. London: Odhams Press, 1944. New York: Grolier, 1958.

The text is that prepared by Arthur Henry Bullen for the Stratford Town Edition, first printed in 1904 by the Shakespeare Head Press, which he founded in 1904. The plays are arranged in the presumed order of composition, and a sketch of Shakespeare's life and a brief synopsis of each play by Sir Paul Harvey (reprinted from *The Oxford Companion to English Literature*) is appended following the glossary. Geoffrey of Monmouth, Holinshed, and the anonymous *King Leir* are cited as the sources.

1503   Farjeon, Herbert, ed. *The Comedies, Histories, and Tragedies of William Shakespeare*. 37 vols. New York: Limited Editions Club, 1935-1941.

The text of *King Lear* (Volume 2, 1939, 122 pp.) is that of the first folio, with occasional quarto insertions. Illustrations are by Boardman Robinson.

1504   *Five Great Tragedies*. New York: Pocket Books, 1939. Reprint. 1943. 574 pp.

The text of *King Lear* is that of the Cambridge Shakespeare (see item 1477) prepared by William Aldis Wright. The introduction, synopsis, and glossary are by John Masefield. The Introduction for the 1947 edition is by Mark Van Doren.

1505   Greg, W. W., ed. *King Lear, 1608 (Pide Bull Quarto)*. Shakespeare Quarto Facsimiles. Oxford: Oxford University Press, Clarendon Press, 1939. 89 pp. See item 1637.

1506   *The Complete Works of William Shakespeare*. Art-Type Edition. New York: Books, 1940. 1300 pp.

This volume includes the Temple notes, a sketch of the life of Shakespeare, and a glossary.

1507 Kittredge, George Lyman, ed. *King Lear.* Boston: Ginn, 1940. 264 pp.

The introductory essay traces the Legend of Lear from Geoffrey of Monmouth through Holinshed, Spenser, Higgins, and the anonymous chronicle play *King Leir.* Shakespeare, in dealing with story matter containing two catastrophes separated by seven years, combined the material into a single tragic catastrophe. One of his most significant additions is the Fool, whom insanity has fitted for his role of chorus as his genius flashes with sporadic insight. Lear's madness, also Shakespeare's addition, is an attack of feverish delirium provoked by the storm and the emotional stress to which he has been subjected. His final moments represent not a relapse into madness but a dissolution. The basis for the text is F_1, supplemented by the 300 lines unique to Q_1; incidental Q_1 readings are also admitted throughout the text. Included also are copious explanatory notes, textual notes, and a glossarial index. See items 1499, 1667, 1689.

1508 Macpherson, Guillermo, trans. *El rey Lear.* Buenos Aires: Editorial Sopena argentina, 1940. 158 pp.

The introduction describes the differences between the quarto and folio texts of *Lear,* the difficulties of translation, and the great diversity of critical opinion concerning the theme of the play.

1509 *Shakespeare's First Folio of 1623.* Boston: Graphic Service Corp., 1940.

Explanatory notes for this positive microfilm copy of the First Folio are provided by William Dana Orcutt.

1510 Kittredge, George Lyman, ed. *Five Plays of Shakespeare.* New York: Ginn, 1941. 264 pp.

The text and introduction of *King Lear* are drawn from Kittredge's *Complete Works* (see item 1499).

1511 Chemin, Camille, trans. *Le roi Lear.* Paris: Aubier, 1942. 317 pp.

This bilingual edition features English and French on opposite pages.

1512   *The Complete Works: William Shakespeare.* Cleveland: World
       Syndicate Publishing Co., 1942. 1173 pp.

       This edition features an introduction to each play along with
       the Temple notes. Additionally, a biographical essay and an index
       to the characters are provided. Designs are by T. M. Matterson, and
       engravings by Alexander Anderson.

1513   Neilson, William Allan and Charles Jarvis Hill, eds. *The Complete
       Plays and Poems of William Shakespeare.* Cambridge, Mass.:
       Houghton Mifflin Co., 1942. 1120 pp.

       In addition to the complete text of Shakespeare's plays, divid-
       ed by genre and arranged chronologically, a general introduction in-
       cludes sections on Shakespeare's life, the chronology of the canon,
       Shakespeare's opportunities, and his achievements. An introduction
       to each play covers matters of text, date, sources, and interpretation,
       and notes are supplied throughout the text. An index to the charac-
       ters in the plays concludes the volume. The copy text for *Lear* is
       F_1, with unique readings and numerous readings from Q_1. The in-
       troductory essay addresses the text, the sources, and the date. The
       skillfully interwoven subplot provides a means of reinforcing the
       tragic impact of the story. Lear's self-will blinds him to the true
       values about him; and, following his disastrous decisions and their
       consequences, he must slowly find his way back to sanity and per-
       ception. At several points, even as early as the moment at Goneril's
       house in Act I, his progress is registered. Disaster reigns at the con-
       clusion, but the Lear who expires with Cordelia dead in his arms is
       a man whom sorrow has ennobled.

1514   *The Tragedies of Shakespeare.* Modern Library of the World's
       Best Books. 3 vols. New York: Modern Library, 1943.
       1266 pp.

       King Lear is included in Volume 2 (pp. 689-785). Notes, both
       explanatory and textual, and a glossary are provided.

1515   *The Comedies and Tragedies of Shakespeare.* 4 vols. New York:
       Random House, 1944.

Notes and glossaries are provided for each volume. The tragedies are illustrated by Warren Chappell. *King Lear* is included in
Volume 4.

1516   Grossman, Reuben, trans. *Lir ha-melekh [The Tragedy of King
       Lear].* Tel Aviv: n.p., 1944. 270 pp. (Hebrew—not seen)

1517   *Shakespeare.* The Viking Portable Shakespeare. New York:
       Viking Press, 1944. 792 pp.

       Based on an informal public opinion poll, this edition prints
       in full the text of seven of Shakespeare's plays—*Hamlet, Macbeth,
       Romeo and Juliet, Julius Caesar, A Midsummer Night's Dream, As
       You Like It,* and *The Tempest.* The next nine, fairly even in popu-
       larity, include *King Lear,* from which brief selections (a total of 115
       lines) are included. The text is that established by George Lyman
       Kittredge (see item 1499).

1518   Cady, Frank W. and Van H. Cartmell, eds. *Shakespeare Arranged
       for Modern Reading.* New York: Doubleday and Co., 1946.
       Reprint. Greenwich, Conn.: Fawcett Publications, 1963.
       1165 pp.

       Shakespeare can be an inexhaustible source of pleasure for
       many whose introduction to the plays has been tainted by the educa-
       tional mandates of the classroom. This volume provides narrative
       synopses of the plays with ample passages of Shakespeare's text in-
       terpolated. The text for the Shakespearean passage is that of the
       Cambridge edition, edited by William Aldis Wright (see item 1477).
       The material on *King Lear* (pp. 940-980), comprised of paraphrase
       and quotation, is followed by a section, "Historical Data," which
       briefly notes the sources and dating of the tragedy.

1519   Errante, Vincenzo, trans. *La Tragedia di Re Lear.* Florence:
       Sansoni, 1946. 198 pp. (Italian—not seen)

1520   Kirchoff, Joseph, ed. *King Lear.* Paderborn: Schöningh, 1946.
       (German—not seen)

1521   Kittredge, George Lyman, ed. *Sixteen Plays of Shakespeare.*
       Boston: Ginn, 1946. 1541 pp.

This edition features an introduction by Arthur Colby Sprague on Kittredge as a Shakespearean critic. The introduction, text, and notes for *King Lear* are drawn from Kittredge's *Complete Works* (see item 1499).

1522   Tieck, Johann Ludwig, trans. *König Lear.* Wuppertal: Marecés-Verlog, 1946. 98 pp.

This bilingual edition features German and English on opposite pages. An afterword by Maurice Maeterlinck is included.

1523   Asen, Abraham, trans. *Kenig Lir.* New York: n.p., 1947. 187 pp. (not seen)

1524   Brooke, Tucker and William Lyon Phelps, eds. *The Tragedy of King Lear.* The Yale Shakespeare. New Haven: Yale University Press, 1947. 202 pp.

This edition represents Tucker Brooke's revising and updating of the 1917 edition by William Lyon Phelps. In addition to the text of the play, the volume includes notes (pp. 152-185), appendices briefly describing the sources (pp. 186-191) and the stage history (pp. 192-193), and an index of words glossed. The folio text provides a better and safer guide than the quarto text, though the latter has been unduly disparaged. It is much too good to be a bad quarto; it probably represents Shakespeare's foul papers, which the compositor found difficult or impossible to read in spots. Conversely, the quarto text is too bad to have served as copy for the folio; presumably only the author could be responsible for the extensive nature of the changes, regardless of what particular manuscript served as copy. In any case there is no reason to doubt Shakespeare's authorship of both versions, and a conflated, eclectic text is presented in this volume. Higgins, Spenser, Sidney, *Leir,* and Holinshed are all cited as sources, with a full reprint of the pertinent passages from Holinshed's *Chronicles.* Our respect for Shakespeare is heightened even more, perhaps, by taking note of his original materials. The stage history notes the lone reference to a contemporary performance, Tate's adaptation in 1681, and the importance of Edmund Kean and W. C. Macready in reestablishing Shakespeare's text. Still there is much truth in Lamb's observation that *Lear* is "beyond art" and "cannot be acted."

1525   *Le roi Lear.* Paris: Le Fleuve étincelant, 1947. 212 pp. (French
       —not seen)

1526   Schlegel, A. W., trans. *König Lear.* Dortmund: Schwalvenburg,
       1947. 90 pp. Reprint. Stuttgart: Reclam, 1950. (German
       —not seen)

1527   Croce, Benedetto, ed. and trans. *Shakespeare.* Bari: Laterza,
       1948. 211 pp.

       The introduction and critical notes for this Italian translation
       are by Napoleone Orsini. Of major concern are the credibility of the
       characters' motivation and the actability of the tragedy.

1528   Harrison, George Bagshawe, ed. *Shakespeare: The Complete
       Works.* New York: Harcourt, Brace and World, 1948,
       1666 pp.

       Copy text for this edition is an amalgamation of the quarto
       and folio texts. Harrison describes briefly the nature of the mis-
       prints and the chaotic punctuation of Q and declares that no fully
       convincing argument has yet explained its peculiarities. The F text
       is based on a copy of Q carefully corrected and extensively revised.
       The play can be dated rather precisely—between February, 1606
       (the publication date of Edward Gresham's *Strange, fearful, and
       true news . . . in the Kingdom of Croatia,* from which Shakespeare
       draws references to eclipses in the sun and moon) and December,
       1606 (the date of its performance at Court according to Q$_1$ title
       page). Harrison provides an especially full account of the sources of
       the play, with passages from Holinshed and Spenser and an exten-
       sive summary of *King Leir. Lear* is above all a tragedy of self-will,
       not of cosmic malignancy or indifference. The concept of Nature is
       explored with every shade of meaning and philosophic misunder-
       standing. The leading image pattern comparing man with members
       of the animal kingdom reinforces the emphasis upon Nature and the
       natural world. In addition to a general introduction, illustrations,
       explanatory notes, and a reading list, Harrison also provides an ex-
       tensive appendix covering a broad range of information on the
       Elizabethan age. See items 1529, 1618.

1529   Harrison, George Bagshawe, ed. *Shakespeare: Major Plays and the Sonnets.* Also issued as *Twenty-three Plays and the Sonnets.* New York: Harcourt, Brace, 1948. 1090 pp.

   The text and all critical apparatus for *King Lear* duplicate the material in G. B. Harrison's *Shakespeare: The Complete Works,* also published in 1948. See item 1528.

1530   Jurna, M. and G. Mari, trans. *Kuningas Lear.* Tallinn: Ilukirjondus ja Kunst, 1948. 196 pp. (Estonian—not seen)

1531   Tieck, Ludwig, trans. *König Lear.* Basel: Birkhauser, 1948. Reprint. Vienna: Osterr. Bundesverl., 1949.

   The introduction and commentary for this German translation are by Ilse Zechner. *Lear* is the most profound creation of Shakespeare's imagination; it embodies the elemental conflict of good and evil in man individually and collectively.

1532   Vallese, Targuinio, ed. *King Lear.* Naples: Pironti, 1948. (Italian —not seen)

1533   Bald, Robert Cecil, ed. *King Lear.* Crofts classic. New York: Appleton-Century-Crofts, 1949. 114 pp.

   This volume includes a general introductory essay, a table of the principal dates in Shakespeare's life, and a selective bibliography. The edition is based essentially on the folio text; passages unique to the quarto are also admitted as genuine, and in a few parallel instances the quarto reading is superior. The introduction covers such matters as the publication and date, the sources, the plot, the characters, and the theme. Shakespeare treats his sources far more freely in *Lear* than in his earlier histories. The double plot, by developing variations on the theme of filial ingratitude, strengthens and intensifies the main plot. Similarly, the Fool's comments, instead of providing relief or contrast as one might expect, contribute to the sense of concentrated economy since his remarks are constantly germane to the central theme. In the tragic conclusion Shakespeare departs most broadly from his sources. Through these structural features the issues of the tragedy seem to transcend the individuals in it as they are faced with events inexplicable in purely human terms.

1534   Campbell, Oscar James, ed. *The Living Shakespeare: Twenty-two Plays and the Sonnets.* New York: Macmillan Co., 1949. 1239 pp.

Based on the text of the Globe Shakespeare, this edition aims at readability and contemporaneity. To that end the introductions to the play move the reader directly to matters of interpretation, and discussion of text, sources, date, and stage history are relegated to a position of secondary importance. The general introduction carries information on Shakespeare's youth and his professional career, Elizabethan London, pre-Shakespearean drama, the stage, Shakespeare's company, his text, and a chronological table. *Lear* is described as Shakespeare's greatest dramatic poem, "an exalted morality play set against a backdrop of eternity" (p. 873). The sub-plot serves dramatically to provide development of fast-paced action long after the main plot has reached a climax in Act II, and it serves philosophically to reinforce and universalize the theme of the child's inhumanity to the aged parent. Lear's story is, further, one of re-demption through love; purged of pride and selfishness, he is re-deemed for a Christian heaven. The culmination of Lear's passion occurs in the scene on the heath, in which the tempest reflects the same cosmic evil impulse as the chaos in Lear's soul. His reconcilia-tion with Cordelia reflects his spiritual regeneration, and the deaths of Cordelia and Lear emphasize their triumph. The discussion of stage history takes special note of Nahum Tate's adaptation.

1535   Duthie, George Ian, ed. *Shakespeare's "King Lear": A Critical Edition.* Oxford: Basil Blackwell, 1949. 425 pp. Reprint. Folcroft, Pa.: Folcroft Publications, 1970. Norwood, Pa.: Norwood Editions, 1977. Philadelphia: R. West, 1978.

The aim of this edition is to establish a text "as near to what Shakespeare wrote as it is possible for us to get" (p. 3). The basis for the F text is a copy of Q brought by an editor into general agreement with a theatrical manuscript (probably the promptbook) containing a shortened version of the play; it omits some 300 lines found in Q. This theory was first advanced by P. A. Daniel and has been supported by E. K. Chambers and W. W. Greg. The Q text is a reported version; it is not a stenographic reproduction (as Alexander Schmidt, F. G. Fleay, Chambers, and Greg argue) but a memorial reconstruction made by an entire company, probably in the summer of 1606 when the King's Men (having left the promptbook in London) were on tour in Oxford, Leicester, Dover, and Saffron Walden. While the result is a far superior text to a memorial reconstruction by a single actor (such as that of Q_1 *Romeo and Juliet* or Q_1 *Hamlet*), it contains typical reporting errors throughout—anticipation and recollection, inversion, insertion of gratuitous exclamations, vocatives, connectives, synonym-substitution, vulgarization, metrical breakdown, omission, patching. This old-spelling edition is eclectic; the basic copy text is F_1 but in some instances Q readings are allowed. The text is much closer to F than that of most modern editions. In addition to the full textual introduction (199 pp.), textual variants at the bottom of the page and textual notes (pp. 357-425) are provided. See items 128, 251, 555, 857, 1389, 1462.

1536   *König Lear.* Brunswick: Westermann, 1949. 126 pp. (German—not seen)

1537   *Korol Lear.* Moscow: Goslitizdat, 1949. 164 pp. (Russian—not seen)

1538   Piàchud, Rene-Louis, trans. *Le roi Lear.* Beaux textes, textes rares, textes inédits, No. 21. Geneva: Pierre Cailler, 1949. 140 pp.

The text of *King Lear* is adapted and translated into French. Also included is an essay by Hilare Theurillat on Rene-Louis Piàchud as a dramatic critic.

1539   Brabander, Gerard den, trans. *Leer om Leer.* Amsterdam: von Oreschot, 1950. 128 pp. (Dutch—not seen)

1540   Dean, Leonard, ed. *"King Lear." Elizabethan Drama.* New York: Prentice-Hall, 1950, pp. 147-240.

The Renaissance was a dynamic period caught between the concept of an ideal, ordered, God-centered universe inherited from

the Middle Ages and the political realities which demanded and rewarded force and shrewdness. Goneril, Regan, and Edmund represent the cool rationalists who through self-discipline can manipulate
the emotionalism and idealism of others. Lear must learn firsthand
how false values can be turned against oneself, and the function of
the Fool is to turn every word to the central fact of Lear's folly and
its growing consequence. The tragedy does not end in despair and
cynicism; its final affirmation comes both positively in the developing perception in Lear and Gloucester and negatively in the self-de-
struction of the rationalists. Lear's madness becomes, not a defense
against the savage truth of the world, but an acutely sensitive realization of it. The text of *King Lear* is that of the Globe Edition.

1541   Engmann, E. A. W., trans. *Mentse Lear.*   Accra: Presbyterian
       Book Depot, 1950. 151 pp.

       Numerous illustrations are provided by the translator. Em-
phasis is upon the purgatorial nature of both Lear's and Gloucester's
experience.

1542   Günther, Alfred, ed. *Konig Lear: Tragodie.*   Reclams Universal-
       bibliotek 13. Stuttgart: Reclam, 1950.

       King Lear is translated into German by W. H. G. Baudissin.
The afterword and textual revision are by the editor.

1543   *King Lear.* New York: n.p., 1950. 54 pp.

       This typescript is Kurt Richard's script of the tragedy as pro-
duced by Robert L. Joseph and Alexander H. Cohen at the National
Theatre in New York on 25 December 1950.

1544   Schaller, Rudolf, trans. *König Lear.* Als Unverkäufl. Buhnen-Ms.
       gedr. Berlin: Henshel, 1950. 139 pp.

       Schaller provides both a critical introduction and a running
commentary on the text.   Specific discussion focuses on the difficulties of translation, especially for a work of such linguistic and
philosophic complexity.

1545   Alexander, Peter, ed. *William Shakespeare: The Complete Works.* New York: London: Collins, 1951. Reprint. New York: Random House, 1952.

The thirty-seven plays, along with the poems and a transcript of Shakespeare's contribution to *Sir Thomas More,* are here reprinted without individual introductions. Such introductions may be found in Alexander's *Introductions to Shakespeare* (see item 1296). The general introduction describes Shakespeare's early life in Stratford and then traces him in London through four periods of his active work as a playwright—(1) arrival in London in 1584 to his joining the Lord Chamberlain's Men in 1594, (2) from 1594 to the opening of the Globe in 1599, (3) from 1599 to the taking over of the Blackfriars' Theatre in 1608, (4) from 1608 to the burning of the Globe in 1613. A brief discussion of the folio and quarto publications is also included, as are reprints of the preliminary matter of the first folio and a glossary. *King Lear,* the masterpiece of Shakespeare's "Third period," is a play not of ingratitude but of the gratitude of a   converted heart. It is a vision of human quality that walks unscathed amidst terrible visions of human degradation. See item 1653.

1546   Craig, Hardin, ed. *The Complete Works of Shakespeare.* Chicago: Scott, Foresman, 1951. 1337 pp.

The introductory essay of this edition provides commentary on the text, the date, the sources, the political background, the ethical interpretation, and the stage history. Q_1 1608, despite its corruptions, is too sound to be classified as a bad quarto. It was probably printed from Shakespeare's revision of his own play, a copy illegible in spots. The clean copy, remaining in the playhouse and thus subject to further alteration, served ultimately as copy for F_1 1623. The most significant source is Sidney's *Arcadia,* since that work is the genesis of tragedy resulting from filial ingratitude and the element of sinful and dangerous intrigue. The stroke of genius was in Shakespeare's combining the two plots and in his creation of the Fool.   While one cannot accept Lilian Winstanley's elaborate scheme of political allegory (*"Macbeth," "King Lear ," and Contemporary History.* Cambridge: Cambridge University Press, 1922),

Lear certainly reflects the contemporary background of intrigue, fear, murder, and violence. The note on stage history emphasizes Tate's adaptation and the most famous actors in the role. A full general introduction covers such matters as the Elizabethan lifestyle, pre-Shakespearean drama, the London Theaters and dramatic companies, the order of Shakespeare's plays, criticism of the canon, the editions, Elizabethan English, and a note on the doubtful and lost plays. A glossary and a list of editions are also included.

1547   Dettore, Ugo, trans. *Re Lear.* Milan: Biblioteca universali Rizzoli, 1951. 136 pp. (Italian—not seen)

1548   Downer, Alan S., ed. *William Shakespeare: Five Plays: "Hamlet," "King Lear," "Henry IV (Part I)," "Much Ado About Nothing," "The Tempest."* New York: Rinehart and Co., 1951. 473 pp.

The brief introduction provided for the text of five of Shakespeare's plays focuses upon Shakespeare's ability to play many roles, that is, his ability to impart life and imagination to the wide variety of characters whose actions comprise the plot. He was highly successful, writing for a commercial theater on whose stage —unencumbered with scenery—the emphasis was upon action with rich costumes and attention to details of processions, battles, duels, and dance. *King Lear,* specifically, is Shakespeare's greatest tragedy. The double plots, more accurately complementary plots, serve each other at every turn. "Not only does the parallel action of Gloucester interpret and humanize the story of Lear, the psychological action and spiritual conflict of Lear magnify the more domestic experiences of Gloucester" (p. xv). Explanatory notes accompany the text of each play.

1549   Holst, Adriaan Roland, trans. *Koning Lear.* Amsterdam: Wereldbibliothek, 1951. (Dutch—not seen)

1550   Entry Deleted.

1551   Burgersdijk, A. J., trans. *Koning Lear.* Leiden: Sithoff, Boekhandlers, 1952. 138 pp. (Dutch—not seen)

1552   Craig, Hardin, ed. *An Introduction to Shakespeare: Eight Plays and Selected Sonnets.* Chicago: Scott, Foresman, 1952. 741 pp.

The volume contains a general introduction, the text of eight plays including *King Lear*, an introduction to each play, and explanatory notes. The text followed is that of *The Complete Works of Shakespeare,* edited by Hardin Craig in 1951 (see item 1546). Q_1 is probably based on Shakespeare's rough but complete manuscript while F_1 is based on a fair copy of that original, a copy revised in the author's hand and difficult to read in spots. Various indications point to the play's being on the stage in 1605, and the publication of *Leir* was apparently in response to the popularity of Shakespeare's play. Certainly, though, Shakespeare was familiar with *Leir* on the boards, and the anonymous play was one of his important sources, along with Holinshed and Spenser, and perhaps *Mirror for Magistrates* and Geoffrey of Monmouth as well. The source for the subplot is Sidney's *Arcadia;* from the source comes also the tragic atmosphere and spirit of the play. *Lear,* however, is of much broader scope; Shakespeare "puts filial ingratitude in its place in the total scheme of things, in the order of the universe, and associates it with social discord and individual sin" (p. 555). Finally, there is a brief consideration of Nahum Tate's adaptation in 1681 and of the most famous actors in the part during the nineteenth and twentieth centuries.

1553   Muir, Kenneth, ed. *King Lear.* The Arden Shakespeare. London: Methuen, 1952; Cambridge, Mass.: Harvard University Press, 1952. 256 pp.

This edition represents a revision of the earlier Arden edition by W. J. Craig, first published in 1901 (see item 1481). Discussions are included of the text, date, sources, stage history, and critical interpretation, as well as appendices providing portions of the source materials. The text is based essentially on F_1; Q_1 readings are accepted, however, where the F readings are corrupt and where the readings are palpably superior. The twelve extant copies of Q_1 contain 167 variants. The date of composition for *Lear* is probably the winter of 1604-1605. Shakespeare need not have seen the 1605 printed version of *King Leir;* he could have been thoroughly familiar with the acting version. Principal sources include the *Leir* play, Spenser's *The Faerie Queene,* John Higgins' account of Cordila in the 1574 edition of *Mirror for Magistrates,* and Sidney's *Arcadia.* To judge from records of performances, the play was less popular than *Hamlet* or *Othello.* After the Restoration Betterton acted Shakespeare's version, but Nahum Tate's adaptation in 1681 provided the text that would hold the stage for 150 years. Kean in 1823 restored the tragic ending but still excluded the Fool and retained the love scenes. Macready reintroduced the Fool in 1838. Henry Irving and Ellen Terry starred in an excellent production later in the nineteenth century, and in the present century notable Lears have included Gielgud, Devlin, Wolfit, and Olivier. Interpretative criticism affords the full spectrum of opinions. Such critics as Thackeray, Allardyce Nicoll, J. Middleton Murry, and Tucker Brooke consider *Lear* a poor play, filled with improbabilities and incongruities. More current criticism has totally reversed this position, though major differences continue to separate those who perceive the playwright as working within the constraints of a teleological universe and those who argue that he is delineating the ultimate horrors of an absurdist's existence. *Lear* is a tragedy both of family and of kingship. "Power corrupts not only the possessor's capacity for loving, but the spontaneity of others' love" (p. liii). Lear's experience leads to a new stage of self-knowledge, and a new Lear is reborn from his reunion with Cordelia. The joy of reconciliation is not an illusion, though it is short-lived. His and Cordelia's deaths are comparatively unimportant; the play makes no concessions to sentimentality, and it is logical that the innocent suffer with the guilty once evil is unleashed. In a pre-Christian setting, Shakespeare builds up from the nature of men—not from revealed religion—the same moral and religious ideas that were being undermined in his own day. See items 342, 516, 814, 857, 859, 1180, 1376, 1462.

1554 Putman, James, ed. *Selected Plays: William Shakespeare.* Cleveland: Fine Editions Press, 1952. 473 pp.

This volume includes *King Lear* along with four other Shakespearean plays.

1555 Smirnovoj, A. A. trans. *Korol Lear.* Leningrad: Iskusstvo, 1952, 231 pp. (Russian—not seen)

1556   Verwey, J., adapt. and anno. *The Tragedy of King Lear.* Pur-
       merend: Muusses, 1952. 117 pp. (not seen)

1557   *The Complete Works of William Shakespeare: The Text and
       Order of the First Folio with Quarto Variants and a Choice of
       Modern Readings Noted Marginally: To Which are Added
       "Pericles" and the First Quartos of Six of the Plays with Three
       Plays of Doubtful Authorship: Also the Poems According to
       the Original Quartos and Octavos.* 4 vols. New York: None-
       such Press, 1953.

       This volume is based on a text established in 1929 by Herbert
       Farjeon (see item 1503) with a new introduction by Ivor Brown.
       King Lear is in Volume 3, pp. 737-827. The text is based on a colla-
       tion of the quarto and folio editions, with marginal notes and "Addi-
       tional Notes" (pp. 828-836) indicating the variant readings.

1558   Sisson, Charles Jasper, ed. *William Shakespeare: The Complete
       Works.* New York: Harper, 1953. 1376 pp. Reprint. Lon-
       don: Odhams Press, 1954.

       Included are a biographical and general introduction, a glos-
       sary, and an index of characters. *King Lear* (pp. 1043-1082) is
       described as a "humbling play" in that it disables the reader's re-
       flective reason. Among Shakespeare's sources may have been the
       contemporary account of Sir William Smith, whose story of the
       division of his estate among three daughters and his subsequent
       misery shocked London in Shakespeare's day. The basic text for
       this edition is the folio, but it is supplemented and corrected where
       necessary by Q_1 1608.

1559   Bernhard, Alfred, ed. *"King Lear." A Selection of the Chief
       Scenes.* Huebers fremdsprachliche Texte, No. 50. Munich:
       Hueber, 1954. 39 pp.

       This translation of *King Lear* into German consists of a selec-
       tion of the principal scenes with an introductory essay and a synop-
       tic commentary.

1560   Harrison, George Bagshawe, ed. *William Shakespeare: Four
       Plays.* New York: Harcourt, Brace, 1954. 172 pp.

This volume includes *King Lear, Henry V, As You Like It,* and *Antony and Cleopatra.* The text and introductory material are based on Harrison's 1948 edition. See item 1528.

1561 Kökeritz, Helge and Charles T. Prouty, eds. *Mr. William Shakespeare's Comedies, Histories, and Tragedies.* New Haven: Yale University Press, 1954. 889 pp.

This facsimile edition of Shakespeare's first folio features a preface (Kökeritz) and an introduction (Prouty). This copy text is the Henry Huth folio now owned by the Library of the Elizabethan Club. The page size is reduced by one-fifth. *King Lear* occupies pp. 773-799.

1562 Shlonsky, Abraham, trans. *ha-Melekh Lir [King Lear].* Merhavya: Sifrit Poalim, 1954-1955. 171 pp. (Hebrew—not seen)

1563 Fust, Milan, trans. *Lear Király.* Budapest: Vj Magyar Kiado, 1955. 189 pp. (Hungarian—not seen)

1564 Kittredge, George Lyman, ed. *The Kittredge Players' Edition of the Complete Works of William Shakespeare.* Chicago: Spencer Press, 1955. 1561 pp.

This volume features photographs of productions of Shakespeare's plays by the Old Vic Company in London, the Royal Shakespeare Company in Stratford-Upon-Avon, and by various other companies throughout England. The introduction and notes are based upon Kittredge's *Complete Works.* See item 1499.

1565 Kurukularaschchi, D. H. J., trans. *Liyar raja.* n. p., 1955. 122 pp. (Sinhalese—not seen)

1566 Saito, Takeshi, anno. and trans. *King Lear.* Tokyo: Kaibunsha, 1955. 425 pp.

The text of *King Lear,* based on the editions of G. I. Duthie (see item 1535) and Kenneth Muir (see item 1553), is translated into Japanese. Extensive annotations are also provided by the translator.

1567   Lodovici, Cesare Vico, trans. *Re Lear*. Piccola Biblioteca Scientifico-Letteraria,1956. Reprint. Collezione di teatro, No. 110. Turin: G. Einaudi, 1967. (Italian—not seen)

1568   Siwicka, Zofia, trans. *Król Lir*. Warsaw: Pánstwowy Instytut Wydawniczy, 1956. 202 pp. (Polish—not seen)

1569   Wolfit, Donald, intro. *The Tragedy of King Lear*. n.p.: The Folio Society, 1956. 131 pp.

The last twenty-five years have seen more performances of *King Lear* than any time since the play was written. The two world wars are, in a sense, "comparable to the titanic struggle that went on in the mind and soul of Lear, conflicts based on greed, ingratitude, jealousy and self-aggrandizement" (p. 3). Today's theater technically accommodates the play more effectively, as well, with fewer intervals and the use of permanent settings that do not obtrude between actor and spectator. Two specific alterations suggested by Wolfit are (1) that Goneril's "marry, your manhood mew" (IV, ii, 68) is a misprint for "marry your manhood—," Messenger [entering] "news" and (2) the rearrangement of Lear's two curses upon Goneril in I, iv, to avoid the clumsiness and incredibility of Lear's exiting only to return four lines later. The text used in this edition is the New Temple Shakespeare.

1570   Zeynik, Theodore von, trans. *König Lear*. Salzburg: Stifenbibliothek, 1956. 174 pp. (German—not seen)

1571   Barnet, Sylvan, Morton Berman, and William Burto, eds. *"King Lear." Eight Great Tragedies*. New York: American Library, 1957, pp. 133-227.

The raw material of Shakespeare's play is rooted in history books, an anonymous play *King Leir,* and a courtly Elizabethan novel. The tragic power was destroyed by Nahum Tate, with his happy ending which held the stage from 1681 to 1838. Lear's anguish is dramatically counterpoised against Gloucester's pain. Kent and the Fool play a role corresponding to that of the Greek chorus. Lear's impatience makes him potentially tragic; through his suffering he must acquire patience and wisdom. In addition to a critical introduction, a biographical note on Shakespeare, a general introduction, and a bibliography are included.

1572   Budd, F. E., ed. *King Lear*. Scholar's Library. London: Macmillan, 1957. 186 pp. (not seen)

1573   Chemin, Camille, trans. *Le Roi Lear*. Paris: Aubier-Montaigne, 1957. 317 pp.

The introduction and bibliography are by A. Mavrocordiato. A reprint in 1976 features a revision of both.

1574   Houghton, Ralph E. C., ed. *King Lear*. The New Clarendon Shakespeare. Oxford: Oxford University Press, Clarendon Press, 1957. 256 pp.

The introduction of this edition provides brief discussions of the tragedy, its date, the sources, the text, and a plot summary. A textual gloss appears at the bottom of each page, and explanatory notes follow the text. A section of previous critical views features excerpts on the play in general from Johnson (see item 168), Hazlitt (see item 2), Keats, Shelley, Maeterlinck; on plot and structure from Dowden (see item 8), Traversi (see item 235); on a comparison with *Hamlet* from James (see item 146); on the play's actability from Lamb (see item 4a), Bradley (see item 9), Granville-Barker (see item 72), Spencer (see item 44); on the characters from Heilman (see item 106), Knight (see item 19), Branson (see item 22), Coleridge (see item 4), MacKail, Lothian (see item 121); on the imagery from Spurgeon (see item 24), Clemen (see item 139); on the scenery from Sewell (see item 288); on the interpretation of the play from Symonds, Swinburne, Raleigh, Knights (see item 283), and Speaight (see item 215). Selections from the principal sources (Holinshed, Sidney, *King Leir*) are also appended, as is a brief synopsis of D. C. Adams' discussion of the Elizabethan staging. The text is eclectic, drawn from both Q_1 (1608) and F_1 (1623), and is essentially that of the *Oxford Shakespeare* edited by W. J. Craig (see item 1481). *Lear* is described as the most universal of Shakespeare's plays, paramountly upholding the value of endurance. It is written at the full maturity of the playwright's powers, the earliest possible date being 1603 (the appearance of Harsnett's *Declaration of Egregious Popish Impostures*) and the latest being 1606 (the performance in December at Whitehall). Six illustrations are included.

1575   Krishnamurthi, S., ed. *Shakespeare's "King Lear."* The Lifco College Classics. Madras: Little Flower Co., 1957. 424 pp.

In addition to the text of *King Lear* this volume includes a general introduction (a sketch of Shakespeare's life and brief discussions of the plays, his tragedies, and the quartos and folios), a special introduction (sections on the date, the sources, the plot, the drama scene by scene, the time of the action [10 days], the plot as tragedy, the functions of the subplot, the anachronisms in the play, classical and other allusions, the main ideas [parent-child relationship; kingship and its obligations; the nature of man, justice, wisdom, and moral order], the pagan atmosphere, poetic imagery, dramatic irony, and persons and places), critical aids (critical and explanatory notes, annotations, character sketches, and critical topics), and supplements (sections on the Elizabethan drama, Shakespeare's theater, great authors on Shakespeare, appreciation of Shakespeare, Charles Lamb's "King Lear," a poetic pageant from the play, parallel passages from plays and poems, a survey of critical opinions on the play, [e.g., Lamb, Coleridge, Hazlitt, Hudson, Brandes], advice to examinees, model questions, and a Shakespeare quiz).

1576   *Lear kiraly.* Budapest: Europa Könyvkiado, 1957. 183 pp. (Hungarian—not seen)

1577   Munro, John, ed. *The London Shakespeare.* 6 vols. New York: Simon and Schuster, 1957. Reprint. London: Eyre and Spottiswoode, 1958.

King Lear is included in Volume 6. The basic copy text is the folio version, with quarto readings adopted only when their merit is clear. The introduction by G. W. G. Wickham includes a brief synopsis of major critical views of the tragedy, and the editor provides extensive textual notes.

1578   Ognjanov, Ljubomir, trans. *Kral Lir.* Sofia: Narodna Kultura, 1957.

Ognjanov, in addition to the Bulgarian translation, provides a critical introduction and extensive explanatory notes. He describes the various sources for *Lear,* emphasizing Shakespeare's modifications such as the addition of the Fool, Lear's madness, and the tragic conclusion.

1579   Tarnawski, Wladislaw, trans., *Król Lear.* Warsaw: Zaklad Narodowy im. Ossolínskich, 1957. 235 pp. (Polish—not seen)

1580   Vera, Fernando Palacios, trans. and adapt. *El rey Lear.* Enciclopedia Pulga., No. 350. Barcelona: Pulga, 1957. 224 pp. (Spanish—not seen)

1581   Wright, Louis B. and Virginia A. Lamar, eds. *The Tragedy of King Lear.* The Folger Library General Reader's Shakespeare. New York: Pocket Books, 1957. Reprint. New York: Washington Square Press, 1960. 125 pp. 1967 (with "Reader's Supplement"). 220 pp.

The text of this edition is eclectic; the basic copy text is F_1, but various readings from Q_1 have been accepted as well as the 300 lines not found in the folio. Spelling and punctuation are modernized, and stage directions are inserted for clarity. Text and notes are presented on facing pages. The general introduction includes information on Shakespeare's life, the publication of his plays, the theater, the history of the Lear story, and the text. References for further reading and illustrations are also included. The interpretative essay stresses the universality of the theme, suggesting that the evil daughters are agents of Fate designed to re-educate and purify Lear. The play is pagan and pessimistic. "Man is in the hands of Fate, an arbitrary Fate that turns the wheel of Fortune mechanically" (pp. xxxix-xl). *Lear* is shot through with the Stoical attitudes of much of the literature of the seventeenth century. See items 1630, 1640.

1582   Alexander, Peter, ed. *The Heritage Shakespeare.* 3 vols. New York: Heritage Press, 1958-1959.

The text and introductions are those of the Collins edition in 1951 (see item 1545). *King Lear* is in Volume 3 (1362 pp.). The general introduction to the tragedies is by George Rylands, with engravings by Agnes Miller Parker.   Rylands observes that *King Lear* adumbrates the spiritual purport of the romances with father and daughter kneeling in mutual forgiveness, oblivious of the worst fate can do to them.   The fundamental and unanswered question posed by the play concerns the cause for human bestiality and hardness of heart.

1583   Alexander, Peter, ed.   *William Shakespeare: Complete Works.* London: Collins, 1958. 1174 pp.

This Players' edition features twenty-four illustrations of Shakespearean actors and actresses of the past and present in their famous roles.   The introductions, glossary, and text are those of Alexander's 1951 edition (see item 1545).

1584   Barka, Vasyl, trans.   *King Lear.*   Hannover: Ukraine u. Welt, 1958. 300 pp. Reprint. n.p.: Ha ropi, 1969. (Ukrainian— not seen)

1585   *The Complete Works of William Shakespeare Comprising His Plays and Poems.*   Feltham, Mass.:   Spring Books, 1958. 1081 pp.

The introduction and glossary are by Bretislav Hodeck, and the preface is by Sir Donald Wolfit, who encourages the reader to gain experience with Shakespeare in the theater. Hodeck describes briefly the date, textual problems, and sources of *King Lear.*

1586   Dissanayake, Hubert, trans.   *King Lear.*   Colombo: M. D. Gunasena, 1958. (Ceylonese—not seen)

1587   *Re Lear.*   Biblioteca Universale.   Milan: Rizzoli, 1958. 144 pp. (Italian—not seen)

1588   Ryl's'kyj, Maksym, trans. *Korol' Lir.*   Kiev: Goslitizdat Ukrainy, 1958. (Ukrainian—not seen)

1589   Saudek, E. A., trans. *Král Lear.*   Prague: Státní Nakladatelství Krásné Literatury, 1958. 199 pp. Reprint. Prague: ILIA, 1962.

The text of *King Lear* is translated into Czech. Introduction and commentary are by Zdněk Střibrný. The reprint is a mimeographed version for actors.

1590   Wilson, Frank Percy, ed. "Three Plays: *I Henry IV, King Lear, The Winter's Tale.*" *Masters of British Literature.* Vol. IV. Boston: Houghton Mifflin, 1958. pp. 261-406.

King Lear is Shakespeare's greatest play in that spiritually it "seems to comprehend all that matters most to man in his life on earth" (p. 265). Lear's spiritual journey to purgation and self-knowledge symbolizes the universal human condition. While *Lear* is not set in a specifically Christian world, it does take place in a world in which belief or unbelief is an important element of characterization. The hidden sources of conduct are examined in both their best and worst extremes. The text and notes are from the edition of W. A. Neilson and C. J. Hill. See item 1513.

1591   Ayyangar, À. Srinivasi, trans. *Mannan Liyar.* Paramakudi: Selbstverl, 1959. (Indian—not seen)

1592   Du Plooy, J. L. and V. H. Vaughan, eds. *King Lear.* London: Macmillan and Co., 1959.

This edition is part of the Shakespeare for South African Schools series. Introduction and commentary are provided.

1593   Grabhorn, Mary, ed. *The Tragedie of King Lear.* San Francisco: Grabhorn, 1959. 103 pp.

Woodcuts are included by Mary Grabhorn. The edition was limited to 183 copies.

1594   Harbage, Alfred, ed. *King Lear.* The Pelican Text. Baltimore: Penguin Books, 1959. 175 pp. Reprint. *William Shakespeare: The Complete Works.* The Pelican Text Revised. Gen. ed. Alfred Harbage. Baltimore: Penguin Books, 1969. 1481 pp.

Introductory material is provided on Shakespeare's intellectual and political background, his life and canon, his theater, his technique, and the original texts. The copy text for *Lear* is F_1, but a few variant readings from Q_1 are admitted as are the 283 lines not in F. Only the frame of a parable-myth could bear the weight of Shakespeare's version of the oft-recounted Lear story. A basic question is whether the play is Christian or pagan. Clearly, while the setting is pagan, the plot seems to be inclusively Christian. Lear, a titan figure, symbolizes mankind—as king, man, and father. His anguish is reminiscent of that of Job, Prometheus, or Oedipus. The Fool makes Lear's errors stand as an *idée fixe* through his constant reiterations. Lear throughout his suffering is the voice of protest; just as his injured self-esteem reaches awesome dimensions in the middle portion, so his hunger after righteousness gives magnitude to the concluding scenes. The play ends as it begins—in allegory—with Cordelia's death reflecting the sacrifices inevitable in "humanity's long, agonized, and continuing struggle to be human" (p. 1063). See item 1462.

1595   Iyengar, A. Srinivasa, trans. *Mannan Lear.* Paramakudi: n.p., 1959.

Iyengar's critical introduction to this translation into Tamil concentrates on the power of *King Lear* to transcend cultural boundaries. A general discussion of the Elizabethan age and its drama precedes a specific thematic analysis of *Lear.*

1596   Marin, Astranda, trans. *El rey Lear and pequeños poemas.* Madrid: Espasa-Calpe, 1959. 156 pp. (Spanish—not seen)

1597   Panikkar, K. M., trans. *Lear Rajavu.* Kottayam: Sahitya Pravarthaka Cooperative Society, 1959.

The text of *King Lear* is translated into Malayalam. This is the authorized translation sponsored by the Sahitya Academy in New Delhi.

1598   Sahinbas, Irfan, trans. *Kiral Lear.* Ankara: Maarif Basimevi, 1959. 168 pp. (Turkish—not seen)

1599   Duthie, George Ian and John Dover Wilson, eds. *King Lear.* Cambridge: Cambridge University Press, 1960. 300 pp.

For this new Cambridge edition John Dover Wilson provides extensive textual notes (pp. 140-276); George Duthie discusses the copy text (pp. 122-139) and furnishes a critical introduction (pp. ix-lv) including sections on sources and date, Lear, Cordelia, Kent, the Fool, Lear's suffering, the subplot, nature, man's double nature, the play's "pessimism," and D. G. James' view of the play; C. B. Young provides notes on the stage history (pp. lvi-lxix). A glossary is also included. The play is dated late 1604 or early 1605, Shakespeare presumably having read *Leir* (published late in 1605) in manuscript. The characters are graphically created. Lear, a monarch of great age, powerful physique, and compelling personality, is victimized by vanity and rashness. Cordelia is conceived as a Christlike figure; attempts to find fault in her refusal to articulate her love are misguided. Cordelia, Kent, and the Fool recognize both the spiritual and practical dimensions of Lear's error. Through suffering the king gains wisdom and attains salvation. The play is not ultimately pessimistic; if the gods are just, they are also merciful in allowing Lear and Gloucester to "die in a state of spiritual health" (p. 1). Duthie abandons his earlier assumption that Q_1 is a memorial text reconstructed by an entire company in favor of a modified view that the source is two boy actors who played Goneril and Regan. The F_1 text is probably "a conflation of 'good' pages from Q_1 supplemented by inserted manuscript leaves to replace corrupt passages of Q_1" (p. 128). The copy text for this edition is eclectic; F_1 is basic, but numerous Q_1 readings are admitted.

1600   Fergusson, Francis and Charles Jasper Sisson, eds. *King Lear.* Commentary by Dudley Fitts. New York: Dell, 1960. 252 pp.

Francis Fergusson's introduction stresses the scope of Shakespeare's vision in *King Lear.* Lear himself is only the center of the tragedy of all Britain at that legendary moment. The form and meaning of the play as a whole are not to be found in the individual speeches but in the interrelationships between them and the general thrust of the story. The vision of reconciliation reached by Lear and Cordelia in Act IV is beyond earthly misfortunes—even the disaster of Act V. If Shakespeare had no consistent philosophy in the play, he did have a consistent vision of our earthly life. Dudley Fitts discusses the style of the play. Specifically, Shakespeare works with the basic cadence of the blank verse line, but he constantly counter-points to create a wide range of variations. In this play in particular the author's experimentation is daring, creating a tone of controlled disintegration unlike anything else he wrote. The prose is also note-worthy, occasionally "heavy cadenced, as though the metrical beat had somehow gone astray and were attempting to break through again" (p. 28). C. J. Sisson's note on the text indicates that the F version is the basic copy text for this edition but that frequent read-ings are admitted from Q_1. Both texts apparently are derived from prompt-copy. Included also are suggestions for further readings on *Lear* and a glossary, as well as a general essay on Shakespeare and his times and a more extensive bibliography by Francis Fergusson. See item 1462.

1601   Jesenka, Zora, trans. *Kral Lear.* Bratislava: Diliza, 1960. (Czech-oslovakian—not seen)

1602   Langford, W. F., ed. *King Lear.* The Swan Shakespeare. Toron-to: Longmans, Green, 1960. 175 pp.

   This edition provides brief sections on Shakespeare's life; the Elizabethan stage; a summary of the plot; the sources; the date; Elizabethan language; Elizabethan grammar; Shakespeare's versifica-tion and prose; critical excerpts from William Hazlitt (see item 2), Charles Lamb (see item 4a), A. C. Bradley (see item 9), Mark Van Doren, the New Hudson edition, and M. R. Ridley (see item 1497); and the chief characters of the play. Additional features are explan-atory notes, review questions for each act, and a set of general questions. There is no indication of the copy text for the edition itself. Described as supremely the play of the breach of family ties, *Lear* is a masterpiece of Gothic drama; in the extensive diversifi-cation of form, aspect, purpose, and expression is a vast and com-plex unity and harmony. Lear's voice is not so much the expression of an individual man responding to cruelty; it is the voice of cruci-fied humanity, and strangely we sense the dominance of good over the principalities of evil despite the accumulation of horrors. The principal figure is admirably depicted in the various stages of demen-tia, the progressive effects of unbridled passions. Goneril and Regan are distinguished in their cruelty, the former acting from ambitions, the latter from sadistic pleasure. The Fool is foolish in name only; his comments both lead Lear to examine himself and provide relief from the overwhelming pathos of the story. Langford dates the play late 1605 or early 1606, stressing the topicality of references to the eclipses and to the Gunpowder Plot of 5 November 1605.

1603   Luarasi, Skender, trans. *Mbreti Lir.* Tirana: Naim Frasheri, 1960. (Albanian—not seen)

1604   Mikami, Isao, trans. *Riya O.* Tokyo: Kawade Shobo, 1960. (Japanese—not seen)

1605   Schücking, L. L., ed. *König Lear.* Rowohlts Klassiker 70. Hamburg: Rowohlt, 1960.

This edition features parallel English and German texts. The translation is by Schlegel and Tieck. An introductory essay by the editor and a bibliography by Wolfgang Clemen are included.

1606   Smith, D. Nichol, ed. *King Lear.* The Warwick Shakespeare. London: Blackie, 1960. 213 pp. (not seen)

1607   Arguile, H. and K. R. Nicol, eds. *King Lear.* Maskew Miller Shakespeare. Cape Town: Maskew Miller, 1961. (not seen)

1608   Collinder, Björn, trans. *King Lear.* Levande litteratur. Stockholm: Natur och kultur, 1961. (Swedish—not seen)

1609   Corteaux, Willy, trans. *Koning Lear.* Klassieke Galerji, 77. Antwerp: Nederl. Boekh., 1961. (Dutch—not seen)

1610   Dashtents, Khackik, trans. *King Lear.* Yerevan: Armenian State Publishing House, 1961. (Armenian—not seen)

1611   Obertello, Alfredo, trans. *La tragedia di Re Lear.* Bibl. mod. Mondadori, 670. Milan: A. Mondadori, 1961. (Italian—not seen)

1612   Peyman, Javad, trans. *Lir Shah.* Tehran: B.T.N.K., 1961. (Iranian—not seen)

1613   Wilson, John Dover, ed. *King Lear.* The Cambridge Pocket
       Shakespeare. Cambridge: Cambridge University Press, 1961.
       145 pp.

       The text of this volume is that of the New Cambridge *Lear*
published in 1961 (see item 1599). All critical apparatus are eliminated except a glossary (pp. 122-145).

1614   Fergusson, Francis and Charles Jasper Sisson, eds. *Shakespeare's
       Tragedies of Monarchy: "Hamlet," "Macbeth," and "King
       Lear."* New York: Dell, 1962. 412 pp.

       Introductions in this volume are by Francis Fergusson, and
C. J. Sisson is the textual editor. The copy for *King Lear* is basically
the folio, supplemented and corrected when necessary from the Q$_1$
1608. Both texts are probably derived from the promptbook, but
Q$_1$ seems to be contaminated by reporting; F printer's copy may
have been an abridged and partly corrected quarto, used as prompt-
copy. A list of doubtful and disputed readings is provided. *Lear* is
"beautifully composed, both as poetry and as a play for the stage"
(p. 266), but it is difficult to produce under modern theatrical conventions because of its imaginative vastness. Among other things,
Shakespeare in the play is suggesting to members of his audience
the horrors that threaten their own society. The division of the
kingdom leads to fragmentation within the individual, the family,
and the community. Basically the theme of the play is the attempt
by various characters with divergent perspectives to find the natural
order in the anarchic kingdom. A brief list of readings on *Lear* is
included, along with a note on the text and a glossary.

1615   Fukuda, Tsuneari, trans. *King Lear.* Tokyo: Shincho-sha Press,
       1962. (Japanese—not seen)

1616   Guthrie, Sir Tyrone, intro. *Ten Great Plays.* New York: Golden
       Press, 1962. 502 pp.

       King Lear (pp. 350-405) is one of the greatest utterances of
the human spirit, but it is not a particularly viable stage play. The
double structure, for example, overloads the plot. Moreover, a
character like Edgar is difficult to play because his role fluctuates

awkwardly between realism and symbolism. Nor are these flaws entirely theatrical. It is the "untidiest, the most at odds with itself, of Shakespeare's tragedies; the sprawling fecundity of that genius, its fiery humanity, are at odds with a theme which demanded a more formal, austere and removed approach" (p. 351).

1617   Harbage, Alfred, ed. *"King Lear." Drama. The Major Genres.* Edited by Robert Hogan and Sven Eric Molin. New York: Dodd Mead, 1962, pp. 65-161.

The text is that of the Pelican edition (see item 1594). Also included are a critical analysis, discussion questions, and excerpts from Nahum Tate's *King Lear.*

1618   Harrison, George Bagshawe and Robert F. McDonnell, eds. *"King Lear": Text, Sources, Criticism.* New York: Harcourt, Brace and World, 1962. 186 pp.

This volume contains the full text of Shakespeare's *King Lear,* selections from five source materials (John Higgins' *The Mirror for Magistrates,* Raphael Holinshed's *The Chronicles of England, Scotland, and Irelande,* Edmund Spenser's *The Faerie Queene,* Philip Sidney's *Arcadia,* and *The True Chronicle History of King Leir*), major portions of Nahum Tate's *The History of King Lear,* and a selection of eighteen critical views ranging from 1765 to 1960. A section on questions and problems is also included, as is a brief selective bibliography.   Critics included are Samuel Johnson (see item 168), Charles Lamb (see item 4a), William Hazlitt (see item 2), S. T. Coleridge (see item 4), Edward Dowden (see item 8), A. C. Bradley (see item 9), Leo Tolstoy (see item 10), Harley Granville-Barker (see item 72), G. Wilson Knight (see item 19), E. E. Stoll, Theodore Spencer (see item 44), George R. Kernodle (see item 64), Robert B. Heilman (see item 106), Edith Sitwell (see item 135), W. H. Clemen (see item 139), D. G. James (see item 146), G. B. Harrison (see item 1528), and J. Stampfer (see item 327). The text, drawn from Harrison's edition of *The Complete Works* (see item 1528), is eclectic; it is based on F_1 with various passages drawn from Q_1 1608.

1619   Laksmikantmohan, trans. *Lear-raju.* Hyderabad: Sri Saravati Book Co., 1962. (Indian—not seen)

1620   Main, William M., ed. *The Tragedy of King Lear.* New York:
       Odyssey, 1962. 239 pp.

       The Globe text of *King Lear* is accompanied by extensive
textual commentary. This commentary is spaced at approximately
twenty-line intervals throughout. In addition each act is summarized
at the end, and there is a general conclusion. The latter describes
Lear as an appassionata play provoking both visceral and philosophic
responses. The theme is the recreation or spiritual rebirth of Lear
through Cordelia's aid. The king passes through "the triple symbolic
lands of hell (rebellion), purgatory (reform), and paradise (obedience)" (p. 221). He moves through his suffering far beyond Stoicism in realizing that Pan, the god of nature, is dead and a power beyond nature ("Cordelia's law") is born; in a sense the play drama-
tizes the fertility ritual of death and rebirth. Above all, the play is
about love, which both fulfills and negates all other achievements.
Appendices provide a description of the texts (in this instance the
folio text is considered superior) and an outline of dominant image
patterns in the tragedy (nature, animal, gods, eye and sight, disease
and medicine, clothes). Bibliographical suggestions are also included.

1621   Bonazza, Blaze Odell and Emil Roy, eds. *"King Lear." Studies
       in Drama.* New York: Harper, 1963, pp. 49-125.

       The introductory comment describes *King Lear* as the highest
level of English tragedy, a level for which the language of literal
reality is too flimsy to bear the limits of grief and joy experienced
by the characters. The language one understands is that of overwhelming emotion. Textual commentary and discussion questions
are provided.

1622   Ch'ien, Ho, trans. *Li erh Wang.* Kaohsiung: Ta Chung Book
       Co., 1963. (Chinese—not seen)

1623   Davidowitz, Harry Solomon, trans. *ha-Malech Lir.* Jerusalem:
       Kiryat Sepher, 1963. 140 pp.

       Davidowitz provides extensive notes for this Hebrew transla-
tion.

1624   Evans, Bertrand, ed. *The Tempest. King Lear.* Literary Heritage.
       New York: Macmillan Co., 1963. 314 pp.

This edition features, in addition to a critical introduction which addresses the theme, date, and sources of the play, extensive study questions on each scene. Also included are comments on the play as a whole, suggestions for composition, and a discussion of Shakespeare and his age (his life, his language, the Elizabethan theater). The critical comment observes that this tale, ultimately from folklore, involves daughters, all of whom share characteristics of the father—two selfish and one prideful. The major focus is on the transformation of a king characterized by selfish egocentricity to a man who reflects genuine concern and compassion for his fellow humans, a theme reinforced through the subplot of Gloucester's experience. The implication is that good does not die in vain, that suffering is indeed a way to salvation.

1624a Fraser, Russell, ed. *The Tragedy of King Lear*. The Signet Classic Shakespeare. New York: New American Library, 1963. 287 pp. Reprint. *The Complete Signet Classic Shakespeare*. General editor Sylvan Barnet. New York: Harcourt Brace Jovanovich, 1972. 1776 pp.

The text is based on F_1, generally considered to stand in close relation to the play as performed, except in spots of misprinting, of omission of pertinent material supplied by Q_1, of inferiority when compared with Q_1, or of emendations canonized by use and custom. A note on the source dates the play 1603-1606 and cites Harsnett, Gresham, *Leir,* Monmouth, Holinshed, Spenser, Higgins, Marston, *The London Prodigal,* Montaigne, and Sidney as sources of greater or lesser moment. The critical introduction describes the tragedy as a structural anomaly; externally it is one long denouement, but internally the rising action is the hero's regeneration. On the heath Lear reaches his nadir; more importantly, though, he also becomes pregnant to pity. An anti-romantic play, *Lear* forces its major figures to confront the full measure of life's horrors and mocks them in their attempts to find rationalization for suffering through any particular philosophic perspective. At the same time, however, it suggests that suffering may at once be purgative and regenerative as well as destructive.

1625 Gheorgiu, Mihnea, trans. *Regale Lear.* Bucharest: Ed. Tineretului, 1963. (Rumanian—not seen)

1626   Gorakhpur, Majnun, trans. *King Lear.* New Delhi: Indian
       Academy, 1963. (Hindustani—not seen)

1627   Ichikawa, Sanki and Takuji Mine, eds. *King Lear.* Tokyo:
       Kenkyusha, 1963.

       The introduction to this Japanese translation covers such
       matters as the political and philosophic tension of the Elizabethan
       age and of the way in which *Lear* both relates to these contem-
       porary concerns and also artistically transcends them. Extensive
       explanatory notes are also provided.

1628   *King Lear.* London: Ganymede Original Editions, 1963. 109 pp.

       Lithographs are by Oscar Kokoschka. The text is based on
       that of the New Shakespeare published by the Cambridge press
       (see item 1599). The press run was limited to 279 copies.

1629   Prōtaios, Georgia and Stathēs Prōtaios, trans. *Hos Vasilias Lēr.*
       Athens: Daremas, 1963. (Greek—not seen)

1630   Wright, Louis B. and Virginia A. Lamar, eds. *"King Lear."*
       The Play's The Thing: Seventeen of Shakespeare's Greatest
       Dramas. New York: Harper and Row, 1963, pp. 517-566.

       The text in this volume is a reprint of that prepared for the
       Washington Square Press edition (see item 1581).   The specific
       introduction to *King Lear* provides both a description of the sources,
       history, and text and a brief critical comment.   Copy text for
       this edition is eclectic.   The basic text is F_1, but Q_1 readings are
       allowed in passages needing correction.   The extremely lengthy
       title on the title page of Q_1 1608 was probably an attempt to dis-
       tinguish Shakespeare's play from the anonymous chronicle play
       King Leir, which had been printed in 1605 and which served as a
       source for the greater tragedy. *Lear* is cosmic in scope; its protag-
       onist "represents the eternal tragedy of an age that has not acquired
       wisdom, and the play in essence is a study of Lear's reeducation and
       purification" (p. 518). The philosophic implications are pagan and
       pessimistic, more likely reflecting the fatalistic and Stoical attitudes
       that characterized much of Jacobean literature rather than some
       personal trauma in the author's life. Appendices provide a summary

of biographical facts about Shakespeare, a discussion of his theater
and dramatic tradition, a selection of early comments on his work,
and a brief bibliography.

1631   Bor, Matej, trans. *Kralj Lear.* Ljubljana: n.p., 1964.

The introduction and notes for this Slovenian translation are
provided by Bratko Kreft. Problems of text, of dating, and of
sources are covered briefly, but the primary emphasis is upon the
difficulties of effectively capturing the emotional power of *Lear* in
translation and on the purgatorial nature of suffering in the principal characters.

1632   Campbell, Oscar James, Alfred Rothschild, and Stuart Vaughan,
        eds. *King Lear.* New York: Bantam Books, 1964. 256 pp.

This volume provides an introduction to *King Lear* and an
essay on Shakespeare's life and times by O. J. Campbell, a discussion
of Shakespeare's theater by Stuart Vaughan, and critical excerpts
from Charles Lamb (see item 4a), William Hazlitt (see item 2), Leo
Tolstoy (see item 10), Algernon Charles Swinburne, A. C. Bradley
(see item 9), Harley Granville-Barker (see item 72), O. J. Campbell
(see item 101), and Lily Bess Campbell (see item 18). The text is
based on the Globe (Cambridge) edition by W. A. Wright and W. G.
Clark. A marginal glossary, explanatory notes, and a selected bibliography are also included. Campbell describes the tragedy as an
exalted morality set against a backdrop of eternity. Lear, purged of
his vices by suffering, "attains not stoic contentment won through
recognition of the ultimate cruelty of things and achieved by with-
drawal into the quiet sanctuary of the soul, but rather he reaches the
Christian equivalent of that ancient virtue, namely love" (p. 3). His
and Cordelia's deaths, a necessary part of the tragic thrust, emphasize the nature of their triumph; it is "the souls of the two that
matter, and in their eternal union their souls are triumphant" (p. 7).
If at the conclusion the world of Lear and Gloucester lies in ruin,
destroyed by both man's passion and by Nature's awesome forces,
it nonetheless has been purged by a kind of purgatorial fire.

1633   Chwalewik, Witold, trans. *Król Lear.* Warsaw: Panstwowy
        Instytut Wydawnicy, 1964. 214 pp.

Chwalewik provides extensive notes and a glossary for this Polish translation.

1634   Collinder, Björn, trans. *De Stora dramerna.* Stockholm: Natur och Kultur, 1964.

Parallel Swedish and English texts are provided on facing pages.

1635   *The Complete Works of William Shakespeare.* Abbey Library. London: Murrays Sales and Service, 1964. 1099 pp.

The foreword for this edition is by Dame Sybil Thorndike, and the text for the dust jacket is provided by Levi Fox.

1636   Hernandez, Luisa Josefina, trans. *"El Rey Lear." La Palabra y el Hombre* (Veracruz), No. 32 (1964), 671-766.

A prefatory essay for this Spanish edition addresses the general characteristics of Elizabethan tragedy and the universality of Shakespeare's tragedy dealing with social injustice and the conflict of two generations.

1637   Hinman, Charlton and W. W. Greg, eds. *King Lear 1608 (Pide Bull Quarto).* Shakespeare Quarto Facsimiles. Revised Edition. Oxford: Oxford University Press, Clarendon Press, 1964. 89 pp.

The entry for *Lear* in the Stationers' Register is dated 26 November 1607. Q_1 subsequently appeared in 1608, called the "Pide Bull" quarto to distinguish it from Q_2, also dated 1608 though actually not printed until 1619. Of Q_1 twelve copies exist, differing in about 150 readings. This facsimile edition is made from the Gorhambury copy (on deposit at the Bodleian) by permission of its owner, the Earl of Verulam. This quarto has more sheets in the corrected state than any other copy. The note to the second impression by Charlton Hinman describes Q_1 as a difficult text but one perhaps preserving a version much closer to Shakespeare'a autograph than was formerly supposed. This statement assumes that the text of Q_1 is based, not on a reported version, but on a transcript of the foul papers that had been rendered virtually illegible in spots from frequent revision. See item 1505.

1638   Entry Deleted.

1639   *King Lear*. London: University Microfilms, 1964.

This text was produced from the original in the British Library by microfilm-xerox in commemoration of the Shakespeare quatercentenary.

1640   McCann, Eric A., ed. *King Lear*. The Falcon Shakespeare. Toronto: Longmans Canada, 1964. 250 pp.

The extensive apparatus of this edition include sections on the date of composition and performance, the sources, the text, the stage history, the early editors (with separate notes on the major contributions of Rowe, Pope, Theobald, Hanmer, Warburton, Johnson, Capell, Steevens, Malone), a reference table including in chronologically arranged parallel columns important events in Shakespeare's life and other significant historical and literary events, the imagery of the play, the relationship of evil to blindness, notes on the characters, dramatic devices in the play, and a synopsis of the critics' comments on (1) the opening movements, (2) the destruction of order, (3) Act III, (4) and the closing movement of the plot. Following the text itself are brief discussions and study questions for each scene and a section of questions on the entire play. The text of this edition is that prepared by the Folger Library (see item 1581); while it is primarily based on F_1, it is a conflation of the Q and F printing. The text is printed on the recto pages, with textual notes provided on the verso pages. The essence of the tragedy is described as the violation of the fundamental bonds of family. Man is brought near indeed to the level of bestiality in the use of his intelligence merely as craft to add a finer edge to his cruelty.

1640a   Muir, Kenneth, ed. *King Lear*. The Arden Shakespeare Paperbooks. New York: Vintage Books, 1964. See item 1553.

1641   "Selección de escenas de obras de Shakespeare." *Cuadernos de Bellas Artes,* April, 1964, pp. 57-107.

Included are selections in Spanish from *King Lear* and six other Shakespearean plays.

1642   Vandiver, Edward P. *"The Tragedy of King Lear." Highlights of Shakespeare's Plays.* Great Neck, N. Y.: Barron's Educational Series, 1964, pp. 262-284.

Featuring excerpts from twenty-three plays, this volume provides selections from the text interspersed with explanation, summary, and comment. Approximately eighteen percent of the text of *Lear* is represented.

1643   Vörösmarty, Mihály, trans. *Lear Király.* Bucharest: Ifjusagi Konyvkiado, 1964. (Hungarian—not seen)

1644   Youle-White, Michael J., ed. *Shakespeare's "King Lear": Total Study Edition.* Toronto: Coles Publishing Co., 1964. 86 pp.

The text of *King Lear*, based essentially on F_1 1623 but with additions from Q_1 1608, is arranged as the middle column in a large three-column page. The right-hand column provides textual notes while the left-hand column includes plot summary, analysis, and occasional comments from other critics. Additionally, an introduction covers Shakespeare's life, his plays, and the Elizabethan theater. This introduction stresses the importance of John Lyly and Christopher Marlowe as forerunners of Shakespeare and of his own stylistic development. A specific introduction to *King Lear* covers critical disagreement concerning the actability of the play and the general meaning, whether positive or negative. The play is described as a powerful tragic exploration of the fact that love, demanded, results in suffering. The opposed factions in the drama repeat conflicting attitudes toward what man is and what man's obligations to his fellow man and to society are. Edmund is especially reflective of contemporary Machiavellian thought.

1645   Bonnefoy, Yves, trans. *Le roi Lear.* Paris: Mercure de France, 1965. 201 pp. (French—not seen)

1646   Curtis, Jean-Louis, trans. *Le roi Lear.* Collection Le Manteau d'Arleguin. Paris: Gallimard, 1965. 285 pp. (French—not seen)

1647   Harrison, George Bagshawe, ed. *The Tragedy of King Lear.* New York: Shakespeare Recording Society, 1965.

This complete text of the performance was issued with the record.

1648   Entry Deleted.

1649   Pasternak, Boris, trans. *Korol Lir.* Moscow: Iskusstvo, 1965. 186 pp.

A postscript by B. Bingerman describes the quality of Pasternak's Russian translation in its principal attempt to reflect the emotional power of Shakespeare's tragedy.

1650   Rotas, Vasilis, trans. *King Lear.* Revised Edition. Athens: Ikaros, 1965. (Greek—not seen)

1651   Tieck, Ludwig, trans. *König Lear.* Bucharest: Jugendverlag, 1965.

Mihnea Gheorghiu, in a preface to this German translation, discusses problems of text, date, and source. Included also is a brief summary of contrasting critical evaluations of the play.

1652   Vörösmarty, Mihály, trans. *Lear Király.* Popular Library Series. Budapest: Szepirodalmi Publishing House, 1965.

The text of *King Lear* is translated into Hungarian with a commentary by Jeno Illes and illustrations by Miklos Borsos. The afterword describes social injustice as the principal flaw in Shakespeare's tragic world. Lear, isolated from the common people for many years, must come to share their agony and their perceptions. A textual commentary is also provided.

1653   Benson, Carl and Taylor Littleton, eds. *"King Lear." The Idea of Tragedy.* Glenview, Ill.: Scott, Foresman, 1966, pp. 104-176.

The text of the Hardin Craig edition (see item 1546) is included along with an excerpt from John Holloway's *The Story of Night* (see item 345) and study questions. Other tragedies represented are Sophocles' *Oedipus,* Ibsen's *Rosmersholm,* Aeschylus' *Agamemnon,* Webster's *The Duchess of Malfi,* and Chekhov's *Uncle Vanya.* A section of critical essays offers comments from Aristotle, S. H. Butcher, Gilbert Murray, Maud Bodkin (see item 21), Francis M. Cornford, Prosser Hall Frye, F. L. Lucas, Maxwell Anderson, Una Ellis-Fermor, Henry A. Meyers, D. D. Raphael, A. C. Bradley (see item 9), Peter Alexander (see item 1545), John Gassner, Joseph Wood Krutch, and Arthur Miller.

1654   Havel, R., M. Herman, and M. Otruba, eds. *Shakespearuv Král Lear v prekladech z doby narodniho obrozeni.* Literarni archiv, Sbornik Pamatniku naradniho pisemnictvi. Prague: Orbis, 1966.

This volume, entitled *King Lear in the Translations from the Period of the Czech National Revival,* features a shortened translation into Czech prose (Prokop Sedivy, 1792), one scene (Josef Linda, 1823), a translation into blank verse (J. K. Tyl, 1835), and Act I (Ladislav Celakovsky, 1856).

1655   Hernandez, Luisa Josefina, trans. and intro. *El rey Lear.* Xalapa, Mexico: Univ. Veracruzana, 1966. 208 pp. (Mexican—not seen)

1656   Joseph, Bertram Leon, ed. *King Lear.* London: University of London Press, 1966. 224 pp.

For this eclectic edition the basic text is F_1, but Q_1 readings are allowed for those lines unique to the quarto and wherever its variants seem preferable to the folio. The critical commentary includes discussion of the sources, Shakespeare's stage and acting, verse and imagery, acting and plot, dramatic irony in the play, the four major stages of the action, the quality of Lear's personality, and the treatment in the tragedy of religion, nature, justice, and free will. Explanatory notes are also included. *Lear* is the tragedy of a man who twice loses his daughter, first when he denounces her in rage for her refusal to articulate the quality of her love and second when he persuades her to go quietly to prison without confronting her sisters. "The really harrowing pity and fear evoked in and by this tragedy are the results of imagining fully what Lear has done to himself; especially tragic is the irony of his persuading Cordelia to let herself be led to prison" (pp. 43-44). To read his final actions as selfish and possessive, however, is to ignore the thrust of what he has learned through his purgatorial experiences and the genuine humility in his present relationship with Cordelia. Ultimately the play, filled with ambiguities, refuses to yield clear answers. "Each individual among us of his readers and his audiences can strike his own balance and decide whether the world of *King Lear* fills us with optimism or pessimism; but we must not forget that we are imagining a world governed by Providence and working through its servants, Fortune, and human beings" (p. 57).

1657   Kalocsay, K., trans. *La Tragedio de Reĝo Lear.* Rotterdam. Universale Esperanto Associo, 1966. 160 pp. (Dutch—not seen)

1658   Entry Deleted.

1659   Pitt, David G., intro. *The Tragedy of King Lear.* New York: Airmont Publishing Company, 1966. 170 pp.

This volume features a general introduction to Shakespeare's life and times, a critical introduction to the play, a brief list of readings, and a series of study questions for each act. The tragedy, following its own logic, demands immediate acceptance as popular entertainment, not long preparatory hours in the study; it is set in a world in which the truths of religion are torn between contesting sects. The importance of the work lies not in its sources but in Shakespeare's composing imagination. The year 1605, with a recent visitation of the plague, financial scandals, and sensational murders, was a time for reflections upon catastrophe. Once Lear abdicates his throne, he is reduced to madness, to childishness, and eventually to total despair. His madness reflects an entire world in convulsion, and it is underscored by the juxtaposition of Tom's pretended insanity and the Fool's professional foolishness. The king's final traumatic moments balance the spectators on a slender edge, and they are subject to an interpretation either of a positive hint of release for the protagonist or of the bitterest blows of fate upon a penitential man whose suffering has already expiated his pride.

1660   Schmiele, Walter, ed. *König Lear.* Frankfurt: Ullstein, 1966. 175 pp.

An introduction describes the methods by which Shakespeare develops a tragedy of elemental proportions from a variety of sources. Extensive notes are also provided. The German translation is that of Baudissin.

1661   Brockett, Oscar Gross and Lenyth Brockett, eds. *Plays for the Theatre: An Anthology of World Drama.* San Francisco: Holt, Rinehart and Winston, Rinehart Press, 1967. 503 pp.

King Lear, along with nine other plays, is included in this volume, which provides a chronological introduction to the drama. Each play is typical of a particular period, genre, or country. Close to medieval drama in its sprawling structure and its intermingling of the comic and the tragic, *King Lear* also reflects classical characteristics in tone and structure. "Lear, like Oedipus, is a compelling tragic figure whose titanic struggle first to control, then to comprehend, his destiny has engaged audiences for centuries" (p. 3). Further analysis is included in Oscar Brockett's *The Theatre: An Introduction* (see item 426).

1662   Clark, W. George and William Aldis Wright, eds. *The Tragedies of William Shakespeare.* Garden City, N. Y.: International Collectors Library, 1967. 378 pp.

The text of *King Lear* is from the Cambridge edition (see item 1477), and the introduction is by Edward Dowden.

1663   Clavel, Maurice, trans. *Le roi Lear.* Paris: Théâtre nationale populaire, 1967. (French—not seen)

1664   Ferguson, Frank A., ed. *King Lear.* Toronto: Clarke Irwin, 1967. (not seen)

1665   Hagberg, Carl August, trans. *Kung Lear.* Stockholm: Wahlstrom and Widstrand, 1967.

The commentary for this Swedish translation is provided by Erik Frykman, who discusses both the political and the domestic dimensions of Shakespeare's theme and the manner in which the double plot both reiterates and counterpoints Lear's experience.

1666   *El rey Lear.*   Madrid: Ed. nacional, 1967.   (Spanish—not seen)

1667   Ribner, Irving and George Lyman Kittredge, eds.   *The Tragedy of King Lear.*   The Kittredge Shakespeares.   Revised Edition.   Waltham, Mass.:   Blaisdell Publishing Co., 1967.   147 pp.

This is the single-volume publication of Ribner's revision of the Kittredge edition, also published as the collected works. See items 1499, 1507, 1689.

1668   Skillan, George, ed.   *King Lear.*   London: French, 1967.   216 pp.

This "acting" edition of the play provides a comprehensive analysis of the action, words, characters, and scene construction. *Lear* never permits the actors to rest from the strain of the highest pitch; the characters "suffer in travail through strife and in the pain of accomplishment" (p. v). The set design should employ a monolithic style, and the stage itself should be divided into three areas. Prefatory sections on a scene-by-scene property plot and lighting plot and on Shakespeare's language are included, and the text itself is accompanied by marginal notes, extremely full interlinear stage and line directions, and illustrations of the staging.

1669   *The Tragedy of King Lear.*   Magnatype Edition.   Pittsburgh: Stanwik House, 1967.   307 pp.

This magnatype edition is prepared for readers having restricted vision.   A general introduction to Shakespeare's life and work is followed by an analysis of *Lear* (the story of the play and an act-by-act synopsis) and a glossary.   The theme is described as the portrayal of filial ingratitude in parallel plots.

1670   Goldman, Mark and Isadore Traschen, eds.   *"King Lear." The Drama. Traditional and Modern.*   Boston: Allyn and Bacon, 1968, pp. 59-166.

The text of *King Lear* is accompanied by G. B. Harrison's notes from *Shakespeare: The Complete Works* (see item 1528). A brief biographical note and a reading list precede the play. The general introduction (for both *Oedipus* and *Lear*) describes the traditional tragic pattern in three phases—the breakdown of established values, the descent into the abyss, and the transcendence and transformation.

1671   Hinman, Charlton, ed. *The First Folio of Shakespeare.* New York: Norton, 1968. 928 pp.

This facsimile text reproduces the correct sheets of the first folio publication of *King Lear,* as determined by a collation of the copies of the folio in the Folger Shakespeare Library. Included are an introduction (the value and authority of the first folio, the printing and proofing, the facsimile) and two appendices (on the variant states of the folio text, on the Folger copies used).

1672   Hoeniger, F. D., ed. *"King Lear." Shakespeare Series: I.* General editor, Northrop Frye. New York: St. Martin's, 1968, pp. 3-162.

This volume includes the text of *King Lear,* along with that of *Twelfth Night* and *Antony and Cleopatra.* The play is accompanied by an introduction, a note on the text, a bibliography, a list of textual variants or editorial emendations, glossary notes, and a section of longer notes. No bibliographical critic has fully explained the relationships between Q_1 1608 and F_1 1623, and like most editions the present one is eclectic. The dominant text is F_1, but numerous Q readings are admitted; indeed, of late arguments for the superiority of Q have been increasing. The introduction discusses the sources, the philosophic backdrop, and the stage history. Structurally the boldest stroke is the double plot through which the *Lear* story is rendered tragic. Not only does Gloucester's experience reinforce that of Lear's; it also as a more realistic narrative provides a link for the audience with their own experience. The curious interplay of realistic and fantastic also creates a powerful atmosphere for the action. Shakespeare adds as well the Fool, the storm scene, and Lear's madness, devices which reflect the King's painful journey to true wisdom. *Lear* may in some respects anticipate the "Theater of the Absurd," but there is a fundamental difference; in absurdist drama the playwright's vision of his stage world is nihilistic; in *Lear* the negative perspective is occasioned by the King's characterization and the world his actions have created.

1673   Jabra, Jabra I., trans. *Ma'sāt al-Malik Lir.* Beirut: Dar al-Nahar, 1968. (Arabic—not seen)

1674   Kim, Jae-Nam, ed. *King Lear.* Panmun Shakespeare. Seoul: Panmun Book Company for the Shakespeare Society of Korea, 1968. (Korean—not seen)

1675   Luarasi, Skënder, trans. *Mbreti Lir.* Tirana: Naim Frasheri, 1960. Reprint. Prishtinë: Rilindja, 1968. (Albanian—not seen)

1676   Entry Deleted.

1677   Ozu, Jiro, trans. *King Lear.* Tokyo: Chikuma Press, 1968. (Japanese—not seen)

1678   Gardner, Stanley, ed. *King Lear.* The New Warwick Shakespeare. London: Blackie, 1969. 100 pp.

Following a brief introduction, the text and the explanatory notes are set on facing pages. The introduction describes Nahum Tate's version in 1681 and analyzes the great diversity of critical opinion toward Shakespeare's tragedy. One of the major motifs involves the imagery of clothing; "Lear begins the play as a monarch who cherishes such trappings of royalty as flattery, affectionate words and manifestations of power, and ends as a 'mere' king" (p. v). Another dominant image is the storm, which physically suggests elemental forces at work and symbolically reflects the acrimony and indifference within Lear that must be purged. While ultimately the tragedy forces us to question the constitution of man and of nature itself, Edmund's belated redemptive cry and the spiritual maturation achieved by Lear and Gloucester render impossible a totally negative response; "the tragedy, in the end, is that such charity and compassion, fostered in reason, should have been overthrown" (p. vii).

1679   Östergaard, V. trans. *Kong Lear.* Copenhagen: J. H. Schultz, 1969. (Danish—not seen)

1680   Straat, Evert, trans. *Koning Lear.* Utrecht: Ambo, 1969.
        (Dutch—not seen)

1681   Mūsā, Fātima, trans. *Al-Malik Līr.* Cairo: al-Hay'a al-Misriyya
        al-Amona li'l-Ta'līf wa'l-Nashr, 1970.

        The introduction for this Arabic translation discusses the diffi-
        culties of translation as well as covering briefly such matters as the
        dramatic traditions in Elizabethan England, of Shakespeare's gen-
        eral artistic development, and of the major differences of critical in-
        terpretation concerning *King Lear.*

1682   Papazayan, Vagram, trans. *Korol Lir.* Erevan: Aiastan, 1970.
        (Armenian—not seen)

1683   Quinn, Edward G., ed. *William Shakespeare: King Lear.* The
        Crowell Critical Library. New York: Crowell, 1970. 235 pp.

        This edition includes a brief critical introduction and descrip-
        tions of the text, sources and date, and stage history. Following the
        full text are selections from Nahum Tate's *King Lear*; selections
        from the sources—*The True Chronicle History of King Leir,* Raphael
        Holinshed's *Chronicles,* and Philip Sidney's *Arcadia*; and selections
        from nine critics ranging from 1765 to 1966—Samuel Johnson (see
        item 168), Charles Lamb (see item 4a), William Hazlitt (see item 2),
        A. C. Bradley (see item 9), G. Wilson Knight (see item 19), Marshall
        McLuhan (see item 376), Jan Kott (see item 348), Maynard Mack
        (see item 530), and Harold Skulsky (see item 600). A brief selective
        bibliography (textual studies, sources, stage history, critical studies)
        concludes the work.   Quinn's introduction summarizes the major
        critical approaches, from that which argues for Lear a moral illumi-
        nation to that which denies a meaningful universe altogether, and
        the editor describes the comic and tragic patterns in the play. Critics
        are agreed that the date of the play can be fixed between the publi-
        cation of *Leir* in May, 1605, and the first performance at the court
        of James I on 26 December 1606. The text of this edition is eclec-
        tic; based principally on F_1, it adopts various readings from Q_1
        1608.

1684   Slok, Johannes, trans. *Kong Lear.* Copenhagen: Berlingake For-
        lag, 1970. (Danish—not seen)

1685   Smith, Jonathan, ed. *King Lear*. New York: Gina, 1970. 95 pp.

This folio-sized Shakespeare Workshop edition of *King Lear* is based upon the folio text except where it is obviously in error. An accompanying booklet lists the most significant variants between F and Q. Spelling and punctuation have been normalized. No introduction or other type of critical apparatus is included.

1686   Elton, W. R., ed. *King Lear*. The Blackfriars Shakespeare. Dubuque, Iowa: William C. Brown, 1971. 91 pp.

An introductory essay on Shakespeare's life and times by the general editor J. Leeds Barroll covers such matters as a biographical sketch, the playwright's London years, his relationship with the actors, his theater and audience, the Elizabethan language, and the printing of his plays. A reading list provides significant titles in each of three particular areas. Then follows an essay on *Lear* by Elton and a brief bibliography, divided into general and advanced. The text for the most part follows the folio; occasional readings from the quarto are allowed, however, where the sense seems to require it. A textual gloss appears at the bottom of each page. The name Lear suggested Learn to its original audiences, thus underscoring the principal theme of the dramatic quest. Members of King James' family are suggested by the names of the characters—Albany was one of his titles, and Cornwall was a title of his elder son. At a time when James in actuality was laboring to bring about the uniting of Scotland and England, the drama depicts the disastrous results of political division. Nahum Tate's version refuses, of course, to see the play as Shakespeare wrote it; so also do the twentieth-century Christian redemptionists like O. J. Campbell (see item 101) and Paul Seigel (see item 255). Lear, in fact—caught between Cordelia's piety, Edmund's atheism, and Gloucester's superstition—moves "from pagan belief to a challenging disbelief in his gods" (p. xiv).

1687   Gress, Lawrence M., ed. *King Lear*. Woodbridge, Conn.: Apollo, 1971. (not seen)

1688   Pasternak, Boris, trans. *King Lear*. School Library of Drama. Moscow: Iskusstvo, 1971.

The text of *King Lear* is translated into Russian. Included also are an essay, "Shakespeare's *Lear*," by B. Zingerman, the text of *Hamlet*, and two essays on *Hamlet*.

1689   Ribner, Irving and George Lyman Kittredge, eds. *The Complete Works of Shakespeare*. Revised Edition. Waltham, Mass.: Ginn, 1971. 1743 pp.

This revision of Kittredge's 1936 edition incorporates advances in the knowledge of Shakespeare's text, of dates, sources, and general historical background. Kittredge's text and many of his notes remain, though the general introduction and the separate introduction to each play have been written anew by Ribner. The introduction features discussion of Shakespeare and the English Renaissance, his life, life in Elizabethan England, the English drama before Shakespeare, Elizabethan theaters and companies, the publication of the plays, a general survey of criticism, a survey of plays in performance, and a bibliography. The copy text for this edition is eclectic; the folio text is used primarily, but readings are allowed from Q_1. The play is dated between 1603 and 1606; the corrupt nature of both Q_1 1608 and Q_2 1608 (actually 1619) is described. A summary of the sources is followed by information on Renaissance naturalism and on the polarized tendencies of critics to see the play as issuing into either despair or regeneration. The notes are extremely full. See items 1499, 1507, 1667.

1690   Rothe, Hans, trans. *König Lear*. Frankfurt: C. J. Bucher, 1971. 155 pp.

The text of *King Lear* is translated into German. Seventeen lithographs by Oskar Kokoschka are included.

1691   Steele, William J., ed. *Shakespeare's "King Lear."* Dublin: Fallon, 1971. (not seen)

1692   Fraser, Russell, ed. *An Essential Shakespeare: Nine Plays and the Sonnets*. New York: Macmillan Co., 1972. 534 pp.

The text of *King Lear* (pp. 379-440) is included, along with a general introduction to Shakespeare's works, a note on the text of

Lear, and an afterword. A suggested reading list on the play provides thirty-four titles. The play is dated late 1606 on the basis of (1) Shakespeare's using an account of solar eclipses by the almanac-writer Edward Gresham which appeared on 11 February and (2) a reference, in the Stationers' Register on 26 November 1607, to the play's having been performed at court on St. Stephen's night of the previous Christmas season (26 December 1606). The afterword discusses the play as Shakespeare's catholic view of reality. Poetic justice is a lie; whether virtue is rewarded in heaven, Shakespeare does not presume to say. The horror of *Lear,* then, not denied. But the play's vision is not despairing or pessimistic. The virtuous is present in human nature as well as the vicious; more important, man is able to grow in the knowledge of himself and in his realization and acceptance of the whimsicality of fortune. A general reading list (criticism, background and biography, reference works) concludes the book.

1693 Entry Deleted.

1694 Herwegh, Georg, trans. *König Lear: eine Tragödie.* Leipzig: Insel-Verlag, 1972.

   King Lear is translated into German. Notes are by Walther Martin, and the afterword is by Robert Weimann.

1695 Hunter, G. K., ed. *King Lear.* New Penguin Shakespeare. Harmondsworth, Middlesex: Penguin Books, 1972. 344 pp.

   This edition features a lengthy introduction; a bibliographical list divided into editions and editorial processes, sources, and criticism; a scene-by-scene commentary; and an account of the text including a list of all quarto passages preferred to the folio (the text is based on the folio), of places where neither the quarto nor the folio text is accepted, and a list of stage directions. The introduction finds the strength of the tragedy primarily in those features unique to Shakespeare's version. The madness of Lear, for example, counterpointed by that of Edgar and the Fool, forces Lear to question not merely the relationship between a man and his family but also the whole sequence of loyalties and duties; his madness brings to the surface truths he could never know in his sanity, and the vision of this madness—despite the late reconciliation with Cordelia —remains a fundamental part of the new value system. Similarly, the careful excision of Christian references permits Shakespeare to explore the problem of Providence in a profound way, leaving unanswered the questions of man's relationship to destiny. The double plot provides both a basis for expanding the action of the play and of diverting attention from the inexplicable speed of the Lear plot. The introduction also contains an analysis of Nahum Tate's adaptation of *Lear* and of the general treatment of Shakespeare's text in the productions of the nineteenth and twentieth centuries.

1696   *King Lear.* New Delhi: Rajpal, 1972. (Hindi—not seen)

1697   Pasternak, Boris, trans. *King Lear.* Minsk: Narodnaya asveta, 1972.

The text of *King Lear* is translated into Russian with an afterword by B. Mitskewich which is concerned primarily with the universal aspects of the tragedy.

1698   Sarkaria, Ranjit Singh, trans. *Liar Potsah.* Patiala: Punjabi University, 1972. (Punjabi—not seen)

1699   Atre, Prahled Keshav, trans. *Samrāta Sīha [King Lear].* n.p., 1973. (Marathi—not seen)

1700   Badawi, Mohammed Mustafa, ed. *Ali-Malik Lir.* Kuwait: Ministry of Information, 1973. Reprint. Kuwait: Wazārat al-I'lam, 1976.

For this Arabic translation of *King Lear* Badawi provides extensive notes in addition to the introduction. Specific attention is directed to the stage history of the play, and the various interpretations of the role of Lear throughout the past three centuries.

1701   Bevington, David and Hardin Craig, eds. *The Complete Works of Shakespeare.* Revised Edition. Glenview, Ill.: Scott, Foresman, 1973. 1447 pp.

The order of the plays—chronological within each genre—is that of the original Craig edition, first published in 1951 (see item

1546). Also, Craig's historical material on the text, dating, sources, and stage history, as well as his notes, are retained. Bevington has rewritten both the general introduction and the interpretative introduction to each play. Basically the text is that of the Globe Shakespeare. Appendices include material on the canon, dating, and early texts, on sources and stage history, a glossary, and a selective bibliography on the various areas of criticism. The copy text for *Lear* is eclectic, F_1 except for 300 or so lines for Q_1 1608. The critical introduction describes the two divergent thrusts in the Lear story—the unwanted parent and the unappreciated child. Paradoxically both Lear and Gloucester must become foolish in the eyes of the world in order to gain the insights of love central to the tragedy. Shakespeare pushes to the limits the concept of a malign or indifferent universe, but the value of love even in defeat and horror obviates the possibility of a nihilistic universe. The meliorating changes in Tate's version are described.

1702   Borgmeier, Raimund, Barbara Puschmann-Nalenz, Bernd Santesson, and Dieter Wessels, trans. *King Lear/König Lear.* Stuttgart: Reclam, 1973. 271 pp.

The English and the German texts are provided on facing pages. The forward is by Ulrich Suerbaum, and the afterword is by Raimund Borgmeier and Barbara Puschmann-Nalenz.

1703   Evans, Bertrand, ed. *The College Shakespeare: 15 Plays and the Sonnets.* New York: Macmillan Co., 1973. 744 pp.

A note in the prefatory material indicates that the text of *King Lear* is eclectic, based on both Q_1 1608 and F_1 1623, though there is no indication of a preferred text. Explanatory notes are included, as is a critical essay (the "Afterword") and a note on the composition of the play indicating the date and the sources. Both the modern theater, equipped with mechanical devices, and film technology provide effective means of producing scenes of the storm on the heath; even so, the folk-tale quality of unreality profits more from the imagination than from physical staging. That is, the mind's eye bodies forth these strikingly archetypal characters better than human actors. A role such as Tom o' Bedlam and a scene such as the assumed leap from Dover's Cliffs "are best acted, no doubt, on the mind's private stage" (p. 562). A general introductory essay covers Shakespeare's life, London and the theater, his contemporary playwrights, the canon and chronology, his use of sources, the texts, his language and verse, along with introductory essays on the comedies, histories, and tragedies and a general reading list.

1704   Halio, Jay L., ed. *King Lear.* The Fountainwell Drama Texts. Edinburgh: Oliver and Boyd, 1973. 192 pp.

Lear is the bridge between Shakespeare's earlier tragedies, in which the protagonists' flaws are at best dimly perceived and the later tragedies, in which the principals knowledgeably embrace their decisions. The double plot both parallels and counterpoints Lear's actions. Lear, for example, endures with titanic determination while Gloucester succumbs to despair; even so, the double plots help the play to expand spatially and temporally. Lear, facing the dark night of his soul, comes finally to know himself and nature. He has fully returned to reality in the conclusion, and his final words represent both amazement and hope. In the critical introduction, Halio provides a note on the text, explaining his choice of the quarto version as his copy text, with occasional folio readings. Following are textual notes, a scene-by-scene commentary, a selective bibliography, and a glossary.

1705   Horsman, E. A., ed. *The Tragedy of King Lear.* Indianapolis: Bobbs-Merrill, 1973. 239 pp.

The introduction to this edition is in three parts—an analysis of the Lear story from folk legend to the Elizabethan period, a summary of critical opinion on Shakespeare's play, and an account of the play as performed on the Elizabethan stage. A section on Shakespeare's text describes the edition of Q_1 1608 (an intermediate between a good and bad quarto) and Q_2 1619 (falsely dated 1608). The folio was apparently based on a copy of the author's manuscript corrected for use as a promptbook. For this edition the copy text, with a few exceptions, is the folio. Appendices include a Shakespeare chronology, excerpts from the principal sources, a note on Shakespeare's English, a discussion of the play's theatrical history, additional discussion of the transmission of Shakespeare's text, and a selective bibliography. Sources discussed and excerpted included

Geoffrey of Monmouth, Higgins, Spenser, Holinshed, *The True Chronicle History of King Leir,* Sidney, Montaigne, Harsnett, and the Book of Job. The diversity of critical views forcuses on the morality structure, the language (imagery), the metaphysical background, the theme of Christian redemption, and the theme of nihilism.

1706 *King Lear.* Guilford, Surrey: Circle P. Publications, 1973. 43 pp.

This edition of *King Lear,* limited to fifty copies, features nine original etchings by Christopher Kent.

1707 Strehler, Georgio. *"Il re Lear" di Shakespeare.* Verona: Bertani, 1973. 267 pp.

In addition to an introduction and explanatory notes by the editor, this edition includes an appendix by Agostino Lombardi, "Irreppresantabile O illeggibile?"

1708 Evans, G. Blakemore, textual ed. *The Riverside Shakespeare.* Critical Introduction by Frank Kermode. Boston: Houghton Mifflin, 1974. 1902 pp.

In addition to the complete text of Shakespeare's plays (including *The Two Noble Kinsmen* and the Shakespearean ascriptions to *Sir Thomas More*), this edition features a "General Introduction" by Harry Levin; "Shakespeare's Text," "Glossary of Bibliographical Terms," "Chronology and Sources," "Records, Documents and Allusions," and "Annals, 1552-1616" by G. Blakemore Evans; and "Shakespeare's Plays in Performance: From 1660 to the Present" by Charles M. Shattuck. Individual introductions to the comedies are offered by Ann (Righter) Barton, to the histories by Herschel Baker, to the tragedies by Frank Kermode, and to the romances by Hallett Smith. Evans provides a "Note on the Text" and a complete list of textual variants among quarto and folio publications at the conclusion of each play. The Lear text (pp. 1249-1305) is eclectic, based primarily upon F_1 but drawing 288 lines and over 100 individual readings from Q_1 and Q_2. Q_1 ("Pide Bull") is a memorial reconstruction bad quarto, probably the result of one person's dictating from Shakespeare's foul papers (presumably incomplete or damaged in spots, in which case his memory of a stage production supplied additional material) to another who copied the lines. The introduction covers in some detail the matter of dating the play (1604-05), the sources, and thematic criticism. A selective bibliography is also included.

1709   Gavruk, Yu, trans. *Korol' Lir: Tragedija.* Minsk: Mastackaja Lit., 1974.

King Lear is translated into Belorussian. The editor also provides a critical introduction and copious textual notes.

1710   Karandikar, Vinda, trans. *Raja Lear.* Bombay: Mouj Prakashan, 1974.

This Marathi translation of *King Lear* features a critical introduction and a running commentary on the text. Points of major interest in the introduction are Shakespeare's sources and the diversity of critical interpretation.

1711   Lott, Bernard, ed. *King Lear.* New Swan Shakespeare. London: Longman, 1974. 212 pp.

The extensive introduction includes discussions in Part I of the significance of *King Lear* today and to its original audiences, the nature of the tragedy, the structure, the sources, the language, and Shakespeare's theater, and in Part II of the characteristics and difficulties of Elizabethan English, the principal characters, the extant texts, a survey of critical opinions, and a selective bibliography. The text and explanatory notes are set on facing pages; the text is eclectic, including the passages unique to both Q_1 and F_1 and in matters of common lines providing the reading which to the editor seems superior. The introduction stresses the timelessness of the conflict— the results of succumbing to foolish emotions and of failure "to appreciate that the young have their own lives to lead, and are best not treated as if they could be moulded into images to please their parents" (p. x). The tragedy is brutal and devastating, with poetic justice operating at the level of the subplot, but the principals do experience a clarification and see life more clearly; they realize that love is not synonymous with flattery, that life is more than ritual and formal pronouncements, and that the guilty are not necessarily brought to justice within the span of our life on earth. The modern stage like the Elizabethan projects a psychological realism that is better able to accommodate the play than realistic or naturalistic productions. The play also lends itself well to film and television techniques, as recent productions by Peter Brook and Grigori Kozintsev attest. Twenty-three illustrations are included.

1712 Mickevica, B., ed. *Korol Lir.* Translated by Boris Pasternak. Minsk: Nar. Asveta, 1974. (Russian—not seen)

1713 Bevington, David and Hardin Craig, eds. *An Introduction to Shakespeare: Eight Plays and Selected Sonnets.* Revised Edition. Chicago: Scott, Foresman, 1975. 378 pp.

Craig's historical information on the text, dating, sources, and stage history is retained. Bevington has rewritten both the general introduction and the interpretative introduction to each play. See item 1552.

1714 Edwards, Phillip, ed. *King Lear.* The Macmillan Shakespeare. London: Macmillan and Co., 1975. 271 pp.

The text for this edition is eclectic; the basic copy text is the folio, but occasional readings are admitted from the quarto. Notes and commentary are arranged on pages facing the text. The critical introduction covers such topics as the greatness of the play, its actability, Lear's mistake, identities and disguises, the purgative nature of suffering, the conflicting philosophies, and the pattern of the action. *King Lear,* more precisely, is quite rightly envisioned as a play about the warfare of good and evil and of the meaning of existence, but it is also the story of familial discord. The double plot enables Shakespeare to broaden the range of the action and to heighten the universality of its appeal. Lear's act of abdication is irresponsible, and his division of the kingdom is an act of political folly. The wrathful explosion against Cordelia is equally indefensible. As a consequence of his rash actions the old king provokes a monumental dislocation of the self, a condition corrected only by his agonizing struggle from arrogance through purgatorial lunacy to humility. The use of multiple disguises in the play—Kent as Caius, Edgar as Mad Tom, a peasant, and a nameless knight—emphasizes the fluidity of man's identity and the artificial quality of social station and clothing. The tension of the play, focusing on two generations, builds upon the conflicting standards of an old world dying and a new one being born. The conclusion of the tragedy presents the feudal values of the old world as a lost cause, while at the same time reaffirming the unchanging nature of the dynamics of human relationships.

1715 *King Lear.* Little Blue Book, No. 255. Girard, Kansas: Haldeman-Julius Co., 1975. 126 pp. (not seen)

1716 Mačabeli, Ivan and Il. Čavčadze, trans. *Korol Lir.* Moscow: Sabčota Sakartvelo, 1975. 236 pp. (Russian—not seen)

1717 Rossi, Matti, trans. *Kuningas Lear.* Helsinki: Tammi, 1975.

The text of *King Lear* is translated into Finnish. An Introduction by Kalle Holmberg covers such matters as the difficulties of translation, the conflicting philosophies in the play, and the lesson of humility and human compassion which Lear is forced to learn.

1718 Tauss, Beatrice, ed. *King Lear.* Shakespeare Parallel Text Series. New York: Simon and Schuster, 1975. 265 pp.

This edition provides on facing pages the text of *King Lear* and a line-by-line contemporary prose paraphrase. A general introduction to Shakespeare's work and Elizabethan stage conventions by the senior editor Maurice Charney is followed by an introduction to *Lear* by Beatrice Tauss that focuses on the quarto and folio texts and the sources of the Lear legend. The tone and texture of the play are Shakespeare's greatest contributions; with its double plot it is concerned with nothing less than the nature of justice, power, the natural order of things, and the meaning of life itself.

1719 *The Works of William Shakespeare.* The Peebles Classic Library. New York: Peebles Press International, 1975.

The text of *King Lear* is included in Volume 10.

1720 Bellay, Jacques, Daniel Benoin, Alain Duclos, and Christian Eychène. *"Le roi Lear" de William Shakespeare. Texte, Analyses, Mise en Scène, Etudes.* Comédie de Saint Etienne:

Centre Dramatique National et Centre d'Etudes et de Re-
cherches Theatrales, University de Lyon II, 1976.

This volume includes four analytic articles, an adaptation and
translation of *King Lear* into French by Daniel Benion, and excerpts
(*Documents*) from Freud (see item 1239), Machiavelli, Peter Quen-
nell (see item 411), L. Febvre, R. Lenoble, and Marshall McLuhan
(see item 376). The articles are "Sur le rôle . . . ", by Bellay,
"Essai d'interpretation . . . " by Eychène, "Quelques éléments pour
une interprétation historique du Roi Lear" by Bellay, and an analysis of the staging of I, i-iii, and I, vi, by Alain Duclos.

1721 Brown, John Russell. *Shakespeare in Performance: An Introduction Through Six Major Plays.* New York: Harcourt Brace
Jovanovich, 1976. 608 pp.

Publication of *King Lear* in 1608 gives evidence of some popularity, but the play could never have been a runaway success. It is
lengthy, complex, and iconoclastic. Breaking the conventional patterns both of revenge tragedy and of rise and fall (de casibus) tragedy, Shakespeare presents a man who begins at the height of his
power and steadily degenerates. The dynamic action is internal as
a character moves from blindness and pride to self-knowledge, compassion, and love; "it is a triumph of the human spirit when all
tangible good is lost" (p. 413). The theme gains emphasis by various
parallel situations among the surrounding characters. A major addition is the Fool, whose function changes from loyal follower to sar-
castic prompter as the play progresses. Comments are included on
major postwar productions—those of Olivier, Gielgud, Laughton,
Carnovsky, Budd, Kozintsev, Brook. It is a theatrical Everest ever
presenting a challenge to actor and director. The text is based primarily on the folio with occasional readings from the quarto. Full
explanatory notes are included along with numerous photographs,
textual notes, and picture credits.

1722 Epperson, James A., ed. *The "King Lear" Experience.* Boston:
Beacon Press, 1976. 162 pp.

An experimental edition, this text attempts to bridge the gap
between the printed word and the shared immediacy of the stage
and to recreate the visual and psychological effects one experiences

in the theater. The language is presented in prose, without footnotes, and the text is illustrated in stark, bold designs on virtually
every page. The introduction describes the thrust of the play as
positive and provocative concerning the nature of man, not despairing and pessimistic. Demanding actors of superhuman power and
directed to a mature audience, *Lear* grows in profundity and mystery as one's familiarity with the work increases. The basic theme
involves the bond between parent and child, but the focus broadens
to a consideration of society and the stage. The tragedy is relent-
lessly secular, a result of mortals acting from human motives. The
afterword describes the textual problem—the corruptions of the Pide
Bull quarto and the relationship to the folio text—and the sources
for the play. Included also are descriptions of eight recent studies of
the play—by R. B. Heilman (see item 106), John F. Danby (see item
116), Russell A. Fraser (see item 368), William R. Elton (see item
559), Marvin Rosenberg (see item 748), Paul A. Jorgensen (see item
194), Maynard Mack (see item 530), and S. L. Goldberg (see item
963). A concluding section includes the full bibliographical material
for these eight studies.

1723   Kot, Jozef, trans. *Kráľ Lear.* Bratislava: Tatran, 1976.

The text of *King Lear* is translated into Slovak. A commentary, provided by A. Bejblik, focuses on the folkloric elements of
the Lear story and the consequent timelessness of its theme.

1724   Halstead, William Perdue. *Shakespeare as Spoken: A Collation
of 5000 Acting Editions and Promptbooks of Shakespeare.*
2 vols. Ann Arbor: Publications for the American Theatre
Association by University Microfilms International, 1977.

Volume 2 includes line-by-line collations of all acting editions
and promptbooks in England of *King Lear* through 1975. The
Globe text (1865) is printed on the left pages, with variants on the
right pages. This work is based on Jaggard's bibliography, Shattuck's
promptbooks, and special library catalogues.

1725   *Le roi Lear.* La Chaux-de-Fonds: Théâtre Populaire Romand,
1977. 157 pp. (French—not seen)

1726   Rosinger, Lawrence. *William Shakespeare's "King Lear" Rendered into Modern Metrical English: With The Original Text.* Dearborn, Mich.:   Henry Ford Community College, 1977, 211 pp.

This volume provides Shakespeare's text and a modernized version on facing pages. The former is based primarily on the folio text, but various readings are admitted from the quarto version. Also featured are a note on the sources and the date of the play and a descriptive *dramatis personae.* The modernization is intended to remove the barriers of Elizabethan language for the present-day student while at the same time being true to the sense and flavor of the original.

1727   Rowse, A. L., ed. *The Annotated Shakespeare.* 3 vols. New York: Clarkson N. Potter, 1978.

Volume 3 includes Shakespeare's tragedies and romances. In addition to a general introduction at the beginning of each volume, an introduction to each play, marginal notes, a bibliography, and an index are included.   Our age is, perhaps, capable of a deep appreciation for Shakespeare's tragedies, both as a consequence of our experience of living like the Elizabethans in an insecure world in which destruction is ever possible and of our psychological perceptions of the human animal.   The Gothic structure of *King Lear,* with its underplot that complicates, enriches, counterpoints, and enforces, sets it apart from the other tragedies, as does its use of the Fool and its mixing of genres.   The text is conflated from the quarto and the folio, with preference given to the latter.

See also items: 294, 1456, 1459, 1462-1463, 1465.

VII. STAGE HISTORY

VII. STAGE HISTORY

1728 Drews, Wolfgang. *"König Lear" auf der deutschen Bühne bis zur Gegenwart.* Berlin: n.p., 1932. Reprint. Liechtenstein: Kraus, 1967.

This volume reviews the various productions of *King Lear* on the German stage before 1930.

1729 Atkinson, Brooks. "The Play." *New York Times,* 16 December 1940, L 27.

This article reviews Erwin Piscator's production of *King Lear* in New York by the Dramatic Workshop of The New School for Social Research, starring Sam Jaffe as Lear. All representational scene barriers were broken down, and the result was a remarkable fluidity of narrative treatment. Jaffe, unfortunately, simply lacked the talent for Shakespeare; with a weak voice and imperfect articulation, he did not possess the instincts for Elizabethan verse. Also, Herbert Berghof's efforts in the Fool's role were masked behind a heavy foreign accent. In a word, the production was flabby and the emotion exterior.

1730 Derrick, Leland Eugene. "The Stage History of *King Lear.*" Ph.D. dissertation, University of Texas, 1940. 293 pp.

Following an analysis of the pre-Shakespearean versions of the Lear story and of the early history of Shakespeare's play, Derrick traces the history of the tragedy on the Restoration stage, of Nahum Tate's revision in 1681 (an act-by-act comparison of the two versions), and of the efforts of Garrick, Colman, Kean, and Macready to restore something of Shakespeare's text. Chapters on *King Lear* during the last century (Phelps, Kean, Booth, Irving, McKinnel, Devlin, Benson, Phillips) and on American productions conclude the study.

1731 Watts, Richard, Jr. "Fun on the Heath." *New York Herald,* 16 December 1940, p. 14.

This article reviews Erwin Piscator's production of *King Lear* in New York by the Dramatic Workshop of the New School for Social Research, starring Sam Jaffe as Lear. The production, unfortunately, is filled with lighting and sound effects, but with very little Shakespeare. Much is appended, including an emblematizing of Cain's killing Abel. Piscator, with his general German pomposity, is mostly to blame. The powerful scene on the heath with the Fool, Edgar as Tom, and the mad Lear becomes only so much rant. Jaffe is ineffective as Lear and Herbert Berghof as the Fool reveals Piscator's hand at its heaviest. In a word, the entire production was mannered and meaningless.

1732   Geddes, Norman Bel. "A Design for *King Lear.*" *Theatre Arts,* 25 (February, 1941), 126.

This notice describes Norman Bel Geddes' scene design for *King Lear*. Geddes sees the characters as primitive, cold, and hard, and the setting as one of pitiless shadow and tempestuous motion. Design and direction are inextricably part of a single scene pattern.

1733   Gilder, Rosamund. "Ring in the New: Broadway in Review." *Theatre Arts,* 25 (February, 1941), 96-97.

This article reviews Erwin Piscator's production of *King Lear* in New York by the Dramatic Workshop of the New School for Social Research, starring Sam Jaffe as Lear. The experiment is praiseworthy, but Piscator neglected the poetry and Jaffe was not up to the title role. "Using Shakespeare's text merely as a libretto, [Piscator] hammered home the fairly obvious thesis—that since the day Cain killed Abel for gain, man has fought man and brother, brother until the world has reached its present state" (p. 97).

1734   Kozintsev, Grigori. *"King Lear."* *The Theatre* (USSR), 4 (1941), 16-32. (not seen)

1735   "Scenic Designs for *King Lear.*" *Theatre Arts,* 25 (February, 1941), 172.

This article provides a sketch of the scene design for Erwin Piscator's production of *King Lear* in New York by the Dramatic Workshop of the New School for Social Research, starring Sam Jaffe as Lear.   Specifically featured is Antonín Heythum's spectacular revolving stage backed by a grey fishnet cyclorama.

1736 Tannenbaum, S. A. "A Unique *King Lear.*" *Shakespeare Association Bulletin,* 16 (1941), 62-63.

This article reviews Erwin Piscator's production of *King Lear* in New York by the Dramatic Workshop of the New School for Social Research, starring Sam Jaffe as Lear. The director's aim was to give the play a modern meaning, and to this end he utilized a symbolic prologue consisting of the Cain and Abel story in pantomime. A revolving stage materially aided the movement of the drama. Jaffe as Lear was every inch a king. His death was one of despair, without hope that Cordelia lives.

1737 Agate, James. *"King Lear."* *Brief Chronicles: A Survey of the Plays of Shakespeare and the Elizabethans in Actual Performance.* London: J. Cape, 1943, pp. 189-205.

Reviews are included of five productions of *Lear* from 1924 to 1943. In each case the leading figure is found to be adequate but not genuinely outstanding. Mr. Gielgud, for example, at the Old Vic both in 1931 and in 1940 is criticized for lacking the adequate physique and the range of talent for the titanic old king. Mr. Carter at the Phoenix Society Theatre in 1924 was too lusty and lacked the proper voice; he was incapable of rising to the challenge of the great scenes.   Mr. Devlin's performance at the Westminister Theatre in 1934 set an excellent, if not great, standard, especially for an actor only twenty-two years old. Mr. Wolfit in 1943 at the St. James' Theater suffered from a broad moony countenance and lacked the necessary range of voice quality.

1738 Blum, Eugene. "Shakespeare in the USSR." *Shakespeare Association Bulletin,* 20 (1945), 99-102.

A surprisingly large number of Shakespeare's plays were being produced in Russia in the early 1940's. More than 200 theaters included Shakespeare in their repertories, nine in Moscow alone. While *Hamlet* was the most popular play, *Lear* at the State Jewish Theater was playing in its sixth consecutive season. Twenty productions of the tragedy were mounted from 1942 to 1944.

1739   *"King Lear* at the Old Vic." *Theatre World,* 42 (1946), 13-20.

This article reviews a production of *King Lear* in London at the Old Vic Theatre, featuring Laurence Olivier as Lear, Margaret Leighton, Pamela Brown, and Joyce Redman as the daughters, and Alec Guinness as the Fool. Olivier dominates the scene with a performance of tremendous dramatic intensity. Pictures are by John Vickers.

1740   Byrne, Muriel St. Clare. *A History of Shakespearean Production.* London: Common Ground, 1947.

This catalogue was prepared for an exhibition in 1947 presented by the Arts Council of Great Britain and the Society for Cultural Relations with the USSR. Consisting of 134 items, the exhibition is arranged chronologically except for the first seventeen, which are intended to introduce the tradition of the theater with a mixture of traditional and modern costumes. Items on *King Lear* include No. 28—Garrick in the storm scene in *Lear* (a copy by R. Houston from the original by B. Wilson, 1761); No. 73—designs for Macready's production in January, 1838; No. 75—properties for Edmund Kean's *Lear* in April, 1858; No. 78—Ellen Terry as Cordelia in 1892; No. 103(2)—the 1940-1941 Old Vic production by Lewis Casson based on Harley Granville-Barker's *Preface* (see item 72); No. 106(8)—the Stratford Memorial Theatre production of 1936 by Komisarjevsky; No. 109—the production by the Braintree Shakespeare Players (boy) Company in 1946; No. 112—the production by the Marlowe Society in 1929; and No. 114—the Old Vic production by Laurence Olivier in 1946.

1741   *"King Lear."* *New York Theatre Critics' Reviews,* 8 (1947), 453-454.

This article includes five reviews of Donald Wolfit's production of *King Lear* at the Century Theatre in New York. Louis Kronenberger, in *PM Review,* calls *Lear* Shakespeare's most tedious play, even while allowing Wolfit some crispness in the production. Richard Watts, Jr., in the *New York Post,* complains that though Wolfit is first-rate the remainder of the cast is flat. John Chapman, in the *Daily News,* calls it a thorough performance in which Wolfit plays the role with a complete lack of trepidation. Howard Barnes, in the

Herald-Tribune, pays tribute to the lead role but finds the other actors unequal to the task. And Robert Garland, in the *Journal American,* calls it an ordeal rather than a play. Even worse than Jaffe's Lear (see item 1729), Wolfit's is loud and prone to excessive gestures, and he is the best in the cast!

1742   Brown, John Mason. "Old Man with a Walking Stick." *Seeing More Things.* New York: Whittlesey House, 1948, pp. 249-254.

The best argument in defense of Charles Lamb's assertion that *King Lear* is unactable is a production like the one in New York with Donald Wolfit in the leading role. His Lear was indeed, in Lamb's words, "an old man tottering about the stage with a walking stick, turned out of doors by his daughters on a rainy night" (p. 254). In Wolfit's production not the intellectual grandeur but only the corporeal infirmity was visible.

1743   Freidkina, L. "*König Lear* in Moskauer Staatlichen Jüdischen Theater." *Theater der Zeit,* 4 (1948), 25-26.

This article reviews a Russian production of *King Lear* at the State Jewish Theatre in Moscow.

1744   Landstone, C. "Four Lears." *Shakespeare Survey,* 1 (1948), 98-102.

This article reviews four productions of *King Lear*: (1) in London, at the Old Vic Theatre starring Laurence Olivier, Margaret Leighton, and Alec Guinness; (2) in Huddersfield, Gabriel Toyne's West Riding production starring Philip Morant; (3) in Bristol, the Bristol Old Vic Company, starring William Devlin; (4) in Liverpool, at the Liverpool Playhouse, starring Abraham Sofaer.

1745   Staples, L. C. "Dickens and Macready's Lear." *Dickensian,* 44 (1948), 78-80.

Two reviews of Macready's *King Lear* attributed to John Forster, editor of *The Examiner,* are actually by Charles Dickens, 4 February 1834 and 27 October 1849. The former gains in importance when one considers that it marked the Fool's return to the stage. Oddly enough, however, the earlier essay is not included in the Centenary Exhibition Catalogue.

1746   Stone, George Winchester, Jr.   "Garrick's Production of *King Lear*:   A Study in the Temper of the Eighteenth-Century Mind." *Studies in Philology*, 45 (1948), 89-103.

Garrick, who considered himself Shakespeare's priest, was caught between the "ideal liking for Shakespeare and a canny understanding of box-office appeal" (p. 91). Even so, his text of *King Lear* started with Tate but ended much closer to Shakespeare. He first appeared in the role in 1742, using Tate's script; by 1754 bits of Shakespeare were being reinstated. The Bell edition in 1773, purportedly Garrick's revised version, restored much of Shakespeare, though Garrick retained the happy ending and a shortened love affair between Cordelia and Edgar. In a word, he vastly qualified Tate's influence on *Lear* after the revised version had held the stage for only sixty years.

1747   Baxter, Beverley. "A Great King Lear." *First Nights and Noises Off.* London: Hutchinson and Company, 1949, pp. 51-52.

Donald Wolfit gave an inspired performance as *King Lear* in the March, 1944, production at the Scala Theatre. The audience was overwhelmingly enthusiastic. By far the finest moment was his agonized speech while holding the dead Cordelia in his arms. Richard Goolden gave a sensitive performance as the faithful Fool. Few, seeing such a performance, would deny Mr. Wolfit's assertion that *Lear* is Shakespeare's greatest play.

1748   Von Heiseler, Bernt. "Shakespeares *König Lear.*" *Zeitwende* (München), 20 (1949), 930-931. (not seen)

1749   Worsley, Thomas Cuthbert. "The Arts and Entertainment: Mr. Donald Wolfit." *New Statesman and Nation*, n.s. 38 (1949), 354-355.

One must accept certain limitations for an evening with Donald Wolfit—namely, that his productions and costuming are of poor quality and that inevitably he surrounds himself with actors of lesser talent. Even so, his role of Lear is justifiably legendary. On the particular occasion of an August, 1949, performance at the King's Theatre, Hammersmith, his ability to bring the conviction of life, of second-childhood senility, to the opening scenes is intensely tragic and moving. The use of electric lights for the storm scene was clumsily handled, and in general Wolfit's performance in the last half was not without flaws. Even so, Wolfit as Lear was a rare wedding of the ultimate challenge and the actor whose talent is up to it.

1750 Boswell, James. *London Journal, 1762-1763.* Edited by Frederick A. Pottle. New York: McGraw-Hill, 1950. 370 pp.

David Garrick in the role of King Lear moves Boswell to abundant tears. The pit was full almost three hours before the performance began (pp. 256-257).

1751 Grün, Herbert. *"Kralj Lear*: Meditacije pred premiero." *Mladinska revija,* 5 (1950), 220-224.

A noted actor describes his meditation on the role of King Lear just prior to an opening night performance.

1752 Miller, E. H. "Shakespeare in the Grand Style." *Shakespeare Quarterly,* 1 (1950), 243-246.

This article reviews a production of *King Lear* by the Brattle Theatre Company of Cambridge, Massachusetts. The production was directed by Albert Marre, with scene design by O'Hearn. The role of Lear, performed by the English actor William Devlin, was the most notable, with the actor in every respect equal to the inhuman demands of the role. Jerome Kilty was brilliant as the Fool, effectively capturing the tragi-comic spirit of man. Indeed, the entire company maintained an unusually high standard of excellence.

1753 Worsley, Thomas Cuthbert. "A Great Lear." *New Statesman and Nation,* 40 (1950), 121-122.

This article reviews a production of *King Lear* at Stratford-Upon-Avon, directed by Leslie Hurry and starring John Gielgud. Gielgud's performance throughout trembled on the verge of greatness—"the grasp, the range, the subtlety, the sureness, the intellectual force, the largeness of conception" (p. 121). The recognition

scene was played with great power and emotion. Maxine Audley
and Gwen Frangcon-Davies were exceptional as the two sisters. Unfortunately, the recorded music overpowers Gielgud's voice at the
beginning of the storm scene.

1754   Heider, Wolf. "Broadway Conquers Shakespeare." *International
       Theatre,* Spring, 1951, pp. 23-29.

       This article reviews a production of *King Lear* in New York
starring Louis Calhern.

1755   Houseman, John. "On Directing Shakespeare." *Theatre Arts,*
       April, 1951, pp. 52-54.

       This article, by the director of a production of *King Lear* in
New York starring Louis Calhern, discusses various theatrical and
economic problems posed in such a venture. In the absence of any
consistent pattern of acting *Lear,* the director must assume a greater
responsibility. Director and actor alike approach any production of
the work with caution; clearly the commercial outcome is in doubt.
King Lear, perhaps more than most plays, reflects the Broadway
anxiety for the smash hit, both in the infrequency of its appearance
and also in the gimmicks which adorn the infrequent productions.

1756   Venezky, Alice. "The 1950 Season at Stratford-Upon-Avon—
       A Memorable Achievement in Stage History." *Shakespeare
       Quarterly,* 2 (1951), 73-77.

       This article reviews a production of *King Lear,* starring John
Gielgud, by the Royal Shakespeare Company at Stratford-Upon-
Avon. Gielgud's performance was the crown of the season, his vocal
virtuosity and his mastery of gestures contributing to the changing
moods of the monarch. The most moving scene was Lear's reconciliation with Cordelia, with Lear bewildered and hollow-voiced.
The set, suggesting a great tree trunk dividing into two branches at
the top, worked well to divide the action into units on the two
halves of the stage.

1757   Williams, David. "On Producing *King Lear.*" *Shakespeare Quar-
       terly,* 2 (1951), 247-252.

While Lamb's assertion that *Lear* is unactable is no longer tenable, the modern director would do well to remember that a successful production depends upon the achievement of both beauty and terror. Fidelity to the text demands an emphasis upon purgative suffering. The set should be simple, and the action unlocalized. The temptation to produce the storm realistically should be avoided; the costuming should be visually striking (not necessarily Anglo-Saxon) and should assist the fundamental conception of character. The evil characters must be realized with utter starkness, and the bestiality of such events as the blinding of Gloucester must be stressed. Conversely, the "creatures of light in this convulsed firmament of a play must be equally emphasized" (p. 250). The development of Albany from a position of moral neutrality to a position of dominance in the resolution of the action is especially significant. These comments were drawn from Mr. Williams' experience of directing the Oxford University Players' production of *King Lear* on its American tour in 1951.

1758   Mitchell, Yvonne. "Playing in *Lear.*" *Spectator,* 4 December 1953, pp. 664-665.

Miss Mitchell, who played Cordelia in a performance of *King Lear*, recalls how shocked spectators were who, visiting the dressing room just after a performance, found her lighthearted and mirthful. In fact, she observes that an actor, if he performs well, is released from the tensions of the role immediately at the conclusion of the play.

1759   Sprague, Arther Colby. "Garrick as King Lear." *Shakespearian Players and Performances.* Cambridge, Mass.: Harvard University Press, 1953, pp. 21-40.

Garrick came forward at the close of a decadent period in acting. Cibber and others had developed virtually a recitative or chanting style; Garrick developed a pantomimic style. His delivery was marked by notable pauses, and he was widely acclaimed for the expressiveness of his face. In the period 1771-1776, he determined to retire, and a long series of farewell performances was initiated. One of his most famous roles was that of Lear. While it was not Shakespeare's version, Garrick did reintroduce much of the original wording that Tate had cut away. A small man, Garrick envisioned Lear as old and physically weak, one who inevitably becomes an object of pity as he endures his great suffering. One of his finest scenes was the storm, in which he was described as evoking pity and terror. Another was the reconciliation scene, described as the most pathetic the stage had ever witnessed. David Garrick, in a word, was the complete answer, a man of immense popularity and considerable talent.

1759a Wadsworth, Frank. "Sound and Fury—*King Lear* on Television."
    The Quarterly of Film, Radio, and Television, 8 (1953-1954),
    254-268.

This article reviews the production of *King Lear* on CBS Omnibus, starring Orson Welles and directed by Peter Brook. The production was not only an abridgement, but a perversion as well. Cut to a playing time of seventy-three minutes, the tragedy lost the entire subplot, much of the Fool's role, and the scene emphasizing Lear's spiritual salvation. The neglect of Lear's spiritual greatness resulted in a pathetic hero, a blustering, truculent, senile old man.

1760   Worsley, Thomas Cuthbert. "The Stratford Lear." *New States-
    man and Nation,* 46 (1953), 100-101.

This article reviews a production of *King Lear* by the Royal Shakespeare Company in Stratford-Upon-Avon. Michael Redgrave as Lear certainly again proves that the play is actable, but the production is marred by a good many failures in casting. Redgrave, however, is first-rate even though his concern for every detail is noticeable and interferes with the free expression of the feeling. Marius Goring was an admirable Fool, and Harry Andrews was excellent as Kent. If Robert Colquhoun's stonehenge-like monolithic setting was distracting in the first half, it did in the second half contribute to the brooding atmosphere.

1761   Kemp, T. C. "Acting Shakespeare: Modern Tendencies in Play-
    ing and Production with Special Reference to Some Recent
    Productions." *Shakespeare Survey,* 7 (1954), 121-128.

George Devine's 1953 Stratford production of *King Lear* was rich in power and poignancy. Michael Redgrave achieved a fair degree of success as Lear. A man of imposing presence and impressive figure, he nonetheless chose to play the role with the fury held in check, suggesting an intensity of thought and a suppressed inner turmoil. He was moving in the mad scene, yet overall was perhaps a bit too much the King couchant. The scenery suggested a megalithic landscape. Especially memorable was Marius Goring as the Fool, who became appreciably less vigorous and more despairing as the action developed.

1762   Lennep, William Van. "Some Early English Playbills." *Harvard Library Bulletin,* 8 (1954), 235-241.

Reproduced from the Harvard Theatre Collection is a printed handbill advertising a performance of *The True and Ancient History of King Lear and His Three Daughters* at the Theatre Royal in Lincolns-Inn Fields on Saturday, 28 March 1724. It is the earliest known Shakespearean playbill of the eighteenth century. Though it carries the phrase "Written by Shakespear," it is of course the Tate adaptation.

1763   Rosenberg, Marvin. "Shakespeare on TV: An Optimistic Survey." *The Quarterly of Film, Radio, and Television,* 9 (1954-1955), 166-174.

This article reviews television productions of four Shakespearean plays, including the CBS Omnibus production of *King Lear* starring Orson Welles. Despite rigorous and sometimes ruthless cutting, the play was powerful, with Welles as Lear especially brilliant in the heath scenes.

1764   Entry Deleted.

1765   Boas, Guy. *"King Lear." Shakespeare and the Young Actor.* London: Barrie and Rockliff, 1955, pp. 37-41.

Lear is less difficult to stage than *Hamlet, Othello,* or *Macbeth. Lear* is not a one-man play; it offers several leading roles; and, while it makes tremendous demands upon the actor playing Lear, it provides adequate time between appearances for rest. The most difficult scenes to play effectively are the storm scenes (in which visual and aural devices are needed in proper moderation with the human voice), the scene with the blinding of Gloucester (if played convincingly, it shocks; if played ineffectively, it amuses), and the final scene with Lear holding Cordelia's body.

1766   Frankfurter, Alfred.   "Controversial Noguchi Sets for *Lear.*" *Art News,* December, 1955, pp. 42-43.

Isamu Noguchi, commissioned to design the Royal Shakespeare Company's production of *King Lear* in Stratford-Upon-Avon starring John Gielgud, attempted to create settings and costumes which would be free of historical or decorative associations. Thereby the timeless, mythical, and universal qualities of the drama could be underscored. Emphasis was on simplicity so that the play would come to life through words and acting.

1767   "Gielgud's Fourth *King Lear*:   The Stratford Company in London." *Illustrated London News,* 30 July 1955, p. 201.

This article reviews the George Devine production of *King Lear* in London by the Royal Shakespeare Company, starring John Gielgud in the title role.   Costumes and decor were designed by the Japanese-American sculptor Isamu Noguchi.   Five photographs depict significant scenes in the production.

1768   Griffin, Alice.   "Shakespeare Through the Camera's Eye 1953-1954." *Shakespeare Quarterly,* 6 (1955), 63-66.

This article reviews television productions of *King Lear* (CBS Omnibus), *Richard II,* and *Macbeth* (Hallmark Hall of Fame).   Peter Brook directed the ninety-minute version of *Lear* with Orson Welles in the leading role.   While the production did evoke a sense of grandeur, the adaptation was generally bad; the entire Gloucester subplot was removed.

1769   Hope-Wallace, Philip.   "Berlin Festival." *Time and Tide,* 36 (1955), 1284.

This article reviews a production of *King Lear* at the West Berlin Shakespeare Festival.

1770   Priestley, John Boynton. "Thoughts in the Wilderness: Candles
       Burning Low." *New Statesman and Nation*, 50 (1955), 155-
       156.

       The production of *King Lear* starring John Gielgud with sets
       by a Japanese-American artist reminds us of how advanced our com-
       munication technology has become; at the same time it reminds us
       of how desolate our age is of creative geniuses. All the fuss about
       decor indicates that the play itself is not burningly alive. Our new
       society is hostile to boldly new creative minds. And we effectively
       hide the old ones under the design of culture.

1771   "A Weird Kind of *Lear*." *Life*, 8 August 1955, pp. 64, 67, 68.

       This article reviews a production of *King Lear* in London by
       the Royal Shakespeare Company, starring John Gielgud. Attention
       is also focused upon the contemporary scenic designs by Isamu
       Noguchi.

1772   Worsley, Thomas Cuthbert. *"King Lear." New Statesman and
       Nation*, 50 (1955), 160.

       This article reviews a production of *King Lear* in London at
       the Palace Theatre by the Royal Shakespeare Company, starring
       John Gielgud. The oriental abstract setting by Isamu Noguchi un-
       fortunately did not aid the performance. The shifting scenes became
       "sillier and sillier as the evening wore on until finally they were, to
       English eyes at least, positively ludicrous." Otherwise, the produc-
       tion was honest and without tricks. Gielgud's Lear was perhaps not
       as successful as his earlier one. He attempted to dominate by voice
       alone. He played the storm scene, however, with absolute mastery.

1773   Brahms, Caryl. "Son of Lear, Caryl Brahms Reviews *Timon of
       Athens* at the Old Vic." *Plays and Players*, October, 1956,
       p. 9.

       This article, with frequent reference to *King Lear*, reviews a
       production of *Timon of Athens* at the Old Vic Theatre in London.

1774   Calendoli, Giovanni. "Re Lear non è un gigante, ma uomo fra
       uomini." *La Fiera Letteraria* (Rome), 9, No. 7 (1 February
       1956), 7.

This article reviews an Italian production of *King Lear* in Rome, starring Renzo Ricci.

1775   Halevi, Moshe. *Darki Aley Bamot.* Tel Aviv: Massadah, 1956.

This autobiography of one of Israel's most distinguished stage directors, entitled *My Life in the Theater,* includes a discussion of his productions of *King Lear* (pp. 162-166).

1776   Hewes, Henry. "Broadway Postscript: No Great Shakes." *Saturday Review,* 28 January 1956, p. 18.

This article reviews a production of *King Lear* in New York, starring Orson Welles in the title role. The performance was heavy and meaningless, with Welles on his initial entrance looking like an overstuffed Schopenhauerian philosopher. He moved through the intermissionless evening without great emotion and expired with a loud belch. Theodore Cooper's rocky backdrop was naturalistically distracting. Perhaps the saving touches were the performances of the Fool by Alvin Epstein and of Cordelia by Viveca Lindfors.

1777   "*King Lear,* New York City Center Theatre Company Production." *Theatre Arts,* March, 1956, p. 20.

This article reviews a production of *King Lear* by the New York City Center Theatre Company, directed by Jean Dalrymple and featuring Orson Welles in the title role. Welles, though performing with a broken ankle, was able to maintain a lofty level, bringing both regality and pathos to the part. The spacious setting and the use of lighting contributed to the large-scale effect of the production.

1778   Lamb, Warren. "Modern Art and the Actor." *Drama,* Winter, 1956, pp. 36-38.

This article reviews George Devine's production of *King Lear* at the Shakespeare Memorial Theatre in Stratford-Upon-Avon. The set by Isamu Noguchi was the center of attention and has been criticized for overwhelming the stage. To the contrary the modern designs demanded a simple, straightforward Lear. The production failed because John Gielgud's agitated performance did not square with this demand.

1779   Heidicke, Manfred. "Shakespeare aus Distanz. *König Lear* am deutschen Theater Berlin." *Theater der Zeit*, 12, No. 7 (1957), 47-48.

     This article reviews a German production of *King Lear* in Berlin.

1780   Hogan, Charles Beecher. "The Plays: *King Lear.*" *Shakespeare in the Theatre 1701-1800.* Oxford: Oxford University Press, Clarendon Press, 1957, pp. 333-361.

     This volume includes notices of 198 performances of seventy-nine productions of *King Lear* between 1701 and 1800. Theaters include the King's Theatre, the Theatre Royal, Drury Lane, Covent Garden, the Haymarket, and the China Hall; and the cast of actors is included in notices from 1751 to 1800. Performances are primarily of the altered version by Tate, with occasional performances of the altered version by Garrick, Colman, or Kemble. A list in Appendix C indicates that the play was performed a grand total of 372 times between 1701 and 1800 and that it ranks sixth in order of popularity among Shakespeare's plays.

1781   Johnson, Charles Frederick. "San Diego National Shakespeare Festival." *Shakespeare Quarterly*, 8 (1957), 531-534.

     This article reviews a production of *King Lear* by the Festival Theatre Company in the Old Globe Theatre in San Diego's Balboa Park. Don Grinderson brought an exquisitely controlled voice and expressive gestures to his finely conceived role of Lear. Suzan Becker's animalistic vigor as Goneril compared favorably with the traditional conceptions of Lady Macbeth. Directed by Allen Fletcher, the play effectively evoked the profound truth that life, not death, is the real tragedy.

1782   Roberts, Peter. "New Plays: *King Lear.*" *Plays and Players*, 5, No. 7 (1957-1958), 24.

     This article reviews Douglas Seale's production of *King Lear* at the Old Vic Theatre in London on 19 February 1958. If Paul Rogers as Lear failed to achieve the heights of a Donald Wolfit, "he at least gives us a good sketch that is complete and finished in itself." His characterization in the initial moments seemed too young for the eighty-year-old king, but it set up an exciting *coup de Théâtre* later as we saw him crumble into dotage in a single scene. The cast was uniformly impressive. Especially notable was Rosemary Webster's Cordelia as a daughter of pride and spirit.

1783 Schulz, Max. *"King Lear:* A Box Office Maverick Among Shakespearian Tragedies on the London Stage 1700-01 to 1749-50." *Tulane Studies in English,* 7 (1957), 83-90.

The fortunes of *King Lear* (Tate's version) in the early eighteenth century run directly counter to the fortunes of Shakespearean plays in general. While, for instance, Shakespeare's popularity waned in the 1720's, *Lear* was played more than three times as often as in the previous decade. Conversely, in the 1730's, while the other tragedies gained in appeal, *Lear* plummeted to virtual neglect. The anomaly would appear to be explained by the presence or absence of an actor capable of effectively performing the role. In the '20's Anthony Bohame emerged at the Lincoln's-Inn Fields as a tremendously popular Lear. The principal actors of the '30's, John Mills, James Quin, and William Paget, were never fully successful in the role. David Garrick's premiere as Lear in 1742 at Goodman's Fields ushered in another period of prosperity for *Lear.* Indeed, by 1756 Garrick began to restore portions of Shakespeare's original text.

1784 "Shakespeare's Plays on Soviet Stages." *USSR,* No. 13 (1957), p. 52.

Photographs are featured from Russian productions of *King Lear, Hamlet,* and *Antony and Cleopatra.*

1785 Brien, Alan. "Mr. Lear's Tragedy." *Spectator,* 28 February 1958, p. 263.

This article reviews a production of *King Lear* at the Old Vic Theatre in London, starring Paul Rogers. The accent was on the psychological realism of the motivation. The text was virtually uncut, and the characters tried mightily to interact meaningfully with each other. Set in ancient Britain, the production was solid and workmanlike, but it never rose to great heights. In a word, the attempt to make everything sensible in turn made the general stage business of torture, disguises, and missent letters all the more unlikely.

1786   Burnim, Kalman A.   "The Significance of Garrick's Letters to Hayman." *Shakespeare Quarterly,* 9 (1958), 145-152.

Two holograph letters in the Folger Shakespeare Library by David Garrick to the artist-scenographer Francis Hayman describe the writer's concept of two major Shakespearean roles—Lear and Othello. Specifically Garrick describes his staging of the heath scene, with Lear upon the ground, Edgar by him leaning on one hand and pointing to the heavens, and Kent attending them. The juxtaposition of Lear's real madness, Edgar's aroused madness, and Kent's urgent concern "will have a fine effect."

1787   Hope-Wallace, Philip.   "Theatre." *Time and Tide,* 1 March 1958, pp. 257-258.

This article reviews a production of *King Lear* starring Paul Rogers at the Old Vic Theatre in London. Despite his effort, it is not difficult to perceive the young character-actor under the beard. The role is adequately played, but Rogers has neither the voice nor the pathos of senility. Likewise, Rosemary Webster lacks the full measure of Cordelia.

1788   McBean, Angus.   "Photographs of Productions of Shakespeare." *Theatre World,* April, 1958, pp. 24-25.

Photographs are included from five Shakespearean plays, including *King Lear* at the Old Vic Theatre in London, starring Paul Rogers and directed by Douglas Seale.

1789   Roberts, Peter.   *"King Lear." Plays and Players,* 5, No. 7 (1958), 25.

This article reviews a production of *King Lear* at the Old Vic Theatre in London, starring Paul Rogers and directed by Douglas Seale.

1790   Rudnitsky, Konstantin.   "Moscow's Mammoth Festival." *Plays and Players,* 5, No. 12 (1958), 16-17.

This article reviews a Russian production of *King Lear* at the Mossoviet Theatre in Moscow with N. D. Mordinov in the title role. The presentation was a part of a dramatic festival involving nearly 500 theaters and some 10,000 actors.

1791 "Shakespeare Lectures at the Oregon Festival." *Shakespeare Newsletter,* 8 (1958), 28-29.

This article includes an abstract of program notes for a production of *King Lear* and three other Shakespearean plays at the Oregon Shakespeare Festival at Ashland, Oregon. Also included are abstracts of the six Gresham Lectures.

1792 "Vintage Shakespeare." *Plays and Players,* 6, No. 6 (1958-1959), 6.

The projected season for the Stratford, England, Memorial Theatre bodes well for a successful centenary year. Among the productions will be Glen Byam Shaw's farewell production of *King Lear* featuring Charles Laughton as Lear, Angela Baddeley as Regan, and Albert Finney as Edgar.

1793 Vrchlická, Eva. "O představení *Krále Leara." Divadlo* (Prague), 7 (1958), 479-480.

A Czech actress reviews *King Lear* as produced at the National Theatre in Prague, starring Jaroslav Prucha.

1794 Worsley, Thomas Cuthbert. "The Old Vic Lear." *New Statesman,* 55 (1958), 266, 268.

This article reviews a production of *King Lear* at the Old Vic Theatre in London. Featuring Paul Rogers in the title role, the production failed largely because of his monotonal voice. The director, Douglas Seale, attempted to cover this flaw by casting greater emphasis upon the subplot. Performances of *King Lear* should await those rare moments when the finest actors of each generation feel impelled to attempt it.

1795 Alvarez, A. "Laughton's Lear." *New Statesman,* 58 (1959), 218.

This article reviews a production of *King Lear* by the Royal Shakespeare Company in Stratford-Upon-Avon, starring Charles Laughton. Unfortunately, Laughton was largely unsuccessful in the role, principally as a consequence of his attempt at originality of interpretation. His senility slipped into pathos, and his mumbling seemed to remove all purpose from the play. Angela Baddeley provided no help by turning Regan into a drunken slut.

1796   Andonov, Mico. *"King Lear* at the National Theatre 'Kr. Sarafov.' "   *Večerni Novini* (Sofia), No. 2348, 10 March 1959.

This article reviews a Bulgarian production of *King Lear* at the National Theatre at Sofia.

1797   Brahms, Caryl. "Nuncle Christmas." *Plays and Players,* 7, No. 1 (1959), 13.

This article reviews Glen Byam Shaw's production of *King Lear* by the Royal Shakespeare Company at Stratford-Upon-Avon, starring Charles Laughton. Laughton's Lear, alas, is too small a vessel for his sail. As a doddering Uncle Christmas, he creeps from scene to scene with petty pace, achieving neither grandeur nor pity. Equally ineffective are Ian Holmes as the Fool, Zoe Caldwell as Cordelia, and especially Albert Finney as Edgar.

1798   Brien, Alan. "Simulation in the Fields." *Spectator,* 21 August 1959. pp. 223-224.

This article reviews Glen Byam Shaw's production of *King Lear* by the Royal Shakespeare Company at Stratford-Upon-Avon, starring Charles Laughton. Visually, the production is a series of colored plates torn from a wicked fairy tale. Laughton's Lear is a "blinking Old King Cole wandering abroad at noon in his nightgown" (p. 223); the Fool is an evil Peter Pan, and Edmund an evil Dandini. The director tailored the play to fit Laughton, but the actor was unable to carry the poetry.

1799   Dzyubinskaja, O. *"Korol Lir* v teatre im. Iv. Franko." *Teatre* (Moscow), 20 (1959), 82-83.

This article reviews a production of *King Lear* at the Moscow Mossoviet Dramatic Theatre.

1800   Gargi, Balwant. "Král bez koturnú." *Literárou noviny* (Prague), 24 October 1959.

This Indian writer reviews Glen Byam Shaw's production of *King Lear* by the Royal Shakespeare Company at Stratford-Upon-Avon, starring Charles Laughton.

1801   McBean, Angus. "Photographs of Productions of Shakespeare." *Theatre World,* October, 1959, pp. 28-29.

Photographs are included from productions of seven Shakespearean plays, including Glen Byam Shaw's *King Lear* by the Royal Shakespeare Company at Stratford-Upon-Avon, starring Charles Laughton.

1802   McBean, Angus. "Photographs of Productions of Shakespeare." *Plays and Players,* November, 1959, p. 12.

Photographs are included from productions of seven Shakespearean plays, including Glen Byam Shaw's *King Lear* by the Royal Shakespeare Company at Stratford-Upon-Avon, starring Charles Laughton.

1803   Matthews, Harold. "A Lowered Lear." *Theatre World,* September, 1959, p. 37.

This article reviews Glen Byam Shaw's production of *King Lear* by the Royal Shakespeare Company at Stratford-Upon-Avon. Charles Laughton is everybody's Lear in that he has stripped the role of majesty and reduced it to Everyman. He possesses that mixture of absurdity and menace frequently noted in savage rulers. Angela Baddeley was fiercely impudent in her role as an alcoholic Regan. In the final analysis one must admit that the martyrdom of man can be demonstrated without majesty. Nevertheless, one misses the grand manner which lends the role political stature.

1804   Slavceva, Sonja. "A Producer's Success." *Bolgaria* (Sofia), No. 12 (1959).

The article reviews a Bulgarian production of *King Lear* at the National Theatre in Sofia.

1805   Speaight, Robert. "Late Season Stratford." *Tablet*, 7 November 1959, p. 963.

   This article reviews Glen Byam Shaw's production of *King Lear* by the Royal Shakespeare Company at Stratford-Upon-Avon, starring Charles Laughton. Laughton's aim for a sweet paternal pathos results in "a slight displacement of gravity." While he is a great actor, this is "not quite a great performance." Shaw has manfully preserved the balance of the play, resisting every temptation to easy cutting. The production crowns his eight years of the directorship of the Memorial Theatre with "a noble integrity."

1806   Stefanov, Vasil. *"King Lear."* *Literaturen Front* (Sofia), No. 16, 23 April 1959.

   This article reviews a Bulgarian production of *King Lear* at the National Theatre in Sofia.

1807   Stojanov, Sašo. "From the Producer's Notebook: The Tragedy of *King Lear*—on the Occasion of the Production at the National Theatre." *Literaturen Front* (Sofia), No. 3, 20 January 1959.

   This article reviews a Bulgarian production of *King Lear* at the National Theatre in Sofia.

1808   Stuiveling, Garmt. "Les van de Levende Shakespeare." *Nieuw Vlaams Tijdschrift*, 13 (1959-1960), 1312-1319, 1432-1437.

   This article reviews a production of *King Lear* and three other Shakespearean plays by the Royal Shakespeare Company at Stratford-Upon-Avon.

1809   "Theatre Abroad: The Storm Inside." *Time*, 31 August 1959, p. 53.

   This article reviews Glen Byam Shaw's production of *King Lear* by the Royal Shakespeare Company at Stratford-Upon-Avon. Charles Laughton's Lear was an "eye-rolling, tongue-lolling, hand-scrabbling, dirty old man." The shock gave way to pleasant surprise, and this version became an effective domestic tragedy. Whatever the critic's reaction, Laughton and his wife, Elsa Lanchester, are convinced that this is truly Shakespeare's Lear.

1810   Trilling, Ossia. "King Lear." *Sydsvenska Dagbladet Snällposter,* September, 1959, p. 3.

This article reviews Glen Byam Shaw's production of *King Lear* by the Royal Shakespeare Company at Stratford-Upon-Avon, starring Charles Laughton.

1811   Vejrazka, Vitezslav. "Shakespeare ve Stratfordu." *Divadelní noviny* (Prague), 28 October 1959, p. 12.

Glen Byam Shaw's production of *King Lear* by the Royal Shakespeare Company at Stratford-Upon-Avon, starring Charles Laughton, is reviewed by a leading actor of the Prague National Theatre.

1812   Burnim, Kalman A. "Eighteenth-Century Theatrical Illustrations in the Light of Contemporary Documents." *Theatre Notebook,* 14 (1960), 45-55.

Eighteenth-century production techniques for *King Lear* and three other Shakespearean tragedies are analyzed through existing documents and seven reproduced engravings. Particular emphasis is on David Garrick's productions.

1813   Byrne, M. St. Clare. *"King Lear* at Stratford- on - Avon, 1959." *Shakespeare Quarterly,* 11 (1960), 189-206.

Charles Laughton's Lear was the centerpiece at Stratford in 1959 for one of the most revolutionary treatments of a major tragedy since the modern-dress Hamlet in 1924. To the displeasure of many in the audience, but nonetheless fascinatingly effective, Laughton played Lear as totally human and realistic rather than portentously grand and magnificent. The lines were spoken softly and matter of factly in the opening scene; Lear was not the ranting authoritarian king but a kind old father deceived in his authority while he attempted to play out his scene with his loving children. This realistic style was maintained throughout, and in the great speeches the spectator—instead of being stimulated by the sheer rhetorical cadence—found himself caught up in the words them-selves. Theatrical effects, even in the storm scene, were never allowed to detract from this simpler and quieter reading which avoided the extremes of pathos and anger. The cast was without exception sympathetic to this rendition; especially notable were the smiling, sexy Edmund, who overtly seemed to temper his ambi-tion with his debonair relish, and the Fool, whose moments of stillness and quiet despair were no less moving than his efforts to distract the king in his grief.

1814   Dobin, E. "Shakespeare Read Anew." *Neva,* No. 6 (1960), pp. 202-204.

Grigori Kozintsev achieves an effective transference of *King Lear* from the stage to the film. He places the legendary hero into a society of contemporary processes, a world in which feudalism is itself being replaced by a society governed by the cash-nexus.

1815   Dolatov, B. and K. Palechek. "Personified by Human Kindness." *Leningradskaja pravda,* 15 March 1960.

This article reviews a production of *King Lear* at the Moscow Mossoviet Dramatic Theatre.

1816   E., S. "The 100th Festival at Stratford-on-Avon." *Teatr,* No. 3 (1960), pp. 186-187.

This article includes a review of *King Lear* by the Royal Shake-speare Company at Stratford-Upon-Avon.

1817   E., Sh. "Students Stage *King Lear* for their Diploma." *Teatr,* No. 6 (1960), pp. 185-186.

This article reviews a production of *King Lear* at the Sarakov People's Theatre in Sofia, Bulgaria.

1818   Merchant, W. Moelwyn. "Costume in *King Lear.*" *Shakespeare Survey,* 13 (1960), 72-80.

Lear on stage presents many imponderables which seem to defy visual interpretation. Not surprisingly, then, more than any other major play of Shakespeare it has provoked a wide variety of creative comment by painters, engravers, and artists in theater decor. The costume designs for Lear, Cordelia, Edgar, and the Fool are traced from the eighteenth century to the present. Various eighteenth-century styles for the Fool have survived, for example, including the "motley," the young and helpless figure, the *commedia dell'arte* figure, and the conventional figure in coxcomb and bells. Cordelia, on the other hand, is found consistently in "tolerably modish costume until Regency Fashions introduced a new 'classical' approach in the last decade of the century." This classical look in setting and illustration persisted until 1832. The mid century featured an argument over the propriety of scenic illustration. Irving's production at the Lyceum in 1892 established the fashion of dating and scenic spectacle which persisted well into the present century. Since World War II the designs have demonstrated a greater eclecticism in both decor and costume. Such comments on staging add another dimension to our understanding of Shakespeare's text.

1819   Obraztzova, A. "Meeting Old and New Friends." *Teatr*, No. 2 (1960), pp. 175-176.

This article reviews a production of *King Lear* by the Royal Shakespeare Company at Stratford-Upon-Avon.

1820   Simonev, E. "They Play Shakespeare." *Sovetskaja kultura*, 6 September 1960.

This article reviews a production of *King Lear* at the Northern Ossetia Musical and Dramatic Theatre.

1821   Szyfman, Arnold. *"King Lear* on the Stage: A Producer's Reflections." *Shakespeare Survey*, 13 (1960), 69-71.

Based on the experience of directing twenty-one productions of Shakespeare's dramas while serving for forty years as director of the Teatr Polski in Warsaw, Arnold Szyfman defends the stage effectiveness of *King Lear*. In particular he takes exception to Margaret Webster, who calls it the least actable of the great tragedies. The one thing that above all must be realized is that a realistic or naturalistic approach will destroy the play. It must be acted as a legend, bearing all the symbolic qualities of a folk-tale.

1822   Zubkov, G.   "The King, the Fool, and Others."   *Sovetskaja kultura,* 19 November 1960.

This article reviews a production of *King Lear* at the Kiev Ukrainian Dramatic Theatre.

1823   "Deep-Freeze Lear in Eskimo Land." *Life,* 17 November 1961, p. 198.

This article reviews an unusual production of *King Lear* by the Canadian Players. The shivering father-king was dressed in Eskimo furs with a weird crown of Walrus tusks. To a member of the audience the setting seemed right—barren and frigid. In effect, the acting was first-rate, and the setting did nothing to impair the effectiveness of the words. Somehow it was easy to imagine a howling blizzard when Lear yelled "Blow, winds, and crack your cheeks! Rage! Blow!"

1824   Dmitriev, Y. *Mochalov: A Romantic Actor.* Moscow: Iskusstvo, 1961.

This biography includes an account of the early nineteenth-century actor in the role of King Lear and four other Shakespearean characters.

1825   Dzuba, V. *"King Lear."* *Sovetskaja Moldavia,* 31 May 1961.

This article reviews a production of *King Lear* at the A. S. Pushkin Musical and Dramatic Theatre in Moldavia.

1826   Hale, John. "Heard But Not Seen." *Spectator,* 25 August 1961, p. 261.

This article reviews the Marlowe Society recordings of *Twelfth Night* and *King Lear.* A masterpiece which bridges the gap between page and stage, the *Lear* recording is marked by the energy and authority of Rylands' production. "All the words are there, so rehearsed and so intelligently spoken that the actors can match their speed to the natural demands of the narrative without losing any of the incomparable suggestiveness of this dense and difficult language.

1827   Hewes, Henry. "The Frisco Kids: San Francisco's Actor's Work Shop." *Saturday Review,* 26 August 1961, p. 26.

This article reviews a production of *King Lear* by the San Francisco Actor's Work Shop. Herbert Blau as director attempts to avoid a solo performance by bringing the subplot to a level of interest equal to that of Lear himself. Michael O'Sullivan plays Lear with a sad and masochistic quality, unfortunately beginning at such a peak of power that he has nowhere to go. The prehistoric atmosphere relates well to modern grotesquerie, and on not a few occasions the audience reacts with intelligent laughter.

1828   Hubler, Edward. "Shakespeare at Princeton." *Shakespeare Quarterly,* 12 (1961), 443-446.

This article reviews a production of *King Lear* and four other Shakespearean plays at the McCarter Theatre in Princeton, New Jersey. Vigorous, exciting, and "oddly youthful," the play was uneven and at times strained the attention of the most experienced theater-goer. For one thing, there was not a sufficient contrast established between the characters at the beginning of the play and the end. Also, the stage was too bare for actors whose elocution was not up to the challenge of Shakespeare's poetry's carrying the full weight.

1829   *King Lear.* London: Argo Record Co., 1961.

King Lear is recorded, complete and uncut, in the text of the New Cambridge Shakespeare edition, by past and present members of the Marlowe Society of Cambridge University. The director is George Rylands.

1830   Lovett, Robert.   "The Southeastern Shakespeare Festival." *Shakespeare Quarterly,* 12 (1961), 471.

This article reviews a production of *King Lear* and two other Shakespearean plays by the Southeastern Shakespeare Festival in Atlanta's Academy Theater. Professional principals were supported by drama students and aspirants, and a modified Elizabethan stage with five acting levels was utilized. The play was directed by John Oettinger; and although the roles were predictably uneven, the performance was effective and at times genuinely moving.

1831   Marder, Louis. "A Frigid King Lear." *Shakespeare Newsletter,*
      11 (1961), 42.

      This article reviews a production of *King Lear* by the Canadian
Players at Timken High School in Canton, Ohio. The performance
illustrates the infinity of man's mind in his attempts to play Shakespeare with gimmicks. Dressed in Eskimo costumes, the actors indeed suggested a primitive setting, but the conception did little to
enhance the genuine power of the play. The pity is the greater since
William Hutt's Lear could have been exceptional if allowed a more
traditional accommodation.

1832   Perkin, Robert L. "Shakespeare in the Rockies: IV." *Shake-
      speare Quarterly,* 12 (1961), 409-413.

      This article reviews a production of *King Lear* and two other
Shakespearean plays in the open-air Rippon Theater at Boulder,
Colorado. J. H. Crouch's production was a remarkable success,
drawing record attendance and provoking the first standing ovations
in the Festival's four-year history. Almost no props were used, and
emphasis rightly fell upon the spoken word. Most outstanding was
K. Lype O'Dell as Lear as a figure of mingled strength and pathos.

1833   Stríbrný, Zdenek. "Obnovený Král Lear." *Národni divaldo*
      (Prague), October, 1961, p. 12.

      This article reviews a production of *King Lear* at the National
Theatre in Prague.

1834   Uhlířová, Eva. "Samota velkýchhercu." *Divaldelni noviny*
      (Prague), 6 December 1961, p. 6.

      This article reviews a production of *King Lear* at the National
Theatre in Prague.

1835   Brook, Peter. "*Lear*—Can It be Staged?" *Plays and Players,* 10,
      No. 3 (1962), 20-22.

      This article records Peter Roberts' interview with Peter Brook,
Director of the Royal Shakespeare Company, during rehearsals of
King Lear at Stratford-Upon-Avon. *Lear,* Shakespeare's greatest
play, is definitely actable on the modern stage. It is not a one-man

play, however, but a stage on which eight or ten characters act out two major and complementary plot strands. One genuine problem is the setting; it must be a primitive, yet sophisticated, society, one that lives indoors, else the inhumanity of turning Lear out-of-doors is lost. Brook notes further that there is no plan for music in this tragedy. The difficult problem of staging the storm was solved, for this production, through the use of thunder sheets in full view of the audience.

1836   Čěrný, Jindřich. "Role." *Divadelné noviny,* 17 January 1962, p. 5.

This article reviews a production of *King Lear* at the National Theatre in Prague, with Z. Štěpánek in the role of Lear.

1837   Gasgoigne, Bamber. "A Lear of the Head." *Spectator,* 16 November 1962, p. 758.

This article reviews Peter Brook's production of *King Lear* by the Royal Shakespeare Company at Stratford-Upon-Avon, starring Paul Scofield. Brook's intelligence and his aesthetic taste merge in a series of unforgettable visual images. A solid play about violent people, this is a totally moving experience. The director's triumph is realized in large measure through the measured brilliance of Scofield and the excellent supporting cast.

1838   Gellert, Rogert. "Scofield's Lear." *New Statesman,* 64 (1962), 715.

This article reviews Peter Brook's production of *King Lear* by the Royal Shakespeare Company in Stratford-Upon-Avon, starring Paul Scofield. An event by any standards, it depicts a *Lear* austere and bleak. Scofield, looking something like a slightly shell-shocked Prussian general, comes nearer to mastering the part than any other British actor of recent memory. His fury was cold, not noisy, and his sarcasm develops a rather cruel strain. Alec McCowen was also brilliant as the Fool. Clearly *King Lear* can be acted for our generation.

1839   Griffin, Alice. "The New York Season 1961-1962." *Shakespeare Quarterly,* 13 (1962), 553-557.

This article reviews a production of *King Lear* by the New York Shakespeare Festival Theater in Central Park. The production was interesting and intelligent, but not shattering. Frank Silvera simply lacked the resources necessary for the title role. His was a minor-key, muted Lear, pathetic but not tragic. Encouragingly, the cast played each evening to a full house of 2,200.

1840 Hapgood, Robert. "West Coast Shakespeare, 1961." *Drama Survey,* 1 (1962), 344-350.

This article reviews a production of *King Lear* by the San Francisco Actor's Workshop. Herbert Blau directs a relatively uncut text with reasonably competent actors. Michael O'Sullivan as Lear, however, shouted from the opening scene; one marveled at the character without being able to identify with him. And the setting added madness beyond Shakespeare with the backdrop of a tent and the characters in Indian dress.

1841 Hewes, Henry. "New Statesman." *Saturday Review,* 15 September 1962, p. 27.

This article reviews a production of *King Lear* by the New York Shakespeare Festival Theater, directed by Joseph Papp. Frank Silvera's Lear is full of the manifestations of senility and silly pride. His performance is intelligent, but it is "too interiorly motivated" to be terrorizing or inspiring. One simply cannot build a tragedy around an easily exasperated old man whose entire concern is with his inner state. The setting, an arrangement of austere monoliths by Ming Cho Lee, is stunning.

1842 Hewes, Henry. "The World of Reasonable Madness." *Saturday Review,* 8 December 1962, p. 51.

This article reviews a production of *King Lear* by the Royal Shakespeare Company at Stratford-Upon-Avon, directed by Peter Brook and starring Paul Scofield as Lear. Brook combines the poetic and the realistic in order to provide a *Lear* for our time. Scofield, as a grey and grizzled leader, is almost teutonic. His meeting with the blinded Gloucester effectively presents a picture of impotence and naked mortality. If the production does not achieve intensely emotional heights, it is "a rich, memorable, and convincing theatrical emotion."

1843   Kreutz, Irving. "The Play as a Poem." *Kenyon Review,* 24 (1962), 745-749.

This article reviews the Marlowe Society recordings of *King Lear* and *Twelfth Night*, directed by George Rylands. The text, complete and uncut, is that of the *New Shakespeare* edited by J. Dover Wilson (see item 1599). The best recording available of Shakespeare, this *Lear* comes to life as a poem. The actor playing Lear uses no tricks; the sense of old age comes from his voice quality and his rhythm of delivery. The entire cast is supremely capable.

1844   Marowitz, Charles. "Lear Log." *Encore,* 41 (1962), 21-23.

The Associate Director of the Royal Shakespeare Company describes production problems in the preparation of *King Lear* by the Royal Shakespeare Company at Stratford-Upon-Avon.

1845   Matthews, Harold. "Royal Shakespeare's Splendid New Lear." *Theatre World,* December, 1962, p. 12.

This article reviews Peter Brook's production of *King Lear* by the Royal Shakespeare Company at Stratford-Upon-Avon. Staged on a bare, grey, and abstract area with the characters garbed in drab long jackets and the thunder created by sheets visibly suspended overhead, the Brechtian production provided a deliberate and unsentimental exploration of the human dilemma. As the king, Paul Scofield was completely credible if not very regal. His darting, speculative eyes and gravelly voice effectively enhanced this portrait of a man who has long survived his act of moral suicide.

1846   "Notice of Production of *King Lear.*" *Theatre World* (1962-1963), p. 209.

The cast is recorded for a production by the New York Shakespeare Festival, directed by Joseph Papp and featuring Frank Silvera in the title role. Pictures are by Friedman-Abeles.

1847   Schumacher, Ernest. *"König Lear* hüben and drüben. Zu Inszen-
       ierungen im demokratischen Berlin und in München." *Theater
       der Zeit,* November, 1962, pp. 24-28.

This article reviews a German production of *King Lear* in
Berlin and in München.

1848   Shvangizadze, N. "The Triumph of Virtue." *Zara vostoka,* 18
       July 1962.

This article reviews a Russian production of *King Lear* at the
North-Ossetia Theatre, starring Tkhapsaev as Lear.

1849   Speaight, Robert. "The Actability of *King Lear." Drama Survey,*
       2 (1962), 49-55.

King Lear has been blessed with several excellent productions
in our time.   John Gielgud's performance at the Old Vic in 1931—
under the guiding hand of Harley Granville-Barker—was a kind of
turning point.   Gielgud returned to the part in 1940 at the Old Vic
and in 1950 at Stratford.   Donald Wolfit's Lear in 1943 was also
highly successful, though he was notorious for surrounding himself
with less talented actors.   In more recent years both Michael Redgrave and Laurence Olivier have successfully accepted the challenge
of the part.   Charles Laughton, on the other hand, failed.   Partially
successful was Speaight's Lear at Immaculate Heart College in Los
Angeles in 1960.   Two points of special interest for that production
were the huge map of England used as a prop in the opening scene
and the sound track of a hurricane used effectively for the storm
scene.

1850   Balk, Wes. "Shakespeare Festivals, 1963: Stratford, Connecti-
       cut." *Drama Survey,* 3 (1963), 294-300.

This article reviews a production of *King Lear* at Stratford,
Connecticut, by the American Shakespeare Theatre.   Morris Carnovsky in the title role was like a sun among stars.   While there were
powerful moments, his role was not well integrated in the company.
The noise in the storm scene at times completely overwhelmed the
spoken word.   Lester Rawlins played the Fool as a cripple with

prophetic insight. While it was a moving performance, the full range of the play was left unexplored.

1851   Barshai, A. "Creative Maturity." *Sovetskaja Kirghizia,* 16 June 1963, p. 4.

   This article reviews a production of *King Lear* at the Kirghiz Drama Theatre in Russia.

1852   Blau, Herbert. "A Subtext Based on Nothing." *Tulane Drama Review,* 8 (1963-1964), 122-132.

   Herbert Blau, director of the March, 1961, San Francisco Actor's Workshop production of *Lear,* asserts that the vital subtext of the play is an environment informed by dark, malevolent gods. Everything proceeds from Lear's line, "Nothing will come of nothing," and the plot is "a dark voyage through the anarchic id" (p. 122). "Nothing" becomes the operative word as Edgar is forced to feel what it is like to become a non-entity; similarly, Lear's madness and Gloucester's blindness tear them from the reality they had known. The setting cuts back behind history, but it also extends to the twentieth century with its saturation bombings, human lampshades, incinerators, and hydrogen bombs. The aim on the heath was total exposure. An electronic score by Morton Subotnick set the scene, at times so penetrating that the clarity of certain lines had to be sacrificed to it. The stage was totally bare of properties. In short, it was a nightmare with the visceral dominance of lunacy. The archetypal Lear becomes acutely human when "something strange, darkling, and horrible comes up, as if from nothing, from the one [he] love[s] most" (p. 132).

1853   Brien, Alan. "Openings/London." *Theatre Arts,* 47, No. 1 (1963), 57-59.

   The Peter Brook production of *King Lear* in Stratford in 1962 bears the stamp and stigmata of our nuclear age. Shakespeare's "opera of the Apocalypse, set to the surging music of an H-bomb storm, could probably only escape whole from the page in an animated cartoon-epic drawn by Picasso" (p. 57). Ignoring certain kinder dimensions of Lear's personality, Brook makes him a tetchy patriarch, a self-made dictator, a robber baron. He consequently is diminished and becomes more a Stalin than a James. We have lost the dimension of both the King and the High Priest. The loss of the elemental Lear is in part the gain of human man of flesh and blood. The impact of this version is indeed powerful, though admittedly it is a partison and partial version.

1854   Clurman, Harold. "Theatre: London's Royal Shakespeare Company Production of *King Lear.*" *Nation,* 196 (1963), 76-78.

This article reviews a production of *King Lear* in London by the Royal Shakespeare Company. Paul Scofield plays Lear with a stern, tight, thoughtful impassivity, and his experience becomes a wild outcry against the human condition and our foolish posturing. Shakespeare's volcanic life, however, is hardly to be conveyed in Brook's shriveled and bleached terms. It is a production trimmed to the measure of our times, but hardly a production one would wish to see more than once.

1855   Dennie, Nigel. "The Eye at Bay." *Encounter,* February, 1963, pp. 49-53.

This article reviews a production of *King Lear* at the Aldwych Theatre in London, starring Paul Scofield as Lear. The setting is neutral, flat walls and negligible shade, so that the action calls the mind's eye into play. The characters are dressed in plain leather. "In brief, all the vivid elements that the 'stage manager' usually values most have been sacrificed, and we are left merely with a plain frame for the gaudy disporting of the words" (p. 52). Nor does Scofield disappoint us; his voice accommodates both tenderness and severity.

1856   Driver, Tom F. " 'As Flies to Wanton Boys.' " *Reporter,* 14 March 1963, pp. 44-46.

This article reviews Peter Brook's production of *King Lear* as absurdist theater by the Royal Shakespeare Company in Stratford. An excellent attempt to allow the play to speak for itself to our own age, this version is admittedly slanted to our own theatrical idiom. Paul Scofield's Lear is a rare achievement, powdery dry in spite of his violence. Most terrifying of all, Lear dies before he can become a tragic hero, and we are "left with no one on stage to put the riddle down by sacrificing himself to the cosmic order" (p. 46).

1857   Dzyubinskaya, O. *"King Lear* at Kiev." *Shelspirovsky Sbornik 1961*. Edited by A. Anikst and A. Shtein. Moscow: The All-Russian Theatre Society, 1963, pp. 282-286.

This article reviews a production of *King Lear* at the Shevchenko Dramatic Theatre in Kharkov.

1858   "Everyman's Disaster." *Time,* 16 August 1963, p. 44.

This article reviews a production of *King Lear* by the American Shakespeare Theatre in Stratford, Connecticut, starring Morris Carnovsky. Lear to Carnovsky is Everyman, and he attempts effectively to suggest the universality of the old king's tragic situation. Stripped of everything but his will to protest, Lear in his final act complains to the gods. Ultimately, what gives Lear dignity is his involvement in his own destruction. Carnovsky, though physically small, so dominated the stage that the remainder of the cast seemed small by comparison.

1859   Frölich, František. "Revoluční insenace Krále Leara." *Divadlo* (Prague), No. 2 (1963), pp. 54-57.

This article reviews Peter Brook's production of *King Lear* by the Royal Shakespeare Company. It is based largely on the notes of Charles Marowitz, the assistant director, and features several photographs.

1860   Hewes, Henry. "Good Company." *Saturday Review,* 29 June 1963, pp. 21-22.

This article reviews a production of *King Lear* at Stratford, Connecticut, by the American Shakespeare Theatre, directed by Allen Fletcher. Morris Carnovsky in the title role begins in a low key, tired and worn, and even in his furious rage he retains a distinctly human size. He snatches at passages in pride or in anger as the spirit moves him. Will Steven Armstrong's movable settings combine with the lighting to produce effective entrances for the characters out of seeming darkness.

1861   Hill, Roland. "Londoner Theater spielen Shakespeare und Brecht." *Frankf. Allg. Zeitg.,* 6, No. 4 (1963).

This article reviews a production of *King Lear* in London.

1862   Hüttner, Johann and Paul Stefanek. "Das Burgtheater (Wien)." *Maske und Kothurn,* 9 (1963), 193-288.

This article reviews seventy-five years of theatrical productions at the Burgtheater in Wien. Pages 196, 197, and 268 involve presentations of *King Lear.*

1863   Joseph, Bertram L. "Shakespeare at Stratford-Upon-Avon, 1962: A Postscript." *Drama Survey,* 2 (1963), 367-374.

This article reviews Peter Brook's production of *King Lear* at Stratford-Upon-Avon by the Royal Shakespeare Company. There is little in the production to delight either the ear or the mind. Scofield's lines as Lear were delivered as staccato prose. In a word he failed to play the role of Shakespeare's tragically grand king. Nor did the remainder of the cast communicate the imagery of the respective characters. The production was a failure because it failed to represent Shakespeare's text.

1864   Kaiser, Joachim. *"Othello* und *Lear* in München." *Theater heute,* August, 1963, pp. 11-14.

This article reviews a German production of *King Lear* in München.

1865   Kalashnikov, Y. *"King Lear* at the Theatre of the Moscow Soviet." *Shekspirovsky Sbornik.* Edited by A. Anikst and A. Shtein. Moscow: The All-Russian Theatre Society, 1963, pp. 281-282.

This article reviews a production of *King Lear* at the Theater of the Moscow Soviet.

1866   Liehm, A. J. "Teatrum mundi." *Literární noviny,* 28 September 1963, p. 9.

This article reviews Peter Brook's production of *King Lear* based on Jan Kott's nihilistic interpretation.

1867   Lukavsky, Radovan. "Anglický Lear v Paříže." *Divadelni noviny* (Prague), 26 June 1963, pp. 6-7.

The Czech actor Radovan Lukavsky reviews a production of Peter Brook's *King Lear* by the Royal Shakespeare Company at the Theatre of the Nations Festival in Paris.

1868   Marowitz, Charles. "Lear Log." *Tulane Drama Review*, 8 (1963-1964), 103-121.

Compiled while Charles Marowitz was serving as assistant director of Peter Brook's 1962 production of *King Lear*, this log is an account of the salient points of rehearsal. From the beginning Brook stressed the pessimism of the play; ironically, as a character acquires sight through anguish and torment he peers only into a void. *Lear* is Beckettian, reflecting "a metaphysical force which ridicules life, death, sanity, and illusion" (p. 104). The character posing the greatest problem is Edgar; from a sober, not-very-bright young man he must evolve through renegade, madman, and faith-healer into potential ruler. The play Brook considers a steep mountain whose summit has never been reached; other climbers are strewn on every side, an Olivier here, a Laughton there. The search especially in the opening scene was to find the subtextual meaning. The Fool is seen as a zany whose quality is ethereal; he is also Lear's conscience. Brook carefully removed the possibility of a catharsis by deleting every touch of sympathy, such as Cornwall's servants' commiseration for Gloucester's fate. For similar reasons a dull, distant storm rumbles at the end, suggesting continued disasters still to come. Marowitz's task of cutting twenty minutes from a later Paris production convinced him anew of the organic unity of the tragedy.

1869   "Notice of Production of *King Lear.*" *Theatre World* (1963-1964), p. 139.

The cast is recorded for the production by the Royal Shakespeare Company, directed by Peter Brook and featuring Paul Scofield in the title role. Pictures are by Angus McBean.

1870   "Notice of Production of *King Lear.*" *Theatre World* (1963-1964), p. 180.

The cast is recorded for the production by the American Shakespeare Festival Company, directed by Allen Fletcher and featuring Morris Carnovsky in the title role. Pictures are by Friedman-Abeles.

1871   Nyssen, Leo. *"König Lear* auf der deutschen Buhne." *Prisma* (Bochum), 1963-1964, 8-11.

This article reviews a production of *King Lear.*

1872   Obraztzova, A.   "Visits to Two Stratfords." *Shekspirovsky Sbornik 1961.* Edited by A. Anikst and A. Shtein. Moscow: The All-Russian Theatre Society, 1963. pp. 322-348.

This article includes a review of a production of *King Lear* at Stratford-Upon-Avon by the Royal Shakespeare Company.

1873   Ogden, Dunbar H. "The 1963 Season at Stratford, Connecticut." *Shakespeare Quarterly,* 14 (1963), 437-439.

This article reviews a production of *King Lear* at Stratford, Connecticut, by the American Shakespeare Theatre. Directed by Allen Fletcher, the production featured Morris Carnovsky in the title role. As the play progressed, Lear was in turn majestic, broken, and old. The storm scene was the center of attention, but unfortunately the sound effects on occasion obscured the spoken word. The Fool, played by Lester Rawlins, was hideously crippled and contributed to the unrelenting gloom of the piece. Douglas Watson as Edmund was especially effective, spicing his role with a constant demonic joviality.

1874   Pryce-Jones, Alan.   "Openings." *Theatre Arts,* August-September, 1963, pp. 12-15, 68-69.

This article, with photographs, reviews a production of *King Lear* by the American Shakespeare Festival Theatre in Stratford, Connecticut. Morris Carnovsky as Lear effectively captures the translation from fairy-tale poetry to cosmic tragedy. He dominated by both size and sound, countered by his cowering Fool played by Lester Rawlins. The acting was uniformly of a high level, and Conrad Susa's background music and the storm sound effects contribute to the power and intensity of the production.

1875   Roberts, Peter.   *"King Lear."*   *Plays and Players,* 10, No. 5
       (1963), 53.

   This article reviews Peter Brook's production of *King Lear* by
the Royal Shakespeare Company at Stratford-Upon-Avon. Here at
last is a performance that bridges the gap between Shakespeare's
vision and ours. The drama is made convincing psychologically, with
Lear not a silly saint and his older daughters not all she-wolf and
spite. The core of the success is Paul Scofield as Lear; his vaguely
countrified accent suggests an earthy and primitive quality, and his
sacerdotal delivery smacks of something primitive and ritualistic.
The only weak link was James Booth as Edmund.

1876   Rosenthal, T. G. "A Great *King Lear*: The Royal Shakespeare
       Company's Production." *Listener,* 3 January 1963, p. 32.

   This article reviews Peter Brook's production of *King Lear* by
the Royal Shakespeare Company in Stratford-Upon-Avon. Brook's
first production since *Titus,* it is revolutionary in its mixture of folly
and grandeur. Irene Worth effectively puts sex into Goneril, and
Scofield's Lear is a barnstorming, self-indulgent performance by a
thorough professional. What one remembers is "the sheer grandeur
of the entire presentation and the power of its central figure."

1877   Savery, Ranald. "Stratford, Connecticut, Festival." *Theatre
       World,* August, 1963, pp. 28-29.

   This article reviews a production of *King Lear* by the American Shakespeare Theatre in Stratford, Connecticut, directed by
Allen Fletcher. The veteran actor Morris Carnovsky was memorable
in the title role, avoiding the pitfalls of sound and fury for their own
sake and yet at the proper moments bringing authority and credibility to his majestic rage. The scenic designs of Will Steven Armstrong were non-realistic, provoking the imagination with movable
columns, decorated frameworks, and banners.

1878   Shank, Theodore J. "English Drama: Elizabethan and Jacobean."
       A Digest of 500 Plays: Plot Outlines and Production Notes.
       New York: Crowell-Collier, 1963, pp. 53-136.

A brief plot summary of *King Lear* is followed by a description of the requirements for casting (among the men one "must
be an exceptional actor"!) and for sets.

1879   Simon, John. "Theatre Chronicle." *Hudson Review*, 16 (1963),
       440-443.

This article reviews a production of *King Lear* by the American Shakespeare Theatre in Stratford, Connecticut. Morris Carnovsky as Lear had only a greasy competence, sometimes pathetic but
never tragic. What dignity he revealed was in the first half of the
play. The supporting cast (except for Douglas Watson's Edmund
and Philip Bosco's Kent) was incredibly weak. Nowhere did the production come near to shaking us; never did it become a tragedy.

1880   Speaight, Robert. "Shakespeare in Britain." *Shakespeare Quar-
       terly*, 14 (1963), 419-432.

This article reviews Peter Brook's production of *King Lear* by
the Royal Shakespeare Company at Stratford-Upon-Avon. Clearly
Brook's conception is that the play is one of despair rather than redemption. While Paul Scofield was brilliant as Lear, the production
was distorted in order to provoke a sense of unremitting gloom.
Cornwall's good servant, for example, was cut altogether, as were
Edmund's lines, "Some good I mean to do despite of mine own
nature." To watch Brook at work on the text is to watch a doctor
involved in a delicate operation. The influence of Jan Kott was
not only present but oppressively so.

1881   Spurgeon, Caroline F.   "Zur Bildersprache des *König Lear.*"
       Prisma (Bochum), 1963-1964, 12.

This article reviews Peter Brook's production of *King Lear*,
starring Paul Scofield.

1882   Sternfield, F. W.   "Music in *King Lear* at the Royal Shakespeare
       Theatre." *Shakespeare Quarterly*, 14 (1963), 486-487.

This article discusses Peter Brook's improper use of music,
both what he included and what he omitted, in his production of
King Lear at Stratford-Upon-Avon by the Royal Shakespeare Company.

1883   Wardle, Irving. "Complex Simplicity." *Plays and Players,* 10, No. 4 (1963), 50-51.

This article, with photographs, reviews Peter Brook's production of *King Lear* by the Royal Shakespeare Company at Stratford-Upon-Avon. Admittedly the production provides an objective reappraisal of the stereotyped pathetic old man as Lear; moreover, it links closely the concept of physical poverty's leading to spiritual progress. It fails in important ways, however. We miss, most importantly, the tragedy of a man's being driven to madness. Paul Scofield in the title role begins and ends robustly, and the general level of his performance is bleakly negative. Excepting James Booth's feeble Edmund, the production's strongest points are the Goneril and Regan households.

1884   Afanasyeva, T. "Once More the Shakespeare Theatre." *Komsomolskaya pervada,* 7 April 1964.

This article reviews the Royal Shakespeare Theatre production of *King Lear.*

1885   Al-Razhidi, Guirguis. "Ittijah Jadid fi Ikhraj Masrahiyyat Shakspir." *Al-Masrah* (Cairo), April, 1964, pp. 64-66.

Contemporary productions of *King Lear* are less concerned with symbolism and stylized ritual than those of past years. The new trend toward realistic presentation and the emphasis on psychological motivation are clearly evident in Peter Brook's production of *King Lear.*

1886   Müller, Andre. "Richard and Lear at Stratford." *Montrealer,* September, 1964, pp. 33-36.

This article reviews a production of *King Lear* at Stratford, Ontario, by the Stratford Festival Theatre. John Colicos was Lear, and the director was Michael Langham. The production was in the romantic tradition, emphasizing man's capacity to suffer and to endure. The reviewer would much have preferred a nihilistic production challenging the existence of God and any form of benevolent or theological control.

1887   Barbu, N. "O impresionantă exegeză shahespeariană." *Iasul Literar,* No. 4 (1964), pp. 83-87.

This article, entitled "An Impressive Shakespeare Exegesis," reviews a production of *King Lear* in Bucharest by the Royal Shakespeare Theatre.

1888   Blau, Herbert. "The Clearest Gods." *The Impossible Theater: A Manifesto.* New York: Macmillan Co., 1964, pp. 227-309.

The most profound method of producing *King Lear* is realized only through an experience with *Godot* and *Endgame*; Beckett, in fact, provides a new vocabulary for *Lear*. A dramatization on the manner of the Apocalypse is encouraged by the events and spirit of the post-World War II world with its lack of center and its ever-present threat of nuclear annihilation. One begins, then, not with *Lear* but with an experience and a *Zeitgeist*; "recent history spreads its terrors behind the scenes" (p. 218). The miracle of *Lear* is that the play leads to a discovery of love amidst the horrors; moreover, it refuses moral exits; that is, it forces a realization that we are responsible for acts of both omission and commission. Costume in this production stressed dress as lending, and accompanying music —electronically produced—produced a kind of drone of vast amplitude. "The task was to maintain the barest semblance of sanity in the realm of unleashed id, entropy running wild" (p. 286). Such an interpretation deals with the "fantasy text" of the play.

1889   Boyadzhiev, G. "His majesty Shakespeare's Servants." *Sovetskaya kultura,* 9 April, 1964.

This article reviews a production of *King Lear* by the Royal Shakespeare Company.

1890   Brook, Peter. "Lear." *Shakespeare auf dem modernen welt-theater.* Velber B. Hannover: Friedrich, 1964, pp. 78-81.

Peter Brook, Director of the Royal Shakespeare Company based in Stratford-Upon-Avon, describes his production of *King Lear* with Paul Scofield in the leading role. The emphasis is on an absurdist philosophical position. Lear and others attempt to find or live by values which exist only in their own deluded minds. Also discussed are the productions by Peter Hall, Fritz Kortner, Laurence Olivier, Günther Rennert, and Giorgio Strehler.

1891   Brook, Peter. "Pas de 'rideau de fer' pour *Le Roi Lear.*" *Le Figaro Littéraire,* 23 April 1964.

Peter Brook, Director of the Royal Shakespeare Company, discusses the problems of taking his production of *King Lear* on tour in Russia and other communist countries.

1892   Brustein, Robert. "Shakespeare with a Few Tears." *New Republic,* 13 June 1964, pp. 30-32.

This article reviews the Peter Brook production of *King Lear* in New York by the Royal Shakespeare Company. A work of admirable intelligence, the interpretation nonetheless provokes a coldness which restrains one's enthusiasm. It is set in an isolated, infertile terrain, and the characters resemble dolmens—ancient, broken, irregular stones. The most intense and original performance is Irene Worth's Goneril. Paul Scofield's Lear is awesome, if not totally satisfactory. What he does achieve beyond question is the feel of old age. Brook's is not the definitive interpretation of *Lear* but rather an essay by a brilliant modern commentator who raises new questions without answering the old ones.

1893   Clurman, Harold. "*King Lear*: The Comedy of Errors." *Nation,* 198 (1964), 591-592.

This article reviews the Peter Brook-Paul Scofield production of *King Lear* in New York by the Royal Shakespeare Company at the New York State Theater at Lincoln Center. The production struck New York without a tear, and expressions of disappointment were common. Perhaps Brook should rightly respond that the play is intended to be cold and unmoving. Certainly the large stage did not technically aid the performance. Scofield lends the part "some of his own innate nobility, a lithic simplicity and an unforced inwardness which compensate in considerable measure for the reduction of Lear's dimension planned in the production" (p. 592).

1894   Coghill, Nevill. "Visual Meaning." *Shakespeare's Professional Skills.* Cambridge: Cambridge University Press, 1964, pp. 1-31.

In numerous instances a director must insert stage directions in Shakespeare's text. Two examples occur in *Lear*. In V, iii, Albany interrupts his comments on the political future of England with "O see, see." We will never know precisely what Shakespeare's Lear was doing at that moment to get Albany's attention. In 1940, the Casson–Granville-Barker production at the Old Vic gave IV, vi, 106-107, a magic touch by having Gloucester kneel when he speaks the line "Is't not the King?" Lear's following lines then strike the spectator, not as a wild and rambling soliloquy, but as a sharp address to Gloucester, who through them is forced to admit his previous guilt of adultery.

1895 Danziger, Marlies K. "Shakespeare in New York, 1964." *Shakespeare Quarterly,* 15 (1964), 419-422.

This article reviews, among other things, a production of *King Lear* at the New York State Theater at Lincoln Center by the Royal Shakespeare Company. This Brechtian interpretation directed by Peter Brook was indeed impressive, as was Paul Scofield's authoritative Lear. Fascinating to watch was his "controlled and economical movement from mere testiness to insight and increasing spirituality, from ignorance to innocence" (p. 419). The stage setting was sparse, and the leather tunics and simple gowns of bronze-brown contributed both to the timelessness of the setting and to its sombre mood.

1896 Davies, Robertson. "Stratford's Festival of Man." *Saturday Night,* August, 1964, pp. 21-23.

This article reviews a production of *King Lear* in Stratford, Ontario, which was the highest achievement by the Stratford Festival Theatre. With no whiff of sentimentality, yet no avoidance of cruelty, John Colicos' Lear reflected not the tragedy of a mythic Lear but of man. The theme of self-recognition applies, of course, to Lear and Gloucester, but it also involves Edgar, who must find his way from a carefree drunken youth to his true identity.

1897 "Double Will from England." *Time,* 29 May 1964, p. 49.

This article reviews a production of *King Lear* at the New York State Theater at Lincoln Center by the Royal Shakespeare Company. Directed by Peter Brook and featuring Paul Scofield, the play suffers the fatal flaw of detachment, inviting one coolly to contemplate Lear's agony rather than to experience it. Scofield relies on technique to serve as passion, and Diana Rigg as Cordelia is equally cool. Alec McCowen as the Fool is refreshingly pensive rather than "hop footedly antic." Brook has shaped a *Lear* that knows its own mind, but "there is a hole in its heart."

1898   Duprey, Richard A. *"King Lear."* *Catholic World*, August, 1964, pp. 327-328.

This article reviews a production of *King Lear* in New York by the Royal Shakespeare Company. Paul Scofield's intelligent and carefully controlled Lear exceeds all plaudits, virtually mocking the assumption that Lear is Shakespeare's most unactable role. The stage is used as an instrument; nothing obtrudes to hamper the drive of the tragedy. Above all, the cast was uniformly brilliant and effective.

1899   Edinborough, Arnold. "Canada's Credible *Lear* and Moving *Richard."* *Shakespeare Quarterly*, 15 (1964), 391-395.

Michael Langham's production of *King Lear* at the 1964 Stratford Shakespearean Festival in Ontario, Canada, does much to dispel any lingering assumptions that Lamb may have been right in his assertion that the play is unactable. John Colicos played a fiercely energetic, whip-carrying tyrant who made the action of the first scene seem credible indeed. He rose admirably as well to the midsection of the play in which agony and suffering function as a wheel of fire to purge his egocentricity. The counterpointing role of Gloucester was also performed with remarkable effectiveness. The emphasis throughout was on human nature—sinning, suffering, destroying, and emotionally creating through the acts of love and forgiveness.

1900   Florova, N. "Glory to man!" *Teatralnaya Zhyzn*, No. 24 (1964), p. 9.

This article reviews a production of *King Lear* at the Khabarovsk Drama Theatre.

1901   Gassner, John. "Broadway in Review." *Educational Theatre Journal,* 16 (1964), 280-289.

   This article reviews, among other things, a production of *King Lear* at the New York State Theater of Lincoln Center by the Royal Shakespeare Company. Directed by Peter Brook and starring Paul Scofield as Lear, the production has many virtues and no serious flaws. The titanism of Lear is regrettably missing in the performance, but the emphasis upon man's inhumanity to man results in a comprehensively satisfactory interpretation. The achievement was one of the total company and not that of Scofield alone. Irene Worth's Goneril was especially powerful.

1902   Gerould, Daniel. "*King Lear* in France and Russia." *Shakespeare Newsletter,* 14 (1964), 62.

   The French and Russian interpretations of *King Lear* express rival philosophies. Both agree in the twentieth century that the tragedy depicts a frightening picture of man's dilemma in an evil world of chaos and injustice. The French maintain that it is a pessimistic picture of the human condition akin to that of the theater of the absurd, a picture of the eternal human condition. The Russians maintain that it depicts the horror of a temporal social condition, that ultimately the view is positive since man can transform and improve his world. These contrasting views have resulted in completely different interpretations of tragedy on the stage.

1903   Gild, David. "Antoine's Production of *King Lear.*" *Shakespeare Encomium.* Edited by Anne Paolucci. New York: The City College, 1964, pp. 135-150.

   Andre Antoine's production of *King Lear,* which had its premiere performance on 5 December 1904, was vitally significant, in effect introducing a new style of French Shakespeare. For one thing the tragedy was given a rapid rhythm that reduced the playing time of the uncut version from some six hours to less than three. For another, realistic details and an attempt at realistic rather than declamatory speech patterns cut away the "overproduction, elegance, and courtliness which had fettered Shakespearean staging for so long" (p. 149). Not only was Antoine the first to bring the authentic text to the French stage; he also utilized a flexible stage with a traveller curtain that, if it was not Elizabethan, did permit the continuous flow of action and also encouraged Jacques Copeau nine years later to establish Elizabethan staging in France. The production was a huge success, playing to capacity houses for several months and prompting Antoine's appointment as director at the Odeon Theatre in 1906. The costumes were lavish and on occasion symbolic; Goneril and Regan, for example, wore rich, pearl-studded gowns and headbands while Cordelia was attired in a simple gown suggesting purity and innocence with her hair falling long and free. Antoine himself played Lear, attempting a level of realism in the storm scene and in Cordelia's death scene never before seen on the French stage.

1904   Golovashchenko, J. "Lear Recovers His Vision." *Tetralnaya Zhyzn*, No. 12 (1964), pp. 29-31.

This article reviews a production of *King Lear* by the Royal Shakespeare Company.

1905   Grack, Günter. "Theater in Berlin." *Christ und Welt* (Stuttgart), 17 (1964), 9, 14.

This article reviews the production of *King Lear* by the Royal Shakespeare Company.

1906   Grodzicki, August. "The Royal Shakespeare Company in Warsaw." *Życie Warszawy*, No. 16 (1964).

This article reviews a production of *King Lear* in Warsaw by the Royal Shakespeare Company.

1907   Guseynov, Kh. "Artistic Maturity." *Izvestia*, 23 May 1964.

This article reviews a production of *King Lear* at the Turkmen Dramatic Theatre.

1908   Hackebusch, Walerij. "Zweite Begegnung." *Wseawit* (Universum-Kiew), 12 (1964), 99-103.

This article reviews Peter Brook's production of *King Lear* by the Royal Shakespeare Company, starring Paul Scofield.

1909   Hapgood, Robert. "West Coast Shakespeare, 1964." *Drama Survey,* 3 (1964), 599-602.

This article reviews two productions of *King Lear*, one by the Oregon Shakespearian Festival Association in Ashland, Oregon, the other by the Los Angeles Theater Group in California.

1910   Hewes, Henry. "The Company Way." *Saturday Review,* 15 August 1964, p. 28.

This article reviews a production of *King Lear* at Stratford, Ontario, by the Stratford Festival Theatre, directed by Michael Langham. John Colicos' performance as Lear was both lyrical and intelligent. His loud growls reflected his human impatience, and his madness was seen as an extension of his chronic indulgence in self pity. Various touches added realism, such as Lear's followers' rape of the maidens and the clear mark of the ropes on Cordelia's neck.

1911   Hewes, Henry. "Real Royalty." *Saturday Review,* 23 May 1964, p. 35.

This article reviews a production of *King Lear* at the New York State Theater at Lincoln Center by the Royal Shakespeare Company. Paul Scofield's Lear was deeply experienced but magnificently controlled. Director Peter Brook was intent upon creating a dark, nightmarish world without histrionics. The settings were simple but unearthly in size, and the costumes seemed to transform the characters into poetic exaggerations of their inner states. Most important, the actors played as a company, brilliantly reacting and responding to their fellow artists.

1912   Houseman, John. *"King Lear." UCLA Alumni Magazine,* May-June, 1964, pp. 34-35.

This article covered an interview with the Director of the Los Angeles Theater Group, with emphasis upon Morris Carnovsky's interpretation of the role of King Lear.

1913   "Howl! Howl!" *Newsweek,* 1 June 1964, pp. 80-81.

This article reviews the Peter Brook production of *King Lear* in New York by the Royal Shakespeare Company. Set on a bare white stage, it was a hard, implacable, revolutionary production bent on molding Shakespeare in the image of our time. The beauty was cold and cerebral, and the play was staged outside of its age and outside of tragedy, transforming it into a black drama of relentless destruction. Paul Scofield as Lear was coldly brilliant, and the remainder of the cast was up to his level. Brook's *Lear*, in a word, reached too deep for tears.

1914   Jelinkova, R. "Royal Shakespeare Company on Tour." *Theatre World,* April, 1964, pp. 6-8.

This article reviews Peter Brook's production of *King Lear* given by the Royal Shakespeare Company on tour in Eastern Europe. Both in Prague and in Budapest the response was overwhelmingly positive. Brook's staging of the play "in its concrete humanity" was described as a true artistic achievement, and Scofield as Lear was touted as mature, moving, and truly unforgettable. Favorable reviews are also noted in Poland and Yugoslavia.

1915   Kaiser, Joachim. "Theater-Tagebuch." *Der Monat,* April, 1964, pp. 68-74.

This article reviews a performance of *King Lear* in Berlin by the Royal Shakespeare Company.

1916   Kermode, Frank. *"King Lear* at Lincoln Center." *New York Review of Books,* 25 June 1964, pp. 4-5.

This article reviews the Peter Brook production of *King Lear* in New York by the Royal Shakespeare Company. A director of imaginative power and sensitive authority, Brook nonetheless marred his efforts by cutting the text to his interpretative measure of a bleak, totally infertile universe. The rot of directorial bright idea spread to Paul Scofield in the title role. The play was studied and brilliantly executed. The difficulty was that "in a traditionless theater the director will pay as much attention to his own sophisticated lendings as to the thing itself, the play" (p. 5).

1917   *"King Lear* ad infinitum." *World Theatre* (Summer, 1964), 135-147.

This article presents a multiplicity of modern views concerning the interpretation and staging of *King Lear*. Illustrations are included.

1918   Kizer, Carolyn.   "Seattle Repertory: One Season." *Drama Survey,* 3 (1964), 565-570.

This article reviews a production of *King Lear* in Seattle, Washington, by the Seattle Repertory Theatre.   Plagued by disaster and unexpected complications in this inaugural year, the company played to only forty percent capacity.   Vernon Weddle as Lear is adequate, at least after the opening scenes.   Archie Smith as the Fool manages to convey a quality of sweetness rare in an actor.   Especially weak is Stephen Joyce as Edgar, who substitutes volume for sincerity, and Harvey Solin's Edmund is equally bad.   Cordelia, too, fails to inspire.

1919   Knight, G. Wilson.   "Some Actual Productions—*King Lear*" and "Contemporary Presentations."   *Shakespearian Production: With Especial Reference to the Tragedies.*   Evanston: Northwestern University Press, 1964, pp. 121-124, 242-270.

The Hart House Theatre production of *Lear* in Toronto in 1935 by G. Wilson Knight made use of a set based on rectangular blocks, so arranged as to symbolize a world fallen apart; such effects lend a kind of visual grammar to the deeper verbal significances of the play.   The Olivier version at the Old Vic in 1946 was ill-conceived.   Lear was played as a slightly fussy but lovable old man; without the fierceness of temper in the opening scenes, he was never able to rise to a pitch of genuine intensity in the mid-section of the tragedy.   His madness was more lyric and rhetorical than fierce.   The part of Edgar suffered especially in the stolid manner of presentation.   Donald Wolfit's Lear in 1947 at Leeds was truly remarkable, a figure inspiring fear; every gesture was that of an old man.   The most impressive production of *Lear* to Knight was that of George Devine at Stratford in 1953; Devine's production at Stratford and London in 1955 with Japanese designs was less effective.   Peter Brook's production of *Lear* at Stratford and London with Paul Scofield was disturbing.   The setting of cream-white slanting side pieces bore little relevance to the tragedy, and Scofield acted Lear with insufficient vivacity and voice modulation; the Fool's costume of ballooning trousers was especially inappropriate. The question is raised of why *Lear* is currently such a popular play. In its blend of tragic assertion with humility, of Renaissance-Nietzschean powers with Christian valuations, it seems to speak directly to our modern world.

1920   Komisarjevsky, Victor. "The Living Voice of Shakespeare." *Soviet Literature* No. 10 (1964), pp. 169-171.

This article reviews a production of *King Lear* in Moscow by the Royal Shakespeare Company.

1921   Kovalev, T. "Meeting in the Anniversary Year." *Nedel'a*, March 15-21, 1964, No. 12, p. 20.

This article reviews a production of *King Lear* in Russia by the Royal Shakespeare Company.

1922   Kralj, Vladimir. "Ljubljanska Drama v Pretekeli Sezoni." *Sodobnost*, 12 (1964), 928-936.

This article reviews a production of *King Lear* heavily influenced by Jan Kott's nihilistic interpretation.

1923   Kulundžić, Josip. "Ritual u slavu reči pesnika—genija." *Pozoriste* (Tuzla), 6, Nos. 2-3 (1964), 139-142.

This article reviews Peter Brook's production of *King Lear.*

1924   Kupke, Peter. "Shakespeare von Engländern gespiclt." *Theater der Zeit*, 19, No. 8 (1964), 23-24.

This article features an interview with Peter Brook, Director of the Royal Shakespeare Company of Stratford-Upon-Avon, in part concerning his production of *King Lear,* starring Paul Scofield.

1925   Lewis, Theophilus. *"King Lear." America,* 20 June 1964, pp. 852-853.

This article reviews the Peter Brook production of *King Lear* in New York by the Royal Shakespeare Company, starring Paul Scofield as Lear. The play itself falls short of tragedy in its conception, but Scofield gives the leading role the finest performance possible. He plays a king we can both pity and respect. Tom Fleming as Kent, John Laurie as Gloucester, Diana Rigg as Cordelia, Irene Worth as Goneril, and Alec McCowen as the Fool also give impressive performances.

1926 Liehm, A. M. "Lear a Romeo." *Literární noviny* (Prague), 29 February 1964, pp. 1-3.

In this interview Peter Brook describes his conception of the modernity of *King Lear* in a nihilistic setting.

1927 McCarten, John. "Melange." *New Yorker,* 30 May 1964, p. 78.

This article reviews a production of *King Lear* by the New York State Theater at Lincoln Center by the Royal Shakespeare Company, starring Paul Scofield. The production left almost everything to be desired, from the acoustics of the theater to the unemotional performance by the featured actor. Alec McCowen as the Fool, Ian Richardson as Edmund, Tom Fleming as Kent, and John Laurie as Gloucester gave the evening at least a semblance of drama.

1928 Machonia, Sergej. "Stratsfordšté u nas." *Literární noviny* (Prague), 29 February 1964, p. 5.

This article reviews a production of *King Lear* in Prague by the Royal Shakespeare Company.

1929 Maretzkaya, M. "Talk with Peter Brook." *Ogoniek,* No. 17 (1964), p. 29.

This article features an interview with Peter Brook concerning the nihilistic interpretation of his production of *King Lear.* Also it reviews the production by the Royal Shakespeare Company.

1930 Markov, P. "Shakespeare on the Moscow Stage. Two Performances by the British Actors." *Pravda,* 8 April 1964.

This article reviews a production of *King Lear* in Moscow by the Royal Shakespeare Company.

1931   Messerer, A. "Paul Scofield and King Lear." *Sovetskaya kultura,* 2 April 1964.

   This article features an interview with Paul Scofield concerning his role as King Lear in the touring production by the Royal Shakespeare Company.

1932   Mordinov, N. "Din tot sufletul." *Secolul,* 20, No. 4 (1964), 69-72.

   The actor of N. Mordinov comments on his interpretation of the role of King Lear.

1933   "Notice of Production of *King Lear.*" *Theatre World* (1964-1965), p. 196.

   The cast is recorded for a performance by the Stratford Shakespearean Festival of Canada, directed by Michael Langham and featuring John Colicos in the title role. Pictures are by Peter Smith.

1934   Obraztzova, A. "Sorrow and Smile of Shakespeare." *Vechern'aya moskva,* 8 April 1964.

   This article reviews a production of *King Lear* in Russia by the Royal Shakespeare Company.

1935   Ogden, Dunbar H. "The 1964 Season of the Ashland and San Diego Shakespearean Festivals." *Shakespeare Quarterly,* 15 (1964), 409-418.

   This article reviews a production of *King Lear* by the Oregon Shakespearean Festival Association at Ashland, Oregon. The play was directed by Angus Bowmer, and Richard Graham performed the title role. The latter, with his cracked nasal twang, was especially effective in the opening scene as a tough, petulant, ranting old man. Unfortunately, however, Graham was not up to the total demands of his role, and consequently he was able to give no sense of growth or development. And the remaining actors more often than not spoke in vacuo, rarely provoking the sense of genuine character interaction.

1936   *The Oregon Shakespearean Festival Association Presents Shake-
       speare.* Ashland: Oregon Shakespearean Festival Association,
       1964.

This 400th Birthday Edition of the Souvenir Program features
photographs of the production of *King Lear* and four other plays.

1937   Pettigrew, John. "Stratford, 1964." *Queen's Quarterly,* 71
       (1964), 434-443.

This article reviews a production of *King Lear* at Stratford,
Ontario, by the Shakespeare Festival Theatre, directed by Michael
Langham. The production succeeded despite minor flaws centered
mainly on an attempt to make the play too realistic. Goneril, for
example, was made too sympathetic in order to be credibly motivated. John Colicos dominated the stage in the title role, even if he
did oversimplify the part a bit. Nonetheless, the audience was trans-
ported by the sheer power of play and production.

1938   Pislaru, Irina. "La Praga cu Peter Brook." *Viata Românească,*
       No. 9 (1964), pp. 170-174.

This article reports an interview with Peter Brook concerning
his production of *King Lear.* His conception of the play, influenced
by the Polish critic Jan Kott (see item 348), envisions the world as
sterile and cruel and, thus, as peculiarly relevant for the mid-twenti-
eth century.

1939   Rischbeiter, Henning. "Peter Brook's *Lear.*" *Theater heute,* 5,
       No. 3 (1964), 24-27.

This article reviews Peter Brook's production of *King Lear* by
the Royal Shakespeare Company, starring Paul Scofield.

1940   Rogoff, Gordon. "Shakespeare's Company." *Commonweal,*
       19 June 1964, pp. 398-399.

This article reviews Peter Brook's production of *King Lear* in
New York by the Royal Shakespeare Company. It is clearly a classic
cast in a uniquely modern mold. Without hero or villain, the play
posits a world in which men test each other's power simply to endure. The readiness for death is a vital issue as the actors move like

petrified figures in a measured dream. The most polished performances are those of Paul Scofield as Lear, Irene Worth as Goneril, Alec McCowen as the Fool, and Ian Richardson as Edmund. The production culminates in Lear's "enduring his going hence with the simple, fragile nobility that is barely left to man" (p. 398).

1941 Saint-Denis, Michel. "Shakespeare et l'Angleterre d'aujourd' hui." *Europe,* January-February, 1964, pp. 48-56.

This article reviews, among other things, a production of *King Lear* by the touring Royal Shakespeare Company.

1942 Shedov, Y. "Guests from Stratford." *Trud,* 8 April 1964.

This article reviews a production of *King Lear* in Russia by the Royal Shakespeare Company.

1943 Simon, John. "Theatre Chronicle." *Hudson Review,* 17 (1964), 421-430.

This article reviews the Peter Brook–Paul Scofield production of *King Lear* in New York by the Royal Shakespeare Company. Brook goes about his Brechtification ruthlessly, with a predilection for the ghastly and the unsavory. Cordelia becomes arrogant, Lear's knights teddy-boys, Albany milk-livered, and Gloucester a fool. Whatever is evil is mitigated and made natural. The title role suffers most of all, and Scofield deserves as much blame as Brook. A sworn enemy of passion, he plays the role without ache, despair, and fury. The cast ranged from Irene Worth's heroic Goneril to John Laurie's boring Gloucester.

1944 Solodovnikov, A. "At the Performance of the Shakespeare Theatre." *Literaturnaya gazeta,* 9 April 1964.

This article reviews a production of *King Lear* in Russia by the Royal Shakespeare Company.

1945 Solórzano, Carlos. "El rey y los inconformes." *La Cultura en Mexico,* 12 February 1964, p. 19.

This article reviews a production of *King Lear* which was "justifiably Mexicanized."

1946   Sontag, Susan. "Going to Theater, Etc." *Partisan Review,* 31
       (1964), 389-399.

  This article reviews, among other things, a production of *King
Lear* at the New York State Theatre at Lincoln Center by the Royal
Shakespeare Company, directed by Peter Brook and featuring Paul
Scofield in the title role. Heavily influenced by Jan Kott, it was
marred by "over-interpretation and too much thought" (p. 398).
The evening was dull, the performance austere, with all the actors
under palpable restraint. Scofield was undoubtedly brilliant, but he
threw much of the part away. The only performance which appeared to thrive on this interpretation was Irene Worth's Goneril.

1947   Stephens, Frances, ed. *Theatre World Annual: 1963,* London:
       Iliffe Books for Theatre World, 1964.

  This pictorial review of the 1963-1964 season includes cover-
age of the production of *King Lear* by the Royal Shakespeare Company, directed by Peter Brook and featuring Paul Scofield as Lear.

1948   Stratford, Philip. "Every Inch a King?" *Canadian Forum,*
       August, 1964, pp. 100-101.

  This article reviews a production of *King Lear* in Stratford,
Ontario, by the Shakespeare Festival Theatre. John Colicos in the
title role was a gruff, grizzled, hard-drinking eighty, an interpretation
which made him credibly authoritarian but left little room for sympathy. Too rough to suffer and too stupid to be tragically mad, he
became pathetic in the last half of the play. The subplot was performed too broadly, especially the role of Edgar, and the unintended
result was almost one of comic relief.

1949   Trewin, J. C. *Shakespeare on the English Stage 1900-1964: A
       Survey of Productions.* London: Barrie and Rockliff, 1964.
       328 pp.

  This volume contains interesting notices and brief accounts of
English productions of *King Lear* in this century. Included are
Norman McKinnel's Lear at the Haymarket in 1909 (one who
"stayed in the foothills of the part" [p. 46]), Frank Benson's
(beardless and strangely habited) in 1914 at Stratford, Russell

Thorndike's at the Old Vic during World War I (a production more famous for Sybil Thorndike's delineation of the Fool), a production at the Phoenix in 1924, Ernest Milton's at the Old Vic on Waterloo Road in 1928 (a Lear that "cut to the brains" [p. 115]), John Gielgud's in 1931 at Sadler's Wells (with Ralph Richardson as Kent), William Devlin's in 1934 at the Westminster Theatre, Randle Ayrton's at Stratford in 1936 (directed by Komisarjevsky, a Lear that caught the "cosmic quality of Lear's desolation and lifted the play into the rare atmosphere when tragedy becomes a purifying influence" [p. 169]), John Gielgud's in 1941 at the Old Vic (directed by Harley Granville-Barker), Donald Wolfit's at the St. James in 1943 (a performance that did emotional justice to Lear), Laurence Olivier's in 1946 (a performance that outshone his production), Gielgud's in 1949 at the Old Vic, Gielgud's in 1953 at Stratford (a disastrous production with sets-geometrical, symbolic shapes by the Japanese-American artist Isamu Noguchi), Stephen Murray's at the Old Vic in 1951 (directed by Tyrone Guthrie), and Michael Redgrave's at the Old Vic in 1953.

1950   Wendt, Ernst. "Vom Umgang mit klasikern: Betrachtungen am Beispiel von drer Molier—und Zwei Shakespeare—Inszenierungen." *Theater heute,* March, 1964, pp. 8-27.

This article includes a review and photographs of a production of *King Lear* in Berlin, directed by Peter Brook, by the Royal Shakespeare Company.

1951   Wyatt, Euphemia Van Rensselaer. "Ripeness Is All: A Study of *King Lear."* *Drama Critique,* 7 (1964), 2-8.

This article reviews the diversity of the major productions of *King Lear* in this century. Specifically discussed are Robert Mantell's in 1905 (directed by William Brady), Sam Jaffe's in 1940 (directed by Erwin Piscator), Louis Calhern's in 1950 (directed by John Houseman), Orson Welles' in 1956, Frank Silvera's in 1962 (directed by Joseph Papp), and Morris Carnovsky's in 1963 (directed by Allen Fletcher). Cited briefly are the most famous British Lears of the eighteenth century and the most famous British and American Lears of the nineteenth century.

1952   Zingerman, B. "Shakespeare Theatre in Moscow." *Teatr*, No. 8
        (1964), pp. 122-128.

    This article reviews a production of *King Lear* in Moscow,
directed by Peter Brook and starring Paul Scofield, by the Royal
Shakespeare Company.

1953   Beckermann, Bernard. "The 1965 Season at Stratford, Connecti-
        cut." *Shakespeare Quarterly*, 16 (1965), 329-333.

    This article reviews a production of *King Lear* at Stratford,
Connecticut, by the American Shakespeare Theatre. Morris Carnovsky returned in the role of Lear and was supported by only an adequate cast. His greatest moments occurred in his soliloquies—his
injunction to the winds, the babbling madness at Dover, the mur-
muring over the body of Cordelia. His triumph, in a word, was as an
individual, not as a member of an acting company.

1954   Blanda, Otakar. "3X Shakespeare." *Divadelni a filmové noviny*
        (Prague), 9 (1965), 9-10, 12.

    This article reviews a production of *King Lear* at Kladno in
Bohemia.

1955   Capriolo, Ettore and Franco Quadin. "Il teatro della crudeltà in
        inghilterra." *Sipario*, No. 228 (April, 1965), pp. 45-47.

    This article describes the aims and objectives of the Royal
Shakespeare Experimental Group in productions of *King Lear* and
Hamlet.

1956   Carlton, William J. "Dickens or Forster? Some *King Lear*
        Criticisms Re-Examined." *Dickensian*, 61, No. 347 (1965),
        133-140.

    The review of Macready's production of *King Lear* in which
the role of the Fool was reinserted on 25 January 1838 was glow-
ingly reviewed in the *Examiner* in a notice from its literary critic
John Forster. Forster, himself indisposed, depended upon a friend
for his analysis. The next issue of the *Examiner*, 4 February 1838,
contains a long review assumed by B. W. Natz in 1908 to be by

Dickens. It now appears that Dickens (the friend) authored the first review and Forster the second.

1957   Chevalley, Sylvie. "Ducis, Shakespeare et les comediens francais (II): Du *Roi Lear* (1783) à *Othello* (1792)." *Revue d' Histoire du Théâtre,* 17 (1965), 5-37.

This article describes theatrical productions at the Comédie-Francais during the time of the Revolution, specifically the adaptations by Jean François Ducis. The appendix lists famous roles of Lear, Macbeth, and Othello.

1958   Davies, Frederick. "John Cowper Powys et le roi Lear." *Lettres Nouvelles,* 13 (1965), 108-115. (not seen)

1959   Harris, A. J. "King Lear in the Theatre: A Study of the Play Through the Performances of Garrick, Kean, Macready, Irving, Gielgud, and Scofield." Ph.D. dissertation, University of Birmingham, 1965. (not seen)

1960   Kamenski, Alexjandro. "Fantasías sobre temas Skakespearianos." *El Nacional,* Supplemento Dominical (Mexico), 18 April 1965, pp. 8-9.

This article describes an exhibit in Moscow of works for set designs for *King Lear* and *Hamlet* by the Russian painter and scenographic designer Alejandro Tishler.

1961   Langr, Antonín. "Národní divaldo v Lublani." *Divaldení a filmové noviny* (Prague), 9 (1965), 9-10, 13.

This article reviews a production of *King Lear* in Prague by the Slovene National Theater from Ljubljana, Yugoslavia.

1962   Mikhoels, Solomon. *Essays: Talks: Speeches: Reminiscences of Mikhoels,* Moscow: Iskusstvo, 1965.

These recollections of the prominent Russian actor include "Working at Shakespeare's *King Lear,*" "On Impersonating a Stage Character in General and on Lear in Particular," and a review of Mikhoel's role of Lear by M. Levidov.

1963   Piens, Gerhard. "The Classic Theatre." *World Theatre*, 14 (1965), 363-372.

This material includes photographs with commentary of German Democratic Republic performances of *King Lear, Troilus and Cressida,* and *Hamlet.* Whereas the term classic demands fidelity to the text, the version of *Lear* suffered from the director's attempt to manipulate the sociological implications.

1964   Rybakov, Yu. "The Kirghiz Dramatic Theatre at the Kremlin Stage." *Sovetskaya Kirghizia,* 13 March 1965.

This article reviews a Russian production of *King Lear* at the Kirghiz Dramatic Theatre in Moscow.

1965   Shattuck, Charles H. *"King Lear." The Shakespeare Prompt-books: A Descriptive Catalogue.* Urbana: University of Illinois Press, 1965, pp. 206-232.

This volume provides an annotated list of 126 texts of *King Lear* which have been marked and used as promptbooks, chronologically arranged, from Joseph Ashbury's for his Smock Alley, Dublin, performance in the 1670's to Glen Byam Shaw's for his Stratford-Upon-Avon performance in 1959. The location of each promptbook is also provided.

1966   Sherley, Lorraine. *"King Lear:* The Stage, Not the Closet." *Shakespeare 1964.* Edited by Jim W. Corder. Fort Worth: Texas Christian University Press, 1965, pp. 59-79.

The full richness of *Lear* is experienced only on stage. And from its earliest recorded performance at court in December, 1606, to the present, it has generally been on the stage in one form or another. Performed at the Globe and at court, then by Davenant's company after the Restoration, it suffered Tate's redaction in 1681; but the efforts of Garrick, Colman, Macready, and Phelps gradually restored Shakespeare's version to the stage. The actability of Lear is attested by the long line of actors who have performed the role—among them Burbage, Garrick, Kemble, Kean, Colman, Macready, Phelps, Irving, and the most distinguished actors of the present century. The crisis years were 1914-1920 when the "New Realism" in the theater was in full force. Shakespeare and *Lear* survived primarily because of (1) the determination of the Old Vic, the Birmingham Repertory Theatre, and the New Shakespeare Company at Stratford, (2) the development of a stimulating body of criticism by such scholars as J. D. Wilson, E. K. Chambers, and Harley Granville-Barker, (3) the rediscovery of the methods of the Elizabethan stage, and (4) the arrival of a great line of modern Lears and receptive audiences.

1967 Šimko, Ján. "Slovinský *Král Lear.*" *Predvoj* (Bratislava), 16 December 1965, p. 14.

This article reviews a production in Bratislava, Slovakia, by the Slovene National Theater from Ljubljana, Yugoslavia.

1968 Bejblik, Alois. "Shakespeare no Kladne." *Rude právo* (Prague), 16 May 1966.

This article reviews a production of *King Lear* and three other Shakespearean plays at Kladno (Bohemia).

1969 Canaris, Volker. "Lear im Niemandsland: Werner Düggelin inszaniert *König Lear* in Düsseldorf." *Theater heute,* 7, No. 10 (1966), 29-30.

This article reviews Werner Düggelin's German production of *King Lear* in Düsseldorf.

1970 György, Eszter, ed. *A magyarországi szinhazek musora: 1965-1966.* Budapest: Institute for Theatre Research, 1966.

This register, entitled *The Repertory of the Theatres in Hungary in the Season 1965-1966,* records the first-night productions of seven Shakespearean plays, including *King Lear.*

1971 Klajn, Hugo. "Kralj umire." *Scena* (Novi sad), 2 (1966), 301-308.

This article, "The King Dies," reviews a production of *King Lear* in Belgrade.

1972   Kozintsev, Grigori.   *"King Lear."   Shakespeare in the Soviet Union: A Collection of Articles.*   Edited by R. Samarin and A. Nikolyukin.   Moscow: Progress, 1966.   (not seen)

1973   Muchraneli, G.   "A Fresh, Talented, Controversial Performance: *King Lear* at the Rustaveli Theater, Tbilisi."   *Zar'a Vostoka* (Tbilisi), 14 April 1966.

This article reviews a Russian production of *King Lear* at the Rustaveli Theater in Tbilisi.

1974   Ofarinov, L.   *"Lear* at the Khamza Theater, Tashkent."   *Pravda Vostoka* (Tashkent), 27 March 1966.

This article reviews a Russian production of *King Lear* at the Khanza Theater in Tashkent.

1975   Theater Review in *Nederlands Theater Jaarbock* (Amsterdam), 14 (1966).

This survey of 1964-1965 productions includes a review of *King Lear.*   Numerous photographs are featured.

1976   Vetsumnietse, B.   "First Acquaintance."   *Sovetakaya Latvia,* 9 June 1966.

This article reviews a production of *King Lear* at the Tula Drama Theater in Latvia.

1977   Wendt, Ernst.   "Die Zeit der Reflektion beginnt: Als Beispiele Hansgunter Heymes *Raüber* in Wiesbaden und Kai Braaks *Lear* in Kassel."   *Theater heute,* 7, No. 12 (1966), 30-34.

This article reviews productions of Hanagünter Heyme's *Raüber* in Wiesbaden and of Kai Braak's *King Lear* in Kassel.

1978   Abirached, Robert.   "Relire les tragigues: de Sénègue à Shakespeare."   *La Nouvelle Revue Française,* 15, No. 179 (1967), 876-879.

This article discusses modern theatrical interpretations of *King Lear* and *Hamlet* by Marcel-Noël Maréchal at the Sail-sous-Couzan and by Tom Stoppard at the Théâtre Antoine.

1979   Aikhenwald, Yu. A. *Ostuzhev.* Moscow: Iskusstvo, 1967.

In this volume of the "Life in Art" series, the actor Ostuzhev discusses his conception of the role of Lear (pp. 249-253, 259).

1980   Andreyev, C. *"King Lear* at the Khamza Academic Theatre, Tashkent." *Pravda Vostoka* (Tashkent), 22 November 1967.

This article reviews a Russian production of *King Lear* at the Khamza Academic Theatre in Tashkent.

1981   Brown, John Russell. "English Criticism of Shakespeare Performances Today." *Shakespeare Jahrbuch* (Heidelberg), 103 (1967), 163-174.

Production standards for Shakespeare's plays can be improved only through a successful wedding of academic and theatrical personnel. Each can learn from the other. Without the interface the director all too frequently lacks the necessary historical perception, and the academician is ignorant of the dynamics of the live stage. Particular attention is directed to Peter Brook's production of *Lear* in 1962 by the Royal Shakespeare Company.

1982   Copeau, Jacques. *"King Lear* at the Théâtre Antoine." Translated by Bernard Dukore and Daniel Gerould. *Educational Theatre Journal,* 19 (1967), 376-381.

King Lear is a tragedy that wounds sensibilities and frustrates traditional logic. Divested of his power, Lear becomes merely an old man, and the stage depiction is constructed upon the eternal conflict of the generations. For Lear the loss of the kingdom is equally as tragic as the desolation of the father. In the use of a single set Antoine captures an effective pace for the sweeping events of the plot. Lear is perhaps noblest in the ignobility of his final moments. "Without majesty, without power, without pride, without voice, the old man is reconciled to the nothingness that his existence has stirred up" (p. 380).

1983   Falkowski, Jerzy. "Szekspir w Odessie." *Teatr* (Warsaw), 22 (1967), 13.

This article reviews a production of *King Lear* at the Stary Teatr in Modrzejewski, Krakow.

1984   Finkel, Shimon. *Bamah Ukla'yim.* Tel Aviv: Am Oved, 1967.

This autobiography (*Stage and Backstage*) of one of Israel's most famous actors describes his experiences in the leading role of King Lear (and Hamlet) in productions at the Habimah National Theatre.

1985   Gerould, Daniel C. "Literary Values in Theatrical Performances: *King Lear* on Stage." *Educational Theatre Journal,* 19 (1967), 311-321.

Every scholar or actor faces the challenge of most fully revealing the possibilities of the text of *King Lear*. Such revelations may range from Solom Mikhoel's Moscow production that focuses on the play as "a parable for our times about the nature of man that reflects the experiences of the revolution and its consequences" (p. 312) to Peter Brook's London production that nihilistically mirrors the grotesque history of modern man. Mikhoel's production in 1935 in the Moscow Jewish Theatre breaks with the traditional Lear of fury, wrath, and power. A puny and bald old man who lives in his subjective illusion of power—a skeptical, world-weary philosopher, he plans the division of his kingdom as a deliberate experiment to test his view of reality. The action of the tragedy involves his gradual awakening to the horrible truths his experiment forces him to experience. His tragedy centers on the bankruptcy of his ideology as his philosophy of individualism proves false. He must learn that he is a part of the human community that also encompasses the beggar, the madman, and the fool. He finds truth in Cordelia only to lose her. Through gesture, sound, and movement, Mikhoel's Lear is orchestrated as "a parable about man's painful recognition of reality" (p. 321).

1986   Grigorian, Anelka. "Serge Zakariadze's *King Lear.*" *Shakespearakan* (Yerevan), 2 (1967), 38-45.

This article presents a discussion in Armenian of the problems of artistic interpretation of the role of King Lear.

1987   Markov, P. *All the Theatres of Various Lands.* Moscow: All-Russia Theatrical Society, 1967.

This volume reviews five Shakespearean plays, including the production of *King Lear* by the Royal Shakespeare Company.

1988   Maulnier, Thierry. "Du *Roi Lear* a *Thyeste.*" *La Revue de Paris*, 74, No. 6 (1967), 130-133.

This article reviews M. Maurice Clavel's adaptation of *King Lear* at the Théâtre National Populaire in Paris.

1989   Naydakova, V. "In the Vastness of Zabaykal'e." *Teatralnaya Zhizn*, No. 22 (1967), p. 19.

This article reviews a Russian production of *King Lear* in Buryat.

1990   "Notice of Production of *King Lear.*" *Theatre World* (1967-1968), p. 196.

The cast is recorded for a production by the John Fernald Company at the Meadow Brook Theatre in Rochester, Michigan. Pictures are by Leslie Howey.

1991   Olivier, Claude. "*Le Roi Lear* au T. N. P." *Les Lettres francaises*, 1184, 1967, p. 26. (not seen)

1992   Schmidt, Dietmar N. "Hersfelder Halbheiten: *Lear, Courage,* und *Belagerungazustand* in der Ruine." *Theater heute*, 8 (1967), 38-39.

This article reviews a German production of *King Lear.*

1993   Senart, Philippe. "*Le Roi Lear.*" *La Revue des Deux Mondes*, 15 July 1967, pp. 281-282.

This article reviews M. Maurice Clavel's adaptation of *King Lear* at the Théâtre National Populaire in Paris.

1994   Shestakov, D. "Confrontation." *Teatr*, No. 1 (1967), pp. 154-162.

This Russian survey of modern English playwriting includes observations on a Royal Shakespeare Company production of *King Lear.*

1995   Soktoyev, A. *"King Lear* on the Bur'yat Stage." *Pravda Buryatii*
        (Ulan-ude), 17 November 1967.

   This article reviews a Russian production of *King Lear* in
Buryat.

1996   Stephan, Erika. "Shakespeares *König Lear* in Dresden." *Theater
        der Zeit,* 22 (1967), 6-10, 32.

   This article features an interview with director Dieter Made
and his co-worker Ursala Puschel concerning *King Lear* as a tragedy
about universal revolution.

1997   French, Philip. "Exemplary Lear." *New Statesman,* 75 (1968),
        524.

   This article reviews a production of *King Lear* by the Royal
Shakespeare Company.   Directed by Trevor Nunn, this production—
six years after Peter Brook's—casts Eric Porter as Lear. "Imaginative
without being gimmicky, this is an 'open' production in the sense
that no single view is imposed upon Lear's situation and, by implication, upon the human condition." Porter effectively captured the
ebb and flow of the King's disoriented mind, the alternating madness
and sanity.   The entire performance was a profoundly moving intellectual achievement.

1998   Kéry, Lázló.   *Shakespeare, Brecht és a Tobbiek: Szinikritikak.*
        Budapest: Magvető, 1968.

   This volume, entitled *Shakespeare, Brecht, and Others: Dramatic Criticism,* reviews eight Shakespearean plays, including *King
Lear.*   Both a Hungarian production of *King Lear* and that of the
touring Royal Shakespeare Company in Budapest in 1964 are
covered.

1999   Kudelka, Viktor.   "Deset premier a jidna jako privazek aneb
        Zmoudreni Mahenovy cinohry?" *Divadelni noviny* (Prague),
        22 (1968-1969), 5.

   This article reviews a Czechoslovakian production of *King
Lear.*

2000   Peet, Malcolm. "Trevor Nunn on Shakespeare, Lear, and the
       Shadow Culture: An Interview." *Tracks* (Coventry Univer-
       sity), No. 5 (Autumn, 1968), pp. 37-40.

   Trevor Nunn, Director of the Royal Shakespeare Company, is
not completely happy with his production of Lear. He considers
himself too young; so, too, Eric Porter (Lear) is only thirty-nine.
Edgar, often considered the actor's graveyard, is one of the most
significant roles in the play. He develops a kind of third morality,
the morality of experience, between the extremes of Edmund and
Cordelia. And he does so by working out his real identity and
reality through a series of disguises (Tom o' Bedlam, lowly peasant,
more powerful peasant). On another subject, too many people
talk glibly without doing things competently, forming a kind of
shadow culture. The critic, for example, frequently does not do
justice to a play either because of his biases or his insufficient knowledge.

2001   Püschel, Ursala. "Theaterschau: Aus Besuchergesprächen uber
       die Dresdener Inszenierung des *König Lear*." *Shakespeare
       Jahrbuch* (Weimar), 104 (1968), 270-273.

   This article surveys a variety of views of a production of *King
Lear* at Dresden.

2002   Roberts, Peter. "Power Politics." *Plays and Players,* 15, No. 9
       (1968), 18-20.

   Trevor Nunn's production by the Royal Shakespeare Company
at Stratford-Upon-Avon places the vocal before the visual by using
no permanent sets. The tent structures appearing in the opening
and closing scenes appear to symbolize the order which Lear (Eric
Porter) destroys through his pride and anger. The costuming starkly
fluctuates between the naturalistic (the storm scene complete with
thunder and lightning) and the stylized (slow motion battle scenes to
the sound of a menacing drone).

2003   Rosenberg, Marvin. "*King Lear* in Germany, France, and Italy."
       Theatre Survey, 9 (1968), 1-10.

   A glance at the major productions of *King Lear* in Germany,
France, and Italy is instructive concerning the tragedy itself and the

cultural and artistic milieu of its production. German stage versions by the end of the seventeenth century mutilated the text badly. The first scene was cut entirely (a change emphatically approved by Goethe), and a happy ending permitted the survival of both Lear and Cordelia. Friedrich Schroeder in 1778 played Lear as pathetic and pitiable. In the nineteenth century Ludwig Devrient, on the other hand, emphasized Lear's senility from the outset, and Anschutz went further in softening and sentimentalizing the figure. The twentieth century's most interesting German production is that of Reinhardt, with its emphasis on the imaginative, fairy-tale qualities. In France the play suffered for years from the dominance of Neo-Classical tastes and from Voltaire's denunciation of Shakespeare as a bloody barbarian. Ducis in the 1780's staged an adaptation, and in the twentieth century Antoine's production in 1904 and Charles Dullin's absurdist version in 1945 are notable. No significant Italian Lears appeared before the mid-nineteenth century. The two most famous actors were Rossi, who emphasized Lear's age, frailty, and growing senility, and Salvini, who stressed the character's giant-sized vigor and grandeur.

2004   Speaight, Robert. "Shakespeare in Britain." *Shakespeare Quarterly,* 19 (1968), 367-375.

This article reviews the production of five Shakespearean plays by the Royal Shakespeare Company at the Shakespeare Memorial Theatre in Stratford-Upon-Avon. The rendition of *King Lear,* directed by Trevor Nunn and starring Eric Porter as Lear, is described as "lucid and true." Peter Hall's retirement from the directorship of the Royal Shakespeare Theatre is also noted, along with a description of his achievements.

2005   Trewin, J. C. "Shadow and Substance." *The Illustrated London News,* 27 April 1968, p. 26.

This article reviews a production of *King Lear* by the Royal Shakespeare Company at Stratford-Upon-Avon, directed by Trevor Nunn. Eric Porter as Lear is commanding and effective, never self-indulgent; his passion never loses itself in rant, and his pathos is true. Other notable performances include Sebastian Shaw as Gloucester, Michael Williams as the Fool, and Norman Rodway as Edmund. Alan Howard leaves much to be desired as Tom o' Bedlam.

2006   Bakó, Endre.   Theater Review in *Hajdu-Biharmegyei Népujság*, 16, 22 January and 2 February 1969.

This article reviews a production of *King Lear* at the Csokonai Theatre in Debrecen, Hungary.

2007   Benyei, Józef.   Theater Review in *Alfold*, No. 5, 1969.

This article reviews a production of *King Lear* at the Csokonai Theatre in Debrecen, Hungary.

2008   Berkovskii, N.   *Literature and Theatre: Essays and Articles.* Moscow: Iskusstvo, 1969.

This volume includes a discussion (pp. 444-452) of a production of *King Lear* in 1941 directed by Grigori Kozintsev.

2009   Boyadzhyev, G.   Theater Review in *From Sophocles to Brecht in Forty Theatrical Nights.*   Moscow: Prosveshcheniye, 1969.

This article reviews a touring production of *King Lear* by the Stratford (Ontario) Shakespeare Company.

2010   Brown, John Russell.   "Ein Epilog: Scholars and Actors." *Shakespeare Jahrbuch* (Heidelberg), 105 (1969), 72-80.

In this contribution to a symposium on *King Lear* at Bochum in April, 1968, Brown is concerned especially with the importance of gestures and of scene designs. He calls for cooperation between theatrical and academic personnel in developing the fullest understanding for and appreciation of *Lear* on the stage. See item 721.

2011   Bundálek, Karel.   "Hra o vášni být milován." *Rovnost*, 18 March 1969.

This article reviews a production of *King Lear* at the Mahen Theatre on 15 March 1969 at Brno, directed by A. Hajda. The text was adapted by L. Kundera from the translation by E. A. Saudek and O. F. Babler. The interpretation was based on Brecht's vision of the tragedy as a play on the "passion to be loved."

2012   Carlisle, Carol Jones.   "Actors' Criticisms of *King Lear.*" *Shakespeare from the Greenroom*: *Actors' Criticisms of Four Major*

Tragedies. Chapel Hill: University of North Carolina Press, 1969, pp. 266-319.

From books, essays, lectures, autobiographies, diary notes, personal letters, and recorded conversations, the author has assembled a wide variety of comments upon Shakespeare's major tragedies by English-speaking actors from the eighteenth century to the present. A major concern about *Lear* in the eighteenth century focused on the preference for Tate's adaptation, along with the modifications of George Colman and David Garrick. Francis Gentleman, Arthur Murphy, and Thomas Davies, for example, spoke against the double plot, a violation of the neoclassical unity of action. The presence of the Fool and the blinding of Gloucester on stage are other offenses against decorum. Not until 1799 did an actor, Charles Dibdin, claim strongly the superiority of Shakespeare's text, a view supported by William Oxberry in 1820 and, most importantly, by William Charles Macready in 1838. For various reasons, among them no doubt the Romantic critics' argument over the actability of the play, the popularity of *Lear* on stage waned in the late nienteenth and early twentieth centuries. Even more recent critics like Margaret Webster and Tyrone Guthrie admit tremendous obstacles to an effective presentation. An important milestone in restoring the play's stage credibility came in Harley Granville-Barker's "Preface" to *King Lear* in 1927. Since then Robert Speaight, who has written at length on the versions of John Gielgud and Michael Redgrave, and Donald Wolfit, himself responsible for almost half of the London performances in the 1940's and 1950's, have contributed to a steady increase in the play's popularity as did Peter Brook's production in 1962 with Paul Scofield in the title role. The shifting emphasis on the nature of the play and the character can also be traced through the actors' comments, from the theme of social protest described by William Poel, to the spiritual renewal as visioned by Lena Ashwell and Robert Speaight, to the deep despair and pessimism argued by Margaret Webster and Peter Brook.

2013   Dolinsky, M. "From Hamlet to Lear." *Literaturnaya gazeta,* No. 37 (1969), p. 8.

This brief notice describes the challenges, both practical and artistic, confronting Grigori Kozintsev in the filming of *King Lear.*

2014   Fritzsche, Max.   "Wortkulisse and Bühnenbild."   *Shakespeare Jahrbuch* (Heidelberg), 105 (1969), 61-65.

Fritzsche describes his experiences as a scenic designer for a performance of *King Lear* at the Schauspielhause Bonn in 1963. Scene design is especially significant in establishing the proper tone for Lear's scenes on the heath. This paper was presented at a symposium on *Lear* at Bochum in April, 1968. See item 721.

2015   Gielgud, John.   *Early Stages: Stage Directions.*   Leningrad: Iskusstvo, 1969.

This volume, translated into Russian by P. Melkova, includes a chapter on Gielgud's Shakespearean Roles in the 1920's and 1930's; the roles of Benedict, Leontes, and Cassius; and the role of King Lear under the direction of Harley Granville-Barker. An introduction is provided by Iv. Kovalev.

2016   Habicht, Werner.   "Spiegelotellen und Gebärdenführung."   *Shakespeare Jahrbuch* (Heidelberg), 105 (1969), 29-39.

The subtext of a play is largely dependent upon the proper enactment of bodily and facial gestures. In *King Lear*, for example, the clasping of hands and the simultaneity of tears and laughter poignantly symbolize without words the force and power of reconciliation between King and daughter. Kneeling can in context indicate either egotistic scorn (as in Lear before Regan) or love and obedience (as in Cordelia before Lear). This paper was delivered at a symposium on *King Lear* at Bochum in April, 1968. See item 721.

2017   Holman, M.   Theater Review in *Host do domu*, No. 2 (1969), pp. 16-17.

This article reviews a production of *King Lear* at the Mahen Theatre on 15 March 1969 at Brno, directed by A. Hajda. The text was adapted by L. Kundera from the translation by E. A. Saudek and O. F. Babler.

2018   Isamoff, F.   "King Lear from the Mountains Jumgal-too."   *Pravda Vostoka* (Tashkent), 2 September 1969.

This article reviews a production of *King Lear* with the Kirgizian actor, M. Ryskulov, as King Lear.

2019   Jorgens, Jack C. "Staging Shakespeare in 1969." *Shakespeare Newsletter,* 19 (1969), 4-5.

This article reviews thirteen stagings of Shakespeare including a performance of *King Lear* in New York by The Roundabout Players, directed by Gene Feist. The stage was a bare 20' by 20' space in the basement of a co-op supermarket in Manhattan. Characters speak from boxes and pedestals. All things considered, the performance was of excellent quality; if this be amateurism, give us more of it.

2020   Koltai, Tomas. Theater Review in *Népszababsáy,* 18 February 1969.

This article reviews a production of *King Lear* at the Csokonai Theatre in Debrecen, Hungary.

2021   Kuner, Mildred C. "The New York Shakespeare Festival, 1969." *Shakespeare Quarterly,* 20 (1969), 451-454.

This article reviews four Shakespearean plays including Gerald Freedman's production of *King Lear* by the Repertory Theatre of Lincoln Center, New York. Lee J. Cobb as Lear too often recalled his role of Willy Loman. While he brought a certain strength to the part, he never caught its lyrical elements. Perhaps the strongest performance was Stacy Keach's Edmund, set against Robert Stattel's Hotspur-like Edgar. The production on the whole was logical and unified, a "realistic drama of family conflicts," but one wished for a bit more incandescence.

2022   Lichtenhahn, Fritz. "Die dramatischen Impulse in Vers and Rhythmus." *Shakespeare Jahrbuch* (Heidelberg), 105 (1969), 23-29.

The role of Oswald is analyzed to reveal the diverse ways in which the role may be enacted. Variations in the rhythmic patterns of his words can create widely different responses. On one extreme he can appear the readily responsible and dutiful servant of Goneril; at another he can appear a toady sycophant incapable of provoking the slightest sympathy from the spectator. This paper was delivered at a symposium on *King Lear* at Bochum in April, 1968. See item 721.

2023   Lindtberg, Leopold. "Spiegelstellen und Gebärdenführung."
       Shakespeare Jahrbuch (Heidelberg), 105 (1969), 39-50.

       The role of King Lear is analyzed for the range of possible in-
terpretations and also, once the particular approach is determined,
for the range of verbal and physical expression necessary within a
given interpretation. This paper was delivered at a symposium on
King Lear at Bochum in April, 1968. See item 721.

2024   Loeffler, Peter. "Zusammenfassender Bericht über die Diskus-
       sion." *Shakespeare Jahrbuch* (Heidelberg), 105 (1969), 65-72.

       The symposium on *King Lear* held at Bochum in April, 1968,
was intended to encourage a wedding of academics and the personnel of the performing arts. Subjects examined include the flexibility
of key roles (Lear, Oswald) in terms of delivery and rhythm, the
vital importance of effective scenic design, and the significance of
the subtext as envisioned through gestures and symbolic actions.
The theme of the symposium was to envision a production of *King
Lear* as a great adventure shared and contributed to both by scholar-
critics and actors and designers. See item 721.

2025   Loney, Glenn. *"King Lear."* *Educational Theatre Journal,* 21
       (1969), 103-107.

       This article reviews a production of *King Lear* by the Reper-
tory Theatre of Lincoln Center, New York, with Lee J. Cobb as a
querulous and ill-tempered King Lear. Barbette Tweed as Cordelia
seemed to have a genuine inner strength, and Goneril and Regan
were played with regal restraint, not like monsters. Contemporary
relevance was saved through emphasis upon the geriatric quality of
the tragedy. The setting by Ming Cho Lee and the costumes by
Theoni V. Aldredge combined to evoke an effective time-setting of
the dawn of England's history.

2026   Marder, Louis. *"King Lear* for TV." *Shakespeare Newsletter,*
       19 (1969), 53.

       This note announces the scheduling of Peter Brook's film
version of *King Lear,* produced by Michael Birkett and starring Paul
Scofield, for CBS-TV in the fall of 1969. The film was shot in a
bleak Danish landscape with sand dunes and frozen sea.

2027   Meersman, Roger. *"King Lear."* *Educational Theatre Journal,* 21 (1969), 223-224.

This article reviews a production of *King Lear* at the Arena Stage in Washington, D. C., directed by Edwin Sherin. In the title role Frank Silvera diminishes the kingly qualities so that the common humanity becomes dominant. Clear in story line and character motivation, the production is graced with an excellent supporting cast. The sets, costumes, and property have a sculptured effect.

2028   Nightingale, Benedict. "An Old, Mad King." *New Statesman,* 78 (1969), 667.

This article reviews a production of *King Lear* in Nottingham, directed by Jonathan Miller and featuring Michael Hordern in the title role. Hordern plays an erratic, egocentric, and sickly Lear who is crawling toward death and peevish to all around him, the "paradigm of the 'geriatric problem' we try so hard to forget nowadays." So detached was the audience that it laughed at the mad scenes. With some relevance to our permissive society, the production by Terry Hand was disjointed at times both physically and emotionally.

2029   "Notice of Production of *King Lear."* *Theatre World* (1969-1970), p. 208.

The cast is recorded for a performance by the Purdue Professional Theatre in Lafayette, Indiana. Pictures are by David Umberger.

2030   Obraztsova, A. "Paul Scofield's King Lear." *Shekspirovsky sbornik, 1967.* Edited by A. Anikst. Moscow: The All-Russian Theatre Society, 1969.

This article in *Shakespeare's Miscellany* discusses Paul Scofield as King Lear in Peter Brook's production. Inspired by Jan Kott's interpretation, Scofield's Lear inhabits a sterile world in which life is without purposeful direction and virtue is doomed to defeat because of its impracticality.

2031   Oppel, Horst. "Wortkulisse und Bühnenbild." *Shakespeare Jahrbuch* (Heidelberg), 105 (1969), 50-60.

King Lear, perhaps above all of Shakespeare's plays, demands a stylized, simplified, and spaciously designed stage set. This atmospheric and symbolic "word-scenery" was, for the Elizabethan, accomplished on a simple, open stage. The contrast between sheltered human habitation and the cold, hostile heath was achieved through a constantly visible tiring-house façade during the storm scenes. This paper was presented at a symposium on *King Lear* at Bochum in April, 1968. See item 721.

2032   Parhon, Victor.   "Turneul Nationallui craioveau."   *România Literară* (Bucharest), No. 23, 6 June 1969.

This article, "Tour of Craiova National Theater," reviews a production of *King Lear* in Rumania.

2033   Piotrovsky, A. I.   *Theatre: Cinema: A Life.*   Leningrad: Iskusstvo, 1969.

This posthumously published volume of an art critic and scholar includes an essay on his reminiscences of a production of *King Lear*, "Lear at the Jewish Theatre."

2034   Popescue, Iona.   "Shakespeare in trei ipostaze discutabile." *România Literară* (Bucharest), No. 24 (12 June 1969), p. 25.

This article, "Three Debatable Aspects of Shakespeare," reviews a production of *King Lear* by the Craiova National Theater.

2035   Ripeanu, B. T.   "Intre Spectacobul de rutina si evenimentul teatral: Consideratii pe marginea unor spectacole Shakespearene." *Teatrul* (Bucharest), 14 (1969), 73-77.

This article reviews productions of *King Lear* and *Macbeth.*

2036   Segedi, I. "Lear and His Children." *Teatr,* No. 3 (1969), pp. 18-19.

This article reviews a production of *King Lear* in Russia by the Kalinin District Drama Theatre.

2037   Shin'ar, Itzhak. "Three New Cinematic Versions of *King Lear.*" *ba-Mahané*, 18 November 1969, p. 31.

The article discusses the film productions of *King Lear* by Peter Brook, Grigori Kozintsev, and Orson Welles.

2038   Stoilov, Bogumil. "Polezni sresci." *Teatur* (Sofia), 22 (1969), 32-35.

This article reviews a Polish production of *King Lear* in the National Theatre in Krakow.

2039   Suchomolova, J. Theater Review in *Mladá fronta,* 5 April 1969.

This article reviews a production of *King Lear* at the Mahen Theatre on 5 March 1969 at Brno, directed by A. Hajde. The text was adapted by L. Kundera from a translation by E. A. Saudek and O. F. Babler.

2040   Theater Review in *Ethnos* (Athens), 12 March 1969, 23 August 1969.

This article reviews a production of *King Lear* by the State Theatre of Northern Greece at Salonica on 7 March 1969 and at the Athens Festival on 22-23 August 1969. The translation into Greek was by Vassilis Rotas.

2041   Theater Review in *Film, Szinház, Muzsika,* 8 March 1969.

This article reviews a production of *King Lear* at the Csokonai Theatre in Debrecen, Hungary.

2042   Theater Review in *Macedonia,* 16 March 1969.

This article reviews a production of *King Lear* by the State Theatre of Northern Greece at Solonica on 7 March 1969. The translation in Greek was by Vassilis Rotas.

2043   Theater Review in *Rovnost,* 15 March 1969.

This article reviews a production of *King Lear* at the Mahen Theatre on 15 March 1969 at Brno, directed by A. Hajde. The text was adapted by L. Kundera from the translation by E. A. Saudek and O. F. Babler.

2044   Theater Review in *Sovetskaya Latvia* (Riga), 24 September 1969.

This article reviews a production of *King Lear* with the Kirgizian actor, M. Ryskulov, as King Lear.

2045   Theater Review in *Svobodní slovo,* 19 March 1969.

This article reviews a production of *King Lear* at the Mahen Theatre on 15 March 1969 at Brno, directed by A. Hajde. The text was adapted by L. Kundera from the translation by E. A. Saudek and O. F. Babler.

2046   Theater Review in *To Vima,* 20 August 1969.

This article reviews a production of *King Lear* by the State Theatre of Northern Greece at Salonica on 7 March 1969 and previews additional performances on 22-23 August 1969. The translation into Greek is by Vassilis Rotas.

2047   Tynan, Kenneth.   *On Stage and Screen.*   Moscow: Progress, 1969.

This volume, translated into Russian, includes an article on Kenneth Tynan's experiences with a production of *King Lear* at Stratford. An introduction by A. Anikst is also provided.

2048   Volfson, A.   "Once More About Classics."   *Teatralnaya Zhyzu,* No. 4 (1969), pp. 18-19.

This article reviews a production of *King Lear* in Russia by the Kalinin District Drama Theatre.

2049   Závodsky, A.   Theater Review in *Lidová demokracie,* 2 April 1969.

This article reviews a production of *King Lear* at the Mahen Theatre on 15 March 1969 at Brno, directed by A. Hajde. The text was adapted by L. Kundera from a translation by E. A. Saudek and O. F. Babler.

2050   Zidarow, Kamen.   "Moite sresci s Vladimir Trandafilov."   *Teatr* (Sofia), 22 (1969), 19-25.

This article discusses Vladimir Trandafilov's experiences in Shakespearean roles, especially those of Hamlet and King Lear.

2051   Copfermann, Emile. *"Le Roi Lear* au Théâtre des Amandiers-de Nanterre." *Les Lettres francaises,* 1970, p. 18.

This article reviews a production of *King Lear* at the Théâtre des Amandiers in Nanterre.

2052   Esslin, Martin.   *"The Alchemist* and *King Lear."*   *Plays and Players,* 17, No. 7 (1970), 43-45.

The production by the Nottingham Playhouse Company at the Old Vic, directed by Jonathan Miller, is not as revolutionary as Peter Brook's, but it is memorable because it is spare, concentrated, and pure. The acting is somewhat uneven, but Michael Hordern as Lear, Peter Eyre as Edgar, and Frank Middlemass as an old and disenchanted Fool are especially strong. The simple set, composed of shifting dark gauze screens, effectively concentrates the play upon the dominant theme of man's mortality and the insight that can spring from madness.

2053   Gromov, V. *Mikhail Chekhov.* Moscow: Iskusstvo, 1970.

A biography of the famous Russian actor, this volume features a discussion of Mikhail Chekhov's experiences in the role of King Lear (pp. 197-200).

2054   *A History of European Theater.* Vol. V: 1871-1918. Moscow: Iskusstov, 1970.

This volume includes a discussion of Max Reinhardt's Shakespearean productions and of the production of *King Lear* by the Meinsingen Company.

2055   Iden, Peter. *"König Lear."* *Theater heute,* 11 (1970), 8.

This article reviews a production of *King Lear* at the Städtische Bühnen in Frankfurt.

2056   Il'ina, L. *"King Lear."* *Leningradskaya pravda,* 25 December 1970.

This article reviews Grigori Kozintsev's film production of *King Lear.*

2057   Josif, Mira. "I. L. Caragiale: Regele Lear de Shakespeare."
        Teatrul (Bucharest), 15 (1970), 51-56.

        This article reviews a production of *King Lear* in the Caragiale
        Theater in Bucharest.

2058   *Krol Lear* w Zielonej Gorze." *Zycie literockie* (Krakow), 8
        (1970), 14.

        This article reviews a Polish production of *King Lear* in
        Zielona Gora.

2059   Lambert, J. W. "Plays in Performance." *Drama,* Summer, 1970,
        pp. 15-28.

        This article reviews a production of *King Lear* by the Notting-
        ham Playhouse at the National Theatre in London, directed by
        Jonathan Miller and featuring Michael Hordern in the title role.
        Hordern successfully played Lear as a man, permitting the divinity
        to come as it would. The king was hunched and grizzled, increasing-
        ly preoccupied with small physical irritations. His tragic stature, in
        such a presentation, was diminished not a whit. The smaller people
        squabbled over the steady wastage of spirit.

2060   Lemarchand, Jacques. "Le Roi Lear de Shakespeare." *Le Figaro
        Litteraire,* 1970, pp. 35-36.

        This article reviews a French production of *King Lear* at Nan-
        terre.

2060a Lipkov, A. "Tested by Fire." *The Screen: Annual Collection of
        Articles and Interviews.* Edited by S. Tchertok. Moscow:
        Iskusstvo, 1970, pp. 109-115.

        This article discusses the problems encountered in Grigori
        Kozintsev's shooting of his film version of *King Lear.*

2061   Lordkipanidze, N. "Scorched Earth of Tragedy." *Komsomol-
        skaya pravda,* 12 August 1970.

        This article summarizes Grigori Kozintsev's production notes
        and describes his experiences in shooting the film version of *King
        Lear.*

2062   Mihailovic, Dusan. "Prvi Beogradski." *Pozorisma kultura* (Belgrade), 1970, 69-70.

This article reviews a Yugoslavian production of *King Lear* at Belgrade.

2063   *Music for the Theatre: Shakespeare.* New York: Gugliatto-Black, 1970.

This monograph lists the music available in mono, stereo, score, or tape for productions of *King Lear* and nineteen other Shakespearean plays.

2064   Shorter, Eric. "Plays in Performance: Regions." *Drama,* Spring, 1970, pp. 27-31.

This production of *King Lear* by the Nottingham Playhouse with Michael Hordern as the king attempted to make something new of the tragedy. Directed by Jonathan Miller, it asked us to believe that Lear got what he deserved and that our lives are indeed solitary, poor, nasty, brutish, and short.

2065   Wroblewski, Andrzej. "Wladza, ktory staje sie czlowiekem." *Teatr* (Warsaw), 25 (1970), 12-13.

This article reviews a Polish production of *King Lear* in the Lubuski Theatre in Zielona Gora.

2066   Zorkaya, N. "Kozintsev Produces *King Lear*: A Report from Narva." *Iskusstvo kino,* No. 3 (1970), pp. 111-123.

Based on interviews with Grigori Kozintsev, this article describes the challenges and difficulties encountered in shooting the film production of *King Lear.*

2067   Abalkin, N. *Fond Memories.* Moscow: Molodaya Gvardia, 1971.

Included in this theater critic's reminiscences is a discussion of Peter Brook's production of *King Lear.*

2068   Anikst, Alexander. "Grigori Kozintsev's *King Lear.*" *Soviet Literature,* No. 6 (1971), pp. 177-182.

This analysis of Kozintsev's *King Lear* sees the film as a brilliantly humanistic description of tragedy resulting from social inequality.

2069   Bauman, H. "Encounter with Shakespeare." *Sovetskaya kultura,* 9 February 1971.

This article reviews Grigori Kozintsev's film production of *King Lear.*

2070   Billington, Michael. "The Uneasy Tradition." *The Illustrated London News,* September, 1971, pp. 54-55.

This article reviews Peter Brook's film production of *King Lear.* The best cinematic versions of Shakespeare are those that exploit the text of a play for its full potential on the screen. This film is such a production, although at times the action seems to get out of hand and lose focus when too many characters are on camera. Paul Scofield gives a superb performance as an unsentimentalized Lear. Other notable performances are Irene Worth's Goneril, Susan Engel's Regan, and Jack MacGowran's Fool.

2071   Blumer, Arnold. "Reibles Lear." *Theater heute,* 12 (1971), 53.

This article reviews a production of *King Lear* in Kapstadt.

2072   Bohme, Irene. "*König Lear* von William Shakespeare." *Sonntag,* 25 (1971), 10.

This article reviews a film version of *King Lear* with scenic design by F. Solter and music by Siegfried Matthus.

2073   Borisova, T. "The Tragedy of Lear." *Sovetskaya Belorussia,* 19 February 1971.

This article reviews Grigori Kozintsev's film production of *King Lear.*

2074   Breytenbach, Phillippa. Theater Review in *Lantern,* 21, No. 1 (1971), 66-69.

This article reviews a production of *King Lear* in South Africa, directed by Uyo Kriege.

2075   Claras, Babis. Theater Review in *Vradini*, 18 March 1971.

This article reviews a production of *King Lear* at the Popular Theater at Piraeus, directed by Manos Katrakis. The translation into Greek is by Vassilis Rotas.

2076   Crouch, J. H. "The Colorado Shakespeare Festival 1971." *Shakespeare Quarterly*, 22 (1971), 381-384.

The 1971 Colorado Festival production of Lear was a mistake of gigantic proportions. Director Robert Benedetti, engaging in numerous deviations from the text, succeeded only in staging a distorted and obnoxious version. Set on what appeared to be a toadstool supporting three priapic posts and peopled with hulking-sulking actors draped in maroon yardgoods, the tragedy muddled through three movements (with scenes freely rearranged)—Before the Storm, The Storm, The Awakening. Lear, Kent, Edgar, and the Fool writhed in orgiastic action through the storm scene, and the awakening was made Lear's reconciliation with Cordelia rather than Lear's confrontation with the blinded Gloucester.

2077   De Vos, Jozef. "Shakespeare in het moderne Zuidnederlandse theater." *Wetenschappelijke Tijdingen*, 30, No. 5, 1971.

This article reviews recent productions in Flanders of *King Lear* and seven other Shakespearean plays.

2078   Emigholz, Erich. "Behrs Bremer *Lear* (Theaterarbeit in Beispielen. 2. Beispiel)." *Theater heute*, 12, No. 12 (1971), 38-39. (not seen)

2079   Fabrizio, Claude. "Le roi Lear et la guerre revolutionnaire." *Les Lettres francaises*, 1971, pp. 13-14. (not seen)

2080   Finkel, Shimon. *Bimvoch Tafkidai.* Tel Aviv: Hinuch-ve-Tarbuth, 1971.

Shimon Finkel, the artistic director of the Habimah National Theater, describes his experiences in the role of King Lear and of other Shakespearean characters.

2081   Gilboa, J. A. Film Review in *Ma'ariv,* 2 July 1971, p. 28.

This article reviews Grigori Kozintsev's film production of *King Lear.*

2082   Gleiss, Jochen. "Shakespeare-Inszenierungen in Dessau, Erfurt, Eisleban und Planen." *Theater der Zeit,* 26 (1971), 24-28.

This article reviews a production of *King Lear* at Eisleban.

2083   "Die Grosse Lears." *Sowjetfilm,* 1971, pp. 7-10. (not seen)

2084   Hapgood, Robert. "Shakespeare in 'Seventy-five: A Review and Guide" by Heironimo Bosch (pseud.). *Satire Newsletter,* 8 (1971), 123-129.

This satirical forecast-review of the kinds of Shakespearean productions presented in 1975 describes, among other things, a screening of Peter Brook's *King Lear* in Sun City.

2085   Harris, Arthur John. "Garrick, Colman, and *King Lear.*" *Shakespeare Quarterly,* 22 (1971), 57-66.

George Colman, not David Garrick, was responsible for restoring significant portions of Shakespeare's text in the mid-eighteenth century.   Colman's restoration was both performed and printed in 1768.   Garrick's more extensive restoration did not appear until John Bell's edition in 1773, and he has been falsely credited with acting the revised text as early as 1756. Evidence suggests that rival actor Theophilus Cibber with his restorations prompted Garrick to retaliate in kind in 1743 but that Garrick's restorations at that time and in 1756 were not significant. Colman in 1768 deleted the love affair between Cordelia and Edgar while retaining Tate's happy ending; he also gave serious consideration to restoring the role of the Fool. Garrick's new text with Spranger Barry in the role did not appear until 1770, and Garrick himself did not act the revised text until 1773. "Colman's work, therefore, emerges as perhaps the most important single contribution towards the restoration of the original text between the time of Tate and the early nineteenth century" (p. 66).

2086   Heinz, Wolfgang. "Gedanken für eine Rolle: Überlegungen zu
       schauspielerischen Vorgangen fur den *König Lear.*" *Theater
       der Zeit,* 27, No. 2 (1971), 11-14.

The role of *King Lear* requires both forcefulness and weakness,
provoking sympathy and detestation. Aspects of Lear's situation are
peculiarly contemporary.

2087   *A History of the Soviet Dramatic Theater.* Vol. 6. Moscow:
       Nauka, 1971.

A production of *King Lear* at the Tadzhyk Theater is reviewed.

2088   Iden, Peter. "Theaterarbeit in Beispielen." *Theater heute,* 12
       (1971), 35-42. (not seen)

2089   Kalkani, Erini.   Theater Review in *Apoghevmatini,* 22 March
       1971.

This article reviews a production of *King Lear* at the Popular
Theater at Piraeus, directed by Manos Katrakis. The translation into
Greek is by Vassilis Rotas.

2090   Keisch, Henryk. "*König Lear* auf dem Bildschirm." *Weltbuhne,*
       1971, pp. 498-500.

This article reviews Peter Brook's film production of *King
Lear,* starring Paul Scofield.

2091   Kozintsev, Grigori. *Deep Screen.* Moscow: Iskusstvo, 1971.

Kozintsev reminisces about his lifetime as a theatrical producer. Specific attention is focused on his productions in the 1950's
in Leningrad of *King Lear, Hamlet,* and *Othello.*

2092   Kozintsev, Grigori. "*King Lear*—The World Premiere." *Lenin-
       gradskaya pravda,* 7 September 1971.

This article records the impressions of the Soviet producer to
the screening of his film version of *King Lear* at the first World
Shakespeare Congress in Vancouver, Canada, in August, 1971. See
item 2123.

2093   Lipkov, A. "The Final Judgment." *Akran Annual Collection of
        Articles and Interviews.* Edited by S. Tchertok. Moscow:
        Iskusstvo, 1971.

        This article discusses Grigori Kozintsev's film production of
King Lear.

2094   Malavetas, Dimitri. Film Review in *Vema* (Athens), 12 Septem-
        ber 1971.

        This article reviews the showing of Grigori Kozintsev's film
production of *King Lear* at the World Shakespeare Congress.

2095   Manvell, Roger. "The Russian Adaptations: Yutkevitch and
        Kozintsev" and "Peter Brook's Film of *King Lear.*" *Shake-
        speare and the Film.* New York: Praeger Publishers, 1971,
        pp. 72-85, 133-152.

        Kozintsev observes that, while *Hamlet* is monodrama, *Lear* is a
multiple tragedy of a civilization crumbling through the evils of inequality and injustice. Through his suffering Lear learns the true
nature of man and society. The music by Shostakovich is designed
to establish the atmosphere. Brook maintains that Shakespeare is
difficult to film because one loses the "free association of image and
thought which is the essence of Shakespeare's kaleidoscopic artistry"
(p. 134). His stylized film of *Lear* is based on his outstanding production at Stratford in 1962. Filmed in 1968-1969 on location in
North Jutland, Denmark, it is an absurdist view of life, a cold, bleak,
desolate assertion that life is ultimately without meaning and suffering is utterly without redemptive quality.

2096   Mennen, Richard E. "The Production of Theodore Komisar-
        jevsky at Stratford-Upon-Avon, 1932-1939." Ph.D. disserta-
        tion, Indiana University, 1971. *DAI,* 32 (1971), 1113A-
        1114A.

        Komisarjevsky's production of *King Lear* at Stratford, Eng-
land, in 1936 was the first symbolic interpretation seen in England. This production is analyzed through use of promptbooks,
photographs, and extensive newspaper accounts, supplemented by
correspondence and interviews with actors in the production.

Komisarjevsky's productions, from 1932 to 1939, are among the most controversial in the history of Shakespearean staging.

2097   Nightingale, Benedict. "Treated Like Meat." *New Statesman,* 82, No. 3 (1971), 310.

This article reviews a production of *King Lear* by the Prospect Theatre Company at the Assembly Hall in Edinburgh. Unfortunately, the acting is perfunctory, without enthusiasm, excitement, or conviction. "So studiedly lifeless is the evening that it must be deliberate: a fashionable exercise in alienation, perhaps?" But if so, it is at best inappropriate to the play. Timothy West's Lear lacks tragic size and depth.

2098   Ognyev, G. "The World Should Change, or Perish." *Komsomolskaya pravda,* 13 February 1971.

This article reviews Grigori Kozintsev's film production of *King Lear.*

2099   Raban, Jonathan. "Homicidal Farce." *New Statesman,* 82, No. 3 (1971), 157.

This article reviews Peter Brook's film production of *King Lear,* starring Paul Scofield. It "looks like an over exposed 8mm movie which has been smuggled out of a disaster area." The actors speak in shell-shocked tones, and Shakespeare's text is "Brooked up" to produce despair without human relief. The film is in the style of a newsreel, with abrupt and jagged shots. In a word, the film "confers on disaster the authenticity of incompetence."

2100   Raphailidis, Vassilis. Film Review in *Modern Cinema,* No. 16 (1971), pp. 23-24.

This article in Greek reviews Grigori Kozintsev's film production of *King Lear.*

2101   Rusu, Liviu. "Drepturile spirituale ale autorului." *Romania literară,* No. 11 (1971).

In this article entitled "The Spiritual Rights of an Author," Rusu denounces the tendency to modernize (and inevitably distort)

Shakespeare. A clear example of the distortion of the theme and spirit is the recent production of *King Lear* in Bucharest.

2102   Sharov, S. "*King Lear*, G. Kozintsev's Film." *Br'auskii rabochii*, 28 February 1971.

This article reviews Grigori Kozintsev's film production of *King Lear*.

2103   Solter, Friedo. "Wolfgang Heinz als König Lear." *Sonntag*, 21 (1971), 7.

This article features an interview with Wolfgang Heinz concerning his experiences in the role of Lear.

2104   Speaight, Robert. "Shakespeare in Britain" *Shakespeare Quarterly*, 22 (1971), 359-364.

The best cinematic translation of Shakespeare since Kozintsev's *Hamlet*, Peter Brook's film version of *Lear* is more moving and more artistically satisfying than his stage version some ten years before. The film—with its wind-swept, snowbound landscape and its castles little more than fortified homesteads—is able to give a geography to the play impossible on the stage. Paul Scofield's Lear is extraordinarily impressive; "his generally slow speech and impassive mien suggests a stupid obstinacy to which the loss of reason is a logical sequel" (p. 362). On the whole, the film focuses rigidly on a Kottian nihilistic interpretation (see item 348). A few modifications are unforgivable, however—the omission of Edmund's deathbed repentance, of the seizure of the incriminating letter from Oswald, of the rebellion of Cornwall's second servant against Gloucester's blinding, of Lear's "Pray you, undo this button." Nonetheless, it is a production that wins one's sympathies and admiration.

2105   Stephan, Erika. "Lass uns der Zeit gehorchen: Shakespeare-Dramen auf grosseu and kleinen Buchnen." *Sonntag*, 4 (1971), 9.

This article reviews a production of *King Lear* in Eisleben.

2106   Surkov, E. "Lear and Others." *Pravda*, 17 February 1971.

This article reviews Grigori Kozintsev's film production of *King Lear.*

2107 Tolchenova, N. "Thoughtful Film." *Ogon'ek,* No. 12 (1971), pp. 20-22.

This article reviews Grigori Kozintsev's film production of *King Lear.*

2108 Urnov, D. "The Pace of Time." *Iskusstvo kino,* No. 4 (1971), pp. 122-136.

This article reviews Grigori Kozintsev's film production of *King Lear.*

2109 Varikas, V. Theater Review in *Nea* (Athens), 22 March 1971.

This article reviews a production of *King Lear* at the Popular Theater at Piraeus, directed by Manos Katrakis. The translation into Greek is by Vassilis Rotas.

2110 Vasil'eva, N. "Dimitri Shostakovich—Cinema Artist. After Recording His Music to *King Lear.*" *Iskusstvo kino,* No. 2 (1971), pp. 128-139.

Dimitri Shostakovich is interviewed concerning his specific aims, general goals, and impressions of the degree of success in his recording of the music for Grigori Kozintsev's film production of *King Lear.* The recording took place in Leningrad in July, 1970.

2111 Yutkevitch, Sergei. "The Conscience of the King." *Sight and Sound,* 40 (1971), 192-196.

Grigori Kozintsev's film version of *King Lear* is a significant achievement in that it demonstrates beyond doubt that Shakespeare can effectively be transposed to film. The challenge is not to retain every line or scene but to use cinematic techniques to capture the dynamic spirit of the tragedy.

2112 Yutkevich, Sergei. "The Price of the Sword. On G. Kozintsev's Film *King Lear.*" *Iskusstvo kino,* No. 5 (1971), pp. 73-88.

This general discussion of Soviet cinema since 1920 focuses on the achievement of Grigori Kozintsev in his film production of *King Lear*.

2112a Zinkevich, E. "Notes for a Study of Shostakovich's Art. Interpretation of Shakespeare." *Sovetskaya muzyka*, No. 9 (1971), pp. 41-47.

This article discusses the musical score for Grigori Kozintsev's film production of *King Lear*.

2113 Andrews, Nigel. Film Review in *Sight and Sound*, 41 (1972), 171-172.

This article reviews Kozintsev's film version of *King Lear* based on Boris Pasternak's translation. Unlike Brook, Kozintsev focuses in the opening scene on the common people, not to isolate the political moment, but to emphasize the sociological themes of his *Lear*. He draws no moral lessons, but permits the stature of the characters to speak for itself. Larger than most conceptions of the tragedy, this version possesses a distinct symphonic quality. Kozintsev's harmonizing of the political and personal values is effected through his skillful alternation of close-up and panoramic shots. He has brought the play fully to life without any strenuous reshaping of the original.

2114 Armstrong, Marion. "Unbearable Masterpiece." *Christian Century*, 89 (1972), 673-674.

This article reviews Peter Brook's film version of *King Lear*. The film is horrible and brutal in its effect, enough for one's lifetime. There is too much battle and too little humanity.

2114a Esslin, Martin. "Un Profeta chi predice la castastrofe." *Sipario* (Milan), 308 (1972), 42-45. (not seen)

2115 Holloway, Ronald. Theater Review in *Plays and Players*, 19, No. 10 (1972), 70-71.

This article reviews Claus Peymann's production of *King Lear* in the Wuppertal Schauspielhaus. Peymann moves precariously between comedy and tragedy, an interpretation which was successful only because of Bernhard Minetti's superb talents in the title role. The conflict between good and evil was emphasized through Edgar's golden armor set against Edmund's black apparel. In the final analysis Minetti's was not a pitiable Lear but rather like "an ancient god walking sceptically and incredulously among his wayward children" (p. 17).

2116   Jackson, Berners W. "Shakespeare at Stratford, Ontario, 1972." *Shakespeare Quarterly,* 23 (1972), 388-394.

The production of *King Lear* at Stratford in 1972 was, without gimmicks or special pleadings, adventurous and even experimental. Director David Williams provided a straightforward reading of the text and a willingness to leave unperturbed the central mysteries with which the play concludes. There were flaws, to be sure— an overly earnest Edmund, a Wagnerian Cordelia, a prolonged battle scene, or overly bloody blinding, but William Hutt was genuinely notable as Lear, from the cantankerousness of the opening lines to the raging incoherence of the storm scenes and the quiet humility of the close. An impressive stage effect was an immense throne, as the play opened, occupied only by the Fool. The subplot was made an effective homiletic complement to the main story.

2117   Johnson, William. *"King Lear." Film Quarterly,* 25, No. 3 (1972), 41-48.

This article reviews Peter Brook's film version of *King Lear*, with Paul Scofield in the title role. The similarities between Brook's techniques and artistic aims are not unlike those of Roman Polanski in his film version of *Macbeth.* From the first Brook forces his action into unnatural shapes. By design no one in the movie can be mistaken for a hero. This, then, is obviously a special view of *King Lear,* the same as that behind his earlier stage production, both of them indebted to Jan Kott (see item 348). In the final analysis Brook's version is neither Shakespeare nor Kott, nor a film worth the effort.

2118   Kiknadze, V. "Unfinished Rehearsals." *Georgian Shakespeariana III.* Edited by Nico Kiasashvili. Tblisi: Xelovneba, 1972, pp. 191-203.

In this volume of essays published to coincide with the opening of the Shakespeare Seminar at Tbilisi State University, V. Kiknadze describes Sandro Akhmeteli's plans for future productions of *King Lear* and *Coriolanus*.

2119   Kopanev, P. *The Art of Translation: Historical and Theoretical Problems.* Minsk: Minsk University Press, 1972.

Kopanev briefly discusses A. Druzhynin's conception of *Lear*.

2120   Kozintsev, Grigori. "Ans der Arbeit am Film *König Lear.*" *Kunst and Literatur*, 20 (1972), 409-425.

This article discusses the challenges to translating *King Lear* from the stage to the film. The aim is to remain true to the text, but various technical features of film permit a director through modification to enhance effects and impact.

2121   Kozintsev, Grigori. "Der gedemütigte König." *Sonntag,* 14, No. 5 (1972), 7.

Kozintsev is interviewed concerning his production of *King Lear.*

2122   Kozintsev, Grigori. "*Hamlet* and *King Lear:* Stage and Film." *Shakespeare 1971.* Edited by Clifford Leech and J. M. R. Margeson. Toronto: University of Toronto Press, 1972, pp. 190-199.

Elizabethan drama was primarily aural, while cinema is essentially visual. The task of the Shakespearean film-maker is to transform the poetic texture into a visual poetry, "into the dynamic organisation of film imagery" (p. 191). The focal point of the opening scene, for example, might well be not a throne but a bench by the fire; his daughters approach him as the fire suggests the family hearth, the ancient glow of the patriarchal fire. Visually the upper and lower strata involved in Lear's experience can be delineated through his towering above other characters in the opening scene, yet kneeling to them later on the heath or in Cordelia's tent. Sound, too, is significant; the voice of human woe, not thunder, should resonate through the play. The cinematic techniques can destroy

Shakespeare's text if the visual becomes an end in itself; they can serve as a means of support and reinforcement if properly adapted to it.

2123   Kozintsev, Grigori M.   "Verfilmter Shakespeare: (Erfahrungen mit der Filminszenierung von *Hamlet* und *King Lear*)." *Shakespeare Jahrbuch* (Heidelberg), 108 (1972), 185-197.

Kozintsev describes his experiences with the film productions of *Hamlet* and *King Lear*. This is a translation into German of Kozintsev's address to the World Shakespeare Congress in Vancouver in 1971. See item 2092.

2124   Entry Deleted.

2125   Lambert, J. W.   "Plays in Performance." *Drama,* Autumn, 1972, pp. 14-30.

This article reviews the production of *King Lear* by the Prospect Company at the Aldwych Theatre in London, directed by Tony Richardson. Timothy West was adequate as Lear as a choleric, elderly old man, as was Ronnie Stevens as the Fool. The remaining members of the cast, however, were not up to their parts; and, with no scenery and only serviceable costumes, there was little else to make the production go.

2126   Lazzari, Arturo.   "*Re Lear* ha affascinato l'Europe." *Giorni,* 22 (1972), 68-69.

This article reviews a production of *King Lear* in the Piccolo Teatro, directed by Giorgio Strehler.

2127   "*Lear* in Wuppertal." *Volksbühnenspiegel,* 18 (1972), 36.

This article reviews productions of *King Lear* featuring Hans Schwab-Felisch and Dietmar N. Schmidt.

2128   Lordkipanidze, N.   "*King Lear.*" *Donatas Banionis.* Moscow: Iskusstvo, 1972, pp. 26-44.

This chapter discusses Banionis in the role of Albany in Kozintsev's film of *King Lear.*

2129   Mikhalovich, A. "Notes on Artists' Inner Maturity." *Iskusstvo kino,* No. 5 (1972), 77-88.

This article includes a variety of letters concerning Kozintsev's *Lear.*

2130   Nemeskürty, István. "A kortársunkká lett Shakespeare." *Filmkultura* (Budapest), No. 3 (1972), pp. 41-49.

Grigori Kozintsev's film version of *King Lear* reveals that Shakespeare is indeed our contemporary.

2131   "Production of *King Lear.*" *Theatre World* (1972-1973), p. 175.

The cast is recorded for a production by the National Shakespeare Company, directed by Philip Meister and featuring John Hostetter as Lear.

2132   "Notice of Production of *King Lear.*" *Theatre World* (1972-1973), p. 186.

The cast is recorded for a production by the Stratford Festival Company of Canada, directed by Jean Gascon. Pictures are by Robert C. Ragsdale.

2133   "Notice of Production of *King Lear.*" *Theatre World* (1972-1973), p. 187.

The cast is recorded for a production by the Theatre Venture '73 Company in Beverly, Massachusetts, directed by Edward Roll and featuring Jeff Corey as Lear. Pictures are by Peter Downs.

2134   Paneva, Lada. "Jaruk spektakul na malij Teatur." *Teatur* (Sofia), 25 (1972), 11-13. (not seen)

2135   Pollack, Daniel B. "Peter Brook: A Study of a Modern Elizabethan and His Search for New Theatrical Material." Ph.D. dissertation, New York University, 1972. *DAI,* 34 (1973), 447A.

This dissertation traces the development of Peter Brook as a theatrical producer. Among his more successful and more controversial productions was *King Lear,* starring Paul Scofield, in 1962 for the Royal Shakespeare Theatre. Taking his impetus from Jan Kott (see item 348), in the production he explored the techniques of Brecht and Beckett.

2136   "*Regele Lear* de Shakespeare." *Teatrul* (Bucharest), 17 (1972), 47.

This article reviews a production of *King Lear* at the Teatr Powszechny in Lodz.

2137   Rosenberg, Marvin. *The Masks of "King Lear."* Berkeley: University of California Press, 1972. 431 pp.

This study seeks an answer to the meaning of *King Lear* through the interpretations of actors, directors, and critics from England, America, France, Belgium, Japan, Sweden, Norway, Germany, Italy, Russia, Czechoslovakia, Romania, Hungary, Bulgaria, and Poland.   Sources include books, essays, periodical reports, memoirs, and acting versions. Additionally the author himself followed a production of *Lear* through two months of rehearsal. The play, with its multiple levels of communication to the senses and the intellect and subject to many styles, resists definition. It is not formless, however. "A firm artistic control makes of the ambiguities and paradoxes a system of reciprocating tensions" (p. 5). While the role of Lear, for instance, can be performed in various ways, the actor must move generally from the pains of civilization with its robed furs to the austere position in which he can voice compassion for "unaccommodated man."   Michael Redgrave describes the role as a constellation in the variety of emotions it requires; the Russian Lear Solomon Mikhoels drew his image from music. On his first entrance he can reflect divine majesty, arrogance, foolishness, or frailty. Cordelia, confronted with the love trial, can profess either speechless incredulity, shyness, or stubbornness; similarly her role can reflect Christ-like innocence or self-willed obstinacy. Lear's references to Cordelia's suitors might reflect pride in her marriageability, a father's teasing, or the darker purpose of possessiveness. The madness can be played on a scale ranging from stateliness to silliness. The final scene with Cordelia dead in Lear's arms is especially difficult. Booth played the moment with a sanity and power not approached before; Kean entered solemnly and with great effort. Gielgud used a sling to make his portage easier and to enhance the image of Lear's strength even in decline; Scofield's howl was all the more effective as a consequence of his granite-like character in earlier scenes; Redgrave acts too exhausted to stand; Salvini even dragged Cordelia heavily behind him. Words fail in this scene in any case; the visual imagery is all important. And so with the tragedy as a whole, Lamb notwithstanding, the kinesthetic qualities are of paramount significance. "They can only be known in performance: the mind's eye, imagining Lear's physical action, can never recreate the totality of the visual poetry that the eye's mind, in the theatre, experiences and organizes" (p. 345).

2138   Rostron, David.   "John Philip Kemble's *King Lear* of 1795." *Essays on the Eighteenth-Century Stage.* Edited by Kenneth Richards and Peter Thomson. London: Methuen, 1972, pp. 149-170.

The existence of the promptbook for John Philip Kemble's production of *Lear* on 20 November 1795 permits a relatively rare insight into the details of an eighteenth-century performance of Shakespeare.   Thirty-eight at the time and anxious to maintain the dominance of Drury Lane over Covent Garden, Kemble was also no doubt motivated to attempt to outdo Garrick in his most renowned role.   The version itself is heavily "Tatefied," far more so than Garrick's.   To Kemble's credit, nonetheless, the study copy reveals a meticulous attention to the details of staging—for example, Lear's hand on his sword restrained by Albany in his anger against Kent in the opening scene, Oswald's simpering cowardice followed by taunting gestures once Kent is in the stocks, the attempt of two "ruffians" (a revealing change in rehearsal from "officers" and "soldiers," indicated by strikeovers) to kill Cordelia and Lear. Kemble's role, emphasizing the age and dignity of Lear, was certainly not without flaw. He stressed too little the King's errors that initiated his cycle of suffering; at times he remained too intellectually aloof from the emotional demands of the moment, and his dry, asthmatic voice and generally poor health prevented his communicating the depths of Lear's passion. If his performance was generally inferior to Garrick's, however, Kemble was especially praised for two scenes—the curse on Goneril and the conversation with Tom o' Bedlam in the hovel.

2139   Sokol, I. *Ekran 1971-1972.* Edited by S. Tchertok. Moscow:
          Iskusstvo, 1972, pp. 65-67.

          This article describes Gritzus' work as cameraman for Kozint-
          sev's *King Lear* and *Hamlet.*

2140   Trewin, J. C. "The Tribe of Ben." *Illustrated London News.*
          August, 1972, p. 44.

          This article reviews the production of *King Lear* by the Pros-
          pect Company at the Aldwych Theatre in London, directed by Tony
          Richardson. Austerely presented, the play featured a "small-scale
          but precisely expressed" performance of Lear by Timothy West
          which was both touching and probing.

2141   Urnov, Dimitri Mihailowitsch. "Zu Grigori Kozinzews Film
          König Lear." *Shakespeare Jahrbuch* (Weimar), 108 (1972),
          175-182.

          Kozintsev presents history as a process of epochal waves, a
          cyclic repetition. This process is underscored by the fact that the
          characters in *Lear* act out contemporary situations in sixteenth-
          century dress.

2142   Zitzewitz, Monika. "Von *König Lear* im Piccolo Teatro." *Die
          deutsche Bünne,* 43 (1972), 16-17. (not seen)

2143   Adler, Doris Ray. "William Charles Macready's 1838 Production
          of *King Lear.*" Ph.D. dissertation, Howard University, 1973.
          DAI, 35 (1974), 391A.

          Macready's production of *King Lear* in 1838, frequently called
          the restoration of Shakespeare's text, is more accurately described
          as an adaptation that reflects Victorian tastes and theatrical conven-
          tions. Admittedly, Macready did reestablish a good bit of Shake-
          speare's text, including the role of the Fool, and he eliminated the
          love story of Edgar and Cordelia. Nevertheless, he omits almost half
          the original play, including Gloucester's blinding and attempted
          suicide; and he introduces a new character, Locrine, into the play.
          In effect, he adapted the play to the Victorian expectation of three
          hours, and he complied with the Victorian standards of piety,
          loyalty, and decency.

2144   Adling, Wilfried. "Historizität und Aktualität in Kosinzews Film *König Lear.*" *Shakespeare Jahrbuch* (Weimar), 109 (1973), 101-102.

Kozintsev stresses, in addition to Lear's domestic crisis, the political ramifications of his action—his relationship with the people and the agony and frustration that he visits upon the nation.

2145   Anosova, N. A. "King Lear on the Screen." *Trudy vesoyugnogo instituto kinematografii,* 6 (1973), 86-120.

This article in *Transactions of the Cinema Institute* describes Grigori Kozintsev's film version of *King Lear* and compares it with earlier film productions.

2146   Baumgart, Reinhard. "Ein deutsches stück?" *Theater heute,* 14 (1973), 25. (not seen)

2147   Braucourt, Guy. "Lear à deux voix." *Nouvelles Litteraires,* 11 March 1973, pp. 20-21.

This brief article compares the film versions of *King Lear* by Peter Brook and Grigori Kozintsev.

2148   Brine, Adrian. "Holland." *Plays and Players,* 20, No. 9 (1973), 61-62.

This article reviews a production of *King Lear* at the Amsterdam Municipal Theatre directed by Hans Croiset. Guus Hermus plays a starkly simple Lear, an interpretation bearing the marks of Peter Brook and Paul Scofield. Exact in every detail, the production nonetheless lacked the spark of enthusiastic magic which informs truly memorable theatrical evenings. In a sense it seemed that there was "more brain than rain" (p. 61).

2149   Červeňsk, Andrej. *"Korbov Lear.* Vypoved herca o tvorbe jednej postavy." *Slovenské divaldo* (Bratislava), 21 (1973), 518-533.

This article provides an actor's insights into the problems and challenges of creating the character of King Lear.

2150   Chaplin, William.   "Our Darker Purpose: Peter Brook's *King Lear.*" *Arion,* n.s. 1 (1973-1974), 168-187.

Peter Brook's refusal to shrink from the horror and cruelty of *King Lear* mocks, not Shakespeare's play, but naive and romanticized notions about it like Nahum Tate's determination to keep Cordelia alive or those who insist that the King experiences a fortunate fall in some sort of Christian atmosphere. In such scenes as Lear's yelling for dinner and overturning the tables in Goneril's home, the director effectively exploits the congruency between disruptive emotional and physical appetite. Similarly, the opening scene eliminates all courtly artifice in order to concentrate upon raw emotion for tonal effect, with the camera panning across a sea of expressionless faces with blank stares to Lear's totemic-like throne from which Paul Scofield in a dry, course voice pronounces the division of the Kingdom. Nor does Brook equivocate about Edgar; he, too, is degraded in his cruelty and in his filth. "Brook's refusal to exaggerate the play's hope and thus its civility and his firm control of emphasis on the amoral, life-obliterating rhythms in the play's deepest spirit become this film's most troubling and memorable achievement" (p. 181). He is effectively able to collapse the sense of contemporaneity and the archaic world, forcing us to live in two dimensions simultaneously and thereby revealing how one can recover the nerve and fidelity of a lost classic without its uniqueness "being sacrificed on the altar either of Literal Faith or Derangement" (p. 186).

2151   Coursen, Herbert R., Jr. "Shakespeare in Maine: 1972-1973." *Shakespeare Quarterly,* 24 (1973), 419-422.

Bowdoin College's Shakespeare Festival featured Ray Rutan's production of *King Lear.* The ambitious and largely successful production ran for only three performances, but it attracted gratifyingly large crowds. The Festival also featured eight recent films of Shakespearean plays.

2152   Fischer-Weimann, Waltrauld. "Der Film *König Lear*: Aufgaben und Probleme der deutschprachigan Synchronisation." *Shakespeare Jahrbuch* (Weimar), 109 (1973), 74-80.

This German film of *King Lear* is a combination of Shakespeare's text, Pasternak's translation into Russian, Baudissin's translation into German, and contemporary German usage.

2153   Horobotz, Lynn K. "Shakespeare at the Old Globe, 1973." *Shakespeare Quarterly*, 24 (1973), 441-443.

The 1973 production of *King Lear* at San Diego was plagued by nagging inconsistency or inattention to detail. The thunder in the storm scenes, for example, obliterated the voices. Lighting effects were obtrusive. Worst of all was the costuming, whether the worn prison uniform of Lear in Act V that would suggest years of incarceration or the decrepit underwear of Edgar that would embarrass even a Bedlamite. Ken Ruta was a quite adequate Lear, and the relatively straightforward production was impressive at times.

2154   Iutkevich, S. *Shakespeare and Cinema*. Moscow: Nauka, 1973.

This volume features a series of essays on twelve film versions of nine Shakespearean plays including "Price of the Sword," a discussion of Grigori Kozintsev's *King Lear*.

2155   Ivanji, Ivan. "Grosse Erfolge deutscher Truppen: Internationales Theaterfestival in Belgrad." *Die deutsche Bühne*, 44 (1973), 24-25. (not seen)

2156   Jäger, Gerd. Review Article in *Theater heute*, 14, No. 10 (1973), 57.

This article reviews a production of *König Lear* in Bremerhaven directed by Gregor Bals.

2157   Jorgens, Jack J. "The New York Shakespeare Festival 1973." *Shakespeare Quarterly*, 24 (1973), 423-427.

Edwin Sherin's production of *King Lear* in Central Park was only partially successful. James Earl Jones as Lear was a fussy, garrulous, crotchety old man, groaning, belching, and chuckling in turn. Mocked and weak, empty in his ravings, he was "a walking dead man" (p. 425) whose death brought a sense of great relief. The best performance was that of Rene Auberjonois as Edgar. "The cast as a whole suffered from flat, colloquial readings, thin voices, and a tendency to 'broadcast' over the loudspeaker rather than act" (p. 426). There were high moments indeed, for instance the duel between Edgar and Edmund, and the general emphasis on the sexual fascination between Edmund and the older daughters. At best, the play was free of Beckett-Kott overtones, but at worst it lacked universality.

2158   Kindermann, Heinz. "Joseph Kainz in seinen Shakespeare-Rollen." *Shakespeare Jahrbuch* (Heidelberg), 109 (1973), 62-77.

The noted German actor Joseph Kainz (1858-1910) was especially famous for his rendition of the Fool in *King Lear*, as well as for the roles of Romeo and Hamlet.

2159   *King Lear*. Dublin Gate Theatre. 4-Sp. Word A9. 1973 (recording).

2160   Kozintsev, Grigori M. "From Notebooks." *Neva*, No. 11 (1973), pp. 200-212.

This article in Russian features insightful comments from Grigori Kozintsev concerning Peter Brook's film version of *King Lear*.

2161   Kozintsev, Grigori. "Gedanken zum Film *König Lear.*" *Shakespeare Jahrbuch* (Weimar), 109 (1973), 56-61.

Lear's path to salvation involves his learning the lesson of humility. He must learn compassion for all men. The film stresses the conflict and agony prompted by a social division in which the masses are controlled and exploited by a ruler initially both indifferent and uncompassionate.

2162   Kozintsev, Grigori. "King Lear." *Problems of an Age—Problems of an Artist*. Edited by Y. Surkov et al. Moscow: Sovetskii pisatel, 1973, pp. 321-326.

Grigori Kozintsev discusses the challenge of realizing the full contemporaneity of *King Lear* while remaining faithful to Shakespeare's text.

2163   Kozintsev, Grigori. *The Space of Tragedy*. Leningrad: Iskusstvo, 1973.

Kozintsev describes his experiences in filming *King Lear* and the difficulties and challenges of translating stage drama into cinema. The Book originated as a series of articles in *Iskusstvo kino* (7-10 in 1971; 1, 4, 6, 8, in 1972; 1 in 1973). See item 2298.

2164   Kuckhoff, Armin-Gerd. "Shakespeare und die Schauspielkunst heute." *Shakespeare Jahrbuch* (Weimar), 109 (1973), 81-87.

The leading idea of Kozintsev's film is that society essentially determines the quality of life and action. The actors successfully convey this deterministic assumption.

2165   Lane, John Francis. "Milan." *Plays and Players*, 20, No. 7 (1973), 62-63.

This article reviews Giorgio Strehler's production of *King Lear* at the Piccolo Theatre in Milan. A convinced Brechtian, Strehler utilized Ezio Frigerio's abstract set of a circus ring filled with a synthetic rubber-like material through which the actors must wade. At the same time, Tino Carraro performed a rather traditional Lear, and the mixture was reasonably effective. Ottavio Piccolo doubled as the Fool and Cordelia, a bit of casting carried through in the similar affection the old king felt for both. The servants' protesting of Cornwall's attack upon Gloucester, omitted entirely by Peter Brook, was given due notice.

2166   Lazzari, Arturo. Theater Review in *Theater der Zeit*, 28, No. 4 (1973), 29-31.

This article reviews Giorgio Strehler's production of *King Lear* at the Piccolo Theatre in Milan.

2167   Leech, Michael. "Canada." *Plays and Players*, 20, No. 7 (1973), 58-59.

This article reviews a production of *King Lear* which the National Theatre of Canada took on tour in Europe, directed by David Williams and featuring William Hutt in the leading role. Hutt succeeds in making Lear a believably foolish old man. And he is

surrounded by a first-rate cast. Especially effective was Edward
Atienza's ashy-faced Fool as a Daumier-like prophet. "It is a memorable *Lear* by a fine and super-capable company" (p. 59).

2168   Melchinger, Siegfried.   Theater Review in *Theater heute*, 14,
        No. 1 (1973), 6-9.

This article reviews Giorgio Strehler's production of *King Lear*
at the Piccolo Theatre in Milan.

2169   Nemec, L.   Theater Review in *Lud* (Bratislava), 2 March 1973.

This article reviews the production of *Kral Lear* presented at
the Ukrajinske narodna divaldo at Presov, directed by I. Ivanco and
J. Sisak. The production was based upon M. Rylskij's translation.

2170   "Notice of Production of *King Lear.*"   *Theatre World* (1973-
        1974), p. 101.

The cast is recorded for a performance at the Brooklyn Academy of Music in New York, directed by David Williams and featuring
Robert Eddison as Lear.

2171   "Notice of Production of *King Lear.*"   *Theatre World* (1973-
        1974), p. 181.

The cast is recorded for a production by the National Shakespeare Festival in San Diego, directed by Craig Noel. Pictures are by
Christopher Darling.

2172   "Notice of Production of *King Lear.*"   *Theatre World* (1973-
        1974), p. 183.

The cast is recorded for a production by the New York Shakespeare Festival Company at the Delacorte Theater in Central Park,
directed by Edwin Sherin and featuring James Earl Jones as Lear.
Pictures are by Friedman-Abeles.

2173   "Other Shakespeare Festivals."   *Shakespeare Quarterly*, 24
        (1973), 453.

The Marin Shakespeare Festival at San Francisco produced *King Lear* along with *As You Like It.* This festival program is not reviewed, but its productions are recorded.

2174   Plieva, G.   *Vladimir Tkhapsayev in Three Shakespeare Roles.* Ordzhonikidze: Iskusstvo, 1973.

The prominent Osetian actor realized perhaps his best roles between 1940 and 1964 as Lear, Othello, and Macbeth.

2175   Reddington, John.   "Film, Play, and Idea."   *Literature/Film Quarterly,* 1 (1973), 367-371.

Peter Brook's film version of *King Lear* is a genuinely successful transformation of a stage play into a movie. Brook utilizes the technical opportunities of video without sacrificing the power and integrity of the dramatic text. Perhaps least successful is the lightning-flash cutting of the storm scene. His choice of location (North Jutland, Denmark) is an attempt to fulfill the language of the play. It is a landscape of the mind, a frigid winter twilight zone. The meeting of Lear and Gloucester is one of the finest accomplishments in any filmed version of Shakespeare. Brook faces life whole—the personal madness, lust, shame, anger, love, rejoicing, and resignation.

2176   Rischbieter, Henning.   *"König Lear* in Wuppertal."   *Theater heute,* 13, No. 5 (1973), 12-14.

This article reviews Claus Peymann's production of *King Lear* in the Wuppertal Schauspielhaus.

2177   Rubin, Don.   "Stratford's Cultural Export: To be (Canadian)   or Not to be."   *Performing Arts in Canada,* 10, No. 2 (1973), 12-15.

This article reviews productions of *King Lear* and *The Taming of the Shrew* which The National Theatre of Canada took on tour in Europe, directed by David Williams. The major question is whether a company calling itself national should not project something of the image of the nation and its people. Poland reacted coolly to *Lear* because it was not on the contemporary cutting edge. Russian audiences, on the other hand, where theater has become so realistic that it is simply dull, reacted enthusiastically.

2178   "Shakespeare für Verbraucher: *Hamlet* in Hildesheim und *Lear* in Bremerhaven." *Theater heute,* 14 (1973), 57. (not seen)

2179   Shvydkoy, M.   "The Ontario Stratford Theatre."   *Teatr,* 9 (1973), 87-92.

This article reviews the production of *King Lear* presented by the Ontario Shakespeare Theatre on a tour in Moscow.

2180   Sisak, M.   Theater Review in *Nove zitta,* 25 February 1973.

This article reviews the production of *Kral Lear* presented at the Ukrajinske narodne divaldo at Presov, directed by I. Ivanco and J. Sisak. The production was based upon M. Rylskij's translation.

2181   Speaight, Robert. *Shakespeare on the Stage.* Boston: Little, Brown, 1973. 304 pp.

Brief discussions are included of productions of *Lear* by Komisarjevsky and Brook and of performances by Phelps, Irving, Gielgud, Wolfit, Olivier, Redgrave, and Laughton.

2182   Stahmer, K.   "Elektronic im Würzburger Theater." *Melos,* 40 (1973), 240-242.

This review article discusses Bertold Hummel's stage music for the production of *King Lear* at the Städtischen Theater in Würzburg on 5 April 1973.

2183   "Strehler über *Lear.*" *Theater heute,* 14, No. 1 (1973), 10-13.

This article discusses Strehler's modifications of *King Lear* in the production at the Piccolo Theatre in Milan.

2184   Svydkoj, M.   "Stratfordskiij teatr iz Ontario." *Teatr,* 34, No. 9 (1973), 87-92.

Thie review article examines the production of *King Lear* at Stratford, Ontario.

2185   Theater Review in *Nove zitta* (Kosice), 18 February 1973.

This article reviews the production of *Kral Lear* presented at the Ukrajinske narodne divaldo at Presov, directed by I. Ivanco and J. Sisak. The production was based upon M. Rylskij's translation.

2186   Theater Review in *Pochoden,* 22 March 1973.

This article reviews the production of *Kral Lear* at the Vychodoceske divaldo at Pardubice, directed by J. Janik. The production was based upon E. A. Saudek's translation.

2187   Trilling, Ossia. "Letters from Scandinavia." *Drama,* No. 109 (1973), pp. 66-68.

This article reviews a production of *King Lear* (Finnish translation by Matti Rossi) in the Turku City Theatre, directed by Kalle Holmberg. Holmberg sees Lear as more the victim of circumstance than of a psychological flaw. The silent background of shadowy servants suggests a doomed and collapsing social structure. The production received tremendous plaudits and led to invitations to stage the play at the Stockholm City Theatre and at the Florence Theatre Festival.

2188   Weimann, Robert. "Lear und das Bild der 'armen nackten Elenden': Zum spezifischen Gehalt der filmischen Umsetzung von Shakespeare Tragödie." *Shakespeare Jahrbuch* (Weimar), 109 (1973), 62-73.

A group of desolate wretches representing the poor, exploited masses appear sporadically in Kozintsev's film both as a reminder of the social dimensions of the tragedy and also to signal particularly important moments in Lear's development.

2189   Whitmore, John. *"The Merchant of Venice, Two Gentlemen of Verona,* and *King Lear."* *Educational Theatre Journal,* 25 (1973), 509-510.

This article reviews a production of *King Lear* by the San Diego National Shakespeare Festival at the Old Globe Theatre in San Diego, California. The director, Edward Payson Call, conceived of *Lear* as a play of titanic excess, and the greatest moments were the scenes of violent conflict and tension. Ken Ruta as Lear managed the wide range from powerful wrath to whimpering childishness. The setting, costumes, and properties reminded one of medieval England and contributed to the brooding sense of a darkened world in which passions and cruelty have run wild.

2190   American Forces Radio and Television Recording of *King Lear.* RU 50-4, 3B. 1974. (recording)

2191   Brook, Peter. "Entre l'humain et l'epique." *Nouvelles Litteraires,* 11 March 1974, p. 20.

Peter Brook comments on his general artistic goals in his film version of *King Lear* and specifically on the textual and subtextual modifications necessary to achieve it.

2192   Canaris, Volker. "Die Moritat vom alten Mann Lear." *Theater heute,* 15 (1974), 6-9.

This review article examines the production of *King Lear* at the Union-Kino in Bochum.

2193   Ciarletta, Nicola. Theater Review in *L'Approdo Letterario,* 20, No. 66 (1974), 128-137.

This article examines the production of *King Lear* at the Quirino Theatre in Rome, directed by Giorgio Strehler.

2194   Elsom, John. "Actors' Carnival." *The Listener,* 91 (1974), 448-449.

This review article examines the production of *King Lear* by the Actors Company at the Wimbledon Theatre directed by David Williams. Robert Eddison was commanding as Lear, a totally narcissistic King. All things considered, however, it would appear that the excess of democracy weakened the performance; the very tendencies to permit the company to make significant decisions prevented the presence of a controlling vision.

2195   Gaydeburov, P. P. *Literary Remains. Reminiscences. Articles. Producers' Drafts. Speeches.* Moscow: All-Russian Theatrical Society, 1974.

This volume dedicated to the prominent actor-producer P. P. Gaydeburov (1877-1960) describes his experience in the role of Lear (pp. 383-390).

2196 Hughes, Catharine. "New York." *Plays and Players,* 21, No. 1 (1974), 68-69.

This article reviews Joseph Papp's production of *King Lear* at the New York Shakespeare Festival in Central Park, directed by Edwin Sherin. Neither particularly good nor particularly bad, it failed to live up to expectations. The leather costumes, non-period setting, and space-age music created a mood confusingly eclectic. James Earl Jones as Lear was interesting but hardly moving, and the remainder of the cast offered at best erratic support. Both Raul Julia as Edmund and Paul Sorvino as Gloucester were exceptionally bad, or at least badly miscast. Somewhat more effective were Douglass Watson as Kent and Tom Aldredge as the Fool.

2197 Hughes, Catharine. "New York." *Plays and Players,* 21, No. 7 (1974), 52-54.

This review article examines the production of *King Lear* by the Actors Company at the Brooklyn Academy of Music. The failure of the arts and costumes to arrive for opening night was only one of many problems. Robert Eddison's Lear was straightforward and clear-cut, but lacking in inspiration. Most effective in the mad scenes, he regrettably was never genuinely stirring. The dominant actor was Ian McKellan in the role of Edmund, at times—despite the virtuoso performance—to the detriment of the play.

2198 Kanters, Robert. "King Lear, Tsar Lear." *L'Express* (1974), p. 42.

This article compares the film versions of *King Lear* by Peter Brook and Grigori Kozintsev.

2199 *King Lear.* Notice of Production, 11 January 1974.

G. Nickolaidis' Greek production of *King Lear,* translated by Vassilis Rotas with scenes and costumes by H. Candrebiotou, was presented at the Mikso Theater on 11 January 1974.

2200   Kloc, Gjunter. "I edin konkreten primer." *Teatur* (Sofia), 27
        (1974), 64-66. (not seen)

2201   *"König Lear."* *Die deutsche Bühne,* 45 (1974), 29. (not seen)

2202   Kozintsev, Grigori. "Ainsi parlait Shakespeare." *Nouvelles
        Litteraires,* 11 March 1974, p. 21.

        Grigori Kozintsev comments on his filming of Shakespeare's
        King Lear.

2203   "Aus den Kritiken zu *Lear."* *Theater heute,* 15 (1974), 6.

        This article reviews Grigori Kozintsev's film version of *King
        Lear.*

2204   Lambert, J. W. "Plays in Performance." *Drama,* No. 115 (1974),
        pp. 41-61.

        This article examines the production of *King Lear* by the
        Royal Shakespeare Company at the Other Place, directed by Buzz
        Goodbody. This cut version removed the political maneuvering, and
        the result was a tense domestic drama. Both the setting and the cos-
        tuming were spare. Tony Church played Lear with a searing intellec-
        tual power; at the opening he was a slightly donnish, aging man,
        while at the end he was an individual in whom humanity had gushed
        too late. Sheila Allen's Goneril was especially effective, but the
        opposite was true of the cockney-Jewish Fool.

2205   Naydakova, V. *The Buryat Soviet Dramatic Theater.* Ulan-Ude:
        Bryant Publishing House, 1974.

        Recent Russian productions of *King Lear* are discussed on pp.
        128-130, 210-212.

2206   *Nederlands Theater-en Televisie Jaarboek.* No. 22, Seizon 1972-
        1973. Amsterdam: Doneto, 1974.

        This 180-page review of the season's stage, television, opera,
        and ballet presentations includes two productions of *King Lear,* along
        with *The Taming of the Shrew* and *Hamlet.*

2207   Nightingale, Benedict.   "The Bard of Barton."   *New Statesman,*
       87 (1974), 456-457.

       The Actors Company production of *King Lear* at Wimbledon
was a disappointment.   Generally the actors were not up to the
challenge of the roles; and, without adequate increases in dramatic
tension, the pace seemed slow and relatively unexciting.   Robert
Eddison, as a gentle, doddery, querulous king, does have a powerful moment, however, as he holds the dead Cordelia in his arms.

2208   Nightingale, Benedict.   "Wet Wallows."   *New Statesman,* 88
       (1974), 628-629.

       This article reviews a production of *King Lear* at the Other
Place.   Tony Church in the lead role is especially effective in the
reconciliation scene with Cordelia.   A resentful, tyrannical Lear, he
realizes with growing amazement that other people deserve and need
pity; and he is transformed in the process.   Buzz Goodbody as director has severely cut the text, omitting France, Burgundy, Oswald,
Albany, and even Cornwall.   As a consequence, Regan is left to blind
Gloucester with her broach.   What the play loses in grandeur, it gains
in intimacy.   The effect is one of private, domestic grief rather than
of political dislocation.   All told, the production was well suited for
the small black square of the Other Place.

2209   "Notice of Production of *King Lear.*"   *Theatre World* (1974-
       1975), p. 176.

       The cast is recorded for a production by the Great Lakes
Shakespeare Festival Company in Lakewood, Ohio.   Pictures are by
James Fry.

2210   "Notice of Production of *King Lear.*"   *Theatre World* (1974-
       1975), p. 202.

       The cast is recorded for a production by the Guthrie Theatre
Company in Minneapolis–St. Paul.

2211   Rischbeiter, Henning.   "'Mich interessiert des Erzählen von
       Geschichten': Gespräch mit Peter Zadak über die Arbeit am

König Lear, über eine neue Arbeitsweise des Regisseurs, über des Verhältnis des *Lear* Zu Zadaks 'Möwe'—Inszenierung." *Theater heute,* 15 (Supplement) (1974), pp. 48-51.

This review article examines the production of *King Lear* at the Union-Kino in Bochum.

2212   Rosenberg, Marvin. "Characterizations of *King Lear.*" *Shakespeare Jahrbuch* (Heidelberg), 110 (1974), 34-47.

The role of Lear is subject to fundamentally different interpretations as illustrated by Tomasso Salvini's titanic but kind Lear, Paul Scofield's arrogant and powerful king, Ludwig Devriant's slightly demented old man, and William Macready's grieved, gentle father.

2213   Simon, John. "Theatre-Chronicle." *Hudson Review,* 27 (1974), 259-266.

This review article examines the production of *King Lear* by the Actors Company at the Brooklyn Academy of Music, directed by David Williams. The performance was "a pure disaster"; even the ship bearing the sets and costumes did not arrive until after opening night. Williams contributed no directorial guidance, except to make the relationships as sexy and sadistic as possible. Robert Eddison played Lear as a "thin-voiced specimen of human pride" more on the brink of whining than of tragic greatness. If this *Lear* had any hallmark, it was the reduction to a demotic level.

2214   Tanyuk, L. S. *Marayan Krushelnitsky.* Moscow: Isskusstvo, 1974.

This biography in Russian of the well-known Ukrainian actor and producer Maryan Krushelnitsky features a discussion of his role of Lear in 1959 at the Acad. Ukr. Franko Theater.

2215   Entry Deleted.

2216   Wilson, M. Glen. "Charles Kean: Tragedian in Transition." *Quarterly Journal of Speech,* 60 (1974), 45-57.

Charles Kean, son of Edmund Kean, was the most popular provincial actor in England in the first half of the nineteenth century. His role of Lear, along with that of Hamlet, was his most famous.

2217   "Zeit für Klassiker? überlagungen aus Anlass der beiden wichtigsten Theater—ereignisse der Spielzeit 73/74: 'Antiken projekt' bei der Schaubuhne, *König Lear* in Bochum." *Theater heute,* 15 (Supplement) (1974), 30-35, 44-47.

This review article examines the production of *King Lear* at the Union-Kino in Bochum.

2218   Cohn, Ruby. "The Triple Action Theatre Group." *Educational Theatre Journal,* 27 (1975), 56-62.

The Triple Action Theatre Group, founded in 1966 by Steve Rumselow, is an experimental troupe combining dramatic text with physical configuration to produce "a dynamic exploration of three spatial dimensions—triple action" (p. 56). The production of *King Lear* in 1973, called *Leir Blindi* (Icelandic for "blind clay"), was essentially absurdist. Actors all issued from a set that resembled a gigantic white beard. From darkness are born, amid rhythmic, panting sounds, both Lear and Gloucester on a totally bare stage. The storm scene is created by four actors tossing a sackcloth to suggest wind while others toss lighted matches across the stage. Gloucester's leap from the Cliffs of Dover is depicted in slow motion. Following their deaths both Lear and Gloucester step forward momentarily, suggesting a resurrection motif, but then they recede into darkness. Then, amid sounds again of rhythmic panting, two more characters are born (Kent and Edgar), suggesting that the whole cycle of man's life with its suffering, blind actions and momentary joys will be played out once more.

2219   Cook, Page. "The Sound Track." *Films in Review,* 16 (1975), 235-239.

This article reviews the score by Hart for the documentary *Portrait in Immortality.* Brief discussion is included on the scoring of scenes devoted to Edmund Kean in scenes from *King Lear, Othello,* and *Macbeth.*

2220   F-a.   Theater Review in *Hlas Ludu* (Bratislava), 5 November
       1975.

   This article reviews a production of *Kral Lear* at the Slovak
National Theatre in Bratislava in 1975, directed by P. Haspra. The
text was translated into Slovak by Jozef Kot.

2221   Gilliatt, Penelope. "The Current Cinema: Take Physic, Pomp."
       New Yorker, 11 August 1975, pp. 42-46.

   This article reviews Kozintsev's film of *King Lear* based on
Boris Pasternak's translation. This tragedy is related to the rest of
the Shakespeare canon. Particular comments are included on the
work of Jarvet and Dol, two members of the cast. Comparisons are
drawn with Kozintsev's earlier film of *Hamlet*, with the Lear story
as developed in Shakespeare's sources (Holinshed, Higgins, *Leir*),
and with *Timon of Athens.* The score of Shostakovich also is
discussed.

2222   Grebanier, Bernard. *Then Came Each Actor.* New York: David
       McKay, 1975. 626 pp.

   This volume contains brief descriptions of performances of
Lear by Garrick, Edmund Kean, Macready, Forrest, Edwin Booth,
Phelps, Rossi, McCullough, Mantell, Milton, Gielgud, Laughton,
Carnovsky, Wolfit, Olivier, Redgrave, and James Earl Jones. Various
productions are discussed in further detail. Accounts are also included of a silent film version in 1916 and of Peter Brook's version
in 1971 with Paul Scofield.

2223   Heilman, Robert B. *The Hero's Self-Understanding in "Othello,"*
       "Lear," and "Macbeth." New York: Jeffrey Norton Pubs.,
       1975.

   This thirty-three-minute cassette (No. 23091) recorded in
1965 examines the movement through adversity to anagnorisis in
three of Shakespeare's major tragic heroes.

2224   Hrabovská, K.   Theater Review in *Nové Slovo* (Bratislava), 13
       November, 1975.

This article reviews a production of *Kral Lear* at the Slovak National Theater in Bratislava in 1975, directed by P. Haspra. The text was translated into Slovak by Jozef Kot.

2225   I., R.   Theater Review in *Práca* (Bratislava), 28 October 1975.

This article reviews a production of *Kral Lear* at the Slovak National Theater in Bratislava in 1975, directed by P. Haspra. The text was translated into Slovak by Jozef Kot.

2226   Kamenistý, J.   Theater Review in *Sinena na Nedeln*, 9 December 1975.

This article reviews a production of *Kral Lear* at the Slovak National Theater in Bratislava in 1975, directed by P. Haspra. The text was translated into Slovak by Jozef Kot.

2227   Kauffmann, Stanley.   "Stanley Kauffmann on Film: Kings and Dancekings." *New Republic*, 6 September 1975, p. 20.

This article describes the difficulties of producing Shakespeare on film. Brief attention is given to the attempts by Forbes-Robertson, Olivier, and others to film *Hamlet, Romeo and Juliet, Henry V, Macbeth,* and *King Lear;* and special emphasis is upon Kozintsev's *Lear.*

2228   *King Lear.*   Notice of Production, 4 July 1975.

Yukio Ninagawa's Japanese production of *King Lear*, translated by Yushi Odajima, was performed at the Nissei Theater from 4 July to 28 July 1975.

2229   Lipsius, Frank.   "Rescuing the Classical Repertoire from Oblivion." *New Hungarian Review*, 16 (1975), 196-200.

This article reviews productions of *King Lear* and *Othello* in Budapest.

2230   Marder, Louis.   "4th Annual Southwork Summer Festival." *Shakespeare Newsletter*, 25 (1975), 29.

The performance of "This Wooden O" by the Bankside Globe Players contains excerpts from *King Lear* with the happy ending provided by Nahum Tate. Directed by Douglas Cleverdon, it was intended to raise money for the construction of a new theater by touring the U.S.A. The role of Lear was ably played by Ron Moody.

2231   *Nederlands Theater—en Televisie Jaarboek: Toneel, Televisie-drama, Opera, Ballet.* No. 23, Seizon 1973/1974. Amsterdam: Doneto, 1975.

This article reviews theater productions of the 1973-1974 season, including *King Lear,* Ionesco's *Macbeth,* Verdi's *Falstaff,* and two stagings of *A Midsummer Night's Dream.*

2232   "Notice of Production of *King Lear.*"   *Theatre World* (1975-1976), p. 174.

The cast is recorded for a production by the American Shakespeare Theatre in Stratford, Connecticut, directed by Anthony Page. Pictures are by Martha Swope.

2233   "Notice of Production of *King Lear.*"   *Theatre World* (1975-1976), p. 183.

The cast is recorded for a production by the Shakespeare Theatre of Maine in Monmouth, Maine, directed by Earl McCarroll. Pictures are by Harry Marshall.

2234   "Notice of Production of *King Lear.*"   *Theatre World* (1975-1976), p. 191.

The cast is recorded for a production by the Asolo State Theatre in Sarasota, Florida, directed by Robert Strane. Pictures are by Gary Sweetman.

2235   "Notice of Production of *King Lear.*"   *Theatre World* (1975-1976), p. 216.

The cast is recorded for a production by the Milwaukee Repertory Theatre, directed by Nagle Jackson. Pictures are by Sorgel-Lee-Riordan.

2236   Oliver, Edith. "The Theatre: Off Broadway." *New Yorker,*
       10 March 1975, pp. 64-65.

This article reviews the production of *King Lear* by the Royal
Shakespeare Company at the Brooklyn Academy of Music, directed
by Buzz Goodbody. Particular attention is directed to performances
by Gwilym and Jameson. The text was considerably shortened, and
several significant characters were excluded. In fact, the play is
better described as gutted than cut. The director explains in a program note that the shortening was necessary to reduce the play for
performance in a school auditorium and to make it acceptable to
sixteen year olds.

2237   Perrin, Michel. "Les Prologues et épilogues de David Garrick."
       Tradition et innovation: Littérature et paralittérature. So-
       ciete des Anglicistes de l'Enseignement Supérieur. Actes du
       Congrès de Nancy (1972). Paris: Didier, 1975, pp. 141-158.

David Garrick's prologues and epilogues to four Shakespearean
plays, including *King Lear,* effectively embellished the performances.

2238   Popkin, Henry. "Theatre." *Nation,* 221 (1975), 189-190.

Peter Brook's earlier production of *King Lear* is discussed
sporadically in this review of his production of *Timon of Athens.*
Brook's settings and staging are discussed in some detail. His attempt was to "translate" *Lear* into plain, unpoetic, contemporary
basic English. "Brook is making a relevant contemporary comment.
The disillusionment of Timon, the degradation of the Iks—that is
where the depression is leading us. Help, somebody!" (p. 190).

2239   Rosenbergová, A.   Theater Review in *Lud* (Bratislava), 31
       October 1975.

This article reviews a production of *Kral Lear* at the Slovak
National Theater in Bratislava in 1975, directed by P. Haspra. The
text was translated into Slovak by Jozef Kot.

2240   Salgādo, Gāmini. *"King Lear." Eyewitnesses of Shakespeare:
       First Hand Accounts of Performances 1590-1890.* New York:
       Barnes and Noble, 1975, pp. 275-292.

From 1681 Tate's version of *Lear* held the stage until 1838, when Macready restored the Fool and most of Shakespeare's play; not until 1845 did Phelps present the play without cuts or rearrangement. Garrick first played Lear in 1756, using a modified version of Tate. Thomas Davies in *Dramatic Miscellanies* reports that he was especially effective in the storm scene and in his moment of reconciliation with Cordelia; he was remarkable in his ability to move from scenes of high passion to those of quiet serenity. When Garrick and his rival Spranger Barry were appearing simultaneously as Lear at Drury Lane and Covent Garden, Theophilus Cibber awards the prize to Barry while Charles Churchill prefers Garrick. James Boaden reports that John Kemble as Lear in 1788 was exquisite, approaching the quality of Michaelangelo in the awesomeness of his delineation. The *Times* wrote of Kean in 1820 that his Lear revealed manifestations of his genius; most masterly was the moment of reconciliation with Cordelia. Dickens praises Macready for restoring the Fool, noting that the Fool's presence allowed Lear to achieve greater effects in his mad scenes. Kean is again praised, this time especially for his Anglo-Saxon setting, by the *Illustrated London News* in 1858. Of Phelps' Lear Henry Morley observes that the king was too infirm to suggest royalty and authority; even so the final moments of the tragedy were signally touching.

2241   Simon, John. *Exploration of Evil: "Dr. Faustus," "King Lear," "The Changeling."* New York: Jeffrey Norton Pubs., 1975.

This fifty-nine-minute cassette (No. 23094) recorded in 1970 examines the nature of the tragic flaw in Faustus, Lear, and Beatrice-Joanna and the forces of evil and temptation in their stage worlds which give rise to tragedy.

2242   Stoklaska, Juliana. "Oskar Strauds Entwürfe zur *König Lear*– Inszenierung Max Reinhardts." *Maske und Kothurn*, 21 (1975), 46-52.

This article discusses Oskar Straud's designs for Max Reinhardt's production of *King Lear*.

2243   Theater Review in *Svobodné Slovo* (Prague), 24 April 1975.

This article reviews a production of *Král Lear* at the West Bohemian Theater in Cheb in 1975, directed by J. Grossman. The text was translated into Czech by M. Lukeš.

2244 Weisinger, Herbert. *The Myth and Ritual Approach to Shakespearean Tragedy*. New York: Jeffrey Norton Pubs., 1975.

This fifty-five-minute cassette (No. 23093) recorded in 1969 describes the patterns of thought and feeling underlying Shakespeare's tragedies. *King Lear* fails as Christian tragedy through the King's regression in Act V into confusion, chaos, and death.

2245 Zavadsky, Iu. *Masters and Disciples*. Moscow: Iskusstvo, 1975.

The reminiscences of a prominent theatrical producer include a discussion (pp. 277, 325-326) of a performance of *King Lear* at the Mossoviet Theatre.

2246 Antokolsky, Pavel G. "G. Kozintsev's *King Lear.*" *Writer's Travelogue*. Moscow: Sovetskii Pisatel, 1976, pp. 283-288.

This article discusses Kozintsev's film production of *King Lear*. Kozintsev's *Lear* in no way mitigates the agony and suffering of the king's experience, but it never loses faith in the value and potential of humanity.

2247 Bejblík, A. Theater Review in *Lidova demokracie* (Prague), 6 January 1976.

This article reviews P. Haspra's production of *Kral Lear*, translated into Slovak by Jozef Kot, at the Slovak National Theatre in Bratislava in 1975.

2248 Condee, Ralph Waterbury. "Goneril Without a White Beard." *Shakespeare Film Newsletter*, 1, No. 1 (1976), 1, 5, 7.

Peter Brook's film version of *King Lear*, starring Paul Scofield, is among nine films discussed as a teaching aid for undergraduate courses in Shakespeare.

2249 Coursen, H. R., Jr. "The Theatre at Monmouth: Summer 1975." *Shakespeare Quarterly*, 27 (1976), 33-37.

The performance of *King Lear* was remarkable both for the use of the subplot to comment on the main plot and for depicting the theme of the confusion of authority. John Fields was an adequate Lear but unfortunately at times tended toward an articulate roar. His final line, "Look there," was expressed effectively staring into space at death, and the Fool was brought in dead with a noose around his neck. The evening's finest performance was Robert Johnson's Fool, with makeup suggesting both the comic and the tragic and action suggesting both total devotion to Lear and also full awareness of his folly.

2250 Cwojdrak, Günther. "Leiden mit *Lear.*" *Die Weltbühne,* 71 (1976), 453-455.

This article discusses the scenic design and background music for a German production of *King Lear.*

2250a Földes, A. "*Lear* király es a csogosipkások." *Nagyvilak* (Budapest), 21 (1976), 1408-1411.

This article, entitled "*King Lear* and the Clowns," reviews a highly controversial production of *King Lear* by the Theatre Twenty-Five in Budapest.

2250b Galey, Matthieu. "Le Roi Lear." *Les Nouvelles Litteraires,* 54 (1976), 29.

This article reviews a production of *King Lear* in Saint Etienne.

2250c Haims, Lynn. "First American Theatre Contracts: Wall and Lindsay's Maryland Company of Comedians and the Annapolis, Fell's Point, and Baltimore Theatres, 1781-1783." *Theatre Survey,* 17 (1976), 179-194.

This article cites records of early performances of *King Lear* and six other Shakespearean plays. The information is drawn from the earliest known theater contracts in America, "Articles to be Strictly observed by the Managers and Performers belonging to the Maryland Company of Comedians" and "Rules to be Observed in the Baltimore Theatre, respecting Benefits." New plays were introduced at benefits to help expand the repertory in America. The first reference to *King Lear* is 17 May 1782 at Mr. Heard's Benefit.

2251   Hapgood, Robert. "The Choreography of *King Lear*: Patterns of Relationship and Isolation in Two Recent Productions in the United States." *Shakespeare Jahrbuch* (Heidelberg), 112 (1976), 115-127.

The major theme of relation and isolation in *King Lear* is bodied out in its choreography or its sequences of physical and metaphysical action. All characters are on stage together in the first scene, for example, but by the end of the scene the social nucleus is broken. The splintering continues until Lear and Gloucester are isolated. Regrouping occurs around Edmund and the group moving toward Dover. At the end the entire group is reassembled with many of them dead. Consider further the wandering Lear followed by the groping Gloucester, the numerous acts and gestures of hate and love, and a rising-falling pattern. These patterns are examined in light of current productions in Monmouth, Maine, and in Stratford, Connecticut.

2252   Kamenisty, J. Theater Review in *Smena na Nedeln,* 9 January 1976.

This article reviews P. Haspra's production of *Kral Lear,* translated into Slovak by Jozef Kot, at the Slovak National Theatre in Bratislava in 1975.

2253   Kennedy, Dennis. "*King Lear* and the Theatre." *Educational Theatre Journal,* 28 (1976), 35-44.

The various revisions of *King Lear,* especially that of Nahum Tate in 1681 (see item 2494), became fair game for the critics' attacks. Not so readily observed is the fact that Shakespeare himself completely revised his own source. His received original was specifically designed for festive comedy. In passing judgment upon any production of the tragedy and whatever liberties it might take with Shakespeare's text, the critic should bear in mind the difficulties involved in a theatrical visualization of the imagination.

2254   Kerndl, Rainer. "Die Trägodie einer späten Erkenntnis: Shake-speare's *König Lear* am deutschen Theater." *Neues Deutschland*, 10-11 (1976), 4. (not seen)

2255   Klatt, Gudrun. "Vom Umgang mit dem Erbe: Zu Friedo Solters Klassiker-In-szenierungen." *Theater der Zeit*, 31, No. 7 (1976), 8-9.

This article reviews recent productions of *King Lear* and *The Tempest*.

2256   "The Long-Awaited Russian *Lear.*" *Soveskii ekran* (Moscow), 3 (1976), 19.

Grigori Kozintsev's film production of *King Lear* establishes tonal and thematic standards which will challenge film makers for generations to come.

2257   Moore, Edward M. "Henry Irving's Shakespearean Productions." *Theatre Survey*, 17 (1976), 195-216.

This highly critical discussion of Henry Irving as an actor and producer of Shakespeare focuses primarily on productions of *Hamlet, The Merchant of Venice,* and *Romeo and Juliet.* Brief attention, however, is devoted to his production of *King Lear* and six other plays.

2258   Müller, Christopher. "*Lear* in deutschen Theater." *Theater heute*, 17, No. 8 (1976), 56-57.

This article reviews recent productions of *King Lear* in Germany.

2259   Nightingale, Benedict. "Howl." *New Statesman*, 3 December 1976, pp. 815-816.

Any doubts concerning Donald Sinden's capabilities as Lear are quickly dispelled in the fresh horror that he evokes from the part. His Lear is an old, undisciplined child consumed by dread and desire. The effectiveness of the role comes through the gradual draining away of egotism; "Sinden chronicles the process by which suffering turns into self-pity and self-love into outward versions of themselves" (p. 815). Especially noteworthy under the direction of Trevor Nunn, John Barton, and Barry Kyle are Barbara Leigh-Hunt as Goneril and Judy Dench as Regan. The emotional power is concentrated in Lear, especially in Sinden's animalistic grunts, especially in the howls of his final entrance. It takes a real actor to make you "shut your eyes and look away for fear of intruding on a grief too awful and intimate to share" (p. 816).

2260   "Notice of Production of *King Lear.*" *Theatre World* (1976-1977), p. 170.

      The cast is recorded for a production by the Alabama Shakespeare Festival in Anniston, Alabama, directed by Martin L. Platt. Pictures are also by Platt.

2261   "Notice of Production by *King Lear.*" *Theatre World* (1976-1977), p. 170.

      The cast is recorded for a production by the Champlain Shakespeare Festival in Burlington, Vermont, directed by Edward J. Fiedner. Pictures are by Charles Trottier.

2262   "Notice of Production of *King Lear.*" *Theatre World* (1976-1977), p. 172.

      The cast is recorded for a production by the Globe Playhouse at Los Angeles, directed by George Coulouris. Pictures are by Mitchell Rose.

2263   "Notice of Production of *King Lear.*" *Theatre World* (1976-1977), p. 176.

      The cast is recorded for a production by the Oregon Shakespeare Festival Company at Ashland, Oregon, directed by Jerry Turner and featuring Denis Arndt in the title role. Pictures are by Hank Kranzler.

2264   "Notice of Production of *King Lear.*" *Theatre World* (1976-1977), p. 223.

      The cast is recorded for a performance by the Trinity Square Repertory Company at Providence, Rhode Island, directed by

Adrian Hall and featuring Richard Kneeland as Lear. Pictures are by William L. Smith.

2265   Pedicord, Harry William.   "Garrick as Adapter-Champion of Shakespeare: Some Problems in Editing the Adaptation." *Shakespeare Newsletter*, 26 (1976), 24.

It is difficult to edit Garrick's adaptations of Shakespeare's plays because in many instances he adapted, altered, and abridged them more than once. He engaged in such modifications for fifteen of Shakespeare's plays, including *King Lear*. His importance as a champion and popularizer of Shakespeare cannot be exaggerated. This is an abstract of a paper delivered in March, 1976, at a meeting of the Shakespeare and Renaissance Association of West Virginia.

2266   Plyeva, G. Kh.   *Heroical and Romantic Ideals on the Ossetinian Stage.* Ordzhonikidze: Iskusstvo, 1976.

A part of the chapter entitled "Shakespeare's Interpretation on the Ossetinian Stage" is concerned with the actor Tkhapsayev and his interpretations of various roles, including that of King Lear (pp. 64-77).

2267   Saccio, Peter.   "The 1975 Season at Stratford, Connecticut." *Shakespeare Quarterly*, 27 (1976), 47-51.

The primitive-setting, Druidical *Lear* with Morris Carnovsky was a disaster. The characters, "heavy with bearskins, robes, capes, and furred gowns" (p. 47), started well, and Carnovsky's initial entry combined measure and authority. But the production fell apart almost immediately, dragging on for three "mortal" hours with incredibly frequent pauses. Even the final moments with Lear over Cordelia produced titters, so bored and uneasy were the spectators. One bright glimpse was Jane White's Goneril, who moved clearly from the controlled greed of Act I to the savage sadism of Act III and the raging frustration of Act V.

2268   Schumaker, Ernst.   "Bewährung vor der Tradition: zur Neuinszenierung von *König Lear* am deutschen Theater." *Berliner Zeitung*, 6 (1976), 6. (not seen)

2269   Seyfarth, Ingrid. "Vom Gebrauch der Macht." *Theater der Zeit,*
       31, No. 7 (1976), 6-9.

       This article reviews a production of *King Lear* in Berlin.

2270   Shattuck, Charles H. *Shakespeare on the American Stage: From
       the Hallams to Edwin Booth.* Washington, D. C.: Folger
       Shakespeare Library, 1976. 170 pp.

       Descriptions are included of performances of *King Lear* by
       Malone, Cooper, Cooke, John Kemble, Edmund Kean, Junius Booth,
       Hackett, Forrest, Macready, McCullough, and Edwin Booth.

2271   Subic, Anastazija. "U slucaju da igrate *Lirà.*" *Zivot,* 50 (1976),
       455-473.

       Anastazija Subic discusses the opportunities and challenges in
       performing the role of King Lear.

2272   Welsh, James M. "To See it Feelingly: *King Lear* Through
       Russian Eyes." *Literature-Film Quarterly,* 4 (1976), 153-158.

       It is doubtful that any film version of *King Lear* before 1970
       successfully met the challenge. Grigori Kozintsev worked toward
       his successful visualization through a production of the Bolshoi
       Dramatic Theater in Leningrad. His film was released in North
       America to the academic audience attending the World Shakespeare
       Congress in Vancouver in 1971. The production is without gimmick.
       His Lear "is placed in a cruel and questioning universe, but it is not
       necessarily an absurd one" (p. 154). The film above all demon-
       strates the deleterious effects of division, fragmentation, disillusion-
       ment, and disintegration. The positive effects of Lear's reconcilia-
       tion with Cordelia are stressed. For one thing, the Fool, now fet-
       tered in chains, stands to one side. For another, Cordelia's parting
       gesture is to kiss Lear's hand. For yet another, his howl rings out in
       agony as we view the rope on which she is hanged. Lear, writes
       Kozintsev, finds true wealth in that moment of harmony. "No
       matter how much more time he has to live, Lear spends these few
       moments as a wise man. He has come to know what is counterfeit
       and what is real" (p. 157). See items 2163, 2298, 2330.

2273   Wilds, Lillian. "One King Lear for Our Time: A Bleak Film Vision by Peter Brook." *Literature-Film Quarterly,* 4 (1976), 159-164.

Despite the rather general disapproval of the critics, Peter Brook's film of *King Lear* is superbly realized. From first shot to last, it has a persuasive and terrifying unity. It begins in total silence, panning across a sea of staring faces to a closeup of Lear, who shatters the silence with the homonymic "Know/No." Brook uses several specific devices to achieve this coherence. He deliberately and systematically cuts all lines and scenes which serve to mitigate the seemingly gratuitous cruelty; omitted, for example, are the lines of the servant who attempts to prevent Cornwall's blinding of Gloucester and the scene in which Edmund recognizes Edgar as his foe and admits the poetic justice of his death. Brook also invents action to suit his vision, such as the scene in which Edgar drags the blinded Gloucester across the snow by one arm. Visual effects also contribute, the stark black and white photography, the shaggy furs suggesting animalistic characters, the devices that remind the spectator he is watching a film and thus block emotional identification. At the end the screen fades to solid white, rounding out the "theme of negation, of empty nothingness, with which the film began" (p. 164).

2274   Arnaud, Claude. *"Le Roi Lear."* *Cahiers Elisabéthains: Etudes sur la Pré-Renaissance et la Renaissance Anglaises,* 12 (1977), 89.

This article reviews a production of *Le Roi Lear* at the Comédie de St. Etiénne à Roanne in December, 1976. The production was based upon a translation and adaptation by Daniel Benoin. The psychological conflicts of life and death, folly and reason, were emphasized through a highly symbolic production replete with excessive gesturing and stylization.

2275   Barthofer, Alfred. "King Lear in Dinkelsbühl Historich—Biographisches Zu Thomas Bernhards Theaterstück, *Minetti.*" *Maske und Kothurn: Vierteljahrsschrift für theaterwissenschaft,* 23 (1977), 159-172.

This article reviews the production of *King Lear* in Stuttgart in 1976, directed by Claus Peymann.

2276   Berlin, Normand. "Peter Brook's Interpretation of *King Lear.*"
       Literature-Film Quarterly, 5 (1977), 299-303.

   Peter Brook's 1962 Stratford production and his 1971 film
version of *King Lear* make a mockery of Shakespeare's tragedy by
reducing it to a monolithic vision of despair and nihilism. Shakespeare is not Beckett or Kott, Brook notwithstanding. "In Shakespeare we come into the world crying and begin a journey which
allows us to ripen. In Beckett we come into the world stillborn"
(p. 300). Every positive and warm touch was cut from the play
to meet Brook's preconceived notions. The character of Cordelia is
a good case in point. In the opening scene she is curt and arrogant,
almost inviting her banishment. In the final scene Lear, instead of
dying with Cordelia in his arms, puts her down, walks off, and ex-
pires alone. Certainly one should applaud filmic and directorial
energy and experimentation, but one must not violate the essential
spirit of the work. And the essential spirit of *Lear* is inclusively
ambiguous, with touches of warmth and cold which make the loss
of love the more poignant.

2277   Bogásci, E.   "*Lear* király—Shakespeare Tragediája a Szegadi
       Szabadteri Játékokon." *Magzar Nemzet* (Budapest), 5 August
       1977, p. 8.

   This article reviews a production of *King Lear* at the Szeged
Open-Air Theatre Festival.

2278   Borisco, Natalija. "Bogdan Stupka." *Teatr,* 9 (1977), 97-104.

   The actor describes his experiences as Edmund in *King Lear*
and as Richard III in a production at the Lvov "M. Zankovetzkaya"
Theatre.

2279   Brady, Leo. "*King Lear.*" *Educational Theatre Journal,* 29
       (1977), 265-266.

   This article reviews a production of *King Lear* at the College
of William and Mary in Williamsburg, Virginia, on 13 November
1976. Performed in Phi Beta Kappa Memorial Hall, the play featured Arnold Moss in the title role. The setting was an arrangement
of paths and rocks backed by a panel that was reminiscent of Stone-
henge. Moss imparted a high degree of composure to the student

actors. Most irritating, however, was the giddiness of the spectators, who seemed anxious to chuckle at every pun but were unable or unwilling to react to the immense pathos of the piece.

2280   Carnovsky, Morris with Peter Sander. "The Eye of the Storm: On Playing King Lear." *Shakespeare Quarterly,* 28 (1977), 144-150.

An actor, unlike the scholar-critic, must thoroughly identify imaginatively with a character. Lear's frustrations, angers, and dawning sympathy must become Carnovsky's personal feelings in a role the actor considers the supreme test of his life's work. Above all, the mystery of the tragedy must be conveyed, the dreadful "day-to-day recognition that it is possible for man to succumb without any particular promise of hope" (p. 147). When Lear's sense of kingship crumbles, he appears to accept tragic necessity and deliberately to expose himself to the forces of nature. In his madness the king is loved by Kent, whose loyalty is ingrained, and by the Fool, who must be both full of love and caustic and lacerating. The final lines over Lear's body ("Do you see this? . . . Look there. . . .") should be spoken with the energy of a startling, new-faced vision. The scene involves one of the closest moments of the actor's interpenetration with the role, his "act of love" (p. 150).

2281   Clurman, Harold. "Theatre." *Nation,* 225 (1977), 92-94.

This article discusses the Royal Shakespeare Company summer season; productions include *King Lear* and Jonson's *Volpone.* While little comment is offered on Shakespeare's play, there is extensive description of the Olivier stage, one of three playing areas at the British National Theatre.

2282   Cournot, Michel. *"Il Re Lear." Le Monde,* 6-7 November 1977.

This article reviews Giorgio Strehler's Italian production of *King Lear* at the Piccolo Teatro in Milan and at the Théâtre de l' Odéon in Paris in November, 1977.

2283   Coveny, Michael. *"King Lear,* Stratford-Upon-Avon." *Plays and Players,* 24, No. 5 (1977), 18-19.

The production of *King Lear* by the Royal Shakespeare Company features Donald Sinden in the title role. Sinden plays the part with "cigar smoke, head down, medals flashing" (p. 18). Directed by John Barton, the play fails to catch fire in any unified way. The nineteenth-century setting contributes little, and Sinden, though with moments of greatness, is not uniformly so. The storm scene is staged complete with wind machine and thunder sheet in full view of the audience.

2284   Dessen, Alan C. "Oregon Shakespeare Festival." *Shakespeare Quarterly,* 28 (1977), 244-252.

The Ashland production of *King Lear* by Pat Patton was "unpretentious, well acted, well paced, and gripping, a collaborative effort that reflected the energy and imagination of many participants" (p. 253). It was staged with no particular thesis, neither nihilistic nor transcendental, and the straightness was refreshing. Moments of horrible brutality and of love and sympathy were given equal emphasis. Rex Rubold was an excellent Fool, using a simian posture as he moved sideways with his head down. Denis Arndt prepared for the role of Lear by immersing himself in the stage history and criticism of the play, and his performance caught the many moods of the old king. Most successful were the scene of his meeting the blinded Gloucester on the heath (IV, vi) and of his kneeling over Cordelia in the final moments.

2285   Evans, Gareth Lloyd. "The RSC's *King Lear* and *Macbeth.*" *Shakespeare Quarterly,* 28 (1977), 190-195.

The RSC production of *King Lear* in 1976 suffered from a mild case of schizophrenia. At one moment naturalism prevailed in the Bismarckian costuming and the very real water of the storm scene; at another, symbolism was predominant in the characterization of the heath scene and the old farm-cart pulled by men in which Lear arrives at his daughter's home. Donald Sinden as Lear had effective moments, emphasizing an authoritarian and peremptory manner. The weakest performance was that of Cordelia; she was insufferably good and consequently lifeless, a quality compounded by the "demure, long-skirtedness we associate with intrepid nineteenth-century lady explorers who wished to insure that coiffure and hygiene kept pace with discovery and exploration" (p. 193).

2286   Fuzier, Jean. *"King Lear."* *Cahiers Elisabéthains: Etudes sur la Pré-Renaissance et la Renaissance Anglaises,* 12 (1977), 81-82.

This article reviews Trevor Nunn's production of *King Lear* at the Aldwych Theatre in London on 1 June 1977 by the Royal Shakespeare Company. While the production was generally excellent, there did seem to be a discrepancy between the highly refined and civilized court costumes (Edwardian costumes) and the primitive barbarity of the acting style. Donald Sinden's cigar-smoking Lear is a case in point. Nonetheless, there were remarkable insights; perhaps the most effective moment was the Dover Cliff scene.

2287   Godard, Colette. *"Le Roi Lear."* *Le Monde,* 5 January 1977.

This article reviews both Georges Lavaudant's French production of *King Lear* at the Maison de la Culture in Grenoble in January, 1977, and a production of *King Lear* by the Comedie de St. Etienne a Roanne in December, 1976. The translation and adaptation were by Daniel Benoin. See also item 2274.

2288   Entry Deleted.

2289   Halio, Jay L. " 'This Wide and Universal Stage': Shakespeare's Plays as Plays." *Teaching Shakespeare.* Edited by Walter Edens et al. Princeton: Princeton University Press, 1977, pp. 273-289.

The performance of *King Lear* at the Delacorte Theater in Central Park in August, 1973, indicates that Shakespeare's plays can be made readily accessible to audiences of a far more heterogeneous class than Shakespeare envisioned at the Globe. Filmed as a live production, it featured the famous Black actor James Earl Jones as Lear and two Black actresses as Goneril and Regan. This performance was of a consistently high standard.

2290   Hare, Arnold. "George Frederick Cooke's Early Years in the Theatre." *Theatre Notebook,* 31, No. 1 (1977), 12-21.

This article includes a discussion of Cooke's role as King Lear, as well as the rest of his known repertory from September, 1773, to 2 October 1775.

2291   Hodgdon, Barbara. "Kozintsev's *King Lear*: Filming a Tragic
       Poem." *Literature/Film Quarterly*, 5 (1977), 291-298.

Kozintsev's avowed intention in his 1970 film of *King Lear*
was to capture the historical process within the tracing of an individual's spiritual life. As Lear was cast Yuri Yarvet, tiny, frail, and
white-haired, while Gloucester was a burley pillar of a man. In
technique the film is of two parts. Part I concentrates on the individual characters with numerous provocative closeups that command our attention and scrutiny. Part II, from the time Lear moves
onto the heath, concentrates on long shots and broad scenes, forcing
us—once we have become fascinated with the individuals—to watch
them act out their fates against a background which suggests timelessness and universality. Particular shots are especially memorable—
the beach scene of Cordelia's wedding to France juxtaposed with the
disharmonious scene of the banishment, a genealogical chart seen
behind Edmund in his opening soliloquy and again behind Edgar as
he flees for safety from his father, Lear's curses—the first uttered
from the castle walls, the second in closeup, the third to the skies
as he is shut out in the storm. At the moment of reconciliation half
of the screen is closeup on Lear and Cordelia, but this vision is set
against a broad scene of soldiers and farmers. At the conclusion life
goes on with peasants in the fields and soldiers moving across the
landscape.

2292   Hughes, Alan. " 'A Poor, Infirm, Weak and Despis'd Old Man':
       Henry Irving's *King Lear.*" *Wascana Review*, 12 (1977),
       49-64.

Henry Irving first appeared as Lear on 10 November 1892, by
which time he had been actor-manager of the Lyceum Theatre for
fourteen years. Clearly he had avoided the play because of critical
predilections against it. His version cut forty-six percent; yet with
the time required to change the elaborate sets it ran for three and
one-half hours. His first entry was magnificent as a white-haired old
chieftain with eyes flashing. The storm scene was presented with
great realism, and Irving played the role for the sympathy a weak
old man could evoke. Similarly, his scene of awakening in Cordelia's
arms was played for its full sentimental value. In the final scene he
achieved a synthesis of love and despair; and the audience was left,

not in total desolation, but with the hint of the existence of benevolent providence moving in mysterious ways. In various respects by
our standards Irving's production of *King Lear* was maudlin and
artificial; nevertheless, he was able to prove both to himself and to
his critics that the tragedy is eminently actable.

2293   Jorgens, Jack J. "Champlain Shakespeare Festival." *Shakespeare
       Quarterly,* 28 (1977), 207-209.

       One of the least-accomplished productions in recent years by
the Champlain Company, *Lear* suffered from inexperienced actors
and a limited budget. Dennis Lipscomb was a creditable Gloucester,
but the play was generally flat.

2294   Jorgens, Jack J. "*King Lear*: Peter Brook and Grigori Kozint-
       sev." *Shakespeare on Film.* Bloomington: Indiana University
       Press, 1977, pp. 235-251.

       As our Western culture grows old both literally and figurative-
ly, *Lear* has replaced *Hamlet* in our esteem as Shakespeare's greatest
play. There are two *Lears,* however. That of Peter Brook is an absurdist nightmare. The crack in Nature is irremedial, and the bleak
existential tale is one of meaningless violence. That of Grigori
Kozintsev is redemptionist tragedy, a man's journey from egocentricity and ignorance to knowledge and compassion. Each director
pursues the logic of his view. Brook, for example, emphasizes the
grotesque comedy of Edgar's deception of despairing Gloucester,
while Kozintsev omits it altogether; Brook omits Edmund's last-
minute repentance, while Kozintsev like Shakespeare suggests the
Christian sense of goodness in the worst of evil. At the end Brook
has Lear's head drop from the frame with only a bright emptiness
remaining; Kozintsev uses the symbol of water and peasants rebuild-
ing to suggest the theme of patience and endurance. In each instance the personal involvement of a talented director transforms
Shakespeare into a personal vision.

2295   Kay, Carol McGinnis. "Alabama Shakespeare Festival." *Shake-
       speare Quarterly,* 28 (1977), 220-223.

       King Lear was the best play of the season for the Alabama
Festival. The fur-covered costumes made the characters look like

beasts of prey (the same costumes used in 1975 at Stratford, Connecticut); here there was no flavor of stale primitivism. Charles Antalosky was a first-rate Lear in this production reflecting the Kott-Brook interpretation of the play. One of the most affecting moments was the Fool's final line, after which he goes to sleep at Lear's feet and dies of exhaustion and exposure.

2296   Kaydalova, O. N. *Traditions and Contemporary Age: Theatre in Central Asia and Kazakhstan.* Moscow: Iskusstvo, 1977.

This volume in Russian includes a discussion of a production of *King Lear* at the Kirghiz drama theatre.

2297   Kozintsev, Grigori. "From the Notebooks of the Producer: Introduced and Edited by V. Kozintseva." *Iskusstvo kino* (Moscow), 7 (1977), 137-156.

The primary focus is on Kozintsev's notes made before and during his work on the Russian film version of *King Lear*. Obvious throughout his comments is his determination to reveal that Lear's salvation involves his regaining a compassion for and identification with the common man.

2298   Kozintsev, Grigori M. *"King Lear": The Space of Tragedy. The Diary of a Film Director.* Translated by Mary Mackintosh. Berkeley: University of California Press, 1977. 260 pp.

Kozintsev, whose film version of *King Lear* was first shown in London in the summer of 1972, views Shakespeare's tragedy as a dramatic symbol of the Apocalypse. By renouncing his despotic power, the king becomes human, but by that point he is caught up in a network of events that sweep him to disaster and destruction. The fundamental tragic irony is that he discovers happiness through a reconciliation with Cordelia only in time to lose her and, within moments, his own life. This diary of events during the filming of the play includes three different kinds of material—the author's meditations concerning the meaning of tragedy and how its universal implications can most effectively be presented cinematically to a contemporary audience, his reminiscences about the development of cinema in the early 1920's in Russia, and the day-to-day difficulties, challenges, and achievements in the actual shooting of the film. Of

particular interest is an account of how Dimitri Shostakovich collaborated on the musical score. See items 2163, 2272, 2330.

2299   Kydryński, Joliusz.   "Holoubek gra króla Leara" ["Gustov
       Holoubek Plays King Lear"] *Zycie literackie,* 27, No. 23
       (1977), 5-6.

       This article reviews a production of *King Lear* at the Dramatic
Theater in Warsaw, with Gustov Holoubek in the title role.

2300   Lipkow, A.   "Joining a Dispute: Problems of Screening Shake-
       speare in the World Cinema and G. Kozintsev's Films." *Is-
       kusstvo kino* (Moscow), 9 (1977), 113-126. Reprint. "Prob-
       leme der Shakespeare-Verfilmung und der Filme Kozinsews."
       Kunst und Literatur, 26 (1978), 412-448.

       The major focus is on Kozintsev's film version of *King Lear*
and his subsequent plans to produce a film of *The Tempest.* Various
techniques unique to this visual medium enable Kozintsev to achieve
significant effects. For example, the final scene, with Lear's death
in the foreground and peasants working in the field in the background, suggests both an end and a beginning, the continuation of
life's cycle in the midst of individual tragedy.

2301   Markham, Rosemary.   "Theatre Review." *Anglo-Welsh Review,*
       59 (Autumn, 1977), 144-145.

       In M ichael Geliot's production of *King Lear* by the Welsh
Drama Company at the Sherman Theatre in Cardiff agony aplenty
was mixed with the counter-thrusts of humanity, energy, and freak-
ish humor. Joseph O'Conor provoked both sympathy and disdain
in the title role, while Cordelia, anything but a sweet lady, was
waspish and implacable, without her father's sense of humor, and
cruel in her treatment of him. "Charles Lamb should have been
invited" (p. 144).

2302   "Notice of Production of *King Lear.*" *Theatre World* (1977-
       1978), p. 98.

       The cast is recorded for a production by the Acting Company
in New York, directed by John Houseman and featuring David
Schramm as Lear. Pictures are by Martha Swope.

2303   Pickard, Roy. "Lee J. Cobb." *Films in Review,* 18 (1977), 525-537.

Lee J. Cobb, interviewed at Pinewood Studies, England, one year prior to his death, described the stage as his real love and movies merely as a means of existence. His happiest moment was as Lear in a production at New York's Lincoln Center, a moment approached by his role of Willy Loman in *Death of a Salesman.* It was the money earned from his role in the TV Western series *The Virginian* that enabled him later to participate in *King Lear.*

2304   Pietzsch, Ingeborg. "Weiter auf der Suche." *Theater der Zeit,* 32, No. 3 (1977), 36-38.

This article reviews a production of *King Lear* at the Budapest Theatre.

2305   Priewe, Anneliese. "Shakespeares *König Lear* am deutschen Theater." *Weimarer Beitrage: Zeitschrift für Literaturwissenschaft, Ästhetik und Kulturtheorie,* 23 No. 3 (1977), 166-175.

The use of recent historical perspective in no way hampers the creativity of productions of *King Lear.* The German production described in this article focuses on the various aspects of power and its use both for destruction and social stability.

2306   Rosenfeld, Lulla. "The Yiddish Idol." *New York Times Magazine,* 12 June 1977, pp. 34-49 passim.

This article describes the productions of *King Lear* and *The Merchant of Venice* on New York's Lower East Side in the late nineteenth and twentieth centuries. The director and leading actor was Jacob P. Adler. His *King Lear* (Gordin's version) was set in nineteenth-century Russia. Lear was not a king but a Jewish merchant of great wealth and authority. This production ushered in a golden era of Yiddish Theater and established Adler as its greatest star. When he died in 1926, hundreds of wailing mourners followed the cortege down the Bowery to the Mount Carmel burial grounds in Brooklyn.

2307   *Sandro Akhmeteli: A Memorial Volume for His 90th Birthday Anniversary.* Tbilisi, 1977. 534 pp.

These essays describe Sandro Akhmeteli's work as actor and later director at the Georgian Rustaveli Theatre. *King Lear* was one of his notable successes as a director.

2308   "Shakespeare and the People: Elizabethan Drama on Video." *Shakespeare Film Newsletter*, 1, No. 2 (1977), 4, 7.

This article discusses television productions of *King Lear* and other Shakespearean plays. James Earl Jones portrayed the principal figure as a once-powerful king, now old and fragile, but above all a king newly conscious of senescence. The production was a film of a 1973 stage performance at the Delacorte Theater in Central Park. The women were wooden, and the audience tended to laugh at the wrong times; but in some ways the small video screen lent an effective intimacy to the scene.

2309   Styan, J. L. "Shakespeare, Peter Brook and Non-Illusion." *The Shakespeare Revolution.* Cambridge: Cambridge University Press, 1977, pp. 206-231.

Based on his reading of Jan Kott's *Shakespeare Our Contemporary* (see item 348) and subsequent discussion with Kott, Peter Brook produced a nihilistic, absurdist version of *King Lear* at Stratford in 1962. The production capitalized on the tension between Renaissance and modern values and emerged as "a metaphysical farce about the blindness of man in an environment of savage cruelty" (p. 218). To the embarrassment and disgust of many literary scholars, the version received acclaim from the audience. Inevitably many Shakespearean values are lost. To render this totally bleak view, changes were made in the text such as the omission of the second servant's objection to Gloucester's blinding and Edmund's last-minute repentance. The production will not soon be forgotten; as Michael Goldman (see item 858) commented, Brook "shows us more of Shakespeare's meaning when he is wrong about it than most of us do when we are right" (p. 223).

2310   Surkov, Ye D. *In the Cinema and the Theatre.* Moscow: Iskusstvo, 1977.

This collection of reviews and essays in Russian includes a discussion of Grigori Kozintsev's stage and film productions of *King Lear* (pp. 298-303).

2311   Szántó, E.   "A szegedi *Lear.*"   *Szinház* (Budapest), October, 1977, pp. 12-13.

This article, entitled "*Lear* at Szeged," reviews the production of *King Lear* at the Open-Air Theatre Festival in Szeged, directed by L. Vámos. Special attention is directed to Vámos as Hungary's leading director and to the importance of this production as a furthur stage in his artistic development.

2312   Traversi, Derek. *Shakespeare's Tragic Structure in "King Lear."* New York: Jeffrey Norton Pubs., 1977.

This forty-minute cassette (No. 23100) recorded in 1965 examines *King Lear* as the most complex and the most universal of Shakespeare's tragedies. Both Lear and Gloucester must move from wrath to self-pity and, finally, to compassion for the plight of others.

2313   Tynan, Kenneth. "Profiles: At Three Minutes Past Eight You Must Dream." *New Yorker,* 53, No. 1 (1977), 45-72.

This article discusses Ralph Richardson's work with such notables as Gielgud, Olivier, and Hall. Lear is a role which has defeated both Olivier and Gielgud. Richardson has avoided both Lear and Hamlet, convinced that he is not of the first division. Lear, however, with its lines of alternate defiance, pity, and humility should be well within his practiced range.

2314   Willson, Robert F. "On the Closing of Gloucester's Door in the Kozintsev *Lear.*" *Shakespeare Film Newsletter,* 2 (December, 1977), 3, 5.

Kozintsev in his film version of *King Lear* in 1970 achieves a powerful synecdoche through Regan's closing the door in Lear's face when she questions his need for even one knight-retainer and again later when Gloucester's servants lock him from the house as the storm approaches. Such a subtextual incident makes Lear's "O, reason not the need" speech more universal in its implications and stresses the sense of Lear's utter isolation.

2315 Bazin, Andre. *Orson Welles: A Critical View.* Translated by Jonathan Rosenbaum. New York: Harper and Row, 1978, 138 pp.

A brief discussion of Welles' version of *King Lear* is included in this analysis of his life and work. His rendition of Lear was controversial and only partially successful.

2316 Billington, Michael. *"King Lear."* Guardian, 12 November 1978, p. 21. (not seen)

2317 Bost, James S. *"King Lear."* *Educational Theatre Journal,* 30 (March, 1978), 108, 110.

The Royal Shakespeare Company production of *King Lear* at the Aldwych Theatre, London, in May, 1977, utilized slashing jabs of white light moving across the darkness of the stage to suggest the relentless struggle between good and evil. The stage image was like a bull ring with the characters entering from behind a wooden stockade that encircles the arena. Edwardian black and white costumes suggested that *Lear* is relevant to modern audiences. The director, Trevor Nunn, set forth a raging Lear who never faltered as he hurled "his own brand of rain and madness into a terrifying and unfathomable world" (p. 110). The Fool is made old, of a piece with Lear, and somewhat like an old vaudeville team he and the king suffer with each other as the storm reaches its peak. In a sterile world man nonetheless possesses a magnificent, if futile, power.

2318 Braunmuller, A. R. and William L. Stull. "Shakespeare in Los Angeles." *Shakespeare Quarterly,* 29 (1978), 259-269.

The Shakespeare Society's production directed by Stephen Roberts was ambitious and adequate, if not superior. The title role was masterfully performed by George Coulouris. The action was well paced, despite the restrictions of the small stage. Coulouris developed an effective sense of tragic inevitability. The subplot clearly intertwined with and defined the main action.

2319 David, Richard. "The Parties Themselves, the Actors." *Shakespeare in the Theatre.* Cambridge: Cambridge University Press, 1978, pp. 85-105.

The Royal Shakespeare Company production of *King Lear* in 1976, directed by Trevor Nunn with Donald Sinden as Lear, was one of the most searching productions of Shakespearean tragedy in England since the war. The action was given an extra-sharp definition and focus by the manipulation of the staging. The playing area itself was reduced and well defined, and the tragedy looked inward rather than outward, concentrating on family tensions and personal passions. The costuming was completely eclectic, drawn from a variety of periods. Throughout the opening scenes the scales of good and evil were delicately balanced with emphasis on Lear's utter irascibility and Goneril's essential reasonableness. An emotional, overwrought, efficient house manager, she is driven to the verge of distraction by the disorder of Lear and his knights. The king's genuine human warmth surfaces slowly through his conversations with the Fool, played as a little old clown who has long served the ruler. The storm sounds were kept in proper balance, but the real rain that poured on the stage occasionally distracted. The words, "Prithee undo this button" referred, not to Lear's throat, but to Cordelia's in his effort to revive her. The spectator in the final analysis was convinced through his tears that "this, if not the only right way to play Lear's death, is a superbly right way" (p. 104).

2320   "Dylan Thomas Reading from Shakespeare's *King Lear* and Webster's *The Duchess of Malfi.*" New York: Caedmon Records. CDL 51158 pl. 592. 1978 (recording)

2321   Galkina, S.   "Tragedy and Time." *Sovetskaya Latvia* (Riga), 14 May 1978.

This article reviews A. Kaltz's production of *King Lear* at the Riga Russian Theatre, featuring M. Hyzhnyakov as Lear.

2322   Georgosopoulous, K.   "I techni tis anagis" ["The Technique of Necessity"]. *Vima* (Athens), 26 April 1978.

This article reviews a Greek production of *King Lear* in Athens. The production generally emphasized the grotesque horror of life and the deterministic factors which delimit the individual's free will.

2323   Hartwig, Joan. "Shakespeare in Louisville." *Shakespeare Quarterly,* 29 (1978), 244-246.

Although the acting was uneven and precarious chances were taken with the cutting of various roles, such as that of Burgundy, the Louisville Repertory Company achieved a notable performance of *King Lear.* The strongest actor was Philip Hoffman in the role of Edmund. Lear was performed by Logan Pope. The outdoor setting in no way diminished the visual effects, but at times the auditory effects were distressing.

2324   Hutchinson, P. William. "Trinity Square Repertory Company: 1976-77 Season. Lederer Theatre, Providence, R. I." *Educational Theatre Journal,* 30 (1978), 122-124.

Under the artistic direction of Adrian Hall, The Trinity Square Repertory Company enjoyed a productive thirteenth season. The most innovative and provocative production was *King Lear.* Set in a dirty, straw-strewn barnyard, the unit was transformed from night to day, indoor to outdoor by imaginative staging and lighting. The costumes, from various periods, were uniformly besmirched. Richard Kneeland was excellent as Lear, though the leading female performers left much to be desired.

2325   Jorgens, Jack J. *Teaching Manual: "King Lear."* Mount Vernon, New York: Audio Branden Films, 1978. 12 pp.

This study manual, written in consultation with Audrey Roth, Michael Flanigan, and Ernest Goldstein, is designed for use with Peter Brook's film version of *King Lear* (England, 1971) featuring Paul Scofield in the title role.

2326   *King Lear.* Notice of Production, 31 March 1978.

M. Katrakis' Greek production of *King Lear,* translated by Vassilis Rotas, was performed from 31 March to 20 April and 2 May to 7 May 1978 at the National Theater of Greece in Athens. Scenes and costumes were by S. Vassiliou.

2327   *King Lear.* Notice of Production, 28 April 1978.

Jerzy Jarocki's production of *King Lear*, with designs by Kasimierz Wisniak and music by Stanislaw Radwan, premiered on 28 April 1978 at the Teatr Dramatyczny in Warsaw. The cast included Gustaw Holoubek as Lear, Piotr Fronczewski as the Fool, and Joanna Orzeszkowska-Kotarbínski as Cordelia.

2328   *Kral Lear.* Notice of Production, 16 December 1978.

Ladislav Panovec's Czech production of *King Lear*, translated by Milan Lukes, was performed at the Horácké Theatre in Jihlava, Moravia. The cast included Jaromir Crha as Lear, Vlastimil Slézak as Kent, Alois Klejzar as the Fool, and Natálie Mukarovska as Cordelia. The scene was designed by Jindřich Boška.

2329   Maby, Edmond. *"Le Roi Lear." Le Provencal,* 27 July 1978.

This article reviews Yves Gasc's productions of *King Lear* in July and August, 1978, at the Festival da Vaison-la-Romaine, the Festival de la Citadelle (Sisteron), and the Festival de la Mere (Sete). The role of Lear was played by Jean Marais.

2330   McNeir, Waldo F. "Grigori Kozintsev's *King Lear* (USSR, 1971)." *College Literature,* 5 (1978), 239-248.

Kozintsev's film production of *King Lear,* which had its Western premier at the World Shakespeare Congress in Vancouver, British Columbia, on August 20, 1971, takes its vision, like Shakespeare's, from the assumption that the cause leading to hard hearts is to be found in the inner mystery of God's nature, not in the outer mystery of the Universe. Neither optimistic nor pessimistic in a doctrinaire sense, it "pictures movingly both man's humanity and his animality as an undeniable dualism, an appalling but not totally disabling contradiction" (p. 247). The film gains its special power from specific cinematic effects—the opening and closing action framed against peasants toiling in the field to suggest the continuing cycle of life, the heath as a frozen wasteland as cold as Goneril's and Regan's hearts, a nightmarish expanse of nothing, Lear on his belly, crawling as he picks flowers, the fiery destruction of the French camp near Dover overrun by the British. See items 2163, 2272, 2298.

2331   Mousseos, Platon. "Six Portrayals by Lambeti and Minotis as Lear." *The Athenian* (Athens) (June, 1978), pp. 36-37.

This analysis of Alex Minotis' appearances in the role of Lear suggests that his performances, while adequate, lacked vitality and depth, possibly because he also served as director.

2332   Oliver, Edith. "Off Broadway." *New Yorker,* 24 April 1978, pp. 94-96.

David Schramm's Lear, performed with the Acting Company, is a merciless depiction of a very old man by a very young one. Clearly in this production the dividing of the kingdom is as insane as his later tirade on the heath. Directed by John Houseman, the production is not flawless, but it is absorbing from beginning to end. Especially notable were Kevin Conroy as Edgar and Dennis Bocigalupi as the "fragile, haunted, and haunting Fool."

2333   Panagho, Emis. "O Bassilias *Lear* sto Ethniko istera apo 20 chronia" ["*Lear* on Stage at the National Theatre after 20 Years"]. *Vradini* (Athens), 29 March 1978.

In part the stage power and fascination of *King Lear* results from its chronicle structure with its pomp and pageantry. The play begins and ends like a chronicle play. At the same time, however, since no young king ascends the throne and since the emphasis is upon the end of an era with the king's death, the added terror of the concept of the end of the world is also present.

2334   Skouloudis, Manoli. "I nanopoisi enos giganda" ["The Belittling of a Giant"]. *Eleftherotipia* (Athens), 21 March 1978. (not seen)

2335   Sotiriadis, N. "Shakespeare's *Timon of Athens.*" *Exormisi* (Athens), 27 August 1978.

Timon of Athens is the draft of a play fully projected in *King Lear.* Whereas *Timon* portrays a man betrayed by his supposed friends, *Lear* projects a man who betrays those who truly love him.

2336   Trewin, J. C. *"King Lear." Going to Shakespeare.* London: George Allen and Unwin, 1978, pp. 204-211.

Instinctively, *King Lear* conjures up Stonehenge-like, primitive settings quite contrary to the 1976 Stratford production of Lear as ruler of a late nineteenth- or early twentieth-century kingdom. It is an extremely difficult play in the theater, despite the gargantuan efforts in this century of John Gielgud, Laurence Olivier, Michael Redgrave, Donald Wolfit, Charles Laughton, Paul Scofield, Eric Porter, Robert Eddison, and Donald Sinden. The Beckettian *Lear* at Stratford in 1962 is the most controversial production of our time. Whatever the interpretation, the scene of Gloucester's blinding is one of the most horrible, a fact that led Lilian Bayliss at the Old Vic to play it just after an intermission so that the squeamish could delay their reentrance. The fool is one of the most challenging roles; he has been played as a very old man, an arch jester, as a youth like a frightened bird (Alan Badel at Stratford, 1950), as a stray from some Tibetan monastery, and, as Alec Guinness acted him so touchingly to Olivier (New Theatre, 1946), as "wry, quiet, and true, with a dog's devotion" (p. 210).

2337   Barnes, Clive. "Shakespeare in New York City." *Shakespeare Quarterly*, 30 (1979), 184-188.

No production has better expressed Shakespeare's view of mortality than John Houseman's production of *King Lear* by the Acting Company at the American Place Theatre in New York on 6 April 1978. The setting by Ming Cho Lee, a shallow saucer flanked with high, bleak-looking walls, helped to create a simple, fluid, cinematic naturalism. The text was presented with no forced conceptualization and with as few cuts as possible. David Schramm appeared as Lear.

2338   Bartholomeusz, Dennis. "Shakespeare in Sydney and Melbourne." *Shakespeare Quarterly*, 39 (1979), 265-267.

The production of *King Lear* by the Alexander Theatre Company at the Alexander Theatre, Monash University, on 27 June 1978 in Sydney, Australia, was a "most rare beast." Directed by Peter Oyston, this modernized version was prepared by the playwright David Williamson. Despite the competent acting, the production was doomed by "language that trivialized the sublime and made the abyss look banal" (p. 267). Lear was played by Reg Evans, Cordelia by Jackie Kerin, and the Fool by Joe Bolza.

2339   Stríbrný, Zdeněk. "Shakespeare in Czechoslovakia." *Shakespeare Quarterly,* 39 (1979), 285-289.

The production of *King Lear* at the Slovak National Theatre in Bratislava on 25 October 1978 is the first attempt to do the play on the Slovak stage. Directed by Pavol Haspra, it suffers from an intermingling of influences, especially those of Peter Brook, Grigori Kozintsev, and Giorgio Strehler. Karol Machata and Gustav Valach alternated as Lear, the former playing a king intensely concerned with his human Calvary and the latter playing a robustly plebeian ruler.

2340   Sykes, Alrene. "Shakespeare in Brisbane." *Shakespeare Quarterly,* 30 (1979), 270-271.

The production of *King Lear* by the Queensland Theatre Company at the S.G.I.O. Theatre in Brisbane, Australia, on 17 May 1978 was a domestic version, with the text cut by one-third and the cast reduced by twelve. Warren Mitchell, if not one of the great Lears, was wholly competent and professional. The director was Alan Edwards, and the stage design by Peter Cooke was spare and flexible.

2341   Trewin, J. C. "Shakespeare in Britain." *Shakespeare Quarterly,* 30 (1979), 151-158.

Anthony Quayle's rendition of Lear in Toby Robertson's production of *King Lear* by the Prospect Theatre Company at the Old Vic Theatre on 24 October 1978 was striking in its lack of any kind of superfluous display. Quayle is a "secure and governing actor," even though he lacks the "more acute pathos." The blinding of Gloucester occurred immediately after the intermission.

See also items: 2, 9, 23, 37, 46, 53, 58, 72, 96, 99, 176, 215, 263-264, 294, 355, 377, 379, 390, 402, 416, 421, 444, 467, 516, 555, 570, 695, 719, 721, 748, 783, 814, 841, 848, 858, 884, 906, 913, 942, 995-996, 1005, 1047, 1080-1081, 1097, 1103, 1185, 1191, 1236,

1456-1457, 1461-1463, 1465, 1480, 1491-1492, 1524, 1534, 1552-
1553, 1569, 1575, 1581, 1585, 1599, 1616, 1618, 1624, 1640,
1656, 1675, 1678, 1683, 1689, 1700, 1703, 1705, 1711, 1713,
1720-1721, 2342-2343, 2347, 2355-2356, 2366-2367, 2376, 2386,
2391, 2393, 2400, 2405, 2408, 2411, 2413, 2415, 2423, 2429,
2432, 2437-2440, 2443-2444, 2447-2448, 2451-2454, 2456, 2461-
2462, 2466-2469, 2472, 2474-2484, 2489-2491, 2494-2495, 2498,
2503, 2509, 2527.

VIII.   ADAPTATIONS, INFLUENCE, AND SYNOPSES

VIII. ADAPTATIONS, INFLUENCE, AND SYNOPSES

2341a Lamb, Charles and Mary Lamb. "King Lear." *Tales from Shake-speare. Designed for the Use of Young Persons.* London: Hodgkins, 1807. Reprint. New York: Weathervane Books, 1975, pp. 117-135.

A simplified version in prose relates the tale of Lear and his three daughters. Shakespeare's subplot involving Gloucester and his two sons is virtually eliminated. The fellow Lear confronts in the hovel, for example, is not Edgar in disguise but merely a poor bedlam beggar. The "judgment of heaven" figures heavily in the conclusion of the play.

2342 Summers, Montague, intro. *Shakespeare Adaptations.* London: S. Cape, 1922. 282 pp. Reprint. B. Blom, 1966. 282 pp.

This volume reprints Nahum Tate's *King Lear* along with two other Restoration adaptations—*The Tempest or the Enchanted Island* by William Davenant and John Dryden and *The Mock-Tempest or the Enchanted Castle* by Thomas Duffett. Extensive notes are provided by Summers.

2343 Spencer, Hazelton. "Tate's Adaptations." *Shakespeare Improved: The Restoration Versions in Quarto and on the Stage.* Cambridge, Mass.: Harvard University Press, 1927, pp. 241-273.

The derisive term *Tatefication* has been coined to describe revision involving romanticizing and sentimental simplification. Nahum Tate's version of *King Lear* was printed in 1681, the year of its first production at Covent Garden. France does not appear in the play; Cordelia's motive in refusing to proclaim her love for Lear is to offend him so that, in turn, Burgundy will reject her. Lear knows of her love affair with Edgar but considers him an undesirable suitor. The Fool also is completely cut from the play. Edgar's motivation for assuming the disguise of Tom o' Bedlam is altered. In Shakespeare it is for self-preservation; in Tate it is to preserve himself for the service of the distressed Cordelia. Edmund openly lusts for both Goneril and Regan while Cordelia disguises herself so that she might seek her father on the heath. At this point Edmund also intends to ravish Cordelia and sends two ruffians to capture her. Edgar rescues her, and they again exchange a declaration of love. Numerous other changes are made, but certainly the most infamous is the happy ending, in which Cordelia's life is again saved by Edgar at the moment of her intended execution. Lear too remains alive. When his kingdom is restored, he bestows it upon Cordelia, who will marry Edgar. Lear, Kent, and Gloucester retire to happy meditation.

2344   Harrison, Thomas P., Jr. "Tennyson's *Maud* and Shakespeare."
        Shakespeare Association Bulletin, 17 (1942), 80-85.

        Although at Tennyson's own suggestion *Hamlet* has been considered the major influence upon *Maud, Romeo and Juliet* and *King Lear* appear to be more important concerning the love story and the youth's madness provoked by the loss of Maud. In particular Tennyson was apparently influenced by the scene of Lear's awakening and his confused recognition of Cordelia in his delineation of the hero's believing that Maud stands silently beside him and the calmness of mind which shortly ensues.

2345   Vandiver, Edward P., Jr. "Longfellow, Lanier, Boker, and *King Lear."* *Shakespeare Association Bulletin,* 19 (1944), 132-134.

        Three nineteenth-century American poets have utilized parts of *King Lear* in their works. Specifically, in Longfellow's "Midnight Mass for a Dying Year," Lanier's "Corn," and G. H. Boker's sonnets we find variations of the motif of the old father and the ministering daughter.

2346   Wilson, Robert H. *"Brave New World* as Shakespeare Criticism."
        Shakespeare Association Bulletin, 21 (1946), 99-107.

        Shakespearean references and quotations permeate Aldous Huxley's *Brave New World. King Lear,* for example, is specifically banned by Mustapha Mond, who rejects history as pure imaginative fabrication. Shakespeare represents the old system of values set in a grotesque contrast with the new. The Fordian era predicted by Huxley, in which the meaningfulness of Shakespeare will disappear, is to a degree already with us. While some readers continue to respond to the original significances of *Lear*, many others now regard it and its treatment of the problem of evil as outmoded as the "Victorian heavy father" (p. 104).

2347   Eich, Louis M. "Alterations of Shakespeare 1660-1710: And an Investigation of the Critical and Dramatic Principles and Theatrical Conventions which Prompted These Revisions." Ph.D. dissertation, University of Michigan, 1948. *Microfilm Abstracts,* 8 (1948), 90-91.

Nahum Tate's revision of *King Lear* was occasioned by the theatrical conditions and dramatic theories of the Restoration. It was the inevitable product of a highly individualized period of English theatrical history characterized by rigid concepts of such matters as poetic justice, didacticism, and the dramatic unities. Tate's version quite literally succeeded in crowding Shakespeare's play off the boards. Alterations of twelve other Shakespearean plays are also discussed.

2348   Severs, K. "Imagery and Drama." *Durham University Journal,* 41 (1948), 24-33.

In a discussion of Shakespearean allusions in T. S. Eliot's *The Waste Land, King Lear* I, ii, 88-92 (the passage in which Cordelia responds "nothing" to the king's request for a declaration of love) is cited as the source for lines 111-120 of Eliot's poem.

2349   Entry Deleted.

2350   Lash, Kenneth. "Captain Ahab and King Lear." *New Mexico Quarterly Review,* 19 (1949), 438-445.

The major Shakespearean influence on Melville is that of King Lear on the creation of Captain Ahab. Both are driven mad by awareness, by their tragic vision. Both, starved and battered by nature, turn their backs on irresponsible man and put their questions to the gods themselves. Lear's madness leads to mumbling insanity;

Ahab's is an obsession. Both die in defeat; but, whereas Lear ends pathetically, Ahab's stature and soul remain unconquered. Lear is more the man, Ahab more the symbol. "Both were kings among men, hands among claws, eyes among the blind" (p. 445).

2351   Hugo, Howard E. "The Madman of the Heath and the Mad-
       woman of Chaillot." *Chrysalis* (Boston), 5 (1952), 3-11.

This article describes the nature and extent of the influence of *King Lear,* especially the scenes of the mad Lear on the heath, on Jean Giraudoux's *La Folle de Chaillot.*

2352   Maxwell, J. C. "Keats as a Guide to Shakespeare." *Notes and
       Queries,* 197 (1952), 126.

Keats in a letter of February-May 1819 to George and Georgi-ana Keats quotes from Shakespeare's *King Lear* that man is a "poor forked creature." The context of the quotation indicates that he had in mind as well a passage from *Measure for Measure* (III, i, 14-17). It is likely that Shakespeare himself had the earlier passage in mind when he wrote *Lear.*

2353   Hook, Lucyle. "Shakespeare Improv'd, or A Case for the Affir-
       mative." *Shakespeare Quarterly,* 4 (1953), 289-299.

The role of the female in Restoration drama continued to be subordinate as a consequence of the tradition handed down from the Elizabethan-Jacobean stage. In the all-male drama, the female parts, played by young boys, are quite limited in range. The women develop off stage, while the focus is on the dynamic quality of the male on stage. Although Nahum Tate admittedly destroys the majesty and profundity of Shakespeare with his adaptation of *Lear* in 1681, a version that would hold the stage for a century and a half, the central importance is the dominance of the female role of Cordelia and her on-stage romantic interest with Edgar.

2354   Legouis, Emile. "La Terre de Zola et le Roi Lear." *Revue de
       Litterature Comparée,* 27 (1953), 417-427. (not seen)

2355   Lief, Leonard. "The Fortunes of *King Lear:* 1605-1838."
       Ph.D. dissertation, Syracuse University, 1953. Abstracted in
       Shakespeare Newsletter, 6 (1956), 22.

This is a study of the alterations of *King Lear* as a reflection of critical taste. Nahum Tate's version, for instance, in 1681 demonstrates the neo-critical principles of compression of plot, clarification of motivation, and simplification of language. Garrick and Colman made additional modifications. Romantic taste swept away the neoclassical standards and spoke of mysterious, poetic unity. Eventually, in 1838 Macready brought Shakespeare's original text back to the stage for the first time in over 150 years.

2356   Noyes, Robert Gale. *"King Lear."* *The Thespian Mirror: Shakespeare in the Eighteenth-Century Novel.* Providence, R. I.: Brown University Press, 1953, pp. 116-174.

The Tate version of *Lear* was extremely popular in the eighteenth century; from 1742 to 1776 the tragedy was absent only five seasons from Drury Lane and only fourteen seasons from Covent Garden. Considering that fact, one is surprised that references in fiction are not more frequent. References include the comment of a stupid woman in Sarah Fielding's *Adventures of David Simple* (1744) and of Lysimachus in Sarah Fielding's *Familiar Letters between the Characters in David Simple* (1747). The Dover Cliff scene is commented on in *The Life and Extraordinary Adventures . . . of Timothy Ginnadrake,* a novel attributed to Francis Fleming, a violinist at the Pump-Room at Bath. Accounts of the acting of the role include Barton Booth in *Memoirs of Sir Charles Goodville* (1753) and of David Garrick by John Shebbare in *Letters on the English Nation* (1755). A distorted version of Lear by strolling players is described in Herbert Lawrence's *Contemplative Man; or, The History of Christopher Crab, Esq.* (1771).

2357   Merchant, W. Moelwyn. "John Runciman's 'King Lear in the Storm,' 1764." *Journal of the Warburg and Courtauld Institutes,* 7 (1954), 385-387. Reprint. *Shakespeare and the Artist.* London: Oxford University Press, 1959.

John Runciman in 1767 at age twenty-three, a year prior to his death, painted his "King Lear in the Storm," reflecting the school of history painting in its organization, but also anticipating romantic painting in its violent interplay of human emotion and the natural elements. The painting comes at a crucial time for *Lear* in the eighteenth century, with critical opinion moving toward the restoration of Shakespeare's text. Runciman clearly was depicting Shakespeare's Lear, standing beside Edgar as Poor Tom, Kent, and the Fool. Lear wears the full Van Dyck dress, however, common to the century's representation of pre-Tudor characters. Since the role of the Fool was excised from Tate's version, the painting could have been little affected by contemporary stage productions. Anomalously, the background of the painting depicts a stormy sea and sky. In general the painting with its highly complex visual imagery captures a sense of extreme tension and helplessness in the old king as he stands before the power of the breaking waves with a ship foundering in the distance.

2358   Holmes, Lawrence Richard. "Joyce's 'Ecce Puer.' " *Explicator,* 13 (1955), No. 12.

Lines 3-4 of Joyce's poem "Ecce Puer" ("with joy and grief / My heart is torn") contain an allusion to Edgar's description of Gloucester's death in *King Lear* (" 'Twixt two extremes of passion, joy and grief, / Burst smilingly").

2359   Chute, Marchette. *"King Lear." Stories from Shakespeare.* Cleveland: World Publishing Co., 1956, pp. 207-220.

Lear is described as the most titanic of the tragedies, a "shattering almost super-human play whose very shapelessness is part of its strength" (p. 207). The plot is then summarized in the form of a prose narrative.

2360   Goto, Takeshi. "Moby Dick and Shakespeare." *Kyushu Daigakue English Literary Proceedings* (Fukuoka), August, 1956.

The Japanese article discusses the significant influence of *King Lear* upon Melville's *Moby Dick.*

2361   Siegel, Paul N. "Willy Loman and King Lear." *College English,* 17 (1956), 341-345.

Both Arthur Miller's *Death of a Salesman* and *King Lear* develop the theme of *Nosce teipsum.* In each case the tragedy occurs because the protagonist is self-decevied and thus makes himself vulnerable to despair and to the manipulation of others.

2362   Tiller, Terence. "The Fool in Lear." *Reading a Medal And Other Poems.* London: Hogarth, 1952, p. 51.

This poem is based on the character of Lear's Fool.

2363   Hammerle, Von Karl. "Transpositionen aus Shakespeares *King Lear* in Thomas Hardys *Return of the Native.*" *Studies in English Language and Literature: Presented to Professor Dr. Karl Brunner on the Occasion of His Seventieth Birthday.* Edited by Siegfried Korninger. Stuttgart: Wilhelm Braumüller, 1957, pp. 58-73.

In a sense Thomas Hardy is the last representative of the tradition and spirit of Elizabethan drama. Living in an area still reflecting many of the older traditions and values, he absorbed Shakespeare in an unusually direct manner. *The Return of the Native* in its general conception and in many thematic and stylistic parallels reveals the influence of *King Lear.* The *Lear* theme of filial ingratitude with its court-heroic milieu is transformed into the mundane world of Wessex, and the tragedy of the cast-out father becomes the tragedy of a lonely, seemingly outcast mother. See item 2377.

2364   Currie, H. Mace. "Notes on Sir Thomas Browne's 'Christian Morals.' " *Notes and Queries,* n.s. 5 (1958), 143.

Browne, in his passage, "Burden not the back of Aires, Leo, or Taurus, with thy faults, nor make Saturn, Mars, or Venus, guilty of thy follies. Think not to fasten thy imperfections on the stars, and so despairingly conceive thy self under a fatality of being evil" (Third Part, Section VII, p. 268) probably had Edmund's passage from *King Lear* in mind: "We make guilty of our disasters the sun, the moon and the stars; as if we were villains by necessity, fools by heavenly compulsion" (II, ii, 134).

2365   Greany, Helen T. "Some Interesting Parallels: Edmund a la Churchill." *Notes and Queries,* n.s. 5 (1958), 252.

Charles Churchill uses a variation of Edmund's soliloquy beginning "Thou, Nature, art my goddess" (I, ii, 1-22) to attack the artificialities of English pastoral poetry in *The Prophecy of Famine* (1763). This Shakespearean inversion is then followed by Churchill's ironic panegyric on Scotland.

2366   Olfson, Lewy. *"King Lear." Radio Plays from Shakespeare.* Boston: Plays, Inc., 1958, pp. 152-167.

Reduced to eight characters plus a narrator, this version is designed for presentation by young people. The radio production can introduce the actor to the magic of Shakespeare without the difficulties of staging. The subplot is totally excised, and the role of the Fool is vastly reduced. In the final scene Lear dies alone—"unnoticed . . . unwanted . . . unloved"—with the lifeless body of Cordelia in his arms. See item 2379.

2367   Halliday, Frank E. "Shakespeare Refined" and "Shakespeare Fabricated." *The Cult of Shakespeare.* New York: Thomas Yoseloff, 1957, pp. 30-43, 76-109.

Nahum Tate's comedy of *King Lear* emphasizes the love element, both that of Edgar for Cordelia and that of Edmund for Goneril and Regan. Edmund even casts lascivious glances at Cordelia. The final act suffers a Tatification in the preserving of both Lear and Cordelia and Lear's restoration to the throne. In spite of Addison's objections this version held the stage until the middle of the nineteenth century. An infamous fabrication of *Lear* by William-Henry Ireland in 1793 is also described.

2368   Kher, D. M. *King Liyar.* Bombay: Vora, 1958.

This monograph provides a paraphrase of the text of *King Lear* along with a critical analysis and commentary.

2369   Muir, Kenneth. "Three Shakespeare Adaptations." *Proceedings of the Leeds Philosophical and Literary Society,* 8 (1959), 233-240.

This study analyzes three Restoration adaptations of Shakespeare—John Dryden's *Troilus and Cressida,* Lewis Theobald's

Richard II, and Nahum Tate's *King Lear.* Other than the happy
ending with Lear's restoration, Tate's most shocking alteration is
the love affair between Cordelia and Edgar. There may be a certain
logic in this closer interrelationship of the two plots, but certainly
it softens the tragic impact of the play. The Fool is cut in the interest of decorum; the mad scenes are shortened and the mock trial
totally eliminated; Edgar reveals himself to his villainous brother
prior to their combat rather than after. Such changes generally
sentimentalize the tragedy and exemplify the mechanical nature of
neo-classical ideas of form. Similarly, the verbal changes reveal a
false taste and a coarse verbal sensitivity. This and other Restoration adaptations stand as a warning to those who would rewrite
Shakespeare in our own age.

2370   Baring, Maurice. "King Lear's Daughter: Letter from Goneril,
        Daughter of King Lear, to Her Sister Regan." *Parodies: An
        Anthology from Chaucer to Beerbohm.* Edited by Dwight
        MacDonald. New York: Random House, 1960, pp. 307-311.

Goneril writes to Regan that she is terribly irritated with her
father for two principal reasons. For one thing he insists on keeping
the Fool though the idiot constantly hops around hitting people
over the head and jabbering nonsense. For another, the old man is
forever mimicking Cordelia's mumbling, sometimes incoherent
speech. In years past the speech pattern was a source of irritation;
now he treats it as a joke.

2371   Cook, F. W. "The Wise Fool." *Twentieth Century,* 168 (1960),
        219-227.

In "Baalam and the Ass" (*Encounter,* 1954, see item 187),
W. H. Auden consciously or unconsciously identifies himself, as
poet, with Lear's Fool. His comments on the function of the Fool
provide clues to the functions and methods of Auden the poet. Note
specifically his tendency toward frivolity in handling serious matters.
"The free artist reminds the readers, as the Fool reminds the king,
of a reality they do not like and which they reject" (p. 222). The
Fool like the poet is wise in his opposition to progress at any cost.
This position is repeated behind the mask of the grinning jester.

2372   James, D. G. "Keats and *King Lear.*" *Shakespeare Survey,*
       13 (1960), 58-68.

During a trip to Carisbrooke in 1817 Keats read deeply in
Shakespeare, especially *King Lear.* Demonstrably this was a period
of extreme significance in Keats' formulation of the concept and
function of poetry. References in his letters suggest that *Lear* was
a point of departure for his deepest speculations about poetry. He
observes that the disagreeableness and repulsiveness of the play are
"evaporated," "buried," and "obliterated" by the spiritual beauty of
Cordelia and Edgar and of Lear's reunion with his daughter. Similar
is Keats' concept that beauty, "proven and impregnable, and bearing, in serenity, the world's evil, [is] the only point from which we
can comprehend, as far as may be, human experience" (p. 63). Both
came to envision sorrow as a heightening of beauty and serenity as a
state containing suffering. Apparently it would be difficult to exaggerate the impact of *Lear* on Keats during this critical time of his
development and maturation as a poet.

2373   Murray, Geoffrey. *Let's Discover More Shakespeare.* London:
       H. Hamilton, 1960.

This volume contains a synopsis of *King Lear* and seven other
Shakesperean plays.

2374   Yoshida, Ken-ichi. *Sheikusupia Monogatari.* Tokyo: Tarumi,
       1960.

This volume in Japanese, entitled *Tales from Shakespeare,* relates in simple prose the story of *King Lear* and five other Shakespearean plays.

2375   Alciatore, Jules C. "Stendhal, Shakespeare and a Fool's Fall."
       Modern Language Notes, 76 (1961), 445.

Either *King Lear* or *Cymbeline* is probably the source of
Stendhal's phrase, "a pris par terre la mesure d'un sot."

2376   Burnim, Kalman A. *David Garrick, Director.* Pittsburgh: Pitts-
       burgh University Press, 1961. 234 pp.

This volume contains an analysis of Garrick's version of *King Lear*, with emphasis on production. Garrick played a significant role in restoring portions of Shakespeare to the Tate version.

2377   Houghton, R. E. C. "Hardy and Shakespeare." *Notes and Queries,* n.s. 8 (1961), 98.

Thomas Hardy in *The Return of the Native* was apparently greatly influenced by *King Lear*. In both stories the climax occurs when a parent is turned away from the comfort and shelter of a home and subsequently dies as a consequence of exposure to the storms on the desolate heath. Verbal parallels reinforce this thematic similarity. See item 2363.

2378   Needham, Gwendolyn B. "Mrs. Frances Brooke: Dramatic Critic." *Theatre Notebook,* 15 (1961), 47-52.

In *The Old Maid* (1752-1755) Mrs. Frances Brooke roundly condemns productions of Nahum Tate's version of *King Lear*.

2379   Olfson, Lewy. *"King Lear." Plays,* November, 1961, pp. 87-96.

The text of *King Lear* is adapted for younger readers for a radio presentation. See item 2366.

2380   Terry, Jean F. *King Lear.* Farnham: Normal Press, 1961.

The text of *King Lear* is paraphrased in modern prose.

2381   De Munnik, Pauline, adapt. *Shakespeare's "King Lear" in Modern English.* Johannesburg: Saga, 1962. 169 pp.

This monograph provides a simplified text of *King Lear* along with a critical analysis and commentary.

2382   Fahnrich, Hermann. "Verdis *Re Lear*." *Neue Zeitschriften für Musik,* 123 (1962), 325-328. (not seen)

2383   Fleissner, Robert F. "Fancy's Knell." *Dickensian,* 18 (1962), 125-127.

The most compelling source for Little Nell's moving death scene is Cordelia's death. Cordelia's inability to communicate with

Lear is the tragic flaw which motivates her death; Lear's description of her as his "poor fool" suggests both affection and a quality of foolishness. Dickens probably considered Cordelia a bit foolish just as he also describes "foolish Nell" in his opening chapter. Nell's death "may have had a cathartic value for him— . . . as a means of solving for him the death of Cordelia, an ending which he may have found hard to justify" (p. 127).

2384   Stopforth, L. M. D., adapt. *"King Lear." Shakespeare Made Easier.* Cape Town: Nasionale Boekhandel, 1962.

The story of *King Lear* is retold in modern English prose.

2385   Viebrock, Helmut. "Keats, *King Lear*, and Benjamin West's 'Death on a Pale Horse.' " *English Studies,* 43 (1962), 174-180.

D. G. James (see item 146) is unfortunately led into generalization and misinterpretation in his comments on Keats' use of *King Lear* as an example of intensity in drama analogous to intensity in art, a quality Keats does not find in Benjamin West's painting "Death on a Pale Horse." Basically, Keats was not speaking throughout the paragraph of *King Lear* but of West's painting, and thus one cannot safely apply all aspects of his statement to the tragedy. More specifically, when Keats observes that in great art the intensity forces "all disagreeables to evaporate from their being in close relationship with Beauty [and] Truth" (p. 176), one cannot read in the analogy that he is implying that the wickedness of Goneril, Regan, and Edmund is made to evaporate by the eventual triumph of the spiritual beauty of Cordelia and of Lear's transformation. Even if the analogy were intended, that reading would violate Keats' aesthetics. For Keats it was not a question of moral good and evil per se but of how the "moral ugliness of human ways and deeds imaginatively presented, is buried or absorbed as ugliness by the artist's achievement in making each part subservient to the whole. . . . The sense of Beauty overcomes every other consideration, or rather obliterates all consideration" (p. 179).

2386   Braun, Margareta. " 'This Is Not Lear': Die Leargestalt in der Tateschen Fassung." *Shakespeare Jahrbuch,* 99 (1963), 30-56.

Both Charles Lamb and a critic for the *London Magazine,* writing ten years apart of their responses to the Kemble production of the Nahum Tate version of *King Lear,* criticize the loss of Lear's inner greatness, of his essential dignity. An examination of Tate's play reveals that such a lessening of the protagonist's character is consciously or unconsciously built into the very structure of the play. First, in order to accommodate the tragedy to the concept of poetic justice, Tate creates a love affair between Cordelia and Edgar and enlarges upon the love affair between Edmund and the two sisters; as a consequence, quite literally Lear is moved from the center to the periphery of the plot. Second, the characters through whom we learn most about Lear—Cordelia, the Fool, Kent, and Gloucester—are themselves so altered (indeed the Fool is eliminated altogether) that their resulting depiction of Lear is also changed. Kent, for example, before Lear's initial entry, laments the weakened and unstable condition of the king. In summary, even considering the demands of the Restoration era which the playwright understandably would attempt to accommodate, the flaws in Tate's conception of Lear force fundamental modifications in the shape of the play and its central figure that cannot be defended.

2387   Buckman, Irene. *"King Lear." Twenty Tales from Shakespeare.* Foreword by Dame Peggy Ashcroft. London: Methuen, 1963. Reprint. New York: Random House, 1965, pp. 152-163.

Dame Peggy Ashcroft describes this volume as an attempt to help young playgoers in their future love for Shakespearean theater by making them readily familiar with the plots of the plays. The synopsis of *King Lear* includes both plot lines and, in its rather full detail, attempts to be reasonably true to the spirit of the play. One exception is that Lear's mysterious final moments are related simply as a period of quiet despair: "But Cordelia was dead and not his love, nor his tears nor his gentleness could bring her back to life again. . . . [A]t last his heart and body really did break, and he fell by the side of his beloved Cordelia" (p. 163).

2388   Gale, Robert L. *"The Prince and the Pauper* and *King Lear."* *Mark Twain Journal,* 12, No. 1 (1963), 14-17.

It is likely that Twain insinuated echoes of *King Lear* into *The Prince and the Pauper* partly as an appeal to his daughters' memories of their reading or acting passages from the play. Resemblances between the two works are numerous but not to the extent of suggesting any sustained intention on Twain's part. Miles Hendon is reminiscent of Edgar, Hugh of Edmund. Little Humphrey the whipping boy recalls the Fool. Many incidents of the plot, as well, recall moments in the play. *"King Lear* seems in this respect and others to have been speaking out over the centuries directly to Mark Twain as he wrote *The Prince and the Pauper"* (p. 17).

2389   Maugham, Robin. *Mister Lear: A Comedy in Three Acts.* London: English Theatre Guild, 1963.

Walter Craine, an aging patriarch, is a writer with three daughters. The two elder resent the male secretary, the father's control of the family, and the youngest daughter's impending marriage. The youngest daughter is cast out when her fiance writes unfavorable reviews of her father's work, and the two older daughters seize control of the estate. Walter, however, marries a wealthy woman, and his secretary eventually marries the youngest daughter. The older daughters, meanwhile, squander this wealth and must eventually beg for reconciliation with their father.

2390   Smith, Albert James. *Shakespeare Stories.* London: Edward Arnold, 1963.

Plot summaries and paraphrases are included for *King Lear* and five other Shakespearean tragedies.

2391   Spencer, Christopher. "A Word for Tate's *King Lear."* *Studies in English Literature,* 3 (1963), 241-251.

Nahum Tate is undoubtedly the most execrated of the Shakespeare adapters; yet, objectively considered, his version of *Lear* is both coherent and entertaining. His added love story of Edgar and Cordelia creates more interplay between the two plots, thus providing more cohesion; the added scene of "Edmund and Regan amorously seated, listening to musick" has a similar effect. Tate also creates a greater plausibility for Cordelia's indifference to Lear in the opening scene. Determined not to be manipulated into a marriage with Burgundy, she refuses to play Lear's game. Lear, in turn, is forced to choose between two kinds of falseness (that of Cordelia and that of her sisters); his error is thus less serious, and the happy ending follows more naturally. By omitting the Fool not only does Tate eliminate a character whose comments are obscure and indirect—in a play he was striving to make clear and explicit; he also diminishes our awareness of the death of Lear's suffering, again rendering the happy ending more plausible. Tate's play is admittedly superficial when compared to Shakespeare's, but it "has an inner consistency of its own. . . . [It neatly brings] several groups of characters through a series of complications to a resolution consisting of punishment for the wicked and reward for the good and the regenerate" (p. 250).

2392   "As They've Liked Him: *Ex Traditione Florilgeium in Dialecticam.*" *North Dakota Quarterly,* 32, No. 1 (1964), 1-6.

Eighteenth-century engravings for *King Lear* are included in material citing four dozen Shakespeare tributes from four centuries.

2393   Ayres, James. "Shakespeare in the Restoration: Nahum Tate's *The History of King Richard the Second, The History of King Lear,* and *The Ingratitude of a Common-Wealth.*" Ph.D. dissertation, Ohio State University, 1964. *DA,* 25 (1965), 6613.

Tate's *King Lear* is an index to the dramatic theory, dramatic practice, language, and theatrical conditions of the period from 1678 to 1682. Tate's Tory sympathies prompted him to select plays appropriate to the troubled times. His aim was to dramatize the evils of usurpation and illegitimate succession. His alterations are not capricious, but are dictated by his political and critical predilections.

2394   Bazagonov, M. S. "King Lear." *Shakespeare in the Red: Tales of Shakespeare by a Soviet Lamb.* Flegon Press, 1964, pp. 40-53.

In this Soviet version the suitors in Lear's court remain for a protracted period. Lear must learn the lesson that old age can be stubborn, inflexible, and aggravating; but once he has realized this fact and the nature of his own conduct, he and his family are harmoniously reunited.

2395   Black, A. J. "A Critical Edition of Nahum Tate's *The History of King Lear.*" Ph.D. dissertation, University of Birmingham, 1964. See item 2494.

2396   Fleissner, Robert F. "Shakespeare and Dickens: Some Characteristic Uses of the Playwright by the Novelist." Ph.D. dissertation, New York University, 1964. *DA,* 25 (1965), 4686.

Dickens was enormously influenced by Shakespeare, most specifically by *King Lear* and *Hamlet.* The *Lear* influence is particularly evident in *Martin Chuzzlewit* and *The Old Curiosity Shop.* The latter involves a death scene from Little Nell in many ways paralleling that of Cordelia. He objected to the appropriateness of "fool" as a term of endearment for Cordelia in Lear's line "My poor fool is hanged" and comes very close to the literal interpretation of the fool's hanging proposed by Sir Joshua Reynolds and I. Griskin.

2397   Heyen, William. "Lear at the Golf Course." *Ball State Teachers College Forum,* 5, No. 3 (1964), 9.

This poem describes an increasingly furious and inept Lear playing golf, showering himself with sand from the trap while the flag waves defiantly from the green.

2398   *Kokoschka. King Lear. Apulian Journey. Hellas. 63 Lithographs 1961-1963.* London: Marlborough Fine Art, 1964.

This monograph includes a catalogue of three limited editions of Kokoschka's work, one of which consists of seventeen lithographs on *King Lear.* Wolfgang Fischer also interviews the artist concerning the impact of *Lear* upon his work (pp. 10-11).

2399   McMahon, Joseph H. "Ducis—Unkindest Cutter?" *Yale French Studies,* No. 33 (1964), pp. 14-25.

This article analyzes the late eighteenth-century adaptations by Jean François Ducis of *King Lear* and four other Shakespearean plays.

2400   Singh, Amrith. "Versions of *King Lear.*" *Journal of English Studies,* 5 (1964), 76-98.

This article focuses on Nahum Tate's adaptation of *King Lear* in 1681 and the various modifications of Tate's version that held the stage and dominated *Lear* criticism throughout the Neo-Classical period.

2401   Green, Roger Lancelyn. "King Lear." *Tales from Shakespeare.* New York: Atheneum, 1965, pp. 271-292.

The plot line of *King Lear* is reconstructed as a prose narrative. Illustrations are provided by Richard Beer.

2402   Klein, J. W. "The Supreme Challenge of *Lear.*" *Musical Opinion,* 88 (1965), 211-213.

Although Shakespeare's drama has inspired numerous musical compositions, *King Lear* has been one work that composers have refused to tackle. Verdi is perhaps the prominent example; he was for years obsessed with the possibilities of an operatic version of the play, but he never could bring himself to the point of composition. Now comes word that Benjamin Britten, encouraged by the librettist Ronald Duncan, will develop an opera on *Lear.* Britten's genius is admirably suited to the tragic subject, and he also has proved himself a born dramatist in his past works. *Lear,* of course, will be Britten's supreme test; if he succeeds, it "may set the seal on his reputation for generations" (p. 213).

2403   Roy, S. N. "Shakespeare in Pre-Raphaelite Painting." *Essays on Shakespeare.* Edited by Bhabatosh Chatterjee. University of Burdwan Memorial Volume. Bombay: Orient Longmans, 1965, pp. 231-246.

This volume includes thirteen essays, published under the supervision of the English Department of the University of Burdwan. S. N. Roy discusses the Pre-Raphaelite painters who were inspired by Shakespeare, including Ford Madox Brown and Sir John Millais on *King Lear.*

2404   Smith, Lain Crichton. "She Teaches *Lear.*" *Times Literary Supplement,* 17 (1965), 520.

This poem based on the *Lear* plot describes the agonies of old age, not the least of which stems from the indifference and lack of understanding of the young.

2405   Spencer, Christopher, ed. *"The History of King Lear."* Five *Restoration Adaptations of Shakespeare.* Urbana: University of Illinois Press, 1965, pp. 271-274, 442-448.

The 1681 quarto of Nahum Tate's adaptation of *King Lear* is printed in full. Five quarto copies have been examined, and the variants are listed in a separate section of notes. Tate's Shakespearean source is apparently Q_2 *Lear,* printed in 1619 but falsely dated 1608.

2406   Hamblem, Abigail Ann. "Lear the Universal." *Cresset* (Valparaiso), 30, No. 5 (1966), 15-18.

This article traces the subsequent use of the Lear story by Turgenev in 1870, by Balzac in 1885, and by Mary E. Wilkins in 1891.

2407   Haywood, Charles. "Negro Minstrelsy and Shakespearean Burlesque." *Folklore and Society: Essays in Honor of Benjamin A. Botkin.* Hatboro, Pa.: Folklore Association, 1966, pp. 77-92.

Portions of Shakespeare's plays furnished excellent materials for parody by the minstrelmen of the American frontier stage. *King Lear* lent itself to many such parodies, and it gave rise to numerous comic songs as well.

2408   Hodson, Geoffrey. "The Nahum Tate *Lear* at Richmond." *Drama,* Summer, 1966, pp. 36-39.

A summer training course for forty-five London teachers at a Georgian Theater in Richmond involves a study of Tate's *Lear* and a comparison with Shakespeare's.

2409   Revyakin, A. I., ed. *Memories of A. N. Ostrovsky by His Contemporaries.* Moscow: Khudozheatvennaya literatura, 1966.

The series of essays in Russian on the nineteenth-century playwright A. N. Ostrovsky includes a discussion of his interpretation of *King Lear* and of its general philosophic influence upon his work. Also included is a passage on his translation of *Lear* and other Shakespearean plays.

2410   Roy, Emil. "O'Neill's *Desire Under the Elms* and Shakespeare's *King Lear*." *Die neuren Sprachen,* 15 (1966), 1-6.

The similarity between *Desire Under the Elms* and *King Lear* extends far beyond the common motif of the education of an old man. Both open with bargaining scenes involving the distribution of land among three children. Like Lear with his map and its unequal division, Eben with his bag of gold assumes that love is measurable and quantifiable. Both act hastily and in wrath, assuming God-like prerogatives, and ultimately both must witness the wanton murder of a favorite child. Lear and Ephraim, blinded by outward appearances, must learn compassion, mercy, and forgiveness; each is mocked by a fool who serves as a voice of the social conscience. In a word, *Desire* is as close to *Lear* as it is to any Greek models; both involve the relationships of child to the parent, of man to the state, and of the gods to men. Lear through madness gains insight into the nature of universal law; Ephraim, on the other hand, is judged mad by a society that itself is mad.

2411   Singh, Amrith. "Versions of *King Lear*." *Indian Journal of English Studies,* 5 (1966), 76-98.

The neo-classical period saw four versions of *King Lear,* the most popular of which was Nahum Tate's, with the Edgar-Cordelia love story. A second version by David Garrick effected a compromise between Tate and Shakespeare. George Colman the Elder came close to restoring Shakespeare; he rejected the Cordelia-Edgar love strand and apparently seriously considered reinstituting the tragic ending. It remained for the romantics like Hunt and Lamb to give full approval to the Shakespearean version.

2412   Smythe, Percy Ellesman. *A Complete Paraphrase of "King Lear."* Sydney: College Press, 1966. 95 pp.

In this complete paraphrase of the text of *King Lear* the stated aim is both to achieve clear, modern expression and also to preserve insofar as possible the spirit of the original, especially in regard to the mood and character of the speakers.

2413   Williams, T. D. Duncan. "Mr. Nahum Tate's *King Lear.*" *Studia Neophilologica,* 38 (1966), 290-300.

The continued popularity of Nahum Tate's *Lear* (1681) for over a century and a half is due in large part to contemporary taste and fashion.

2414   Balakirev, M. A. *Chronological Outline of Life and Work.* Leningrad: Muzyka, 1967.

This description of the work of the eminent Russian composer focuses at times on the music which he wrote for *King Lear* (pp. 43, 46, 53-55).

2415   Black, James. "An Augustan Stage-History: Nahum Tate's *King Lear.*" *Restoration and 18th-Century Theatre Research,* 6, No. 1 (1967), 36-54.

This article describes the adaptations made by Nahum Tate for his *Lear* in 1681 and describes the productions of this version which held the stage for many years.

2416   Black, James. "The Influence of Hobbes on Nahum Tate's *King Lear.*" *Studies in English Literature,* 7 (1967), 377-385.

One of the major influences on Nahum Tate's adaptations of *King Lear* was Thomas Hobbes, whose concept of man's acting purely on self-seeking principles was given stage life in the modified character of Edmund. Tate saw in Shakespeare's villain "an adumbration—if not an actual type—of the Hobbesian 'natural' man and took pains to make [him] more exactly Hobbesian than he found him to be" (p. 385).

2417   Golata, John   *"Père Goriot* and *King Lear."   English Journal,* 56 (1967), 1288-1289.

Père Goriot like *King Lear* is concerned with a father who too late realizes that his daughters are ingrates. Royalty and the common man as fathers are vulnerable to the same mistakes; and in any social class words of love are not necessarily sincere. Students exposed to both of these works come to understand how deeply complex are the duties and responsibilities of parenthood.

2418   Margolis, John D.   "Shakespeare and Shelley's Sonnet 'England in 1819.' "   *English Language Notes,* 4 (1967), 276-277.

The opening line of Shelley's sonnet "England in 1819" distinctly echoes Shakespeare's *King Lear.*

2419   Prager, Leonard.   "Of Parents and Children: Jacob Gordin's *The Jewish King Lear."   American Quarterly,* 18 (1967), 506-516.

Jacob Gordin's *The Jewish King Lear* is no travesty but a drama involving the binding together of two generations, reflecting the anxiety of the early immigrant Jews in America that they would lose their children to the modern world, to Gentile America. First performed in 1892, it is not great drama but it celebrates family and folk cohesion. Gordin borrowed from Shakespeare the plot scheme of the wilful father, David Moyshele, who imprudently divides his riches among his daughters, rejects his youngest, Taybele, because she refuses to flatter him, and suffers agonizing consequences. *King Lear* is thus transformed into a story of an "Eastern European Jewish immigrant who places his hopes in his children, who looks to them for an ultimate answer regarding the meaning and value of his departure from one world and his entry into another" (p. 516).

2420   Sewall, Richard B.   "Ahab's Quenchless Feud: The Tragic Vision in Shakespeare and Melville."   *Comparative Drama,* 1 (1967), 207-218.

Both Shakespeare and Melville developed deeply tragic views of life, and both were highly critical of their own times. The leading question in both *Moby Dick* and in *King Lear* concerns the nature of malicious agencies that operate on man to render him susceptible to tragedy, to a quenchless feud. Lear is a furious old man bent on vengeance; his peculiar white whale is the monomaniac vision of his daughters.

2421　Tremewan, P. J. "Balzac et Shakespeare." *Année balzacienne* (1967), pp. 259-303.

Balzac was thoroughly familiar with Shakespeare's work. *King Lear* and three other plays (*Romeo and Juliet, Othello, Richard III*) had a particularly extensive influence upon his work.

2422　Bayley, John. "King Lear and Father Sergius: A Parallel." *Forum for Modern Language Studies,* 4 (1968), 64-69.

The fact that *King Lear* profoundly affected Tolstoy is revealed in the intensity of his attacks upon the play. Father Sergius' pilgrimage seems directly modeled upon Lear's spiritual adventure.

2423　Brix, Brigitte. "Shakespeare's *King Lear*: En analyse of tragedien og dens kilder med en oversigt over de sceniske bearbejde ser af teksten og den litteraere kritik heraf i England indtil 1838." *Extracta,* 1 (1968), 53-61.

This article focuses on the adaptations of Shakespeare's *King Lear* between 1681 and 1838 and on the dramatic centrality of such matters as the function of the Fool and the tragic ending involving Lear's loss of the crown and Cordelia's death.

2424　Fleissner, Robert F. " 'The Rape of the Lock,' I, 16: A Parallel." *American Notes and Queries,* 7 (1968), 23.

The source of Pope's line, "And sleepless lovers just at twelve awake" (I, 16), is not Chaucer but Shakespeare's *King Lear*; it is a parodistic reversal of the Fool's final quip, "And I'll go to bed at noon" (III, v, 92). Pope mocks the tradition of going to bed at noon by comically observing that noon is the time for an amorous, wakeful life.

2425   Gillon, Adam.   "Joseph Conrad and Shakespeare: Part II."
       Conradiana, 1, No. 2 (1968), 15-22.

   Both in theme and in specific phraseology Conrad is indebted
to *King Lear* in "End of the Tether." Also discussed are influences
of *Hamlet* on *Lord Jim*.

2426   Markels, Julian.   *"King Lear* and *Moby Dick*: The Cultural Con-
       nection." *Massachusetts Review*, 9 (1968), 169-176.

   King Lear exerts a decisive influence on *Moby Dick* primarily
because both protagonists experience a form of madness that leads
not to degeneration but to an encounter with vital truth. The two
works artistically pose questions and answers that are instructively
similar; they " 'anatomize' nature to see whether it is demonic, conclude that its brutality is indifferent rather than intelligent, and
recommend an attitude toward its perils that we may broadly describe as humanist Stoicism. *King Lear* works out the problem
through the ethics and consciousness of a feudal culture in crisis, and
Moby Dick through the corresponding elements in the anticipated
crisis of a democratic culture" (pp. 170-171). *Lear* embodies the
philosophic conflict of Hooker and Hobbes, *Moby Dick* the crisis of
a single cultural consciousness tested for the first time against the
absolute condition of reality. The waste and destruction in each
culture are disastrous, but Edgar and Ishmael survive as evidence
that there is hope if man will fulfill his human responsibilities with
the necessary sufferance.

2427   Ruoff, James.   "Kierkegaard and Shakespeare." *Comparative
       Literature*, 20 (1968), 343-354.

   King Lear, along with three other Shakespearean plays, was
profoundly influential upon Kierkegaard. The philosopher considered Shakespeare to be a kindred spirit who articulated a "deep,
ineffable secret" through artistic sublimation.

2428   Scragg, Leah.   "Shakespearean Influence in *Herod and Anti-
       pater.*" *Notes and Queries*, n.s. 15 (1968), 258-262.

   The characterization of Antipater as a bastard child of Herod,
certain elements of the plot, and a number of verbal echoes suggest

that one source of Sampson's play is the subplot of Shakespeare's *King Lear.*

2429   Sharkey, Peter L. "Performing Nahum Tate's *King Lear*: Coming Hither by Going Hence." *Quarterly Journal of Speech,* 54 (1968), 398-403.

Various characteristics and mannerisms established effectively for Tate's version of *King Lear* have continued to plague productions since the restoration of Shakespeare's text. Tate, for example, wrote the psychology of the ruling passion into the play. Lear's mad curses and ravings, Edgar's and Cordelia's protestations of love, Edmund's vow to gain revenge—"each is a rhetorical cameo session or locket of the single passion ruling the corresponding character, and the scenes in which they appear are essentially rhetorical frames" (p. 400). The actor in Tate's version is required to move suddenly from heights of passion to extended prosaic valleys, and individual talent established legendary Lears in the eighteenth century, especially Garrick's sentimentalized sick and dotty old king. The legacy of Tate's interpretation haunts modern productions in a tendency to histrionics that has led more than one twentieth-century Lear to heights of passion in cursing Goneril which he finds it impossible to sustain or surmount; occasionally, too, there is excessive concern for the portrayal of Lear's pathology.

2430   White, William. "Uncollected Whitman on Lear." *Shakespeare Newsletter,* 18 (1968), 41.

Walt Whitman, when editor of the Brooklyn *Daily Times,* quoted Lear's comment to the elements that they "owe [him] no subscription," observing that it would be nice to be able to say the same thing of his readers.

2431   Adling, Wilfield. "Gorki und Shakespeare: Zur Shakespeare—Rezeption im dramatischen Spätwerk Maxim Gorkis." *Shakespeare Jahrbuch* (Heidelberg), 105 (1969), 89-103.

This essay compares Shakespeare's *King Lear* with a cycle of late plays (after 1928) by Gorki. Abiding thematic similarities overshadow the necessary differences due to sociological conditions.

2432 Gascoigne, Bamber.   "Will They Ridicule our Shakespeare?"
       Stratford Papers 1965-67. Edited by B. A. W. Jackson. Ham-
       ilton, Ontario: McMaster University Library Press, 1969,
       pp. 29-50.

       This article discusses the difficulties of maintaining the original
tone and impact in the adaptation of Shakespeare's plays. Specific
attention is directed to Nahum Tate's *King Lear* (1681) and a
Japanese version of *The Merchant of Venice* called *The Strange
Affair of the Flesh of the Bosom* (1877).

2433 Osborne, Charles. "Verdi and *King Lear.*" *London Magazine,* 9,
       No. 8 (1969), 84-88.

       Verdi for personal reasons was never able to bring himself to
complete an operatic version of *King Lear*, although he considered
it the greatest of Shakespeare's works and constantly spoke of his
intentions to do so. He planned to create a four-act opera with
four principal singers. Quite possibly music composed for this opus
found its way into other works of Verdi.

2434 Swaminathan, S. R.   "Keats and Benjamin West's *King Lear.*"
       Keats-Shelley Journal, 18 (1969), 15-16.

       It is likely that Keats in his reference to *King Lear* in his
famous "Negative Capability" letter is referring not to Shakespeare's
play but to Benjamin West's painting of the storm scene in *King
Lear.*   Lear is depicted taking off his clothes with the comment,
"Off, off, you lendings! Come, unbutton here."

2435 Vassilious, Spyros. *Lights and Shadows.* Athens: n.p. , 1969.

       This volume of three hundred sixty-three scene paintings of
Spyros Vassilious includes examples from *King Lear* and three other
Shakespearean plays.

2436 Williams, A. E. "Le Mythe du Shakespeare français." *Revue de
       Litterature Comparée,* 43, No. 1 (1969), 98-107.

       This article compares Tristan L'Hermite's *La Folie du Sage*
with *King Lear.*

2437 Hunter, G. K., ed. *"King Lear": 1820.* Adapted by R. W. Elliston. London: Cornmarket Press, 1970. 68 pp.

This text, bearing the name of the celebrated comic actor and the lessee of Drury Lane from 1819 to 1826, is another document in the long journey from Nahum Tate's adaptation (1681) back to Shakespeare's original version. It is apparently the text Edmund Kean used in his debut in the role at Drury Lane on 24 April 1820. The play could not be performed during George III's insanity, but was released for performance when he died on 29 January 1820. The text retains much of Tate, including the full Edgar-Cordelia love story. Reintroduced, however, is the scene of Lear's recovery to sanity. Elliston in the introduction describes the setting and costuming as Saxon and quotes at length pertinent passages from Holinshed. He is apologetic for the pandered text but observes that the "public taste long ago decided against the sublime, but terrible, catastrophe of the original" (p. a).

2438 Hunter, G. K., ed. *"King Lear": Charles Kean 1858.* London: Cornmarket Press, 1970. 90 pp.

The text of this version of *King Lear* is a photographic reproduction of that used by Charles Kean in his production at the Princess' Theatre in 1858. It is an entirely Shakespearean text, that is, Nahum Tate's additions have disappeared; but Tate's influence remains in the excising, stitching together, and reconstructing (for example, the joining of the two heath scenes III, iv and III, vi). The text is heavily cut; about one-third of Shakespeare is gone, including I, v; III, v; III, vii; IV, iii; and IV, v. In part the cuts provide the time necessary for realizing Kean's inordinate interest in historical detail, a concern reflected in his "Historical and Explanatory Notes" printed at the end of each act. The attention to scenic detail also resulted in part from the final disappearance of the stage into a proscenium frame during this period.

2439 Hunter, G. K., ed. *"King Lear": Cumberland's Edition c. 1830.* London: Cornmarket Press, 1970. 67 pp.

The text of this facsimile of *King Lear*, first performed by Edmund Kean on 10 February 1823, reintroduces Shakespeare's tragic ending; otherwise it is largely Nahum Tate's version. It was first printed in Dolby's *British Theatre,* VI (London, 1924) and was subsequently reprinted in Cumberland's *British Drama, 1830-1831.* The facsimile was made from a copy of Cumberland's in the Birmingham Shakespeare Library. George Daniel, in his prefatory remarks, speaks of *Lear* as the most affecting of all tragedies, depicting a harrowing picture of human misery. "Lear, wandering over the barren heath, amidst storm and tempest, with a broken heart, and a bewildered brain, is so transcendently sublime and awful, that antiquity must acknowledge the supremacy of Shakespeare, and bow to the immortal" (p. 6). Garrick, Kemble, and Cooke are notable past Lears, but Kean is to be praised for returning in part at least to Shakespeare's text. Included also are a list of costumes for each character and the cast of characters for Drury Lane in 1824 and Covent Garden in 1828.

2440　Lippincott, Henry F., Jr. "Tate's Lear in the Nineteenth Century: The Edwin Forrest Promptbooks." *Library Chronicle,* 36 (1970), 67-75.

　　　The promptbooks of Edwin Forrest reveal that Tate's version of *King Lear* played in America until 1872, over a quarter of a century longer than has generally been supposed. Moreover, his text is far from "pure Tate." The script runs slightly more than half as long as Shakespeare's.

2441　Ryan, Sister M. Rosario. "Dickens and Shakespeare: Probable Sources of *Barnaby Rudge." English,* 19 (1970), 43-48.

　　　Various parallels are described between Dickens' novel and *King Lear* and *Macbeth* to display the extent of Shakespeare's influence on the nineteenth-century novelist.

2442　Balakirev, M. and V. Stasov. *Correspondence.* 2 Vols. Moscow: Muzyka, 1971.

　　　Volume 2 contains a discussion of M. A. Balakirev's music for *King Lear.*

2443　Cohen, Ruth. Theater Review in *Yediot Aharonot* (Tel Aviv), 7 October 1971.

This article reviews Edward Bond's production of *Lear* at the Royal Court Theatre in London.

2444   Esslin, Martin.   "Edward Bonds *Lear* uraugeführt."   *Theater heute,* 12 (1971), 62.

This article reviews a production of Edward Bond's *Lear* at the Royal Court Theatre in London.

2445   Gardner, C. O.   " 'No Worst There is None,' and *King Lear*: An Experiment in Criticism."   *Theoria,* 36 (1971), 11-37.

T. S. Eliot's claim that the past is "altered by the present as much as the present is directed by the past" is well illustrated by Shakespeare's *King Lear* and Hopkins' sonnet, "No worst, there is none." The number of Shakespearean memories recorded in Hopkins is remarkable. Clearly in the very title Hopkins is recalling Edgar's comment, upon seeing his blinded father, that the worst has not occurred so long as one can articulate the idea. More specifically, word echoes such as "grief," "woe," "sorrow," "world," "mind," and "all" contribute greatly to the theme. The effect is not one of imitation but of enhancement and enrichment as Hopkins writes on the same theme and in the process establishes resonances with the earlier work. The enriching influence works in reverse equally well as Hopkins' poem helps to underscore the concept of "religious questioning and probing, the cry of agony thrown out to the Gods" (p. 26). The poem, moreover, encapsulates the sufferings of Lear, Gloucester, and Edgar, and the complexity of its final line reiterates the profound ambiguities of the ending of the drama, the ambivalent assumption that "a loving inscrutable wisdom informs even the cruellest blows of fate" (p. 34).

2446   Hildebrand, William.   "Jupiter, Demogorgon, and Lear: A Note on the Sources of *Prometheus Unbound* III. i. 19."   *Serif,* 8, No. 3 (1971), 11-13.

In *Prometheus Unbound* and *The Cenci* Shelley pays Shakespeare "the ultimate devoir of one artist to another: formal and stylistic imitation" (p. 11). Specifically, Lear's line indicating that his revenges on Goneril and Regan will be "the terrors of the earth" (II, iv, 284) is the source of *Prometheus Unbound,* III, i, 19, in which Jupiter describes his "fatal child" by Thetis as "the terror of the earth." Not only is the phrasing virtually identical; both lines also refer to filial ingratitude, and in both instances the fate of the victim provides the possibility of renewal for the survivors.

2447   Holmstrom, John. "Lear, Royal Court." *Plays and Players,* 19, No. 2 (1971), 42-46, 53.

This article reviews Edward Bond's grim production of *Lear* at the Royal Court Theatre.

2448   Lambert, J. W. "Plays in Performance." *Drama,* Winter, 1971, pp. 14-31.

This article reviews Edward Bond's production of *Lear* at the Royal Court Theatre. Essentially, the interpretation views the play as a piece of masochistic horror.

2449   Martin, George. "Verdi, *King Lear* and Maria Piccolomini." *Columbia Library Columns,* 21, No. 1 (1971), 12-20.

Throughout his career Verdi refers sporadically to his intention to compose an opera based on Shakespeare's *King Lear.* A letter in the Columbia University Library sheds light on one specific attempt to do so. Verdi's letter, addressed in August, 1856, to Vincenzo Torelli, the Associate Secretary of the Teatro San Carlo in Naples, indicates his desire to have Maria Piccolomini sing the soprano lead. Although she was much in demand in London and Paris, she agreed to appear in Naples for five months, from 15 October 1857, to March, 1858. For unknown reasons the negotiations failed, and once again the opera was not written. Some critics and biographers have suggested that subconsciously Verdi was never able to work on *Lear* because the subject was too painful; Verdi himself in his earlier years lost his daughter, son, and first wife in rapid succession.

2450   Oppel, Horst. "Shakespeare-Tagung in Frankfurt 1970—Bericht der Arbeitsgruppe zum Thema 'Shakespeare und die bildende Kunst.' " *Shakespeare Jahrbuch* (Heidelberg), 106 (1971), 7-9.

Illustrations of Shakespeare can attempt realistically to depict a particular moment in the action or abstractly to capture the spirit and theme of the play in a single, composite scene. King Lear, for example, can be portrayed realistically in the opening court scene, or he can be the abstract symbol of dejection and loneliness. The only real danger is that an illustration might severely limit the spectator's impression of the play.

2451   Tierney, Margaret. "He that Plays the King." *Plays and Players*, 19, No. 2 (1971), 18.

Harry Andrews, who played Lear in Edward Bond's production of *Lear* at the Royal Court Theatre, is interviewed concerning his experiences and challenges in the role.

2452   Weightman, John. "Stage Politics." *Encounter*, 37, No. 6 (1971), 29-31.

This article reviews Edward Bond's production of *Lear* at the Royal Court Theatre. The tone is totally black, a vision "of a humanity of ferocious beasts."

2453   Arnold, Arthur. "Lines of Development in Bond's Play." *Theatre Quarterly*, 2 (1972), 15-19.

This article discusses the major plot lines in Edward Bond's *Lear* and compares the structure of the play with that of Shakespeare's tragedy.

2454   Berwinska, Krystyna. "Teatr polityczny czy teatr okrucienstwa?" *Teatr* (Warsaw), 27 (1972), 9-11.

This article reviews Edward Bond's production of *Lear* at the Royal Court Theatre.

2455   Besser, Gretchen. "Lear and Goriot: A Re-evaluation." *Orbis Litterarum*, 27 (1972), 28-36.

King Lear is in many respects a model for Balzac's *Le Père Goriot*. Despite the absence of confirmatory documentation, there are many remarkable points of resemblance. Primarily, the plots are similar; in both a doting father, unwise in his love and duped by flattery, commits the fateful error of ceding his entire fortune to his children. In both narratives a subplot reiterates and intensifies the basic theme. Character resemblances, other than that between Lear and Goriot, are also striking; Victorine, for instance, is reminiscent of Cordelia in her saintly virtue and long-suffering patience, and Edmund like Rastignac is driven by a relentless ambition to succeed at any cost. The primary difference lies in the degree of awareness of the two protagonists. Lear comes fully to distinguish flattery from genuine affection, while Goriot is a willing victim of his own delusions. Moreover, *Lear* is a cosmic tragedy, whereas the setting and characters in Balzac are reduced to lifelike dimensions. If not, however, in personality or station in life, Goriot walks in Lear's shadow "in his enraged fatherhood" (p. 36).

2456 Bond, Edward. *Lear*. New York: Hill and Wang, 1972; London: Eyre Methuen, 1972. 88 pp.

Lear attempts to protect his kingdom against the Duke of Cornwall and the Duke of North by tyrannically forcing his subjects to build a protective wall. Farmers constantly rebel and tear down at night that part of the wall built during the day. Lear is shocked when he hears that his daughters Fontanelle and Bodice have married the two dukes. Claiming that he is mad, the daughters take control and open their arms to Lear's enemies, their husbands. One form of tyranny has replaced another, and a guerilla warfare develops, led by Cordelia, wife of a gravedigger's son who befriended Lear and whose ghost accompanies him. Cordelia's forces eventually prevail, and Fontanelle and Bodice are both executed. The warfare is ceaseless, however, and eventually the land is turned to waste. Lear, meanwhile, is treated as a prisoner, first by one side and then the other. Through his suffering and eventually his blinding, he develops a compassion for the common man and a realization that justice and law are nothing more than labels used for the method of exploitation by those in power. Finally Lear realizes the wall is a symbol of oppression, and he is shot to death attempting to tear it down. In the "Author's Preface," Bond describes man's aggression as a consequence of his living in unnatural conditions—urban, crowded regimented groups, working like machines. "Act One shows a world dominated by myth.   Act Two shows the clash between myth and reality, between superstitious man and the autonomous world. Act Three shows a resolution of this, in the world we prove real by dying in it" (p. xiv). See item 2509.

2457   Cohn, Ruby. "Beckett and Shakespeare." *Modern Drama,* 15 (1972-1973), 223-230.

Both Beckett and Shakespeare are possessed by the theme of nothingness. While this theme is reflected throughout the canon of both playwrights, the common ground has been made especially obvious in the recent Beckettian productions of *King Lear* by Peter Brook (see item 1890) and Herbert Blau (see item 1888).

2458   Frazer, Winifred L. "King Lear and Hickey: Bridegroom and Iceman." *Modern Drama,* 15 (1972-1973), 267-278.

Lear, in IV, iv, 199, about to be reunited with Cordelia, comments that he will "die bravely, like a smug bridegroom." Eugene O'Neill, in making the bridegroom of love also the iceman of death, utilizes the same ironic paradox; his iceman, Hickey, is the bridegroom Lear, who will "die bravely." Both Shakespeare and O'Neill utilize the double meaning of death as the cessation of life and the culmination of sexual orgasm. Although he shot Evelyn, Hickey in effect has been killed by her possessiveness; he and the others in Hope's No Chance Saloon are all victims of woman as both seducer and destroyer. Lear, likewise, caught up in a latent incestuous drive, is destroyed by a love that leads him to curse all of mankind: "Crack nature's moulds, all germens spill at once / That make ingrateful man!" "In the Garden sex and death were *born* together, and two great playwrights have ironically dramatized, by means of a *deadly* serious joke, the curse under which mankind has ever since labored" (p. 277).

2459   Gicovate, Bernardo. "Presencia de Shakespeare en la poesia de Juan Ramón Jiménez." *Sin Nombre,* 3 (1972), 76-83.

King Lear, among four other Shakespearean plays, is discussed as a source for allusions to imagery and character in Jiménez's early poetry.

2460   Green, Lawrence D. " 'Where's My Fool?'—Some Consequences
       of the Omission of the Fool in Tate's *Lear.*" *Studies in Eng-
       lish Literature,* 12 (1972), 259-274.

The Fool in Shakespeare's *King Lear* provides a focus on the
protagonist from numerous angles and acts as a device through
which Lear vents his passion and by which to measure the progress
of his madness. Tate's elimination of the Fool turns Lear's dialogue
and extended responses into dramatic monologue and consequently
internalizes the character. Such actors as Betterton, Boheme, Garrick, Colman, and Barry were forced, in other words, "to create a
metaphoric context outside of the lines themselves, to have a private
understanding of what gave rise to Lear's speeches and actions, . . .
to create an internal reality for Lear apart from the play" (p. 269).
By the time Macready reintroduced the Fool in 1838, this fascination of critics and actors with the psychology of Lear's character had
become so firmly established that it has carried over into Shakespeare's play as well. Even some current stage productions depict
Lear in self-conversation, mentally isolated in his own private world
while the Fool scampers about uttering needless paradoxes. The result is a loss of the needed interplay between the two characters.

2461   Hazan, Ruth. Theater Review in *Al ha-Mishmar* (Hotam, Israel),
       14 July 1972, pp. 16-17.

This article reviews Edward Bond's production of *Lear* at the
Royal Court Theatre in London.

2462   Levison, William Samuel. "Restoration Adaptations of Shake-
       speare as Baroque Literature." Ph.D. dissertation, University
       of Illinois-Urbana, 1972. *DAI,* 34 (1973), 730A.

Nahum Tate's version of *King Lear* in 1681 is characteristic
of the prevalent baroque style in its largeness of conception and execution, its adherence to classic or neoclassic principles, its glorifica-
tion and appeal to the senses, and its tendency toward excess.

2463   Meckier, Jerome. "Dickens and *King Lear*: A Myth for Victorian
       England." *South Atlantic Quarterly,* 71 (1972), 75-90.

Dickens never attempted   a tragedy comparable to *King
Lear,* but he did employ situations from the play to comment on

Victorian society's state of the soul. The grandfather and Nell in *The Old Curiosity Shop,* Dombey and Florence in *Dombey and Son,* and Gradgrind, Louisa, and Sissy Jupe in *Hard Times* are all reworkings of the Lear-Cordelia relationship. Perhaps, of course, Dickens found an objective correlative for his own childhood unhappiness in the tale of a cast-off child who returns to aid the parent, but more importantly he seized upon the motif as a myth for his culture, "in which the hard-hearted, deluded father figure, who refuses or perverts the love he receives from an affectionate daughter, became mid-century England, industrialized, materialized, even Benthamized, an England casting out, in the persons of Nell, Florence, and Louisa, all the emotions, feelings, and attributes of the heart that Dickens felt were essential to any genuine millenium" (p. 76). Each of the three novels concentrates on a different aspect of the Lear story—*The Old Curiosity Shop* on the death of Cordelia and the response of the grief-stricken father, *Dombey and Son* on Lear's plight with the comfort of the silent and long-suffering Cordelia, and *Hard Times* on the climactic scene of Lear's falling dead beside his daughter.

2464   Tough, A. J. *"Wuthering Heights* and *King Lear." English,* 21 (1972), 1-5.

   Wuthering Heights seems undeniably to owe an artistic debt to *King Lear.* The quality of the emotional impact is quite similar, each creating a sense of elemental passion and power played out against the backdrop of a storm-swept heath. The principal focus in both is the intensity of the protagonist's suffering, an anguish so intense that he curses those he loves and from which death is a welcome relief. There are differences, of course. Lear endures all while Heathcliff, with touches of both Edmund and the evil sisters, also inflicts pain. More importantly, *Lear* ends with a catastrophe in which the hope is at best a gleam; *Wuthering Heights* through the development of a second generation provides a kinder and more positive resolution.

2465   Weintraub, Stanley. "Shaw's *Lear." Ariel: A Journal of International English Literature,* 1, No. 3 (1970), 59-68. Reprint. *"Heartbreak House:* Shaw's *Lear." Modern Drama,* 15 (1972-1973), 255-265.

King Lear stands grimly and insistently behind Shaw's *Heart-break House* with its mad Captain Shotover, an old man of eighty-eight, and his three daughters, an ingenue and two sisters in the middle forties. A "modernized *King Lear*," as Shaw described it, *Heartbreak House* deals also with "the increasing inhumanity that increasing civilization seems paradoxically to bring . . . ; the dominating drive of the female of the species; the inevitable humiliation and defeat of the idealist and the dreamer; the misleading appearances we mistake for reality, dramatized through symbolic unclothing" (p. 263). In some ways Shaw's play is an inversion of Lear's—his daughters at the end live and thrive in their open cynicism while Lear's are defeated and dead; Shotover became delusively satisfied that all is for the better while Lear perceives his world crumbling. Both, however, reflect the "Lear dimension" (p. 258), and Kent's statement, "Break, heart, I prithee break" (V, iii, 312), perhaps even suggested Shaw's title.

2466   Wendt, Ernst. "London zum Beispiel: Viele Erfahrungen und einige Nutzanwendungen anlässlich von fünf Aufführungen." *Theater heute*, 13, No. 1 (1972), 24-27.

This article reviews productions of Edward Bond's *Lear* and Peter Brook's *A Midsummer Night's Dream.*

2467   Williams, Gordon. "The Problem of Passion in *Wuthering Heights.*" *Trivium*, 7 (1972), 41-53.

Heathcliff like King Lear is ambivalent and unpleasant at the same time that he commands tragic sympathy. The very name may well have been suggested by *Lear*, "at once stressing the mystery of the man and identifying him with the wild, natural setting" (p. 51).

2468   Entry Deleted.

2469   Arnold, Arthur. "Lines of Development in Bond's Play." *Theatre Quarterly*, 2, No. 5 (1973), 15-19.

This discussion of Edward Bond's dramaturgy includes an analysis of his adaptation, *Lear.*

2470   Boring, Phyllis Z. "More on Parody in Valle-Inclán." *Romance Notes*, 15 (1973), 246-247.

Valle-Inclán's *Romance de lobos* is, among other things, a parody of *King Lear*. Just as Lear divides his kingdom among his daughters during his lifetime, Montenegro distributes the inheritance to his sons. In both instances the children prove ungrateful and hostile, and the principal wanders in virtual exile with one who speaks the truth with a prophetic voice—the Fool and Fuso Negro. Whereas Lear is a tragic figure, however, dying of a broken heart after his alliance with powerful armies, Montenegro leads a band who turn cowards and flee when he orders them to charge the house held by his sons.

2471   Cook, John A. "The Fool Show in *Roderick Hudson.*" *Canadian Review of American Studies*, 4 (1973), 74-86.

Henry James began work on *Roderick Hudson* in the same year he reviewed Turgenev's *A King Lear of the Steppes*. Thus prompted, he "extrapolated significant elements from Shakespeare's play in order to create a similarly ironic tragedy around the issues of irresponsibility, rashness, and lack of trust" (p. 74). Like *Lear*, the novel has a fool figure who mirrors these qualities and a father-figure who victimizes the innocents in his charge.

2472   Dark, Gregory. "Edward Bond's *Lear* at the Royal Court." *Theatre Quarterly*, 2, No. 5 (1973), 20-31.

This article comprises a casebook from 13 June 1971 to 29 September 1971 (the date of the initial performance) of the preparation for production of Edward Bond's *Lear* at the Royal Court Theatre in London.

2473   Delrose, George. *An Updated Version of Shakespeare's "King Lear."* n. p., 1973. 135 pp.

Shakespeare's text is paraphrased, with emphasis on readability for the young contemporary reader.

2474   Domin, Hilde. "Grundsätzliches zu Edward Bonds *Lear.*" *Frankfurter Hefte*, 28 (1973), 762-766.

This article describes the fundamental philosophic and socio-logical principles underlying Edward Bond's version of the Lear story.

2475   Esslin, Martin. "Un Profeta Chi Predice la Catastrofe." *Sipario,* No. 308 (1973), 42-45.

This article reviews the production of Edward Bond's adaptation of *Lear* at the Royal Court Theatre in London.

2476   Gooch, Steve. Theater Review in *Plays and Players,* 20, No. 8 (1973), 66.

This article reviews a production of Edward Bond's *Lear* at Dartington College, Devon, directed by John Roche.

2477   Gross, Konrad. "Darstellungsprinzipien in Drama Edward Bonds." *Die neueren Sprachen,* n.s. 72 (1973), 313-324.

Edward Bond's version of the Lear story demands a consistent visual realism only sporadically present in Shakespeare's play.

2478   Holloway, Ronald. Theater Review in *Educational Theatre Journal,* 25 (1973), 108-110.

This article reviews a production of Edward Bond's *Lear* at the Frankfurt Theater in Frankfurt, Germany, directed by Peter Palitzsch.

2479   Hughes, Catharine. Theater Review in *Plays and Players,* 20, No. 10 (1973), 62-63.

This article reviews the production of Edward Bond's *Lear* by the Yale Repertory Theatre, directed by David Giles.

2480   Iden, Peter. "Ein unzumutbares Stück—oder unzumutbare Aufführungen?" *Theater heute,* 14, No. 3 (1973), 24-25.

This article reviews productions of Edward Bond's *Lear* in Vienna, Frankfurt, and Munich.

2481   Nathan, M. Theater Review in *Ma'ariv Daily* (Tel Aviv), 17 May and 27 December 1973.

This review article examines the production of Edward Bond's *Lear* at the Royal Court Theatre in London.

2482   Pfefferkorn, Eli.   Theater Review in *Ha-Aretz Daily* (Tel Aviv), 1 November 1973.

This review article examines the production of Edward Bond's *Lear* at the Royal Court Theatre in London.

2483   Filler, Witold.   "Bond i jego na wierzchu [Bond Has the Upper Hand]." *Teatr* (Warsaw), 29, No. 7 (1974), 4-5.

This article reviews a production of Edward Bond's *Lear* at the Teatr Wspólczesny in Warsaw.

2484   Grew, Zygmunt.   "Oczy Lira." *Zycie literackie* (Kraków), 21 April 1974, pp. 7, 13.

This article, entitled "The Eyes of Lear," reviews a production of Edward Bond's *Lear* at the Teatr Wspólczesny in Warsaw.

2485   Klotz, Günther.   "Erbezitat und zeitlose Gewalt." *Weimarer Beiträge,* 19, No. 10 (1973), 54-65. Reprint. *Shakespeare Jahrbuch* (Weimar), 110 (1974), 44-53.

The immediate cause of the confrontation between Lear and his daughters in Edward Bond's *Lear* is their marriage to his two arch enemies—the Duke of Cornwall and the Duke of North—but the rhythm of the conflict between the old and young generations and of the ceaseless struggle for power and wealth is the more fundamental catalyst.

2486   Moshe, Nathan.   "The Shock Theater of E. Bond." *Ma'ariv* (Tel Aviv), 17 May 1974, pp. 22-23.

This article (in Hebrew) examines Edward Bond's dramatic technique and the particular qualities of the adaptation which lend it a particularly macabre quality.

2487   Müller, Andre.   "Über die 'linken' Greuel: Bemerkungen zu Bonds *Lear.*" *Theater der Zeit,* 28, No. 4 (1973), 31-33.

This article discusses both the physical horrors and the political implications in Edward Bond's *Lear*.

2488   Nelson, Cathryn A.   "Echoes of *1 Henry IV, King Lear,* and *Macbeth* in *Wit's Triumverate.*" *Shakespeare Quarterly,* 25 (1973), 357-358.

The author of the anonymous comedy *Wit's Triumverate, or The Philosopher* was thoroughly familiar with Shakespeare's *King Lear.* In addition to an echo of *1 Henry IV* and *Macbeth*, the lines "Gyants, Arm'd-men, mee thought, I sawe, Halfe-Horse, / Half-man, iust Centaure-like. / Why so are all, the upper part of Man, the other / half is beast, divided by the girdle" closely resemble *Lear,* IV, vi, 126-129.

2489   Sullivan, John.   "Un *Lear* original la Royal Court." *Contemporanul,* No. 25 (1973).

This article reviews Edward Bond's Production of *Lear* at the Royal Court Theatre in London.

2490   Sullivan, John.   "Teatrul Powszechny din Lodez: Regele Lear de Shakespeare." *Teatrul,* No. 6 (1973), p. 47.

This article reviews the production of Edward Bond's *Lear* at the Lodz Theater.

2491   Oppel, Horst and Sandra Christenson.   *Edward Bond's "Lear" and Shakespeare's "King Lear."* Mainz: Akademie der Wissenschaften und der Literatur, 1974. Abstract. English and American Studies in German. Summaries of Theses and Monographs. Supplement to *Anglia,* 1974. Tübingen: Max Niemeyer, 1975, pp. 146-147.

Such twentieth-century productions of *King Lear* as Peter Brook's (see item 1890) and Charles Marowitz's (see item 1868) have encouraged Edward Bond to plunder Shakespeare at will for his own drama. Ultimately, however, Bond's creative powers appear limited in comparison with their magnificent foil. In both versions Lear, deeply shaken, clings obsessively to the thought of his ungrateful daughters. Bond deletes the function of Cordelia, subsuming a part of it in the role of the Gravedigger's boy; so, too, Edmund is deleted, a part of his function subsumed in Warrington. One essential difference is that Shakespeare focuses on personal tragedy whereas Bond concentrates on a society "that revels in aggression and has pledged itself to inescapable thoughts and deeds of destruction" (p. 10). The wall is the dominant symbol for man's uninhibited craving for power. A second essential difference is in the playwrights' delineation of common man. In both plays common man is delineated in stark contrast with his superiors, but Shakespeare tends to depict him as a simplistically good creature willing to risk life and limb in opposition to the tyranny of a villainous lord; Bond's common men cover the wider range of guiltless victims, conformers, and accomplices.

2492   Svaglic, Martin J. "Shelley and *King Lear.*" *Nineteenth-Century Literary Perspectives: Essays in Honor of Lionel Stevenson.* Edited by Clyde de L. Ryals. Durham: Duke University Press, 1974, pp. 49-63.

In *A Defense of Poetry* Shelley describes *King Lear* as "the most perfect specimen of the dramatic art existing in the world." His adulation in part stems from Shakespeare's blending of comedy with tragedy, in particular in the function of the Fool. More importantly, Lear symbolizes Shelley's tyrannical father-king who must be chastened and brought to terms; in the process Cordelia functions as a Beatrice Cenci without her flaw, in returning kindness and forebearance for injury. Moreover, as Lear experiences a moral purgation in moving from egocentricity to love, Shakespeare is able to inculcate sound moral principle without overt didacticism. Finally, Shelley had come to believe that no effective social reform was possible without the spiritual regeneration of the individual members of society; *Lear*, more successfully than anything Shelley himself wrote, combines the abstract message with effective concrete dramatic plot.

2493   Benston, Kimberly W. "*The Duchess of Malfi:* Webster's Tragic Vision." *Gypsy Scholar,* 3 (1975), 20-36.

Just as Webster's *The Duchess of Malfi* is philosophically and thematically reminiscent of *King Lear*, so there are many verbal and structural echoes as well. The Duchess, like Lear, "must suffer the stripping away of prefabricated protective masks and confront an evil world's irreducible facts of pain and death. As Lear in his progress from pride to knowledge is forced ultimately to contemplate unaccommodated man, so the Duchess must eventually confront life without possession and with her honor obscured. Her capture, torture, and murder carry the play, like Lear's sufferings in the storm, into a wider universe which transcends common experience. Finally, like Lear she rejects insanity, a form of renouncing responsible involvement in a world seemingly without ultimate value and order; both protagonists in their final stage of development form an existential armistice with objective reality, determined to uphold those bonds and values which one can only devoutly wish existed in actuality.

2494   Black, James, ed.   *The History of King Lear* by Nahum Tate. Regents Restoration Drama Series. Lincoln: University of Nebraska Press, 1975, 111 pp.

Tate's version of *Lear* first appeared in print in 1681 with four additional quarto publications during his lifetime—namely1689, 1699, 1702, and 1712. All texts are derivations from Q_1, which serves as copy text for this edition. Tate's fundamental changes involve his elimination of the Fool, the restoration of Lear to his throne, and a successful romantic relationship between Edgar and Cordelia. The version held the stage until Kean's restoration of the tragic ending in 1823 and Macready's restoration of the Fool and the full text in 1838. It also was revived on several occasions in the mid century. Most recently the play was performed in Richmond, Yorkshire, and London in 1966. See items 294, 566, 570, 595, 715, 719, 808, 893, 913, 948, 1001, 1046, 1058, 1081, 1463.

2495   Dark, Gregory.   "Edward Bond's *Lear* at the Royal Court." *Theatre Quarterly,* 2 (1975), 20-31.

This article reviews a production of Edward Bond's *Lear* in London at the Royal Court Theatre.

2496   Gillon, Adam.   "Joseph Conrad and Shakespeare: Part Five: *King Lear* and *Heart of Darkness." Joseph Conrad:*

Commemorative Essays. Edited by Adam Gillon and Ludwik Krzyzanowski. New York: Astra Books, 1975.

Heart of Darkness like *King Lear* offers a paradoxical view of man, with good and evil inextricably joined as necessary aspects of human nature. More specifically, the novel parallels the linguistic and philosophic revelations of Shakespeare's play. Marlow and Kurtz, like Lear and Gloucester, must learn to distinguish between language and truth, and they must come to understand the tremendous gap between emotion and idealism. The elaborate rhetoric of the characters gives way in both instances to a bare simplicity of expression suggesting that love needs no words and demands no high-sounding slogans. Conrad's world of unreason, rapacious folly, and madness, in a word, recapitulates Shakespeare's view of a darkness both physical and spiritual.

2497   Hainsworth, J. D.   *"King Lear* and John Brown's *Athelstan."* *Shakespeare Quarterly,* 26 (1975), 471-477.

One night before Garrick opened at Drury Lane in John Brown's *Athelstan* on 27 February 1756, his rival Spranger Barry opened at Covent Garden in the role of Lear. Garrick apparently chose his role in part because it afforded certain parallels with Lear through which he could mount a challenge to Barry. Moreover, it provided an ending resembling *Lear* through which Garrick could test the practicality of his desire to discard Tate's happy ending in his future productions of Shakespeare's play.

2498   Knapp, Bettina L.   "The Paris Theatrical Season: 1974-75." *Drama and Theatre,* 12 (1975), 110-114.

This article reviews a production of Edward Bond's *Lear* in Paris. The director, Patrice Chéreau, describes the contemporary adaptation as a vision of our time. It is, however, more like Grand Guignol than modern drama, a work devoid of conviction and depth. The fault lies in the insipid play, not with the acting.

2499   Entry Deleted.

2500   Morley, Patricia. " 'The Road to Dover': Patrick White's *The Eye of the Storm." Humanities Association Review,* 26 (1975), 106-115.

Shakespeare's *King Lear* is a major paradigm for Patrick White's novel *The Eye of the Storm.* The "road to Dover" is a metaphor for life's journey toward death, and the novel presents two Lears, one who traverses this road successfully and one who does not. Lear himself, of course, has two faces—the one worthy of reverence and love, the other despicable in its folly, cruelty, and baseness. The major characters in the play are driven to death, but that death is either demonic (Goneril, Regan, Edmund) or apocalyptic (Lear, Cordelia, Kent). The successful Lear in the novel is Elizabeth Hunter, who dies in her home, having cheated the old people's home of another victim. Her cathartic experience in the cave-like wine cellar in which she takes refuge from a cyclone on Brumby Island is analogous to Lear's experience in the hovel on the heath. The unsuccessful or "plasticine" Lear is Sir Basil Hunter. Knighted for his acting, he nonetheless can never escape the haunting memories of his failures, and to the end he remains trapped in his ego. He dies, in signal contrast to Elizabeth Hunter, a "slightly surreal Fool" (p. 112).

2501   Pedersen, Lise. "From Shakespearean Villain to Shavian Original Moralist: Shaw's Transformation of Shakespeare's Richard III and Edmund the Bastard." *McNeese Review,* 22 (1975-1976), 36-50.

Shaw's Andrew Undershaft in *Major Barbara* has obvious Shakespearean predecessors in Richard III and Edmund. Like Richard's physical deformity and Edmund's illegitimacy, Undershaft's illegitimacy and poverty provide him the incentive to defy society by whatever unscrupulous means are necessary. All three men thoroughly understand human nature and thus are able to manipulate others to their own advantage. Each, moreover, is guided by a cold rationality; Edmund, for example, uses the love of Goneril and Regan purely to advance his own interests. All three scorn the naivete and the conventional morality and religiosity of those around them; the very morality and credulity of Gloucester and Edgar are the focus of Edmund's attack. There are fundamental differences, however, and these differences point up Shaw's persistent criticisms of Shakespeare—that he categorized his characters too melodramatically as villains and heroes and that the villains merely repudiate conventional morality rather than setting forth their own original concept of values. Undershaft from first to last proclaims the superiority of his moral code to the accepted one, even morally defending the destruction and murder which are the products of his munitions factory.

2502   Reader, Willie. *"King Lear* as a Partial Source for Browning's 'A Serenade at the Villa.' " *Browning Society Notes,* 5, No. 1 (1975), 25-26.

The Edgar-Gloucester mock suicide provides the allusive structure for Browning's "A Serenade at the Villa." The contrasting speeches which the lover imagines his lady to deliver form a parallel to this event from Shakespeare. In the first the lover offers himself, Edgar-like, to help guide the lady; in the second she scorns his offer and demands to die in peace. The darkness and pain of Gloucester's blinding seem to haunt the entire poem; indeed, once the allusion is recognized, the metaphoric level almost overwhelms the literal.

2503   Schwarze, Hans-Wilhelm. "Edward Bond: *Lear.* Analyse, Interpretation und Vorschläge für die Behandlung im Unterricht der Sekundarstuffe II." *Praxis des neusprachlichen Unterrichts,* 22 (1975), 363-371.

Edward Bond's *Lear* is discussed as appropriate subject matter for the German school system.

2504   Shapiro, Arnold. " 'Childe Roland,' *Lear,* and the Ability to See." *Papers on Language and Literature,* 11 (1975), 88-94.

King Lear, the most obvious source for Browning's "Childe Roland to the Dark Tower Came," provides an ironic framework for the dramatic monologue, a perspective for better understanding of the central figure. Roland, more specifically, is the reverse of Edgar in his behavior, embodying values that the latter pointedly rejects. Whereas Edgar through the agonizing experiences with his blinded father develops a capacity for genuine perception, Roland never measures up to the ideal of truly seeing; obsessed with a bleak view of existence and totally without sympathy for his fellow creatures, he is characterized by a moral laziness and blames others—the cripple, the treachery of his former comrades—for his own passivity, cynicism, and despair. Nature in *King Lear* is equally ugly and people equally treacherous; yet Edgar never succumbs to despair. Roland, in a word, is best understood in comparison with the character whose memory he is intended to recall. Unlike Edgar he undergoes no transformation, no growth in sympathy and awareness. Instead, he creates another picture with himself at the center.

2505   Smith, Grover. "Lamb and *Lear* in 'Little Gidding.' " *T. S. Eliot Review*, 2, No. 2 (1975), 2.

T. S. Eliot's phrase "impotence of rage" in "Little Gidding" is a direct echo of Charles Lamb's description of King Lear as a figure of "corporal infirmities and weakness, the impotence of rage." According to Lamb, Lear's leading quality is helplessness; Eliot's analogy bears the further frustration and agony of realizing that his rage, directed at the folly of mankind, is to no avail.

2506   Stratmann, Gerd. "Edward Bond, *Lear."* *Das zeitgennössiche englische Drama.* Edited by Klaus-Dieter Fehse and Norbert Platz. Frankfurt, n.p., 1975, pp. 274-298.

Edward Bond's *Lear* is a powerful delineation of man's destructive potential when his mind, impelled by pride, is controlled by an obsession which prevents meaningful communication.

2507   Strongin, Carol Diane. "The Anguished Laughter of Shakespeare, Chekhov and Beckett: An Exploration of Their Tragicomic Drama." Ph.D. dissertation, Brown University, 1975. *DAI*, 37 (1976), 302A.

The tragicomic vision perceives the world as incapable of sustaining man's aspirations to tragedy and man as incapable of attaining the liberation of comedy. Tragicomedy deals with suffering that does not ennoble and repression from which there is no escape. It offers the audience neither catharsis nor liberation. In several of Shakespeare's plays, including *King Lear,* one can trace the beginnings of a line of modern tragedy that leads through Chekhov to Beckett.

2508   Truchlar, Leo. "Lear oder die Pornographic der Gewalt." *Revue des Langues Vivantes* (Brussels), 41 (1975), 133-138.

This discussion of Edward Bond's *Lear* centers on the destructive and debilitating aspects of power.

2509   Cohn, Ruby. "Lear Come Lately." *Modern Shakespeare Off-shoots.* Princeton: Princeton University Press, 1976, pp. 232-266.

In the twentieth century, especially since World War II, *King Lear* with its cruelty and agony has enjoyed its greatest popularity. By emphasizing the theme of filial ingratitude through the addition of a subplot and by the addition of the storm with its strange trio of madmen, Shakespeare has given cosmic resonance to the Lear legend. The play exhibits a remarkable linguistic variety—"ceremonious blank verse, staccato pentameters, ballads, dialect, and amazingly flexible prose" (p. 234). The first offshoot was Nahum Tate's adaptation in 1681, with its happy ending involving the restoration of Lear to the throne and the love affair between Cordelia and Edgar. Edmund Kean briefly restored the tragic ending in 1823, and Charles Macready returned to the full Shakespearean version in 1838. At the turn of the present century the play became a whipping boy for Leo Tolstoy (see item 10). Both G. Wilson Knight in *The Wheel of Fire* (see item 19) and George Orwell (see item 66) came strongly to the play's defense. Freud (see item 1239) finds in Cordelia a symbol of death, while Bertold Brecht praises Shakespeare for his realism, observing that the tragedy traces the decline of feudalism. This theme is further developed by Marshall McLuhan (see item 376), and Jan Kott (see item 348) analyzes the play as absurdist drama. Four dramatic offshoots have appeared in the last seventy years. Gordon Bottomley's *King Lear's Wife* in 1915 depicted Queen Hygd as a frigid and demanding wife of Lear to whom many of the later tragic moments can be traced. *Mister Lear* by Robin Maugham (see item 2389) in 1956 reduced the play to utter triviality. In 1969 the Italian production by the Gruppo Sperimentazione Teatrale was improvisational theater based on four highly visual scenes—the frivolous activities of Lear's court, the civil war, Lear's madness, and Lear's death. Edmund Bond's *Lear* (see item 2456) in 1971 achieved considerable power in its own right.

2510   Duncan, Joseph E. "The Child and the Old Man in the Plays of Edward Bond." *Modern Drama,* 19 (1976), 1-10.

A child-old man relationship is a recurrent motif in Edward Bond's plays, among them his adaptation of *Lear* (pp. 7-9).

2511   Gervais, David. "James's Reading of *Madame Bovary.*" *Cambridge Quarterly,* 7 (1976-1977), 1-26.

Flaubert was rereading *King Lear,* which he considered the greatest reach of Shakespeare's art, when he was in the final stages of writing *Madame Bovary.* His pity for Lear reflects a religious sense of man's place in nature; man's transcendence involves an awareness of, not an escape from, the sense of human frailty. The development of one's full potential through love, as revealed in Shakespeare, is the very quality Emma Bovary is never able to achieve.

2512   Gillon, Adam. "Joseph Conrad and Shakespeare, Part Four: A Reinterpretation of *Victory.*" *Conradiana,* 8 (1976), 61-75.

This discussion of Shakespeare's influence on Conrad concerns both general themes and specific phrases drawn from four plays, including *King Lear.*

2513   Gradman, Barry. "*King Lear* and the Image of Ruth in Keats's 'Nightingale' Ode." *Keats-Shelley Journal,* 25 (1976), 15-22.

The allusion to Ruth in Keats' "Ode to a Nightingale" ("Perhaps the self-same song that found a path / Through the sad heart of Ruth, when, sick for home, / She stood in tears amid the alien corn") is a conflation of the Biblical Ruth and of Shakespeare's Cordelia from *King Lear.* Keats uses three allusions to suggest the timelessness of the bird's song; it is heard by "emperor and clown" (figures from the historical past), by Ruth (figures from the Biblical past), and in "faery lands" (figures from the realm of pure imagination). Probably Keats had Lear and the Fool in mind with the "emperor and cloud" allusion, and the conflation of Cordelia and Ruth occurred, perhaps unconsciously, in the second allusion.

2514   Guthke, Karl S. "A Stage for the Anti-Hero: Metaphysical Farce in the Modern Theatre." *Studies in the Literary Imagination,* 9, No. 1 (1976), 119-137.

Using illustrations from *King Lear,* Guthke argues that Shakespeare is responsible for the spirit and sense of metaphysical farce central to modern absurdist drama.

2515   Hoge, James O., Jr. "Tennyson on Shakespeare." *Texas Studies in Literature and Language,* 18 (1976), 147-170.

King Lear, among other Shakespearean plays, was a strong influence upon Tennyson's philosophy and his art. The comments are drawn from Hallam Tennyson's notes on his father's life and work.

2516   Jacobs, Henry E. and Claudia D. Johnson. *"King Lear." An Annotated Bibliography of Shakespearean Burlesques, Parodies, and Travesties.* New York: Garland Publishing, 1976, pp. 39-40, 90, 156-157.

Nine comic adaptations of *Lear* are cited, dating from 1868 to 1964.

2517   Mieczyslaw, Brahmer. "Entre Shakespeare et l'Arioste: Notes sur *Balladyna* de Słowacki." *Revue de Littérature Comparée* (Paris), 50 (1976), 116-120.

Słowacki's drama contains numerous allusions to Shakespeare. The "fairy" tragedy *Balladyna* combines with the fairyland romance of Ariosto's *Orlando Furioso* and with plot motifs from *A Midsummer Night's Dream, Macbeth,* and *King Lear.*

2518   Muir, Kenneth. "The Case of John Ford." *Sewanee Review,* 84 (1976), 614-629.

Brief attention is afforded *King Lear,* among other plays, in the discussion of Shakespeare's influence upon John Ford.

2519   Oppel, Horst. "Edward Bond, *Lear.*" *Das englische Drama der Gegenwart.* Edited by Horst Oppel. Berlin: E. Schmidt, 1976, pp. 222-238.

This essay discusses the place of Edward Bond's *Lear* in English absurdist drama.

2520   Baxter, John. "The Stone Angel: Shakespearian Bearings." *Compass,* 1 (1977), 3-19.

In several basic narrative respects Margaret Laurence's *The Stone Angel* bears comparison with *King Lear*—the extreme age of the protagonist, the thwarted dynastic ambitions, the dispossession of the central figure by those of the younger generation, the determined Machiavellianism of the younger figures. A major focus in both works, as well, is on the protagonist's confrontation with death, a focus involving one's proper evaluation of life even at such a woefully late moment. The inhabitants of Shadow Point are reminiscent of the two wandering over the heath "more sinned against than sinning," just as Edgar's leading Gloucester to a renewal of faith is analogous to Murray Lees' encounter with Hagar. Finally, the hallmark of both works is the effective mixing of styles.

2521   Bogdanova, P. "The Tragedy of Turgenev's Lear." *Teatr,* 12 (1977), 74-75.

This article discusses a television film production of I. G. Turgenev's *A King Lear of the Steppes,* produced by A. Vasilyeva. One of the notable characteristics of this adaptation is the introduction of Lear's soliloquies into the production.

2522   D'Avanzo, Mario L. " 'Childe Roland to the Dark Tower Came': The Shelleyan and Shakespearean Context." *Studies in English Literature,* 17 (1977), 695-708.

The possible sources for Browning's "Childe Roland"—that is, sources that depict life as a test, trial, and pilgrimage—are manifold, but two major pieces, Shelley's "The Triumph of Life" and Shakespeare's *King Lear,* most strongly "inform the craft and meaning of Browning's poem and reveal his creative process" (p. 696). Edgar is Roland's model for his fortitude, for his ordeal seen through to a final affirmation and the triumph of love. Roland, like Edgar, must confront and overcome despair with Stoical resolve, and he must accept life with all its flaws with the attitude that "ripeness is all." The theme of pride in *Lear* in many ways is reflected in Roland's trials and isolations. Edgar's remark upon seeing his blinded father ("And worse I may be yet; the worst is not / So long as we can say 'this is the worst' ") "assures man of hope and fortitude. If hope thrives in man's lowest state of fortune, it is clear why Roland, in an analogous condition to Edgar's, can dauntlessly resist, symbolically announcing his affirmation of the quest and of life" (p. 708).

2523   Franke, Jeannette. "Elemente des Theaters der Grausamkeit and des Absurden im Werk des englishchen Dramatikers Edward Bond." Ph.D. dissertation, University of Mainz, 1977.

An analysis of Edward Bond's *Lear* and *Bingo,* this study focuses both on the general characteristics of absurdist drama and on the relationship of Shakespeare's *King Lear* to Bond's play.

2524   Herman, Josef.   "The Painter and Literature."   *Essays and Studies,* 30 (1977), 70-72.

Literature can awaken the creative energies of a painter, but a basic transformation must occur. Where literature conveys a variety of viewpoints, the painting is a compressed entity confined to a single mood on a single surface. *King Lear* inspired Herman's painting of a single individual with, off to the distance, the Fool playing a flute. Both the Fool and the natural setting were totally indifferent to this suffering, isolated individual. The thrust of the painting is the horrendous loneliness of Lear.

2525   Pendelton, Thomas A.   "The Return of *The Broken Lance.*" *Shakespeare Film Newsletter,* 2 (December, 1977), 3.

The Broken Lance, a movie Western in 1954 featuring Spencer Tracy, Robert Wagner, and Richard Widmark, is an adaptation of Jerome Weidman's 1940 novel *I'll Never Go There Anymore.* Even though the story involves a father's dominance over his sons and focuses on the familial unit, any connection with *King Lear* is tangential at best.

2526   White, Michael. *"King Lear* and the Aesthetics of Eighteenth-Century Drama." *South Central Bulletin,* 37 (Fall, 1977), 97.

The apologetic posture of most scholars dealing with eighteenth-century adaptations of literature inhibits the exploitation of their true value, which is to analyze them for the insights they afford into the rationale intrinsic to the critical tenets of their own age.

2527   Williams, Aubrey. "Of 'One Faith': Authors and Auditors in the Restoration Theatre." *Studies in the Literary Imagination,* 10 (1977), 57-76.

This article includes a brief discussion of the appeal of Nahum Tate's *King Lear* (1681) to eighteenth-century audiences. Specific attention is directed to the accommodation of the tragic story to the demands of poetic justice.

2528   Borowitz, Helen O.   *"King Lear* in the Art of Ford Madox Brown." *Victorian Studies,* 21 (1978), 309-334.

The young members of the Cyclographic Club, who were later to become the Pre-Raphaelites, disillusioned with the industrial dehumanization of their world, looked back with great reverence on the great men of the past. Shakespeare ranked only below Christ; and, for the leader Ford Madox Brown, *King Lear* was the supreme literary achievement. Artistic influences from Germany provided him a compositional format for his first *Lear* sketches, just as the Victorian stage productions spurred his later *Lear* works. Brown's etching *Cordelia* was the frontispiece on *The Germ* and in turn influenced Henry Irving's stage production. Apparently, it was Cordelia's drama rather than Lear's which most attracted him; perhaps the reason is to be found in the fact that her symbolic value—a total honesty stiffened with pride—well characterizes his own dealings with the art establishment of his day.

2529   Habicht, Werner. "Edward Bond: *Lear." Englische Literatur der Gegenwart 1970-1975.* Edited by Ranier Lengeler. Düsseldorf: Bagel, 1978, pp. 22-31.

Edward Bond's *Lear* is discussed both as an adaptation of Shakespeare's play and as an example of contemporary absurdist drama.

2530   Lowrey, Robert E. "The Theme of Legitimate Succession in Nahum Tate's *King Lear.*" *Publications of the Arkansas Philological Association,* 4, No. 3 (1978), 18-24.

The theme of legitimate succession is central to Tate's adaptation of Shakespeare's play. This emphasis was especially timely, coming only three years after the Popish Plot of 1678, in which, according to Titus Oates, Charles II was to be assassinated and James II placed on the throne. The restoration of Lear and, in turn, the reestablishment of Cordelia as next in line to succession have a topical counterpart in the continued rule of Charles II and the lawful establishment of James as the heir apparent.

2531   Oppel, Horst. *Die Vorgeschichte zu "King Lear" im Lichte moderner Adaptihnen.* Akademie der Wissenschaften und der Literatur, Mainz. Abhandlungen d. Geistes—und Sozialwissenschaftlungen Klasse, 1978, No. 9. Wiesbaden: Franz Steiner, 1978. 64 pp. (not seen)

2532   Reimann, Aribert. *King Lear* (opera, 1978).

This operatic version of *King Lear,* with Libretto by Claus Henneberg, was commissioned by the Bavarian State Opera. It was produced by Jean-Pierre Ponnelle at the Munich Summer Music Festival in 1978 and was subsequently reviewed by William Mann in the London *Times,* 26 July 1978, p. 13.

See also items: 2, 23, 37, 58, 264, 294, 329, 334, 358, 390, 413, 425, 427, 625, 653, 686, 715, 719, 729, 814, 832, 848, 913, 995-996, 1017, 1047, 1097, 1185, 1236, 1283, 1330, 1456-1457, 1462-1463, 1465, 1486, 1492, 1524, 1552-1553, 1571, 1581, 1617-1618, 1656, 1678, 1683, 1689, 1695, 1700-1701.

INDEX

INDEX

References are to item numbers

A. S. Pushkin Musical and Dramatic Theatre, Moldavia, 1825
Albalkin, N., 2067
Abel, Lionel, 388
Abell, Adam, 1324; *The Roit or Quheill of Tyme,* 1324
Abenheimer, K. M., 60, 457
Abirached, Robert, 1978
Abrams, M. H., 260
Accedens of Armoury (Legh), 1276, 1343
Actability of the play, 72, 223, 244, 263, 1491, 1527, 1614, 1821, 1898, 1966, 2012
Acting Company, New York, 2302, 2332, 2337
Actors Company, 2194, 2197, 2207, 2213
Adams, John C., 96, 1574
Adams, Joseph Quincy, 96, 98, 1253, 1354, 1369
Adams, Robert P., 291, 548
Adamson, Elgira, 419
Addison, Joseph, 913, 2367
Adelman, Janet, 1180
Adler, Doris Ray, 1103, 2143
Adler, Joseph P., 2306
Adling, Wilifried, 2144, 2431
Adventures of David Simple (Fielding) 2356
Aeschylus, 31, 182, 1020, 1653; *Agamemnon,* 325, 1653
Aesop, 94
Afansyeva, T., 1884
Agamemnon (Aeschylus), 325,

1653
Agate, James, 1737
Ahab, Captain, 2350
Aikhenwald, Yu. A., 1979
Akhmeteli, Sandro, 2118, 2307
Alabama Shakespeare Festival, Anniston, Alabama, 2260, 2295
Alaham (Greville), 901
Albany, an actor's view of the role, 2128, 2138; his alignment with positive forces, 64, 233, 275, 539, 667, 793, 795; his archetypal qualities, 210, 543, 1124; as a character of developing wisdom, 30, 288, 309, 342, 351, 500, 532, 626, 674, 889, 964, 1418; the distortion of his role, 942, 1387a, 1894, 1943, 2208; his inability to comprehend, 576, 759, 1005; as the final arbiter, 18, 162, 309, 313, 354, 400, 532, 658, 865, 914, 939, 1049; as a potential political liability, 250, 277; his relationship with Goneril, 561, 565, 661; his relationship to King James, 658, 1686; his role in Q and F compared, 1454; his speech pattern, 79, 265; a spokesman for the general woe, 119, 246, 731; his tragic futility, 317, 461, 599, 764, 838, 973, 983; a victim of Lear's truancy, 622; a victim of treason, 792; his war against Cornwall, 325